It Is Written

Other Books by

PHILIP LEE WILLIAMS

NOVELS

Emerson's Brother
The Campfire Boys
A Distant Flame
The True and Authentic History of Jenny Dorset
Blue Crystal
Final Heat
Perfect Timing
Slow Dance in Autumn
The Song of Daniel
All the Western Stars
The Heart of a Distant Forest

POETRY

The Flower Seeker: An Epic Poem of William Bartram
Elegies for the Water

NONFICTION

It is Written: My Life in Letters
In the Morning: Reflections from First Light
Crossing Wildcat Ridge: A Memoir of Nature and Healing
The Silent Stars Go By

CHAPBOOK

A Gift from Boonie, Seymour, and Dog

It Is Written

My Life in Letters

PHILIP LEE WILLIAMS

MERCER UNIVERSITY PRESS Macon, Georgia

35 Years of Publishing Excellence

MUP/ H886

Published by Mercer University Press, Macon, Georgia 31207

1400 Coleman Avenue
Macon, Georgia 31207

9 8 7 6 5 4 3 2 1

Books published by Mercer University Press are printed on acid-free paper that meets the requirements of the American National Standard for Information Sciences—Permanence of Paper for Printed Library Materials.

Library of Congress Cataloging-in-Publication Data

Williams, Philip Lee.
It is written : my life in letters / Philip Lee Williams.
pages cm
ISBN 978-0-88146-493-1 (hardback : acid-free paper) -- ISBN 0-88146-493-7 (hardback : acid-free paper)
1. Williams, Philip Lee. 2. Authors, American--20th century--Biography. I. Title.
PS3573.I45535Z46 2014
813'.54--dc23
[B]

2014023715

Contents

Acknowledgments

I would like to extend my deepest thanks to the following for permission to quote from their letters to me and use other materials: Randy Latimer (for the estate of the late Raymond Andrews), Molly Friedrich, Harvey Klinger, Kevin Meyer, Chuck Searcy, Pete McCommons, John Wilson of *Books and Culture* magazine, Margaret Quinlin, Edward Hudson, Buster Hudson, Marc Jolley, Linda Rowley Williams, Whisperin' Bill Anderson, and Bill Contardi. This book could not have been written without their help. I would also like to thank my sister, Laura Jane Kuncaitis, my brother, Dr. Mark Williams, and our father, Marshall Williams, along with Anderson, Klinger, and Contardi for reading and commenting on the manuscript.

MERCER
UNIVERSITY PRESS

Endowed by
TOM WATSON BROWN
and
THE WATSON-BROWN FOUNDATION, INC.

This book is for Linda

1

New York City, 1991

My literary agent, Harvey Klinger, and I settled in a taxicab and headed east across Manhattan to a party in the soft early June light, while I was digging in my pocket to find a ridiculously large bill to give to the cabbie. I had been drinking at Harvey's apartment after a day gawking around the American Bookseller's Association Convention, where I saw—like two different species—towering former NBA star Wilt Chamberlain and tiny sex therapist Dr. Ruth Westheimer standing close to each other ready to promote upcoming books.

The day had already been a success. My editor-to-be at Random House's jazzy new Turtle Bay Books imprint, Joni Evans, had found me at the Jacob Javits Center on West 34th Street where the ABA was meeting and immediately hit me up for a stick of gum while she looked me over. She'd just bought my new novel, *Final Heat*, for an advance of $67,500, which was a huge sale for me (and a decent one for Harvey, who made the deal), and I would have waxed her car if she'd asked. She wanted me to take her close—but not too close—to the Peachtree Publishers exhibit, since she was inheriting me from Peachtree and wanted to take a gander at my former editor, Margaret Quinlin. (I was actually in New York to promote my final Peachtree novel, *Perfect Timing*.) A record crowd of 36,000 would attend the convention—maybe the high point for independent booksellers in the U.S. I felt like a drone in a kicked-over ant mound. Later in the day, Joni and I had taken a cab to Turtle Bay Books's beautiful brownstone on East 51st St., where we worked on the manuscript in her still-unfinished office. The novel was an extremely dark, violent, and frightening book set in Mississippi. Later, friends and strangers almost unanimously berated me for writing it.

"I just *love* your books," said one older woman acquaintance. "Except for *Final Heat*. Oh my God I hated that one. *Hated* it. I can't *tell* you how much I hated it." A reviewer for *Athens Magazine*, in the Georgia town where I lived and worked at the University of Georgia, savaged the book and accused me, among other things, of being obsessed with breasts, something that seriously annoyed me, since I had been an old-line feminist and vocal Equal Rights Amendment supporter. *The Atlanta Journal-Constitution*, however, said it was "daring" and a "hell of a read." And Harvey couldn't have been more supportive. I believed the *AJC*. That was months in the future, though.

I had worked with Joni on my book then taken a cab back to the Penta Hotel on 7th Avenue at 33rd St., across from Madison Square Garden where I could barely sit on my unmade bed, awaiting the party that night at the brownstone to christen the new Random House imprint. I had arrived, in fact, at the sorry state of believing my own press. Famed film producer Richard Zanuck still had my novel *All the Western Stars* under contract for a movie, and MGM would in the not-too-distant future pay me a ridiculous amount to write the screenplay. Ron Howard and Brian Grazer had optioned already *Perfect Timing* for a movie as well, and smaller production companies were calling, too, looking for options on my other books. (I would a few years later sell rights on an unpublished novel to Meg Ryan and her company, Prufrock Pictures.) Soon, I would be rich and famous, no doubt. People would yield to me on sidewalks, whispering my name.

Also on the trip was my good friend and fellow Georgia writer Terry Kay, who had sold a superb new book to Peachtree which would come out that fall—*To Dance with the White Dog*. But Terry and I didn't see much of each other during ABA because I was busy trying to jump ship.

I made it to Harvey's apartment on West 57th Street around seven, and once there I began to drink, my preferential poison being bourbon and water, far more the former than the latter. He was a very good agent and much better known in New York City than I was as a writer, but he allowed me to pretend, which I thought was decent of him.

"So who's gonna be at this party, anyway?" I asked. I already knew the whole Turtle Bay crowd would be there, including Joni and the other editors, Juli Grau, Susan Kamil, and Karen Rinaldi, who in coming years would establish themselves as movers and shakers in New York. I should report that all the editors of Turtle Bay—and this made it newsworthy—were women. They were all brilliant, young, and seriously hungry for success. *The New York Times* even ran a major feature story on Turtle Bay a couple of months before, calling it the Big Apple's "glitzy new imprint." It would last only two years before Random House pulled the plug, but it still managed to buy books from me, A.S. Byatt, Ann Beattie, Erica Jong, and celebrities such as actor Michael Caine. In all, the imprint published just twenty of those books before it folded, mine among them, perhaps a badge of honor or the answer to a "Jeopardy!" question, or both.

"*Everybody*," he said. "Don't do anything stupid."

"Me?" I cried. "Me? Surely you jest."

"Maybe ease off on the booze a little," he said, laughing. I toasted him and drank up. Harvey and I had a love-hate relationship from the beginning. He hated the fact that I could be stubborn and write novels he didn't like, and I hated the fact that he only wanted to represent things he might conceivably sell for cash money. What kind of an agent would treat a writer like that? I would sometimes send him a novel I'd worked on for a year, and he'd call and say, "Nah, this ain't it, kid. Go write something else." I'd scream and rage after I hung up for a couple of days and then go beg the Muse for yet another reprieve. I'd written *Final Heat* in just such a fit, balled in an almost fetal position of shaking rage, taking my characters through vast depredations and considerable bloodshed. Though it had strengths, I was very unsure of its overall quality, but I sent a copy to Harvey and awaited the dreaded rattle of his rue. The phone rang one Tuesday.

"Phil Williams," I said, answering the phone.

"In the flesh," said Harvey, his habitual greeting, creepy, but true-Harvey anyway. I asked him what was up, knowing full well my novel was up and that he was either going to dismiss it in less than ten syllables, or say he loved it.

"So, what about it?" I asked, paying no attention to proper narrative build-up.

"This is the most commercial thing you've ever written, kid," he said, "and you don't even know it." I could hear him grinning over the phone. He may have said the writing was good, but I can't remember, to be honest. He *did* say he thought he could sell it. I didn't believe him, of course. Writers who have been publishing for a while know precisely how much they dare believe with their whole hearts and how much they should ignore. (I should note here that although he always called me and, I presume, other male clients "kid," I am actually slightly older than he is.)

"Oh?" I said.

"Have you ever heard of Joni Evans?" he asked. "She's got influence in town. And she's got this new imprint, Turtle Bay Books? I'm sending it to her."

"Ummm."

"Stop talking to me and go write," he said.

"Okay." He hung up. Harvey never had much time for idle chat. That was one of the reasons he was a great agent.

I should backtrack a little to Harvey's apartment, which was small but elegantly appointed in Midtown. He also has a home in Bucks County, Pa., and I presumed, therefore, that most of his clients were much more successful than I was. In fact, he seemed most pleased by my sale to Random House because it happened on his birthday.

That was also the long weekend when I last laid eyes on one of the best friends of my life, novelist Raymond Andrews. The day before I met up with Harvey and went to the Random House event, the Peachtree crowd had a dinner party at Rosa's, a pleasant Mexican restaurant, and Ray (who had a book out from Peachtree), sweet-talked beers off several of us as always and then in the end thanked Margaret Quinlin for the meal, even though we were going Dutch. We all adored Ray and would have bought him anything, and we all knew he had very little money. She paid for his dinner without blinking an eye, and we walked back south the ten blocks or so to the Penta. I didn't know it then, but Ray was having a terrible time. He lived most of the year in a house his brother, the artist Benny Andrews, owned not far from me, near Athens, but he came back to New York late spring each year and took his summers in the city where he'd spent most of his adult life. That night, when we got back to the hotel, he wanted to go drinking at O'Reilly's, our favorite Irish pub across the street from Madison Square Garden, but I was exhausted and told him I'd see him back in Athens. My wife, Linda, was pregnant, and I had too many things on my mind. (She didn't make this trip to New York, though we'd come together several times before.) We shook hands in front of the Penta, and I never saw him again. He came back South in the early fall, and, busy with Linda's pregnancy and the birth of our daughter Megan, I only talked to Ray on the phone a couple of times. A week before Thanksgiving, he wrote a suicide note and then shot himself near the gazebo in the yard of his home about ten miles from my house. We were shattered, but all that lay in the future.

Harvey probably had high hopes for me in those days, meaning I might make us both a great deal of money. This had all come as a tremendous shock to me, since I'd considered myself a literary writer, though I *had* made a considerable amount of money off movie options. I barely remembered writing *Final Heat,* the novel Joni bought along with books by several other writers, for her new imprint. I had been in a cold rage for some reason or another one summer and wrote the darkest, most hellish tale I could concoct. It lay around for a while until on a whim I sent it to Harvey, who was serially rejecting everything else I sent him. I should have known it would be his kind of book, and it was.

I was forty-one years old and proud as only a fool heading for a fall can be.

By the time we got to the party at Turtle Bay's new-paint-smelling townhouse, I was woozy with bourbon, so Harvey steered me through the place. I had tipped the cabbie twelve dollars for an eight-minute ride, and he thought I was nuts. I found myself, for some reason, in the kitchen with the caterers, then I was hanging out in a small garden behind the brownstone, where people mingled and drank. I struck up a conversation with Anne Beattie, who had just signed with Turtle Bay. I have no idea what I said. I presume I acted like a Fellow Writer, but she clearly had no idea who I was. I then flung my arm around the shoulder of an older gentleman and chatted with him for a while about how much I loved New York, how much I loved Random House, and, generally, how important I was. He looked at me with mild horror and finally escaped, glancing over his shoulder at me. I felt like a panhandler begging for quarters. I went on an expedition to the bar and ordered another free drink. Harvey came up, mildly mortified.

"Jesus, kid, do you know who that was?" he asked.

"I didn't catch his name," I slurred.

"You ever heard of Si Newhouse?" he asked.

"Vaguely."

"He owns all this."

"All of what?" Harvey made an expansive gesture with his arm.

"Random House, half of New York. *All of this.*"

"Oh my God," I said, cringing. "Does my voice sound slurred to you?"

"You need to get some air," he said. We were standing in the garden behind the brownstone.

"Where would we go for that in New York City?"

I talked to a lot of other writers that night, remembered none of their names, hugged Joni like we were old friends, introduced myself to the other editors, and generally made a fool of myself. Some time around midnight, I remember sitting with Harvey in the Hard Rock Café, watching the waitresses go through a dance routine (only in New York) as I sipped a Coke that didn't seem to clear my cluttered head. Later, he poured me into a cab and sent me downtown to the Penta, and I remember lying in the back seat looking up the shafts of skyscrapers toward the stars, thinking I was F. Scott Fitzgerald and that my life would now be played on a much larger stage.

I might have remembered that fiction is built on illusion, but somehow the fact that life is built the same way apparently escaped me.

He leans over to pick up a twig that has fallen with a clack on to another, downslope from his house, toward Wildcat Creek. That dry but sweetened sound reminds him of something he cannot quite place. He is sixty-three and stands against a spring-green dogwood tree until the pain passes. The rue anemones have flowered and faded. Trilliums sift the sunlight onto the forest floor with their stalks alone, now that the blooms have gone. Below, the creek unwinds its sparkling ribbon. He picks up the twig and turns it in his hands, looks up to see where it had once clasped and then let go, the larger limb from which it has suddenly vanished. A jet's contrail seems to stretch from tree to tree across the creek like a clothesline, before it, too, lets go and floats off into blue.

2

Dirt Roads and Convicts

The idea of being a serious novelist didn't occur to me until I was in my late twenties and only then because my wife kept telling me to write fiction because I like to run my mouth so much. Growing up, I lived in a family in which poetry and classical music were next to the gods, and fiction was next to invisible. My mother read novels sometimes, but I had a sniffy superiority about poetry that began at sixteen when I started my career with a poem called "Metamorphosis," about the lava-outlined bodies of slow-footed residents of Pompeii I'd seen in *The National Geographic*.

Here are the first two stanzas, just to squash any notions of precocity:

> I am a child, but
> I know my fate.
> It is foretold by my ancestors
> who say much, but
> believe nothing.
>
> I live here in the city
> And things don't please me
> Because I am scared
> of vengeance—vengeance
> of the Gods.

Well. It goes on like that for several handwritten pages, complete with a few stanzas almost directly cribbed from T.S. Eliot's "The Hollow Men." I doubt I saw the irony. When I finished it on November 3, 1966, (I was already dating my work for posterity), I felt in my heart that Walt Whitman's place in American literature was growing more tenuous by the moment. While our house was a hotbed of Wordsworth and Beethoven, I'd actually spent much time as a boy blowing things up, playing army, and watching my father launch himself improbably from one interest to another. One day he might be designing and building an electronic organ, and the next he would be playing the same half page of a Chopin Polonaise over and over on our remarkably ugly upright piano which he had painted a color called "chamois buff" but which we always called *"shammy buffet."*

We lived on the outskirts of the small north central Georgia town of Madison between 1953 and 1960. By the time I was six I loved to go with my older brother (by eighteen months) Mark to the deep-green woods behind our house. Once there I spent hours in the silvery solitude I craved like a drug. Our father was principal of Morgan County High School (starting in 1955) and also taught chemistry and physics. Our house was within walking distance of the school, a collection of worn-out redbrick buildings that had originally been part of Madison A&M School in the Teens, Twenties, and early Thirties. We would play in the chemistry lab amid the ripe stench of whatever sulfur compounds we could concoct after school or on weekends when everyone was gone. Mark knew something about chemistry, but I seemed slow and daydreamy, though I was far less dense than my parents might have suspected. That never stopped me from mixing chemicals just to see if they'd catch fire. Mother kept house and took care of her family, surely a full-time job if ever there was one. When she had time, she listened to opera, read fiction and poetry, played baseball with us, and cleaned us up for church on Sunday.

She and my father had both served their country during World War II, he in the U.S. Army Air Forces, and she in the WAVES, the Navy's volunteer unit for women, so we all had a healthy sense of military pride, and Mark and I often shoveled up foxholes in the pasture behind our house so we could get better "shots" at the beef cattle the county kept back there. (The county owned our house and all the land, though the concept of renting meant nothing to me.) Our sister Laura Jane was born in the early fall of 1959, and by then I was almost ten and Mark eleven. Soon she grew beautiful blonde hair and brought a perpetual and infectious giggle into our home.

Our father's mind did not work like our friends' fathers'. He was wildly interested in everything, from ancient history to contemporary politics, and he knew a ridiculous amount about all of them. Some time in the late 1950s, he decided we should start finding Indian village sites in Morgan County, logging them on a map, and making artifact collections that we kept separate from each other. We spent hours in the summer or on Sunday afternoons during the school year walking slowly like bent old men in the freshly plowed and rained-on sienna fields looking for potsherds and projectile points, beginning what was the first systematic county site collection ever done in Georgia. All along we planned to donate the artifacts to the University of Georgia as a scientific collection, and we did. (Mark is now an archaeologist at the University of Georgia and in charge of the site file for the whole state, but more on that later.) Years later, in 1967-68, our father, Mark, and I would work as volunteers with a team from the University of South Carolina in excavating Fort Prince George, a British colonial outpost in Pickens County, South Carolina, just across the river from our parents' home county, Oconee. I even found the cornerstone of a building in the fort with 1761 carved in large numerals and 1770 and some initials in a much smaller size. Laura Jane came along several times, too, and even though she was very young she still remembers her days at the site decades later. Those were dramatic times and cemented our lifelong love of history.

Madison itself was a somewhat unusual town, having been founded in 1809 on the edge of what was still Indian Territory, though no Indians had actually lived in the area for almost one hundred and fifty years by then. Manifest Destiny manifested itself in Georgia starting from Savannah and moving upstate, so Madison, for example, is much older than Atlanta. For a time, the Georgia Railroad reached the end of the line in Madison, meaning that a class of wealthy planters rose in the county (their wealth built on slavery), and along with them the leisure time that only the wealthy could then afford. With leisure came a love of the arts, and so by the time we moved to Madison in the dusty summer of 1953, the town had a long history of tolerating, if not embracing, artists and the arts. When I started writing poetry in high school and publishing it in the local paper, nobody treated me like I was weird.

Mark and I fought much of the time, which, as brothers only eighteen months apart, we were required to do. He was always taller and faster, however, so it was relatively easy for him to hammer me, run me over with his bicycle, or throw rocks at me and get away with it. Oddly, that never got in the way of our friendship, and we've barely had a serious disagreement since we got out of grade school. Mark was highly competitive, something of a nerd, wearing glasses early, and a Brain. He was tall and thin, with dark curly hair and deep brown eyes like mine. He played high school football and was a star on the track team. Not wanting to get killed at those sports, I played golf, in which I was enthusiastically mediocre. (Laura Jane, with her blonde hair and green eyes, would grow up to be a Brain, too, becoming valedictorian of her senior class in high school and being superb at anything she tried.)

We lived on a dirt road that kept our living room orange in the summer, back in those pre-air conditioned days when the windows were all open from May until October. My mother cleaned constantly, singing as she was apt to do. (She sang pop songs from the radio to us when we were small, and I grew up knowing all the lyrics to songs by Frank Sinatra, Nat King Cole, and Patti Page, words that I still remember.) Mark and I played army in the ditch by the road, pausing only to hold an occasional imaginary beauty pageant in which our mother was the sole contestant. She won the title of Miss Old Buckhead Road by a vote of three to nothing. (We discussed changing the title to Old Miss Buckhead Road, which she thought was funny.) We had a white fox terrier named Flipsy and an ebony mongrel named Mac. We named our cat Gym because we found him at the high school campus in an abandoned gymnasium, which in the mid-Fifties was full of pigeons and a great place to play. (Originally part of the long-gone Madison A&M school, the gymnasium was unsafe and would be torn down not long after we found Gym.)

Mark and I subscribed to *Boys' Life*, began a stamp collection, and camped out in the woods across a field behind our house, sometimes leaving on Friday afternoon and not coming home until Sunday morning in time for church. I will never forget the marvelous smell of an open campfire in those woods. Our parents weren't afraid. The idea of being worried didn't seem to occur to any of us. Hell, I used to hang out with the *convicts* who worked the fields behind the high school. "Trusties," they were mostly middle-aged black men serving long stretches, and in mid-afternoon they would take a brief break in the only shade they had—beneath their tractors in the middle of the field. I sat under there with them and talked, and they were courteous and kind and even gentle, and I loved them. If a guard was present, I can't remember him. Once, I walked all the way home to get two Goody's headache powders for one convict friend who felt sick. Mother gave them to me without asking a question.

From my earliest memories, our house was full of the arts and sciences in almost equal proportions. Our father didn't need an invitation to start reciting the reams of poetry he'd memorized in high school or college, from long stretches of Shakespeare plays to Wordsworth (a favorite), or even the high-camp humor of Robert W. Service's "The Cremation of Sam Magee," which at one time he knew virtually whole. Mother knew almost as much poetry by heart, so it wasn't at all unusual to hear one or the other break into Keats or Browning, though Mother wasn't half as hammy or theatrical as Daddy. They both also knew classical music, at least what was on the radio or our small collection of 78 rpm records. We actually had *Messiah* on 78s, on idiotic twenty-four scratchy sides that had to be changed every three minutes, as if Handel had composed about two hundred pop songs instead of an oratorio. When long-playing records arrived in the mid-1950s, Daddy slowly began to obtain Mahler and Bruckner, and I grew up more addicted than an opium eater to the Late Romantics. By the time I was in my early teens, I had listened to Bruckner's Fifth Symphony hundreds of times.

We had a houseful of paints and paintings, too. Our father had been an artist for years, and as for all good Renaissance men, too much of a good thing wasn't enough for him. When we'd catch the whiff of Damar varnish, turpentine, and oil paints drifting through the house, we'd know he was at it again. I used his exact combination of varnish, oil, and paint for years before I finally got sick of having to take an hour for clean-up and shifted to acrylics, which you can throw all over the house and still clean up with soap and water. Daddy painted one really lovely dog scene, did a nice portrait of our mother when she was young, and also did an astonishing old woman from a newspaper photograph. He didn't write poetry anymore, though when President Kennedy was killed in 1963, he sent one of his older poems straight to Mrs. Kennedy and got in return a black-bordered thank you note, one of probably a million sent out, though for years I imagined Jackie herself in widow's weeds, stuffing it in the envelope with copious tears. He had also composed some pieces for piano in his youth, and his scores were like the Dead Sea Scrolls to me—artifacts of great mystery and value. In mid-life I took up alabaster carving just so I could do something he'd never tried.

Until I was nearly grown, I thought Mark, Laura Jane, and I had had a typical southern childhood, and it came as something of a shock to find that other fathers didn't recite Wordsworth while cutting the grass or conduct Beethoven's Fifth along with a record. I think Mother knew it all along.

I was nine years old when the epiphany came.

I have always been suspicious of those Saul-on-the-road-to-Tarsus conversions that change drunks into saints or politicians into human beings. (To be fair, the former happens far more than the latter.) There's something remarkably uniform and suspiciously phony about tales of waking up and seeing the Truth. In retrospect, the garden behind Turtle Bay's brownstone would have been a reasonable place for my own lurch into the True Limelight. *This* epiphany, though, was the Real Thing, a life-changing event. The day is so indelible that in memory it feels like a scene from *The Odyssey* or *The Canterbury Tales*. I've told myself that it couldn't have been so clear to me, that maybe I dreamed it all. But my father agrees with my version completely. It was a warm day, and I seemed to pause in luscious mid-air in our back yard, playing on the swing Daddy had made for us, an abandoned fire hose looped around the outreaching limb of a pecan tree. You could sit in the cradle of the loop and swing five, six feet off the ground. I would look upward toward the heavens sometimes and instead of sky spot a vile black snake hanging above me in the limbs and peeking down, pursing its lips and clearly preparing for the kill. That summer we were besieged with a Biblical *plague* of black snakes, nasty-tempered five-footers with a vicious bite. (I knew, having stupidly tried to pick one up, since Mark and I routinely played with king snakes, and I didn't see why this one wouldn't like to be petted, too.) I had been swinging as high as I could rise and then leaping out just shy of the arc's apogee to fly. So far, I had broken two U.S. and three Olympic records. The crowds were going wild. I made a scuffmark in the dirt with my Keds every time I broke the record.

"Phil, come inside, there's something I want you to hear," my father called from the back steps. I was keeping one eye on the masses and one eye on the malevolent serpent that was flickering its bifurcated tongue at me two limbs up. In the past year, I had dreamed of being as strong as Tarzan (who will always look like Johnny Weismuller to me) and was gaining on Mark in footraces. (This meant that in a one-hundred-yard dash, he'd only beat me by forty yards, but anyway.)

"Okay," I said, and I dusted my jeans off and stepped into heaven.

Inside, he had on the radio tuned to WGKA, Atlanta's AM classical music station that sometimes came in, and the unnamed orchestra played something martial and stirring. I sat there listening, wondering why he'd ruined such pleasure for the thousands outside watching my heroics, when suddenly everything changed, utterly, as Yeats might have said. The music was the overture to an opera named *Fra Diavolo*—a Robin Hood-like character, this Brother Devil—by an Eighteenth Century French composer named Daniel Auber. Classical music had always been around the house—I couldn't remember life without it. But until that moment it was just aural wallpaper, the background of life, and I paid only spotty attention. Mother cooked supper, happily pregnant with Laura Jane as I remember, and Mark might have been building a radio or just being a Brain and a Nerd. That music though—my *God*, that music—it hit me with the force of a revelation. Suddenly and instantly, I *knew*. I saw the whole world before me, and I knew that I was going to be an Artist of some kind, knew it as certainly as my next breath. The overture to *Fra Diavolo* is a wonderful piece of music, and it probably ranks in the second ten thousand of the world's most popular classical pieces. But it infected me like typhus; my palms began to sweat, and I felt like laughing and crying at the same time. How did my father know to call me then, at that precise moment? And why? Does True Art ordain itself? Here I was in a small north Georgia town, in a frame house on the edge of the country, with a cat named after a gymnasium, and a new sense of vocation.

From that day, I was *mad* for classical music. I started listening when my parents quoted Shelley and Byron. I began to read poetry myself in the dogeared copy of *Palgrave's Golden Treasury* that my father had lugged around with him during the War. When he painted, I hung out with him and watched as he mixed his colors and media with the precision of the chemist that he was. I prowled over the section on visual art in our copy of *The Popular Educator's Library* and learned about Salvador Dalì. And yet that was the problem. In *A River Runs Through It*, Norman Maclean said, memorably, that in his house as a boy there was no clear line between religion and fly-fishing. In our house, there was never a clear line between art and science. To me, science seemed like an art, and art seemed like a science. Both were intoxicating mixtures of curiosity and inspiration. I grew up wading through archaeology, radio electronics, chemistry, and physics. (Daddy took to building bombs with cardboard pillboxes, black gunpowder, orange fuses, and medical tape during those innocent pre-terrorist days. He exploded them for his high school physics students to demonstrate the speed of sound. He also built rockets and balsa wood airplanes.) On the arts side, our house was a hotbed of poetry, music, painting, and the occasional piece of fiction, too.

In those same years, I had a secondary epiphany, one somehow just as powerful as the first but visual and intuitive. The north side of our yard sloped down to a majestic oak tree that stood between our house and a tiny deep-banked creek that lay between us and the Teacherage, a rambling building near the high school that had been built as a girls' dormitory and later used by teachers in the old A&M days. Here is what happened: I was alone outside. It was late fall, and all the leaves had fallen from that oak tree and the others around our yard. Though sunlight still streaked the sky to the west in lovely shades of pumpkin and pink, the moon and stars were already coming out, too. It was almost time for supper, as the evening meal was universally known in the South. And I was standing not far from the oak, looking west into the setting sun when I had an overwhelming sense of peace and a knowledge that I would do something important with my life. Other writers and artists have reported similar times of speechless intuition. Willem De Kooning had such a moment looking out into the harbor in his boyhood Rotterdam. I remember that I wore a jacket and that I felt as if I slipped entirely out of my body and saw myself standing there, small and fragile, yearning. The air was crisp and clean, as if a cold front had gone through. Perhaps it had. But somehow I knew that I was meant to live a different life, and that I would not be like others I knew. It may well be that almost everyone has such moments, but from talking to many people, I doubt it. I felt more alive, more sure, and more at peace at that moment than I ever did for the rest of my life. I took it as a summons and a challenge. *God,* it was wonderful.

In those early days, Mark had almost no interest in anything but the science side of the family and certainly didn't care for writing as art. Later, he became a solid writer with numerous edited books, scholarly papers, and archaeological site reports to his credit, though, as an undergraduate at the University of Georgia, he once, in a paper, used the phrase, "For some, that may be too big of a pill to handle." I was the exact opposite, becoming more and more sure of myself in the world of the arts and finding anything past long division as easy to follow as the Sears Catalog in Cuneiform. Later,

Laura Jane would take up both sides, becoming an exceptional pianist and a fine registered nurse who now teaches medical procedures to would-be licensed practical nurses.

But following that epiphany, my course was set as surely as a planetary orbit. After supper that night, I went back to our fire hose swing and touched the sky feet-first like Frost's swinger of birches, not caring that the black snake had dripped off the limb in the heat and glared at me, wringing its malevolent but metaphorical hands with nasty anticipation. I never did know an omen, even when it looked me in the eye.

He loves the ice colors of winter, the cinereous trunks in low daylight, mars-black on a crescent moon night. He has always heard that old people cannot tolerate the cold, grow phototropic as daffodils, but he loves a day when words become visible. The timberwolf stripes of white oak and hickory rise, seasonal guardians, just outside his study's window. Some of them have grown old, too. Sun off Wildcat Creek at noon in January turns the water cadet gray. He tries so hard to love the days when the gunmetal hues go away and green returns, when the woods fill with trilliums and rue anemones. But he cannot. He only feels fully himself when the last leaf (except for beeches) has dropped down to the forest floor, and cold darkness blows in from the northwest.

3

Also, a Whiff of Aromatherapy

We moved into Madison from our house in the country when I was ten, and my father had left his job at the high school to take a position in Athens, which meant he had to commute twenty-eight miles each way. He never seemed to mind, but then politics was the only thing that ever got him extremely exercised. He would still do things like play the "Polka and Fugue from *Schwanda the Bagpiper*" on the stereo and dance around the living room with unrestrained glee.

Laura Jane, as I said, was born in 1959, and when she was five, my mother and her friend Barbara Engle started a private kindergarten they called Magic Land, and Mother was in her element, teaching and nurturing, something she and Barbara did for twelve years. Mark and I fought less because I was too smart to get pummeled as often once I became a teenager.

By the time I was fourteen, I decided that I wanted to be a composer of symphonies and concerti. I read biographies of Beethoven and Brahms, of Schumann and Schubert, noticing that they didn't have exactly normal lives. Few of them married, for instance, and Schumann celebrated his art by trying to drown himself in the Rhine and then starving himself to death. To me, this was just wonderful. I loved the fact that Wagner, for instance, was a cheapskate who never paid his debts and engaged in serial philandery. Sure, there was always some killjoy like Richard Strauss who got rich and stayed married to the same woman for fifty years, but there was also a Hugo Wolf to offset the killjoys. Wolf, who wrote exquisite songs, wound up in an asylum mad as the March Hare. The lesson was this: If you are a great artist, *the rules do not apply*. They didn't apply to Liszt, who fathered children out of wedlock and lived like the Shah of Turkistan. They didn't apply to Tchaikovsky, who was what my townsmen in those long ago days would have (sadly) called a fruit or something worse, but who was beloved anyway. Any fourteen-year-old in America adores those to whom the rules don't apply. And just before I turned fourteen I saw, on "The Ed Sullivan Show," a British pop band that didn't seem to follow too many rules, either. I loved rock and roll, pop, and what we now call Americana music. I'd like to say that seeing the Beatles on TV was a second epiphany, that it prefigured a period of debauchery and artistic madness, but in truth I was always a Good Boy, and the idea of misbehaving in public horrified me. I knew which side my hair was parted on. We did have some strange goings-on in the family, and I had one uncle who'd died a suicide and another who'd called the day of his own death like Babe Ruth calling his home run, but when I grew up, I found virtually everyone else I spoke to had similar stories or worse. (My family looks like a clan of saints when balanced against Zelda Fitzgerald's.)

We first moved to a small, boxy house on Poplar Street in Madison, then around the corner to a larger and nicer home on Foster Street, where, at this writing, my father still lives, ninety-one years old and flourishing. (Mother died in 2008, and I still grieve.) As always, Mark and I shared a room. That was a necessity. I didn't like sharing it with his *mouse* during the weeks he kept it in a cage and ran experiments on it for a high school biology class. He and our father had built a unit with a counter that clicked every time the mouse moved, so Mark could graph its day-night activity. All night long, I heard this *click-click-click*, and finally it was even driving Mark crazy, and we stuffed pillows, socks, and underwear over the device, just managing to avoid suffocating the rambling rodent.

"I think it was tenth grade biology with Mrs. Ridgeway," Mark remembered decades later. "It was using an ultrasonic motion detector... The counter was a green clacking counter very similar to a car odometer—it simply counted more times if the mouse was moving around more. It was relay-driven and totally electromechanical. I simply was documenting the change over day-night, etc. I still have the counter! Wish I had the ultrasonic unit also—we sold it. Our loss of sleep was a small price for the advancement of science!"

That was our house when I was growing up.

At age fourteen, I began to compose and to take piano lessons from Kathleen Reid, who lived with her family on a quiet street I could reach through the woods about two hundred yards from our house. Mrs. Reid was a conservatory-trained musician of such transcendent brilliance in all areas of music that I still, at this late date, feel honored to have known her. She *was* music in Madison for forty years, and she died much too young in 2001 from aplastic anemia. I absolutely adored her, though starting piano at fourteen meant I was about six or seven years behind where I should have been. But I already knew so much about music history and theory that she enjoyed teaching me as much as I loved taking from her. I would gain moderate competence as a pianist by the time I graduated from high school, but I never got much better as a sight-reader, though I could play almost anything by ear after hearing it once. (Laura Jane, by contrast, never could improvise at all, though she could sight-read *anything,* a talent I have coveted my whole life. She has always wanted to have *my* improvising skills. Life isn't fair!) To this day, I can see a movie and then two or three days later go to the piano and play the main-theme music in any key, a seriously useless but sometimes amusing talent. Mark had studied piano with Ms. Reid for one year, in the first grade, but it had been such a misfire with his scientific bent that my parents hadn't even made me do it—I started lessons when I had to *beg* for them. Mark still remembers his only recital, playing a piece called "Buster's Little Indians," and leaving out a third of the short piece. He later became quite a fine guitarist and a superb bassist, and for years he played with a band of crazy archaeologists and beer addicts who called themselves Slant Six, the name taken after one of the best auto engines ever designed. Perfect. I remember seeing Slant Six play once when they came on at a club around 1 a.m. (This was some years before the all-woman punk-rock trio called Slant 6.) He also played in a bluegrass band called Georgia Southern Grass for a year in the late 1970s.

The first thing I composed was a sonata for solo violin. I had heard plenty of violins on records (and my father had started taking me to concerts in Athens and Atlanta), but I couldn't play one. On one of those trips we even saw Aaron Copland conduct the Atlanta Symphony Orchestra playing his Third Symphony. We owned my father's father's fiddle, but none of us could sound a note on it. (My grandfather had died in 1935 when my father was twelve.) Much of my knowledge was, therefore, theoretical, something that never stopped me from acting as if I knew everything. Mark and our father share this character flaw, though Laura Jane and Mother were blissfully free of it. I was also by then quite a good trombonist, playing in the high school band, and so I composed brief pieces for my trombone, too. In fact, it was in those years that I began to fanatically schedule my time so that I could cram an insane amount into each day, especially a Saturday. Here's how it would look:

7:00-8:00—Read from Grout's *History of Western Music*
8:00-8:15—Breakfast
8:15-9:15—Listen to Act I of *Die Meistersinger*; make notes for my opera
9:15-10:15—Practice trombone
10:15-11:05—Practice piano
11:05-12:00—Read from *Medieval and Renaissance Music*
12:00-12:15—Lunch
12:15-1:15—Nap
1:15-4:00—Compose

This kind of thing went on for months at a stretch, I regret to say. Now, fifty years later, I still manage my time in much the same way, like the Roadrunner on amphetamines. I feel as if I've wasted my entire day if I haven't at least written and composed (maybe painted, too) before ten in the morning. James Dickey did the same thing, early and late in his life, and at one period, according to Henry Hart's biography, Dickey drew up schedules that "accounted for every half-hour of his day." I thought my mad love affair with creative work was about as bad as it got. Then I read in Isaac Asimov's obituary that he had written *five hundred* books. I felt like a complete loser for weeks. By the time I was sixteen, I had been composing steadily for two years, much of it for solo piano or trombone, though I'd tried a few harder things and would eventually finish a fully scored (though small) symphony by the time I was nineteen. That November, however, my father gave me the large blank book and my life shifted directions. Maybe it wasn't enough only to be composing, studying music history, and practicing the piano and trombone. I was being a slacker. I should be writing and painting, too.

I know, I know. It appears that I was manic-depressive, suffering from what we now neatly call bipolar disorder, except that I never had the depressive stage. If anything, I was manic-(slighty less)-manic. I've wondered at times over the years where this nutty approach to life comes from, and my only defense is that my brother and father are exactly the same, so I don't think it was from a brother-brother competitive drive. Apparently, it is genetic. My wife once found me reading a book about

Flannery O'Connor, listening to a symphony, and watching a Braves game with the sound on the TV muted.

"I'm also doing a little aromatherapy," I said, pointing toward the incense in its burner on the coffee table. Linda looked at me the way she looks at me. Believe me when I say this isn't the palaver of a braggart. I can also sit for hours looking at ant mounds or watching sinuous dunes form and reform beneath the flowing water of our creek, but it doesn't feel as nice to me as seeing just how much I can cram into one morning. Anyway, my father gave me this large blank book, and in the front, with moronic self-importance and redundancy, I wrote the following:

VOL. I
OPUS
POETRY, VOL. I
AND OTHER NOTES

Four years later, when I was a sophomore in college, I had progressed sufficiently far to know my first efforts at writing had been, well, putrid. This was fortunate. Unfortunately, I wrote the following on the page facing my grand title:

NOTE:

Most of these poems constitute a first attempt in this medium, but a man with one eye is king in the land of the blind.–Philip L. Williams, 1970

If I had wanted to be a prodigy at fourteen, I was, apparently, still something of a stuffed-shirt ninny at twenty, which now, well past sixty, I admit without shame. I was, to wring out the final drops from the metaphor, just another man with no eyes in the land of the blind. I should backtrack a little, though.

I had been writing already, but nothing so high-minded as poetry. I had always been a ham, grabbing the microphone of our reel-to-reel tape recorder and shouting jokes from the back of *Boys' Life* whenever Daddy was trying to do some serious documentary work. Mark and I had also taken to reading *Mad* magazine, which I absolutely adored. (There's an unwritten doctoral thesis on the influence of *Mad* on mid-century American humor.) Under the influence of *Mad*, TV sit-coms, and the kind of old-fashioned comedy records my parents' friends would sometime bring over to play, I began to write what might generously be called "sketches"—little playlets with cheap set-ups and sophomoric gag lines, though sometimes with a mildly appealing surrealistic quality. (My feeling was that if Dalí could melt a watch, anything was possible.) I wrote a number of these sketches and read them to the family, and whether it was out of relief when they were over or from genuine mirth, they laughed, which made me write more of the things.

One Thursday I came home from school and found *The Madisonian*, our local weekly newspaper, on the dining room table, folded open to one of my sketches! It was, as I recall, about an expedition by early geographers to find the point where Georgia, South Carolina, and North Carolina meet. I was nothing if not topical. It seems my doting father had taken my handwritten playlet to Adelaide Ponder, the paper's editor, and later one of the most influential people in my life, and she'd printed it without hesitation for reasons I have never comprehended. Byron said that one morning he "awoke and found myself famous" when the London papers printed the first installments of his epic poem *Childe Harold's Pilgrimage*. I didn't awaken famous the next day, but my friends teased me mercilessly, and I found to my amazement that I liked it. So I wrote more, and my father dutifully took them to the newspaper office on Jefferson Street, and Mrs. Ponder dutifully had them set into type. Writing poetry had not occurred to me then, much less fiction. What I wanted to do was write for *Mad*.

So when my father gave me the blank book, I was unsure what to put into it. Should I write some sketches? Just why I decided to write a poem about the dead of Pompeii escapes me now, though it seems in some ways a perfect adolescent theme. My second poem was equally unexpected, thirteen couplets and one additional line just to make sure my point got across. I called it "Sic Semper Tyrannis," which of course means "Thus Always to Tyrants," and is the state motto of Virginia and the phrase John Wilkes Booth shouted just after he shot President Lincoln. My poem was about a sadistic plantation overseer who beats his slaves and gets his just desserts when he's struck by lightning. The first two couplets are worth printing:

In midst of night the wind did howl
And moaning cries from beast and fowl

Did fill the nearby cotton fields
Which now lay heavy with their yields.

To this day, I'm not sure how a chicken can make a "moaning cry," but I didn't let small details like that stop me. I hit new heights with a poem called "Life":

Ha, ha, ha
Blah.
Twinkle, klink, click
Buzz blat, splat
Poof
The End
Of life
Or death.

This was clearly *good stuff.* After some argument with my girlfriend in November 1967, I started a poem with the line "Pity the poor fool who calls himself happy," thereby anticipating another great poet, Mr. T. But at least it was an improvement over moaning chickens. So I was launched as a poet and comedy writer. My classmates began to ask me to help scribble their theme papers, which I considered a great honor. And it took a little pressure off my classmate and friend Sandra Stapp, who got begged for help almost daily. Sandra somehow managed to be hilariously funny and effortlessly brilliant at the same time, making her the one Brain of whom nobody was ever jealous. Sandra did everything perfectly—math, English, French, social studies, living a lovely life as a human being—she was *always* right. My next-door neighbor, classmate, and good friend Charles Parker also helped me get through high school, especially in math. Thanks, Charlie.

I was composing and writing and painting, and I remember one painting I called "Beyond the Bitter Crescent," in which I managed to cram about three pounds of oil paint on a nine-by-twelve-inch canvas board. I also did a female nude, which I painted entirely from uneducated guesses and smudged images from hijacked and hidden copies of *Playboy*. Mostly I did still-lifes, leading my friend Edward Hudson, who is a real artist, to coin an imaginary conversation between two people fictionally looking at one of my paintings in a gallery: "Is that a Williams?" "It must be. It has a vase."

About this time I starred in a play for the first time in my life. It was also the last time I was ever in a play, and the character I played, named Richard, got run over by a car halfway through. Because we had no way to get me off stage, I had to fall down and spend the second half of the one-act lying behind a prop after I'd been slaughtered. The play was done in front of an audience of maybe a thousand at the state Y-Club conference at Rock Eagle State Park near Eatonton, Georgia, and afterward, my phone didn't ring off the hook from agents trying to hire me. In fact, on stage I sounded like someone with English as a second language trying to read a phone book. At least the critics didn't kill me. But the imaginary car did.

My parents pretended everything I did was wonderful, which encouraged me to commit further horrors on the English language. Since I knew nothing at the time about orchestration, I began a symphony. How hard could it be? All through high school I was like this, I'm embarrassed to say, but little by little, I was learning to separate the poor from the less poor, and sometimes I wrote a line with enough sparkle to let me know I was on a path that might lead me to castles in the sky.

The last day of his work life at the University of Georgia, he tries to feel something deep and lasting. It is January 30, his birthday. For weeks he has been listening on YouTube to a 1970 recording of David Crosby and Graham Nash singing "Guinnevere," and he is wistful, certain that his work life has meant little beyond helping pay his family's bills. He opens the venetian blinds and looks over the characterless parking lot that is squeezed between the Chemistry Building and Sanford Stadium. A truck empties a Dumpster with a hideous screaming clang. He knows he will not come back to campus anytime soon. He hopes that people will stop asking him when he will write full time.

4

Russian Leather and Getting Blocked

I found my first real girlfriend in the eleventh grade. Her name was Emma[1], and she had china blue eyes, a wild sense of humor, and an astonishing talent for music. She composed pop songs that were professional, and she had a belt-it-out alto that could break glass or hearts. For our last two years of high school, Emma and I were inseparable. She had a wonderful, unladylike laugh, said whatever was on her mind, and was completely realistic about her future, unlike yours truly, who was still planning to make Beethoven look like a loser. I don't remember how she came to be my girlfriend, but she must have broken up with someone else and been on the rebound. I had dated, of course, but I'd known most of the girls since we were in the first grade, and they seemed more like sisters. Emma and her piano had moved in from another state much later.

On a typical date, I would pull a red velveteen sweater over a white dickey and then douse myself with enough Russian Leather to save Yellowstone from a wildfire. I washed my hair four times with Prell until it had so much static electricity I could repel stray cats. I was also courteous and had very good manners. I wasn't a complete romantic idiot, though. With my friends Wayne, Larry, Bill, Edward, Terry, Ted, and many more, we rode around at night on the dirt roads of Morgan County, some of us drinking bootleg beer from quart bottles and smoking Swisher Sweet cigars, behavior that passed for Very Bad in the 1960s. We talked about girls and music and golf, argued about baseball and football. None of them held it against me that I was a Published Arthur, as Morgan County lingo denoted those who wrote. I had a knack of bailing out at just the moment we were about to get into trouble. I was never sure if it was intelligence or cowardice,

---

[1] Name changed, in case she shudders at the thought of me.

but I rarely had any serious problems until I got kicked out of the high school band.

I had also turned into quite a fine trombonist. I practiced all the time (see my schedule, above), and by ninth grade, I was first chair in the MCHS band's trombone section. I was quite vain about this and about my "diaphragm vibrato," a way of slightly wavering the tone to give it more musicality. Most high school trombonists do it by rapidly moving their slides, but I did it by controlling my breath. I had a golden tone and technique to burn. In the summer between the tenth and eleventh grades, we had band camp as usual at Camp Daniel Morgan, nine miles from Madison on the grounds of Hard Labor Creek State Park, which never, so far as I knew, had an obstetrical ward. I think the name came from something involving convicts or wives, but the funny thing was its *Morgan* name. Our whole county, in the heart of Dixie, in a town where part of Sherman's troops had come through on the March to the Sea, was named for a man from—*New Jersey*. He was a patriot in the Revolution, but in truth Madison was never much for the *Waw-wah* (as we called the Civil War) anyway, despite the protestations of the UDC. Oh, we celebrated Confederate Memorial Day every year, but there had always been an undercurrent of apostasy and well-deserved guilt when it came to the Old South.

I digress. Not long before camp that year, eight nurses had been murdered in Chicago, shocking the country. Everyone was edgy and watchful, and that made it a dubious time for a group of non-band-members from our high school to swim across an arm of the lake and sneak into camp in the middle of the night. It was the kind of prank that went on all the time, but pulling it that year was seriously stupid. I was naïve and afraid, not to mention half asleep. None of the boys who broke in were friends of mine, but some band girls saw them running through the woods and alerted the band director. The next day, he kicked our whole cabin of boys out of the band, which was an unbelievable shock to me, since I had nothing to do with what was meant as a harmless prank. But that's life, and our director had his reasons. You can't fool around with fear. I would like to say that turned me into a rogue and a scoundrel, that I was in and out of trouble for the rest of my teenage years. Han Solo, not Luke Skywalker. Not true, though. I was mortified, horrified, and so ashamed I barely left the house for weeks.

That fall I had to take a physical education class in school for the first time in my life, since I was no longer in band. My friends accepted this with appropriate hilarity. We played touch football in what was essentially a pasture behind the football field during PE, sometimes calling time-out to smoke a Bull Durham cigarette in the shadow of the stadium's ticket booth. As a football player, I was slow, but I wasn't weak. At thirteen, I had gone mad for weightlifting and bodybuilding, a regular Charles Atlas, and I'd trimmed myself up. Still, I was not large, and the school was full of farm boys who could sling a hundred-pound sack of cattle feed on to a pickup truck with one meaty hand.

We chose teams and huddled. Whoever called the play always said the same thing to me: "Block Grant." That's right, Roger Grant[2]. Roger was a genial boy, easy to like, and stronger than the proverbial ox. He wasn't tall, but what he lacked in height he made up for with a kind of cheerful menace. *Nobody* could block Grant, least of all me. But I didn't want to be a bad sport, so I'd line up opposite Grant on every play.

"You're dead meat, Grant," I'd say, and he'd just smile at me, a grin of obvious, gentle, and frightening power. Maybe I'm misremembering this, but it seems Roger started running in place just before the ball was snapped every time to gain torque, not that he needed any. Then the center snapped the ball back, and Roger slammed over me like a dump truck over a centipede. I would try to block him, but he would flatten me in one fearful rush, and I'd land on my back, watching Grant's feet coming over my head toward the quarterback.

"Damn it, I told you to block Grant," the quarterback would say.

"I tried," I would answer with an almost inaudible squeak. I was told to block Grant again. This became a running joke during PE football games, so that when the quarterback was giving the play, everybody else on the team would turn to me and say, with the perfect unison of the Mormon Tabernacle Choir, "Block Grant." I spent that entire "season" getting laid flat on every offensive play we ran, and Roger never stopped smiling. He often helped me up after the plays and managed to look sheepish.

Emma didn't seem to mind that I was such a loser in sandlot football. I did play on the golf team, for instance, and was just good enough to be fourth on a four-man team, usually shooting around 83 or 84. (The region

---

[2] Name also changed.

tournament in both our junior and senior years was the morning after bibulous and sleepless proms, and we hit the first tee looking like Napoleon's soldiers after a Russian winter, but that's a story whose full details I won't divulge here.) I had been on the tennis team in the ninth grade, in those days of all-whites and wooden rackets with screw presses, but I had given up tennis for trombone.

I showed my esteem for Emma by writing her reams of bad poetry and composing songs with such a high sugar content they should have been banned for diabetics. If she thought I was being a dip, she never let on, at least not to me. And that was one of the problems. Even after several years of writing and composing, I wasn't getting any better. I knew I wasn't a Keats yet, but I was hoping I was no worse than Rod McKuen. In looking back now on the archives, which I have stupidly kept, I can say I was putrid in a sincere kind of way. The fact that I was reading almost nothing of real value probably had something to do with things.

I did have two favorite books, both of which I read the summer of my fifteenth year. The first was *Les Miserables*, which should ideally be read at fifteen. I slogged with Jean Valjean through the sewers of Paris the same way my daughter, thirty-eight years later, would follow Harry Potter's adventures. I just absolutely and hopelessly adored Victor Hugo's great book. The other was an unexpected pleasure, too, *The Agony and the Ecstasy* by Irving Stone. I think each of us has books that are tremendously important to us as youngsters, even though we know they aren't Shakespeare. Hemingway obsessively read Capt. Marryat's boys' books, for instance. *The Agony and the Ecstasy*, of course a biographical novel of Michelangelo, was probably the single most important book of my entire life. I realize I shouldn't admit this, that I should say that on a stormy night, I read *King Lear*, and it changed me forever. (That *did* happen, in my defense, but not for a few more years.) In truth, though, I began to read Stone's novel obsessively, and I kept it checked out of the library for probably three years. I now have five or six copies, and whenever it is a damp, drizzly November in my soul, I read the book, and it takes me back to my youth when all things still seemed possible.

I didn't want to be a writer like Irving Stone, though. I wanted to be Michelangelo, to paint, sculpt, write poetry, design buildings, and in general be the perfect Renaissance Man. Quite a goal for someone getting knocked on his ass by Grant every day. My own father was my guide, and I can say that I'm at least a well-meaning and hard-working polymath even today. The only difference between me and Michelangelo is that genius thing.

Emma and I made something of an odd couple, I'm afraid, mostly because of my doe-eyed infatuation and continuing disbelief that she would go out with a boy who wore Russian Leather and a dickey. I liked her high spirits, though, her amazing musical talent, and that laugh. Soon enough, she saw through me. During the summer after our senior year, while I was waiting to go to college, and she was looking for a job, she broke up with me. I didn't see it coming at all, and when she gave me back my Bad Poetry and sappy songs, I should have burned them out of pride. But I had not yet developed a sense of shame, and so I kept every page of what was more a courting strategy than an attempt at literature.

The only good thing I soon learned is that I couldn't have gotten much worse.

Sharp light has always broken him. In summer, he can bear the heat though he does not like it. What he cannot bear is the tropical light. So he dives down deep into a sheltering darkness, behind curtains and blinds, air conditioner set on sixty-eight, a different season from the one ten feet away. Look at him in photographs as a boy, and he is always squinting, forever tilting his head against the sun. In this one, he is standing with his brother Mark (who wears a Davy Crockett T-shirt) and his mother and father. It is June 1956, and they are at the house of his father's older brother. He has a large bandage on his head from an accident a couple of weeks before. His mother's hands are on his small shoulders, protective. Even though he smiles, the light hurts his eyes, hurts the small boy's brown eyes.

5

Flight of the Starling

When it comes to religion, I'm the child of a mixed marriage, since my father was a Southern Baptist and Mother was a Methodist. My parents didn't compromise by becoming Presbyterians, however. Mother did what all good wives did in the 1940s—she turned Baptist. In those days, unlike today, there wasn't much difference between them. In fact, most protestant denominations in my childhood 1950s were different only by tradition and hymns, with a few odd variations in worship services. The Methodist Church was right across the street from Madison Baptist, and we were all friends. Nobody thought much about it.

I wanted to be baptized, but I kept putting it off because I was terrified of standing in front of the congregation of Madison Baptist Church and having my head held under water by Preacher Sheffield, our kind old pastor whose faith never wavered, though his hands sometimes did. I was afraid he'd lose me in the font and have to call the fire department, and by the time they pulled me out, I'd be dead. I didn't want to be saved and croak at the same time, so I kept finding ways to avoid the whole thing as my friends, one after another, got dunked. None of my Methodist buddies had to face possible drowning and public humiliation, since they sprinkled over there, which seemed much more civilized.

We got a new preacher with the euphonius name of Tucker Singleton when Preacher Sheffield retired, but one summer night when I was about nine, I was at a party at the parsonage with my parents and lots of others, when Preacher Sheffield, who was still around, asked me to step with him back toward the garden. Uh oh. I knew where this was going. They were sending in somebody from the Hall of Fame to recruit me. This was serious.

"Phil," he said, "have you been thinking about giving your heart to the Lord?" he asked when we got to the corn. What was I going to say? You know, I think religion is the opiate of the masses? I'd like to, but I just washed my hair?

"Yes, sir," I said dutifully.

"Then we need to get you baptized soon," he said drumming his fingers on his thin cheek. "In three Sundays."

So that was it. I was going to be drowned just about the time Laura Jane was going to be born. It was all a set-up. But I realized that I couldn't get out of it this time, and so I grimly put my affairs in order—I had to decide who would get my Robin Hood men and my Roy Rogers six-guns. My brother Mark was out of the question, since at that time he was still dutifully throwing rocks at me and running me over with his bicycle. Maybe I'd leave them to some poor child who had been deprived of having an inch-tall rubber figurine of Friar Tuck.

The day came, and I still hadn't made any decisions about my possessions, which, the more I thought about it, the poor wouldn't want, either. Preacher Singleton had tutored me in baptism for a few weeks, telling me what to expect. Drowning wasn't, apparently, among the commonly listed side effects, though a New Life in Christ was. I had this idea that I'd come up from the water (if at all) glowing with the New Life, shining like a lightning bug, seraphic. But then I started wondering if the New Life might be accompanied by electricity, and I knew from my gadfly scientist father that water and electricity weren't friends. While he did build bombs and rockets, I was fortunate he never tied me to the huge Tesla coil he and Mark had constructed and tossed me in the creek to see what might happen.

The morning of my baptism, I was shaking like a maple leaf in an F-5 tornado, but at least I was allowed to wear blue jeans into the baptismal pool, something that seemed wonderful to me. I had always thought blue jeans were an offense to God, like snickering during communion. What I didn't know was that I had to wear a baptismal robe over my T-shirt and blue jeans—something that looked remarkably like a very small woman's gown. So not only was I going to be drowned in front of all my friends, it was going to be in a *dress*.

When the time came, I stepped down into the pool of coolish water, and immediately my jeans weighed about eighty pounds, and my dress floated on the surface of the water like a lily. And of course I had to pee. I was told that God would be watching all this, too, no doubt rolling around and laughing, pointing me out to Mrs. God and saying, "Wait for it. You're gonna *love* this." The pool had a curtain, so Preacher Singleton let me get situated before it was drawn back, as if revealing the Wizard of Oz or an execution. I glanced into the congregation, and everybody in the place was looking at me as I swatted my dress to try and make it sink. In those pre-air conditioned days, the tall stained glass windows were open, and a bird descended to the closest sill to watch, too. For a moment I hoped it might be a dove, a sign from God, but on closer inspection it turned out to be a starling.

I was shaking by now, worrying about electricity, trying to keep my dress down, needing a bathroom desperately. I wondered for a moment if a baptismal font was like the city swimming pool, which was about one-eighth urine on any given day. I knew that I couldn't pee in the baptismal font without being damned for all eternity, though having to wear a dress in front of two hundred people was close enough to damnation already. Preacher Singleton began the ritual, and I was repeating some promises we'd rehearsed, and I meant them, but about that time I noticed that my blue jeans had soaked up so much water that I wasn't sure I could walk back out of the baptismal pool or, perhaps, even come back up after he dunked me.

I glanced at the congregation. Mark was grinning like a coyote about to be thrown a piece of meat. Everyone else seemed delighted except for sweet old Mr. Ralph Collier, who was lying asleep on the front row, having gone through his ritual shouting of *amen* several times before he dozed off. I was saying things, but I wasn't thinking too much about them, when suddenly, I felt Preacher Singleton's hand on the back of my neck, and he was pulling me backward into the water, from which I was to rise full of the spirit.

I rose, instead, blowing water like a whale from my nose, though nobody could see it since my dress had floated up over my head. I was sure at this point that I was dying, and I swatted at the dress, staggering from the burden of my blue jeans, which alone weighed enough to sink the *Titanic*. And God *knew* I needed a bathroom. I finally got the dress off my face, gasping and shivering from the water, which now seemed horribly cold. Everybody in the congregation seemed ecstatic except for Mr. Collier, who was happily snoring and clearly in the middle of a dream. The curtains closed, and Preacher Singleton went out to change quickly, since he had to get back to the pulpit. I started to get out, but then my dress and my blue jeans began to drag me backward into the water, and I grabbed the edge of the pool and managed to stagger up the steps, dripping and shivering. At which point I dedicated myself to God—to getting *even* with him, I mean.

Fortunately, this phase didn't last long, and for much of my life, I've been in a pew on Sunday mornings. I left the Baptist church in college as I changed, and for many years I was a member of the ELCA, the moderate branch of the Lutheran Church. I'm not sure being spiritual has ever been considered cool to people in their late teens or twenties, but I didn't have a choice. After that morning, God and I began a lifelong argument, but it was one of good cheer and at times quite scholarly. At least I stayed above the water and not beneath it.

He has never liked his own face. In the mirror, his backward twin looks haunted and hidden. He ducks from photographs because the flash can trigger migraine auras. But there is more. That odd gene, too, that his hair has never gone gray—people suspect him. He realizes how stupid it is to dislike one's own face, how self-centered, how pointless. He is proud of what he has done, and loves all his family, more than he can easily say. But he wonders if some moral weakness is visible, some deeper sorrow writ in flesh and bone. He writes from the unhappiness he sees in that face, unhappiness that is largely absent from how he presents himself to others. He wonders if it turns away because it hides a great secret, one too painful to see. Please, he says to the mirror, please do not look at me.

6

No Regard for Money

My graduating class from Morgan County High School in the spring of 1968 numbered about sixty-five. We had survived many things together, from the assassinations of President Kennedy and Dr. Martin Luther King, Jr., to a raging new war in Vietnam. Robert Kennedy was killed a few days after graduation. (He, Dr. King, and civil rights pioneer John Lewis have been my lifelong heroes.) I had not been permanently maimed blocking Grant, though some days I was sure being crippled would be easier. The band, amazingly, survived without me.

I never doubted what would come next in my life. I would attend the University of Georgia, where Mark was already a student and where our parents had both graduated in 1948. (Laura Jane was already, as I said, on her way to being a Brain like Mark, but I had only graduated because my algebra and geometry teacher, the fabled Alma Quillian, took pity on me and helped me through formulas that I never understood. To this day, when I see x=*anything*, I start to have a panic attack.) I knew by the time I was fourteen that I would major in music.

Of course, I had to audition for the music school, which I did that spring. My friend Dera Goodner, an accomplished pianist who was already at UGA as a keyboard major (she was Mark's age), agreed to accompany me as I sang a couple of the *Songs of a Traveler* by the English composer Ralph Vaughn Williams. Just why I thought I could be a voice major escapes me now. The truth was I wanted to major in theory and composition, but everyone in music had to have an "instrument," and since I'd been cashiered from my trombone-playing days, my light baritone voice was my only hope. As a pianist, I was still just adequate. So I prepared as hard as I could, trying to infuse my miniscule technique with some personality. Unfortunately, I sounded, on high notes, as if I was trying to call for help while drowning in tapioca. Dera coached me as well as she could, but my tone was the musical equivalent of being run over by Grant. By the time my audition came, I was shaking so badly that I feared I'd sound like the old lady in our church choir who had turkey wattles and howled on high notes somewhat like the "fowl" in my ill-fated poem. Dera launched into the songs, though, and I had to sing, so I did. By the time I finished, my judge (and I, presumed, high executioner) Professor Pierce Arant, a man whose surpassing dedication to excellence I would get to know well in the next few years, was nodding.

"That was very nice," he said when I finished. I wasn't sure if I'd actually done acceptably, or if they were so desperate for students they would have admitted James Brown to the vocal program. As far as I knew, Puccini had not written "I Feel Good." Once back outside, I was so relieved I gave myself a metaphorical high-five (a physically demanding move) and then realized I'd locked my keys in the car. Miserable, I slunk back inside and scouted around until I found a coat hanger in the choral rehearsal room, pilfered it, and crept back out, unfolded it, and began to fish for the lock, which in those days, designed for the convenience of thieves, was an easy-to-reach button on top of the door. I was making some progress when I realized someone was standing beside me: a campus cop.

"I suppose this is your car," he said dubiously.

"I just auditioned for the music department," I said in a strangled voice. "I'm from Madison." He clearly wasn't impressed with my accomplishments or pedigree. "I was nervous and locked my keys in the car. Pretty stupid, huh?"

"It happens," he said, which, when translated, meant Yes, it's pretty stupid. Fortunately, I managed to catch the lock and pull it up about that time, and he wandered off while I got in and lay my forehead on the steering wheel, sweating and breathing like Pavarotti after "Nessun Dorma."

As it turned out, that day was the high point in my career as a music major. I had kept up my composing and writing, and I believed that a career in either would be my ticket to fame. You'll notice I didn't say fortune. That's because we grew up with virtually no regard for money, since neither of our parents ever talked about it at all. We were given to believe that if you had enough money to pay your bills and have some left over for books, records, and components for rockets, radios, or Tesla coils, that was all you needed.

From the beginning, that fall of 1968, I was in trouble as a music major. First of all, my advisor accidentally signed me up for Women's Glee Club. I came in the room and sat down at the appointed time and realized that all the other singers had pins from Tri-Delt and Phi Mu, and that I was the only male in the room. There was a considerable amount of giggling and pointing. For a brief, electric moment I thought about staying. It took me two *days* to get things straightened out. Nobody told me, either, that I had to sign up for a practice room at the beginning of fall quarter, since I was taking a class in piano, too. I wound up begging the pastor of the Lutheran Campus Center to let me practice there, since Mark's girlfriend went to church there. Dubious, but trying to be a good guy, he gave me late-night access when I was too tired to play a scale, much less Mozart.

In three weeks I realized that I was so far out of my league I needed to change majors. Emma and I had broken up by then, so I had no future as a professional musician, no girlfriend, and the suspicion that being sandwiched between two Brains in our family left me in the Moron Slot. I was also living in Reed Hall, a near-medieval dormitory on a stately quadrangle, with my good friend from Madison, Larry Walker, who was working nights at a local printing plant and came in at all hours. Larry was a great guy, intelligent, talented in many things, and a *real* football player who'd been a linebacker on the MCHS team while Grant was knocking my lights out in the PE class. Larry was a tremendously gifted guitarist, too. But even a fine man can't be quiet eating a vending machine dinner at three in the morning, and I was getting little sleep, though our noisy hall-mates had as much to do with it. One morning I got up, groggy from being awakened about nine times, stepped into the hall, and confronted a cheerfully clucking chicken that had apparently been kidnapped and then freed. It was walking slowly down the empty hall, singing placidly. I could tell it wasn't a music major, either. I went back to bed and missed class.

After one quarter, during which I had shamed myself in courses such as Brass Methods, I knew that the life I'd planned for the past four years would not happen. I was stunned and bereft, and in that state of eighteen-year-old confusion, I did the only sane thing that came to mind: I looked for a major that didn't require math. That ruled out all the sciences, which was fine with me, since Mark was struggling hideously as a physics major, and I had no intention of having my father tie me to his Tesla coil and teach me the finer points of static electricity. (A born teacher, he would stop eating to deliver a fifteen-minute lecture on organic solvents or Etruscan history, something we came to expect at any moment.) It was frankly quite a relief to have half of the learned world off my radar.

After music, I loved literature the most, but this was in the middle of the Vietnam War, and I had a college deferment, and graduating with an English degree in those days was the equivalent of asking to be posted on the Cambodian border with a Red Ryder BB gun and a Wham-O slingshot. I needed something more practical. When I told this to my voice teacher, the aforementioned Pierce Arant, he suggested, with the quiet sarcasm at which he was a virtuoso, that I look into motel management.

"Music just wasn't what I thought it was going to be," I whined in his office, which in those days was in the basement of the Fine Arts Building. "I wanted to study periods of music, like, like, the Medieval and the Classic, and the...the...."

I was stuck trying to remember, and my hands shook. He pointed to a tape recorder on the shelf.

"If that tape recorder right there [*pointing*] fell off that shelf and crashed to the floor it would be...."

"Baroque!" I shouted miserably. He tented his fingers and nodded. At last I'd gotten something right.

I went through the course catalog like a religious nut seeking biblical ciphers. One morning it dawned on me: journalism! As a journalism major, I could substitute something called "physical science" for math. This physical science turned out to be a cross between high school chemistry and physics, with almost no math. This would also allow me to write for a living. So, with great élan, I changed my major to—*television directing*? I did, God help me, though to this day I cannot quite remember why. I had the choice of three "sequences" in the journalism school: radio-TV-film, print journalism, or advertising. I had already begun working summers at *The Madisonian* with Adelaide and Graham Ponder, writing everything from obituaries to feature stories and sports, but for some reason, I looked into the future and saw myself performing a job whose stress level was just a notch below that of air traffic controller. I'd almost melted down while singing a couple of songs. I'm sure I would have been a dandy TV director. (In truth, I wound up as editor of an "alternative" newspaper later that was more stressful—

and fun—than any television control room, but I'm getting ahead of myself.) I coached myself into believing that journalism was a choice I'd made, but the truth was I'd bailed out of music from fear and cowardice. John Berryman once said that a central dilemma of our culture is that a man can live his whole life not knowing whether or not he is a coward. Hah.

I also moved out of Reed Hall and back home to Madison, where I wouldn't have to fend off noisy hall-mates or feral chickens. My father had been working in Athens for several years by then, and so I commuted with him after that through four years of college, and though he'd sometimes cue me into the latest Dead Sea Scrolls research or the likely identity of Jack the Ripper, or lecture me about the stupidity of my increasingly left-wing political views, we mostly rode in a congenial silence.

That fall, needing to write, I decided to compose a grand essay called "The Necessity for a Creative Existence." I took my blank book and made a title page to that effect, turned one leaf, and began writing: "Any theory of existence viewed from a single position or idea must be considered incomprehensible." I knew I was in trouble already, and my essay lasted exactly eighteen-and-a-half lines before I gave it up. I was nineteen in January 1969, and it was getting pretty clear that I wasn't going to be a child prodigy. I *had* painted a number of pictures, and I finished my symphony that winter, but I was just posing for something I hoped to be. Any time I got near the really hard work, I fled, as I had from being a music major.

Since it had been so difficult to get into the Men's Glee Club, what with my detour into the women's group, I decided I would stay in that class, and I kept it up until the last quarter my senior year, touring with the guys, making an LP, and generally having a fine time. We sang well, drank a lot of beer, chased women, and generally pretended we were in Seventeenth Century Heidelberg, minus the saber scars. One time we sang in Beethoven's Ninth with the Savannah Symphony Orchestra, and after a rousing performance, we went back to the hotel, quickly achieved an appalling degree of inebriation, and ran amuck. We followed three stewardesses to their room as they checked in and, on the balcony, we sang "Delta is ready when you are!" in three-part harmony. They laughed but then called the house detective on us. One fine bass in our group wound up standing on a coffee table in the lobby singing "Old Man River" *a capella* while we cheered him on. (My artist friend from Madison, Edward Hudson, was also in the glee club, and he can vouch that I'm not making this up.) Dr.

Arant lectured us mightily, threw up his arms, got red in the face. He called us names. We deserved his rebuke, but as always, he forgave us and made us work twice as hard. He almost dared us to quit, but few ever did because we were so damned good that every rehearsal was like a cocktail of gin and adrenalin. Some of our performances approached transcendence. He passed away a few years ago, and I hope the heavenly choirs are behaving and listening to him.

Television in 1969 barely resembled what it does today. Field cameras, electronic or videotape, did not exist. All stories done outside the studio had to be *filmed*, then the film had to be developed and edited before it could be shown on the six o'clock news. The studio cameras at the University of Georgia weighed about three tons a piece, and it took two large men to dolly them around. It also took about ten trillion candlepower to light sets for these beastly cameras, and the lights were blisteringly hot, but the cameras wouldn't operate in heat. This meant the studios had to be kept at the average temperature of McMurdo Station in deepest winter, even when the cameras and the lights were off. We didn't even have color cameras in the studio, making do with cast-off black-and-white Vidicon cameras that commercial stations could donate and, I suppose, write off on taxes as an educational expense.

As usual, I began majoring in TV directing while having absolutely no idea what I was doing. My ignorance was so vast that I couldn't even summon enough emotion for cowardice. We learned to operate cameras and studio "switchers," to read the news, to run the "board" in mock radio studios. My favorite professor was a floppy-haired and attractively smug young man named Larry Aldridge, who was funny and who put up with us when we played with the equipment for fun.

So I was launched into college, minoring in English and history, while learning to direct TV programs, something I had no intention of ever doing in Real Life. My writing had almost stopped, I'd managed to fail in music—the only thing I ever really wanted to do—and I was living at home again with my parents, Laura Jane, and a Siamese cat named Slob.

I was going nowhere fast when fate, with a giggle, made sure I came face to face with Jaws.

What is the soundtrack of his life's movie? Something of deep romantic love and pain, meaning music that is rather idiotic but honest. He can see the audience laughing when the Main Theme *kicks in as he walks on the trails he built all over his family's land. Not that again! Then there's the* Retirement Suite, *music for flute and harp, the wistful uselessness of age. The audience goes for popcorn. Put on the cartoon! someone shouts from the back, and a wave of giggles breaks on the shoal of the stage down front. Here is the* Autographing-When-No-One-Comes *theme, and it's getting pathetic in here. Well, it ain't* Apocalypse Now! *a man in the back shouts. The soundtrack of his life's movie is out of control. He dashes up into the projection booth and tries to stop the film, but the reel keeps unspooling. This is the* So-What? *theme, as he grins and shrugs, as if to say, Take it or leave it. This is the truth of me.*

7

No Sudden Movements

In the summer of 1970, I headed south with my friend Edward Hudson and his family on a weeklong houseboat cruise in the Florida Keys. Edward was the sole person in Madison who had the same attitude toward Art that I did. He was a spectacular visual artist, and I also painted, though I wasn't remotely in his league. By 1970, though, we were twenty, out of our teenage years, and into a deep need for Art in a serious, constant way. From the first, I had no interest in popular authors or the idea of writing to make money. Maybe being famous like Byron could be amusing, but I wanted to create lasting works as Shelley or Wordsworth had, and to me Art was about transcendence, not about money. I was just getting to know modern authors such as Cummings and Stevens and Pound and Ginsberg, and the excitement of discovery was, as it always is for the young, absolutely intoxicating.

Edward and I began to dig deep into our own areas of the art world. In addition to already being a superb hand with oil paints and a pencil, he knew classical music as I did, since his mother was an excellent pianist and piano teacher. He also played the piano beautifully by ear and had a wicked sense of humor that matched mine. At the same time, we lived fairly normal lives, and he was also on the golf team and quite a bit better than I was. His father was an officer at a local bank, and that summer, he rented a houseboat for a week. We would pick it up, I think, on Matecumbe Key off the coast of south Florida and spend the week wandering around the islands and Florida Bay, going any place we chose. In addition to Edward's mother and father, his brother, universally known by his nickname Buster, came along. (They had an older sister, Janie, who was already grown and off living her life. What wonderful people.)

The driving trip from Madison to south Florida was suitably hilarious, and Buster was every bit our equal in nutty words games and humor heavily influenced by Monty Python. The boat was squat and slow, but we had a delightful time, and not long before sunset one day, I caught a huge red snapper that I cleaned and cooked for dinner that night. I also brought a notebook and wrote a few poems when I had time. By then, I was reading more and more and beginning to write from a new place—one that excited me tremendously. I fell madly in love with the poetry of Walt Whitman, and I began buying anthologies and seeing with increasing joy the new writing of the Fifties and Sixties in America. I also sensed for the first time that I might have talent that could work with my ambition if not quite match it.

All the way to the tip of Florida on the drive down, we joked about sharks. You have to realize that this was four years before Peter Benchley's novel *Jaws* came out and five before Stephen Spielberg's film of it did. (I have a six-degrees-of-separation tie to the film of *Jaws*: The producers of that picture, Richard Zanuck and David Brown, bought the movie rights to my novel *All the Western Stars*, but that was eighteen years in the future. I even have a minor tie to the novel—see the chapter on my first literary agent, Molly Friedrich.) The idea that we might actually encounter a shark, however, seemed ridiculous.

The John Pennekamp Coral Reef State Park is just south of Key Largo, seventy nautical square miles of gorgeous underwater architecture. We had already on the trip made it to Key West and toured Ernest Hemingway's house, but this was almost eight years before the onset of my Hemingway obsession. At that point, I had no interest whatever in writing fiction. I considered poetry a higher art (and still do), and I wanted to be two things: a fine poet and a great composer. Still, Hemingway's house jazzed me, and six-toed cats, descendants of the polydactylic fuzzballs that Ernie kept there decades before, dripped out of trees as we passed under them, languidly looking at us in the drowsy heat. The Nobel Prize-winning author of *The Old Man and the Sea* had shot himself in Idaho nine years before, but his ghost still seemed to linger in Key West. I was still thinking of Hemingway and long-form fiction when we dropped anchor in Pennekamp, which is the country's first underwater park, formally opened as such in 1963.

The water where we sat bobbing in the Atlantic Ocean, maybe half a mile offshore, was only about seven or eight feet deep. The day was gorgeous and hot, and we planned to snorkel through the coral formations and admire their natural artfulness. By then, Edward and I both had begun to see the world in a new way, and he taught me how to see color—something few people, in truth, really know how to do.

"It's amazing," Edward said, as we both rose at the same time from the sea floor, breached the surface of water, and blew out our snorkeling tubes.

"I can't believe it," I nodded. "I never thought I'd get to see anything like this."

We went back down, and this time I came down feet-first on to the coral and immediately cut a long gash in my foot. I glanced down through my diving mask and saw a murky trail of bright blood as it drifted from my foot like smoke off a candle. A bolt of pain shot through me, and I cursed my luck and swam back to the boat. After hauling myself up the ladder and on deck, I found the first aid kit and bandaged my foot, more or less stopping the bleeding.

"Maybe you shouldn't go back in with it bleeding like that," said Jean, Edward's mother.

"I'll wear my tennis shoes," I said. In retrospect that seems like a nutty solution, but I was thinking of my foot leaking blood, and I thought that a sneaker, along with the bandage, might keep the bleeding stanched until later. I knew the chance of seeing such a gorgeous undersea world might never come again. So I sneakered-up and climbed back down the ladder into the water that connects the Gulf of Mexico to the Atlantic Ocean. Moving through the water with canvas shoes on was awkward at best. I thrashed and splashed and soon enough was several hundred yards from the boat. I had been practicing coming up just beneath the surface of the water, blowing out my snorkel, and going back down—the whole point of the device, after all. And when we went back down, I began to stay longer and longer, rising like a whale to expel water from my tube, taking a deep breath of sea air, and resuming my minutes as a submariner. The reef's formations were gorgeous, and huge fish of many species finned through them, waving hello or goodbye. I don't know how long I stayed down without taking my head out of the water this time—maybe twelve minutes or more—and I rose just beneath the surface and accidently ingested a bit of water and so came on into the glare of tropical light. When I did, I found myself in a huge and spreading pool of salty, highly aromatic blood, and from the boat, the rest of our party screamed my name. I licked my lips and realized I could *taste* blood, and for a moment I became disoriented as I treaded water.

"Phil! Phil!" the voices shrieked shrilly from the houseboat. "Shark!" One glance and I could see that everyone had made it back to the boat but me. The wake of drifting blood was so large that at first I thought I'd reopened my cut and was bleeding out. But in a moment I knew it couldn't be from me. In fact, it was from the just-killed tarpon three feet from me, bobbing in the low waves. Everyone still screamed my name and waved at me, but fear began to cast some kind of acoustical shadow over the hot surface of the water. The tarpon bobbed toward me, and I could see that it had been bitten in two, and the part left—with a bite mark like one on a child's sandwich—was more than three feet long. That's when I saw fins cutting the water five feet to my left.

The distance from dorsal to tail was staggering. And I knew instantly, irrevocably, that it was a shark. It thrashed and bowed, gnashed and chewed. My body turned carmine, burgundy, scarlet. A great shudder wracked my bones and flesh, and I inhaled sharply, waiting for the blow, for the tearing, for the end. The pain from my cut foot grew intensely as brine ached its way deep into the cut. If my crewmates shouted, I heard nothing now. If they leaped and waved, I was unaware. I could only see the roiling of the shark. It rolled to its side once, and a hank of flesh three inches long flashed off one tooth.

Abruptly, I remembered what I'd heard all my life: *Don't make sudden movements around sharks in the water. Be as still as you can.* But I was in a spreading vat of sea-borne blood, and the creature that had caused it was almost close enough to touch. The tarpon's head section, meanwhile, bobbed idly right next to me, its open and staring eye a biblical warning of hubris. My fight-or-flight instinct swelled in me like a tidal wave. I slid the diving mask over my face, bit down on the snorkel, and began to swim, heavy-footed and splashing, in my sneakers, trailing blood from my cut foot. Now the sound of my friends came back, and I could see them waving, moving, terrified. One cannot swim quietly or elegantly in the sea while wearing sneakers. I felt my breath go out and not return. I gulped at the heavy, spicy air, but nothing seemed to sink down into my lungs. A raspy gasping sound came from my throat, and though I tried to smooth my strokes and my flutter kick, I must have seemed like a Sunday buffet to the shark. The tarpon's blood came with me. It cloaked and coated me. I smelled of blood and salt. Then I was swimming more strongly, faster, harder, as I got nearer and nearer the houseboat. I realized that my friends were now screaming and making noise and looking past me in the water, not trying to help me aboard but hoping to scare the shark away from me. Then hands were reaching down for me as I made it to the ladder on the boat's starboard side.

I grabbed the third rung up, and, almost poisoned with adrenalin and fear, came flying up over the side of the boat and landed with a thud amid-decks, gasping, gagging, and looking down to see if one foot or the other was gone. I was whole. I was safe. I had made it. The others screamed and waved and threw a few disposable shipboard things at the shark, and I stood, shaking, and got my first and only look at the whole shark. It was *huge*. A shattering shudder came through me, and I calculated it was probably at least fifteen feet long, possibly a bit more.

"Bring it around!" someone shouted. I felt faint and fell to my knees and then my seat.

"Got it!"

I couldn't say who was talking, but the boat, now under power, veered to starboard, and Edward and Buster were looking for something, found a huge pair of pliers, and when the boat settled in the water, they began to lean over the side and reach down into the water. Their father was happily snapping pictures of anything that moved.

"It's a sh…." I tried to say. "Don't reach into the…."

In fact, they were catching the remains of the *tarpon*, and with the kind of strength that only youth keeps, they managed to haul it over the side and on to the deck. This section of the fish alone was *enormous*. I looked at it dully, and I realized that I was trembling uncontrollably and that I stank of drying blood and brine.

"Are you all right? Are you all right?"

Voices, thick and next to me. I began to realize that my coming aboard, the capture of the tarpon's remains, and someone checking on me had happened in probably thirty seconds.

"I think so," I said. I did not recognize the voice that came out of me. It was husky, distant, older. We began to head toward land slowly, and the puttering engine of the houseboat was a beautiful sound. I realized, though, that I could not stop shaking, and I didn't stop for almost four hours. A great breaking sound wanted to rise in me; tears pushed at me. But I simply sat there and trembled. And even when we got back to land and docked, I could not stop.

In the film *Jaws* there is a scene in which the ocean scientist Matt Hooper, played by Richard Dreyfuss, tries to explain what a shark is to a doubtful listener. Hooper says this:

"Mr. Vaughn, what we are dealing with here is a perfect engine, an eating machine. It's really a miracle of evolution. All this machine does is swim and eat and make little sharks, and that's all."

We never knew the exact species of the shark into whose territory we had blundered. If it *was* a Great White, the kind in the book and the film, it was nowhere near as large as the one we see when Chief Brody (Roy Scheider) tells the old sea captain Quint they're gonna need a bigger boat. But it was still terrifying, easily large enough to bite a full-grown man in *half.*

Edward's father, gleeful at our escape and in possession of a trophy, found a seaside taxidermist that day and had what was left of the tarpon stuffed and mounted. It still hangs, more than forty years later, over a mantel in the Hudsons' lake house, though Edward's parents have now passed away.

We all have close calls with death during our lives. For most, it's a lucky swerve on a highway that saves us. In thinking back over it, there was no way I should have lived through that event, with an oozing foot and drifting in the blood of a tattered tarpon while a shark longer than a sofa was in a feeding frenzy. But I did.

And for the rest of that summer, working at our local newspaper, *The Madisonian*, realizing I had cheated the hangman, I began to think of what I could accomplish as a writer. And I knew I had to stop my indifferent dating and find me a woman. Earlier that year, I had, but neither of us knew it yet. Soon, though, I'd be in full-chase mode myself.

A rainy Tuesday in the Strand Bookstore at 828 Broadway, and he is just past middle age and in trim good shape. Is that woman looking at me? Is she? No, she's looking at Thai cookbooks. He feels the weightlessness of pages. Once, he overheard two women talking about subscribing to the National Geographic. *Do you get it to read or to smell? one asked the other. Yes, he thought. I understand. Now he inhales Biography and wonders of lives lived, well or not, of his need to be in Byhalia with defibrillator paddles, ready to shock William Faulkner back into his life. A young man in jeans and a T-shirt comes soaking, dripping inside, his hair Einstein-wild. He wants to be a writer. He can be read all the way from Military History, from Bonsai Gardening.*

8

The Girl with that Attitude

She came walking into our biology lab at the last minute in spring quarter of 1970, her silky brown hair parted sharply down the middle and held up off her long neck with a barrette in the back. Only one seat was still open, and it was next to me. I had dated some in college and even thought I was going with a pretty girl named Yvonne, but when she quit returning my calls or meeting me on campus, I knew that *she* had seen through me, too. This was getting depressing.

"I'm Linda," the girl in lab said as she settled next to me. She smelled wonderful, some exotic scent that other girls hadn't discovered yet.

"*Melinda*?" I asked. She had something of a northern accent, and I found her hard to understand. She shook her head, rolled her eyes.

"Just Linda," she said.

She looked at me through beautiful blue-green eyes, and wore lovely skin, a ready smile, and an attitude. Her nose had a slight bump in the middle, giving her face considerable beauty and character. Linda was the anti-Southern Belle. She smoked Vantage cigarettes, had long, thin fingers, and wore bell-bottom jeans covered with peace patches. Unrest on college campuses all over America was epidemic, and unhappiness about the Vietnam War and much else had finally gotten to Athens. I had been changing myself. I had spent my high school years (alas) more worried about grades and girls than about the Civil Rights Movement or the growing war in Vietnam. I was talking on the phone with Emma the night Dr. Martin Luther King, Jr., was killed, and she was the one who told me about it. I recall being stunned and shaken, but I failed to rush into the streets. Now, however, with the war turning endless, with casualties rising and no end in sight, I found myself being energized by the Left, and despite the fact that I was maturing, still being interested in beer and girls. I did not want to get shot in Vietnam, obviously, but I knew people who *were* going, and I found it profoundly disturbing.

I grew my hair long, almost shoulder length, infuriating my father, who was a Goldwater Republican and was sure long hair meant I was running a Communist sleeper cell out of the Physics Building where his office was located. (After leaving the teaching business, he'd run a radio and television repair business for a few years in Athens before being recruited as an electronics design engineer by UGA.) Our most furious argument was over the Sgt. Pepper mustache I grew, about which I was almost idiotically vain. I doubt my father seriously thought I'd follow him into the Right Wing, but he must at least have been hoping my liberal phase would pass. Much to his sorrow, I'm just as much a Progressive/Green/Lefty forty years later.

Linda's hair was waist-length and gorgeously, shimmeringly healthy. I didn't know it, but she had a boyfriend at the time, a philosophy grad student, and she was hanging out with a crowd that read Frantz Fanon, James Baldwin, Simone de Beauvoir, and others of the prophetic-and-pissed persuasion. (Those writers had plenty to be angry about, and I learned from them soon and still find myself in a self-righteous swivet about three times a day over the world's injustices. Like my connection to the film of *Jaws* through Richard Zanuck, I would, many years later, have a minor connection to Baldwin.) By this time, my early disinterest in science had changed radically, and a gene for the love of the natural world had kicked in. Linda was almost worse than I was in math and didn't have a clue about science.

"There!" she cried once as my lab partner. "I see the amoeba!"

"Um, that's an air bubble," I said.

"Do air bubbles have a nucleus?" she asked seriously.

"Not generally," I said. Then I made up a wild lecture about the wonders of microscopy, complete with technical matters I'd learned from my years as a kid in my father's high school chemistry lab. I think I bragged, *sotto voce,* about being a writer and composer. She saw through me instantly, which was an epochal relief. But she still liked me, something I have ranked over the years with the Miracle on Ice. I've often wished Al Michaels had been there to announce her acceptance of me for who I was. ("Do you believe in seeing through morons? *Yes!*") To me, science was more or less a game, and I enjoyed playing it. In high school, I had a chemistry teacher who was intelligent, young, and beautiful and not quite up for the Marx Brothers quality of our class. We were so wild that at mid-year she separated the Good Students from the Bad Students and swore, like Scarlett O'Hara, that as God was her witness, she'd never teach to the Bad Students again. Of course, I was with the Bad Students. The fact that I spent the last twenty-seven years of my career as a professional science writer at the University of Georgia would probably have struck most of my fellow Bad Students as something meant to induce a case of the giggles.

During that spring quarter of 1970, Linda and I made good lab partners. I was good with a microscope, and she was good at reading Jean-Paul Sartre and Chinua Achebe, at rage-smoking and ignoring the lab completely. I got us through, though, and when the quarter ended, I sighed to be leaving and losing her. But clearly, I was not in her league. I had met her once or twice that quarter when she lived in Myers Hall (to study—that was my cockamamie story, anyway), and it turned out she knew Joan Norton, a lifelong friend of mine from Madison, who also lived in that dorm.

During the summers of my college years, I worked at *The Madisonian* as a reporter, working hard to get better with each story. Mark, who had started as a physics major at UGA, changed to anthropology and would later earn his doctoral degree and become the leading expert on the archaeology of Georgia's Oconee River Valley. Laura Jane was making A's and re-establishing the family's good name after my years in high school. (No small feat, that.) I found out that I had no interest in covering government meetings, since they are hideously dull and are probably listed somewhere in the Canon of Tortures for the Spanish Inquisition. I loved writing feature stories—not the kind of drool-inducing pablum one sees on local morning television stations—but pieces in which I tried to dig deeply into a person's life or background. Each of these stories was informed by a mini-plot, so by the time I did become a novelist, I already had an idea how to structure a story effectively. That summer, girlfriendless and wan, I tried to become a Serious Artist, composing nonstop and trying to write. I wrote about fifty pages of a novel and asked my mother to read it. She did, alas.

"Well, it's not as good as…." and she inserted the name of a weak popular novelist whose name I have mercifully forgotten. That was it. She handed me the sheets, and I took them in the backyard and burned them. It was probably one of the high points for fire in all its interactions with humans. Prometheus, eat your heart out. Don't ask my mother something if you don't want to hear the truth about it—that was the gold standard when

I dealt with her. I can't remember much about that manuscript except that it was set in South America (where I'd never been) and involved an old man and a donkey cart. I'd never seen a donkey cart, either. My mother saved me about three years in my development as a writer by initiating that summer's auto-da-fé.

I spent the rest of that season almost being eaten by a large aquatic predator and seriously considering my own mortality. On the first day of fall quarter in 1970, I was walking past Memorial Hall on the UGA campus with, I am sure, a vacant look on my face.

"Pssst!" It was a girl's voice, and in those days it might have been the first syllable of a vocal brawl between the Young Americans for Freedom and the Weather Underground. I braced and turned, and there was the Chick with the Attitude that I'd gotten through the Biology 102 lab the spring before. I smiled, but then thought: Holy Shit! I can't remember her name! Melina. Melamia. *Delamia*. Linda! But I'd never known how to pronounce her last name, which I remembered how to spell—Rowley. Was the first half of her last name pronounced "row" as in a fight or "row" as in "row, row, row your boat?" I had no idea. Fortunately, the girl sitting with her solved it for me.

"Rowley, I'm gone to class," said the girl, who I later found out was Linda's roommate, Kathy. And she pronounced the first syllable of Linda's last name like "row, row, row your boat." So I knew that much: *roll*-y.

It was late September, and a cool breeze blew Linda's gorgeous long hair over her shoulders. She wore dangly gold peace-symbol earrings, a sporty crimson jacket, blue-jean bell bottoms, and that attitude. Her eyes were bright blue (they shifted according to her mood and the light—whenever they turned a flat green, I fled), and she smiled at me with what I took to be a slight superiority and amusement at remembering me from class the spring before. We chatted for a bit, and for some reason, I saw what I thought was an opening. Her smile dazzled me. She was quite thin and seriously beautiful, and I was tired of always losing the girl.

"So, where are you guys living?" I asked. Turned out she and Kathy were renting an apartment in an older house on Barber Street. "Ah. Well, maybe I'll see you around some time."

"Maybe you will." She said hi to someone passing by, and I hated the guy, even though I didn't know him. In fact, to my surprise, I wanted to go kick the everloving *shit* out of him.

"Um, are you usually here about this time of day?" I asked her, trying to act cool despite my clear desperation.

"Might be. I'm around."

"Yeah. I'm around, too," I said, trying to look cool and failing worse than the Bay of Pigs Invasion. "Well. Maybe I'll run into you." I smiled at her and turned.

"You want my phone number?" she asked. She waited for me to find a piece of paper in my billfold and take dictation. The only thing I could find was one of the little cards with my name on it from my high school graduation invitations. (What kind of addlepated ninny would be carrying *that* around in his billfold? Gentlemen [and women] of the jury, you have no choice but to convict the defendant.) I wrote down her number. And to this day, I still have that card. I could not have been happier if I'd single-handedly solved the Enigma Code during World War II.

"I'll call you sometimes," I said.

"If you want to," she shrugged.

But she had an interest in me, even if it was slight, and I decided I wasn't going to take no for an answer. So I began to develop a plan that made the Normandy Invasion look like an impromptu picnic. Within a few days, I invited her to go to a UGA football game with me—a safe first date. At first she said she wasn't sure and would get back to me. I found out years later that she already *had* a date for the weekend, but she ultimately broke it to go with me. The only problem is that we wouldn't be going to the game and out after it alone. We were going with her roommate, Kathy. And Kathy's boyfrend. And Kathy's parents. And Kathy's boyfriend's parents. And *Linda's* parents. I had planned a quiet dinner out and then perhaps a party somewhere—it was easy in those days just to wander into a kegger with no one asking who you were or much caring. Plus my freshman roommate and high schoool friend Larry Walker had joined a fraternity, and I'd visited him there several times, so that was an option. Instead, after the game, we went back to Linda and Kathy's apartment and got seriously toasted. All of us. So much for my plan for winning the intramural snuggling championships.

Their hippified apartment consisted of a huge sunny kitchen, a cheerfully cluttered area used as a den, and two bedrooms. The house had probably once been the home of some prosperous merchant, but the passing years had cut it up into apartments, and exhausted plaster and divots in the walls had changed it entirely. Kathy and Linda had sutured some of the cracks with posters, and a cheerful messiness cloaked the rest of the shuddering architecture. By ten that night, we were all laughing riotously and drinking like Sahara survivors. Kathy's father, a pharmacist from Kentucky, told screamingly funny stories, and Linda's dad, an executive in Atlanta, laughed until he couldn't breathe. My parents were teetotalers, and I could not even imagine getting wasted with them. I had no idea how to act, but trying to keep up with the partiers as we drank was a huge mistake.

"Hey, I know where we can go eat," said Kathy's boyfriend. "The Swamp Guinea!"

I had vaguely heard of it, a legendary fish-and-beer place in the country north of Athens, so in short order we all piled into a couple of cars, and I snuggled as close to Linda as I could. She held my hand and rubbed the back of my thumb with hers, and I nearly howled with mad joy. Maybe I could be a drunken poet after all. I remember getting lost as we drove and taking a long, *long* time to get there—it was almost eleven when we pulled up. But the place was still hopping, and I started to skip minutes—like a stone being bounced over a stream. I blinked and we were sitting before gigantic plates of fried catfish and hushpuppies, waiting for Kathy's father to finish a story. I couldn't make anything of the punchline, but Linda's father did, falling apart with wheezy, silent laughter. I blinked again and saw someone stuffing catfish we hadn't been able to eat into his suit coat pockets for a later snack. I'd never seen anything remotely like it. And through it all, I kept my eyes on the girl, and oh my *God* did I like what I saw. Even though I was seriously messed up, I managed not to disgrace myself more than anyone else did. And I knew, while I was driving home to Madison a few hours later, rapidly getting sober with the windows down on a cool night, that I'd be calling her again, that even if she said no, I'd never take that for an answer. I would never again forget her name or how to pronounce it. I had the girl, but I was unsure if I could keep her. Once, the following year, Linda said something in her typically decisive way, and, laughing, I said to her, "Wow, you really don't fool around, do you?" My hopeful double entendre (I was hoping she *did* fool around) was lame, but so what?

"I do not," she said, beautifully smiling.

"Will you put that in writing?" I asked.

"Yes, I will," she said. And she took out a stick of Wrigley's spearmint gum, unfolded the wrapper, and wrote on its inside:

I, Linda K. Rowley,
DO NOT FOOL
AROUND!
Linda K. Rowley

I still have that artifact of college love, too, so I can remember those first lovely days when I was chasing her with all the purpose of a shark chasing a tarpon.

The movers are coming to take him to the country, to pack them off to woods and ghostly contours, hidden terraces built when this was cotton land. In the woods are rusted guitar strings of barbed wire, playing wind. He has made it back. The smell of conifers, the wintering fill of Wildcat Creek. She has never lived in the country, his girl, his beloved, and he wants to teach her to track, to know colors by their sounds and smells. She is expecting their second child. Their son is unsure he wants to leave. Even this much deadfall is impossible. Years' worth will take machines and time, but he doesn't care. In the night, foxes come. Opossums rise. Deer pose, already statuary in the just-lit mist. He can see it all before it occurs. The movers are coming to take him to the country.

9

Falling in Love with a New Poetry

That October, I bought a book that changed my life. To this day I can't remember where in Athens I found it, because this was 1970, long before the large chains came. Although I was aware of some contemporary poetry, it was almost all "serious" and "academic," and the only verse I knew that came even close to being really modern or progressive was that of e.e. cummings, who had died eight years before. I remember going to the poetry section and shuffling through the usual stuff, when I saw before me a thick anthology with a strange, whimsical, all-red cover. It was called *An Anthology of New York Poets*, edited by Ron Padgett and David Shapiro. I opened it and fell in love.

It is hard to explain to young people of today how insular and even parochial we all were before the Internet. I prowled Barnett's News Stand in downtown Athens looking for poetry magazines and books, but they had very little back then that I wanted to read. (I still miss that shop terribly, though.) The UGA Library had the usual suspects such as *Poetry* magazine and university-related literary journals. But there was an entire literary world out there that was invisible to young people like me. And I had it in my *hands*. The problem was that the book, even in paperback, was astronomically expensive: $3.95. I could get four meals for that in those days. But I opened it to page eleven and began to read a poem by one James Schuyler:

> Under the French horns of a November afternoon
> a man is raking blue leaves
> with a wide wooden rake (whose teeth are pegs
> or rather, dowels....)

That *voice*! And as I flipped other pages, the poems were like a newly discovered galaxy, and I saw poets whose names I did not know, anymore than I knew Schuyler: Kenneth Koch, John Ashbery, Frank O'Hara, Ed Sanders…my hands literally trembled. I had no idea then that many of the poets in the volume were gay, but so, probably, was Walt Whitman, and he was my idol. (When I discovered this some months later, it was one of my first lessons in tolerance and understanding. My small world was small indeed, but I would need to know the larger world if I were to become a writer.) That night, I went home to Madison and dug through all my drawers until I came up with about $4.50 and literally prayed that the book would still be there when I came back the next day. I dashed in, and there it was, and I bought it, went out into the sharp, cool, October air, and my world changed forever.

There never really was a "New York School of Poets," at least not in the sense of "The School of Athens" from ancient days. It was simply a group of writers who were thick as thieves with the visual arts community in New York City and who decided the world of 19th century Realism was limiting and maybe not so Real after all. Bit by bit, and through them, contemporary European poetry also began to open to me: Pierre Reverdy, Raymond Roussel, Antonin Artaud, and many more. I gathered from the book that the leading poet of the New York School was O'Hara, who had died young, being run over by something like a dune buggy (or "water taxi") on Fire Island four years before. And yet it was almost impossible then to find out more about these writers. Even the now-venerable *American Poetry Review*, through which one could discover non-academic contemporary poets, didn't come along until 1972. The only real way to know about current literature was to live where it was being produced or to buy anthologies of it. But this was a pathbreaking book, and I felt strongly that nothing like it had ever appeared in the U.S.

Some of the poets in it became lifelong passions: Schuyler, O'Hara, Koch, John Ashbery. The poems of others, such as Ted Berrigan, seemed more like dashed-off random thoughts, interesting though they were. The parallel "school," influenced by Allen Ginsberg, of "first thought, best thought" had never interested me as this did because I simply don't believe in that idea (it's too half-baked to call a theorem). But neither did I believe in poems overworked until their formal flawlessness made them cold and unapproachable. At the same time, much of William Carlos Williams seemed a tad precious to me, and though I loved Cummings's love poems, many of his efforts seemed typographically self-indulgent to no clear end. In short, I had found a crack in the door, and the light that streamed in was epiphanic, blinding. My writing changed *immediately*. I began writing verse similar to O'Hara's "lunch poems" and "I-do-this-and-I-do-that poems." Doubt, fear, elation, pop culture references, smug dismissal—all began to crop up in my writing and thinking. About the closest I could get to the New York School of Poets in terms of actually buying books *was* the work of Ginsburg and his cohort, and so I began to save money and buy volumes from the Pocket Poets Series from City Lights Books, including early printings of *Howl, Kaddish,* and *Planet News*. And I began to realize that even in Athens, Georgia, in 1970, there were others who had a serious interest in contemporary writing and reading.

Most of what I wrote was bad, of course. But it was no longer laughably bad, and I began to understand that if I wanted to be a fine writer, I had to be a *much* better reader, and I had to know the literature of my own time. Because of the Padgett and Shapiro book, my interest in poetry as a whole exploded. Oddly, it also served to take what small interest I had in prose fiction and drown it in the nearest Henry Jamesian puddle. From there, that fall I worked my way backward and sideways and was poking through books in the UGA Library when I found an enormous volume of fractured poetry that seemed to combine several threads coming together in me. It was absorbed with history and filled with bizarre crackerbarrel comments and strong opinions. And it made no concessions whatever to things the reader didn't know or couldn't even find out. It looked to me like a magnificent shaggy beast. The name of it was *The Cantos,* and it was by a poet named Ezra Pound. I checked it out, and suddenly I was breaking through at light speed. Many years later, when having dinner with Pound's daughter Mary de Rachewiltz, I told her the story of discovering *The Cantos* and how that act, along with the discovery of *An Anthology of New York Poets,* changed my life. I knew by then, of course, of Pound's multiple failures as a human being, and indeed his nutty near-treason during World War II. But she accepted my praise with modest gratitude.

I am old now, but sometimes when I visit the UGA campus and see a young woman or man sitting on a bench and intensely reading a volume of poetry or a novel, I hope it's not for class, that it is a discovery that brings the same utter and lasting joy I found there so very long ago.

I only lived in Reed Hall for one quarter in the fall of 1968 before moving home and commuting for the rest of my undergraduate years with my father. Part of this was practical, since I had to pay for most of my college myself from summer-job savings, and living at home was cheaper. But there was more behind my decision, and I knew it even then. From childhood I have been hypersensitive to sounds, light, and the general busyness of the world. I was happy enough howling around Morgan County at night with my high school friends, but by late 1970, I knew well enough that I craved solitude, silence [or at most the gorgeous sounds of classical music], and dim light. I *did* love sports and sometimes played golf, but in general I set myself a private course to attack and defeat Western Literature, to know it as well as a would-be writer can.

After our date to the football game and the Swamp Guinea, I was wholly smitten with Linda Karen Rowley and began chasing her from one end of the University of Georgia campus to another. I learned and memorized her class schedule so I could "accidentally" bump into her as twenty thousand kids wandered from class to class.

"Hey! What are you doing here on the bridge by Sanford Stadium? How are your classes going? Can I kiss you?"

Of course I didn't say the last one, and after a time, I'm sure she began to catch on to my dippy ruse. No one in the history of physics or chaos theory ever ran into someone by chance as much I did, and my path seemed to cross hers two or three times a day. I managed to buy her a Coke in the Bulldog Room a few times while she parried my courting swordplay with baffled amusement. And I began to borrow the family car (I wouldn't own one myself until I graduated from college in the June 1972) and drive from Madison back to Athens (twenty-eight miles each way) to take her on real dates. We especially liked Village Inn Pizza on Prince Avenue, a small venue that showed old black-and-white silent films while patrons munched on yeasty pizza and drank frosted mugs of ice cold beer. I polished my *bons mots* to a giddy gleam for those dates, throwing in quotes by everyone from Jacques Lacan to Bobby Kennedy.

In my studies, meanwhile, I began to understand more about who I was and what I loved. I'd prepared for four years to be a music major when I came to college. I wanted to be Gustav Mahler, to write huge symphonies, not to seek fame but to have it seek me. In high school I had checked out Milton Cross's *Encyclopedia of the Great Composers and Their Music* from

Madison's library about twenty-five thousand times, and I knew somehow that being a well-known Artist (in the big sense) was inevitable for me.

Then, after I came to Athens, I stayed a music major exactly one quarter when I discovered that I was among the least well-prepared for it. Coming from a town with almost no real links to the outside world beyond the Atlanta daily paper we got and the evening news on TV, I simply didn't know what I didn't know. The whole world was that way. Halfway through that fall 1968, I fell apart, realizing that no one could make a living as a Great Composer and that I would have to work ten times as hard as the other music students just to catch up. So I changed to journalism, as I have said earlier. That was the practical part of me, but the scholarly side, and it was strong, decided on a split academic minor in English and history. And God, did I love those classes. In English, I had a number of marvelous teachers, including George Marshall, a kind, gentle, and generous specialist in Victorian literature; Coleman Barks, the poet and famous future translator of the Persian mystic writer Rumi; and Marion Montgomery, who lived, wrote, and taught at the intersection of literature and philosophy. There were others, too, such as the marvelous history professor and well-published writer Lee Kennett.

I took one early-level English course taught by a graduate student I'll call Mack Garfield. He was a sniveling, supercilious bully and made fun of our class, giving us the impression that he knew all literature by heart, and we knew nothing and never would. One day he asked each of us to write a poem and turn it in by the end of the week. This wasn't a creative writing class—the English department in those years didn't even recognize creative writing as part of English literature. (Coleman's "hobby" of *writing* literature was fine, but my sense was that it didn't add to his scholarly credentials, at least not then. Later, he would be recognized as one of America's best-selling poets and translators, not to mention living his life as an utterly wonderful human being.) Most of the students dashed off something that looked like poems, turned them in, and forgot about them. I worked probably fifteen hours on my poem that week, rewriting it dozens of times until I felt it was the best I could do. That Friday I turned it in, and Garfield nodded and sneered as he laid it with some others.

"Could I ask what these are for?" I asked, braving his bully's demeanor. Instead he laughed, a kind of superior snort.

"Sure you can," he said, his upper lip actually curling. "I'm having a party at my place tomorrow night, and we get drunk, and I read them out loud. Funniest thing you've ever heard in your fucking life."

I froze and felt a rage rise in me. The son of a bitch was using us for his *amusement.* I decided that I was going to cold-cock him. He was a thin, weasley little shrimp, and I could have done it without much effort. The room had emptied, and we were the only ones standing there. Then I knew I could do nothing, just as he knew it. He had all the power, and we could only be checkers in his wretched parlor game. I turned and walked out. He never brought those poems back up and never gave them a grade, and nobody else knew why we wrote them. But I wrote down his full name so I wouldn't forget it, and years later I Googled him, and he had vanished from the face of the Earth. No big surprise and no loss, but I have to admit my Schadenfreude Meter went off the scale.

After buying *An Anthology of New York Poets,* I began to write much more than I ever had in the past. The Milton Cross books, even though about composers, showed me how creative people can make a life through their art. I also began to broaden my reading, both in poetry and fiction, making lists of writers I admired and why. The first poem that actually had a huge impact on me was one by Karl Shapiro called "Auto Wreck," which I originally discovered in a high school literature textbook. I have always had a copy of it in my billfold to remind me from where my love of literature came. It's there as I write these words, in fact. But as 1970 turned into 1971, I was digging more deeply into American and English literature and also into history, a passion that some days rivaled my love of poetry and fiction. I was also in those years looking over my worried shoulder at my Draft Board. The sheer madness of the Vietnam War howled in the background of my college years, and on December 1, 1969, the first draft lottery had been held, and my birth day, January 30, was number 164, and that was high enough to guarantee I would not be inducted into the Army and sent to my slaughter. Still, no one felt safe, and the rage we felt against a pointless war in which 58,000 Americans would ultimately die infected everything we thought or did. And American deaths were only part of that sad story. More than a *million* Vietnamese soldiers and civilians died. (At the same time, I feel compelled to say that I admire veterans without restraint and have a lifelong interest in military history.)

At Christmas 1970, I got a card in the mail from Linda, sent from her family home in Decatur, a suburb east of Atlanta. It was a simple note, but to my astonishment and delight, she signed it "Love, Linda." Maybe it was just a standard valediction—I have had women friends (and a few men) who *always* sign themselves with love, meaning no more, really, than "sincerely." But in those days, I convinced myself that she did care about me. When winter quarter began in January 1971, it was obvious that we were a couple, and that I was in love with her. I never could quite tell where she stood, though, because she was a genius at keeping her feelings closed and her options open. But we were spending more time together between classes, and she was exclusively dating me by then.

I also bought another totemic volume: a paperback copy of Charles Norman's biography, *Ezra Pound*. Of course I had already checked out Pound's *Cantos* from the UGA Library many times and read as much of it as I could, but until I managed to buy Norman's book, I knew very little about Pound and the exciting days of his early years in London and Paris. Above all, those were times of small literary magazines and tiny collections of poetry. So I began to plan a printed collection of my own poems, and I thought I knew how I could do it.

Winter turned into fresh-smelling spring, and by then I had gotten to know Linda's wonderful family well. She was the oldest of five children, with Gail, Melody, Donna, and Brian in descending age order below her. Brian was only six years old. Their father, Fred, was a native of Harwich Port, a small seaside town on Cape Cod, and Marie, their mother, was from Carrollton, Georgia.

"We're going to the Cape to visit my grandparents in July," Linda told me as we sat outside Park Hall, the English department building that spring. "Would you like to go with us? We'll be gone ten days or a couple of weeks."

In truth, I would have slain an army of Visigoths to spend an extra *hour* with her. By then I was working each summer at my hometown newspaper, *The Madisonian*, as a reporter and job printer, so I'd have to get permission. But I was sure I could.

"I would *love* to go to Cape Cod," I said. I had never been north of North Carolina at the time. (Years later, my first literary agent admitted that by the early Eighties she'd never been *south* of Long Island, but I still felt hopelessly parochial when Linda invited me to the Cape.) And so that July we all crammed in the family car with Fred driving, and we made the slow, hilarious trip north from Georgia to Massachusetts. My world began to expand. Harwich Port, a lovely small town, is only a few miles up the coast from Hyannis Port, and Linda's grandfather was a doctor who, in addition to his private practice, was a member of the staff at Hyannis Hospital, so I felt almost like a member of the Kennedy family. I learned to shell-fish in the aromatic tidal flats, to drink more alcohol than I thought I was capable of holding, and to eat fresh lobster with a tiny fork and a large bib. We also toured the Cape, going to family property on Sheep Pond near the town of Brewster, driving out to Provincetown, one of the artiest villages on the East Coast. And we discovered a spectacular used- and rare-book shop called Parnassus in the town of Yarmouth Port. (It's still there.)

"Look at this," I said to Linda as we came back around the stacks one day. I'd found a book published by New Directions that looked interesting. "Have you ever heard of this man, Kenneth Patchen?"

"I don't think so," she admitted.

The book was a novel first published in 1941 called *The Journal of Albion Moonlight*. On the back, liner notes said, "Inspired by one of the finest lyrics in the English language, the anonymous pre-Shakespearian *Tom O'Bedlam*...Kenneth Patchen sets off on an allegorial journey of his own in which the far boundaries of love and murder, madness and sex are sensually explored." I bit, and the hook sunk deep. The 313-page volume set me back $1.95, but it was my first real opening into avant-garde fiction, and from that stone, I fell into a widening pool, in love with experimental poetry and fiction and much *out* of love with the "well-made, realistic" story. That night, I read the first twenty pages or so, and I felt a voice growing within me. By lamplight, I wrote in the front, so I wouldn't forget:

P. Williams
Yarmouth Port, Mass.
July, 1971

Linda and I took long, romantic walks on the beach, which was only a quarter of a mile from her grandparents' house. And one evening, when we held hands and padded down the sand at sunset, I knew how I'd bring my first book to its birth.

That summer of 1971 and for much of the following summer after we'd graduated from UGA, Linda and I wrote letters to each other. Comparatively few people write actual U.S. Postal Service-mailed letters anymore, but in those days, a first-class stamp cost eight cents and long-distance phone charges were far outside my budget. In the hot months of 1971, Linda always expressed both her love and her reservations. As I discovered new poets, I had told her I wanted to buy some books for her. She answered this way on August 3:

> I appreciate very much your idea about the books—but you know you could save that money and be even further ahead in your savings than you already are. Sometime you might want to buy something and if you've got the money it would be nice. I know how it is not to have the cash when you want it. Anyway, I want you to get the poetry books you have been wanting to get.... Again, I thank you now and in the future for the poems you have created—perhaps those mean more to me than almost everything else I have ever had or been given. Hopefully I will be able to create some lines of value before long....

In early September, I was still courting her hard, and the quality of my work was steadily improving. She wrote me on September 8:

> It's hard to believe you have composed another song already—I don't know if I have gotten over the shock of this one yet (pleasant shock, I must add). I really don't know how you have any time to be bored—you've been pretty busy all summer, between all your creations, etc....

That summer she had somehow gotten a hardback copy of *The First Circle* by Aleksandr Solzhenitsyn, and it knocked me dead. I spent several letters trying to nag her into reading it, but she was reading another book popular that year, *Future Shock* by Alvin Toffler. Little by little, she began to talk of our days as if they might last further than we'd originally thought:

> You'll have to come over some time when there's a full moon—I've heard it's beautiful walking up Stone Mountain at night when there's enough moonlight. It will have to be a cool night or I probably won't make it. We'll have to go over there during the summer anyway—since you haven't been there in such a long time. In case you didn't notice—this is a projection into the future....

By late summer, plans for my self-printed volume of verse were taking shape:

> I'm started to get excited about your soon-to-be printed book of poetry. Just from looking through the books [typed collections of hundreds of my poems] I would have a hard time picking out the ones I wanted to print. There are a lot of what I consider really good poems—and there are many more that I like regardless of whether or not I think they're good....

I have dozens of letters from that summer and the next, but maybe that gives a flavor of her writing. By the fall of 1971, we were starting our junior year at the university, and I knew I had a long, long journey ahead as a writer and as a suitor trying to keep the girl close to me. But by that time I was madly sure that I would never quit working to win both of those battles.

We live, always, in the decade of our greatest happiness. The Seventies never end. Turn on the radio, and the Eagles are singing "Take It Easy" still. The war is winding down finally, and he won't be drafted, not now, but it isn't the Seventies. It's the early Nineties, and he feels astray, lingering in the wrong life, and yet knowing those who have saved him so far and who will again are at a hug's length. He can't believe it has happened, the film deals, the visits to New York and California, lines of people just to see him. It is all artificial, pointlessly true. Already he has begun to lose his keys, to misplace proper nouns. But he will not misplace his beloved girl, his Megan, his armful, his saving grace. He takes it easy now, and it is the right life, and he rocks her by the fire, which warms its hands on their flames.

He looks at his son, his strong and intelligent boy, just back from wilderness survival training, scratched from hair to boot. He and Linda named him Samuel Brandon and call him by his middle name. On the porch, a cool wind carries the scent of burning leaves. No one burns leaves anymore. No one has to survive in the wilderness. But nothing is past when inside book and memory, and so they walk with Wordsworth, listen to the deaf Beethoven as he stamps out the Credo from his Missa Solemnis. *He knows that we go on living when the body ashens or lies down for its sanctified sleep. Brandon is throwing gum balls at a shadow, boots unlaced, hunter's knife belted at his waist. He raises his head. The father wonders if he has scented something different, something wild.*

10

Planting *New Seeds*

The butter churn of poetry more often than not brings forth only clabbered milk. That's the kind of comparison that sends editors into a frenzy of mirth and despair. A seasoned judge of others' work can see in a moment if the would-be poet or short story writer has read more than a metaphorical thimbleful of accomplished literature. And over a lifetime as a writer, I'm always a bit stunned by how many people desperate to be authors have read little but occasional junk. In 2013, getting creative work out is easy with a blog or on Twitter or even Facebook. Self-publishing is rampant. And there are thousands of online journals where writers can try to gain a pen-hold in the world of literary art. But back in the early 1970s, publishing a volume of poetry was expensive, and that made it rare. Highly accomplished poetry has never made money. I had two clear and present reasons to get published, though. First, I wanted to be the new Keats, the new Pound, the new Ginsburg. And second, I wanted to win the girl. I knew, even then, that the second motive wasn't about Art. But I also didn't give a damn. At the time, I didn't know Oscar Wilde's dictum that "All bad poetry springs from genuine feeling. To be natural is to be obvious, and to be obvious is to be inartistic." Even if I had known it or had it tattooed on my ass, it probably would not have stopped me from publishing (or rather printing) my first book, *New Seeds*, in the fall of 1971.

My reading by then had far outraced that of the general fan of poetry in the American South. I had grown to love poems that, like those in the *Anthology of New York Poets*, shone a light into a world between Serious Art and Pop Culture. While important poets like Frost were swinging on birches, Frank O'Hara would start a poem called "Steps" by saying

> How funny you are today in New York
> like Ginger Rogers in *Swingtime*

I was too stupid in those days to realize I could impress Linda more by repairing her apartment's plumbing or working on her car engine. (I couldn't do either, which probably made the issue of strutting my malehood moot.) But I had plenty of poems for a forty-page book, and I also had an ace up my proverbial sleeve. At *The Madisonian*, where I worked during the summers, we also did job printing on small Multilith offset presses, and I talked my mentor and friend Adelaide Ponder, editor and co-owner of the business with her husband Graham, into letting me use the presses at night to print *New Seeds*. I knew how to run the presses, though about as well as I could repair the engine on my parents' 1962 Chevrolet. Billy Arthur, though, was a master at printing. The genial and technically accomplished Billy had worked at the newspaper for awhile, along with his wife, the quiet and delightful Peggy. So that summer of 1971, I paid Billy to work overtime and help me put *New Seeds* together. If this didn't get me the girl, *nothing* would.

By early fall, long back from Cape Cod, and with classes starting for a new quarter, I was slowly assembling a small volume. It didn't bother me that each poem seemed to have been written by a different man, if not a different species. The influences of O'Hara and Schuyler and even Aram Saroyan (another of the New York poets) was obvious, though. This wasn't your mother's moon-June poetry. Some of it was terrible, of course. I was twenty-one years old in an era when contemporary poetry was hard to find. But it did rip the covers off who I was as a young man and a writer. One poem called "Song for Silence (Thoughts on Dante # 6)" prefigured my lifelong adoration of Dante and my willingness to steal from a poet like Paul Simon. I wrote the author-description for the back of the volume and said about myself, apparently without shame or guile: "He writes on many themes, but always exhibits striking imagery and a deep concern for man and nature. As he says, his poetry is a search to 'probe reality through sensitive reaction to both the real and dream worlds.'"

Hee.

Linda seemed impressed when I presented her with a copy of it, though I suspect she was more relieved that I would stop talking about it. Loyally, she showed it to an English professor she admired, and the prof admitted to liking only one *line* in the whole book, which in retrospect might not have been so bad. A small esoteric bookstore in Athens called The Hobbit Habit agreed to carry my book, which I published under the name by which everyone knew me: *Phil Williams*. Only in 1984 with the publication of my first "real" book did I begin to publish with my full name. Even early, self-published books have their value, though. A signed copy of *New Seeds* is now worth a pretty penny.

During much of 1971, Linda and her friend Kathy lived in a trailer on the south side of Athens, and as the days passed and our relationship deepened, I started to stay over with her, lying to my parents, of course, about where I was. (I *did* often hang out with my friends Larry and Edward, also students at UGA, who lived in a blacklighted apartment in a lumber-and-roaches complex called Durlan Courts, just off Prince Avenue. I drank more bourbon and beer in that apartment than many poets do in half a lifetime, I'm proud to say.)

My classes in English and history absorbed me. I had developed a love of Russia that I translated into a course-focus on the rich history of that country. I also began a lifelong love of philosophy, especially Nietzsche, Foucalt, Kant, and Wittgenstein. (Well, I *tried* to read Wittgenstein. I'm still trying.) But I was majoring in televison directing, an idiotically hopeless endeavor. In fact, the following spring, as a final project for my major, my assigned partner was happy to amuse me and produce on videotape the first act of Samuel Beckett's *Waiting for Godot*. Why the college let us get away with such lunacy when the major was about working in television stations, I have no idea. And since we had total control of the project, we decided to be the actors and "hire" a student friend to direct and produce it. I played Vladimir, and my project partner was Estragon, and he was fairly good. I was putrid. Fortunately, the black-and-white videotape was recycled for another project after we graduated, so there's no damning evidence of my complete inability to act. But it was a gleeful shot over the bow of the *S.S. Propriety*.

I was writing poems by the dozens, by the *hundreds*. And I began to read my way through literary histories in the Main Library at UGA. In those days, T.S. Eliot was God Revealed in academia, and though he'd died in London just before my fifteenth birthday, his ideas in both poetry and criticism had swamped American universities. Alas, it turned out that Eliot had overshot the mark, though no one can doubt the effect of "The Waste Land," and a couple of dozen other poems on the history of Twentieth Century poetry. As much as I loved poetry, the literary life, and Linda, I was far more fearful of what might happen when I graduated after spring quarter in 1972. By the first of January that year, Linda and I had been dating for a year and a half, and even though we were still young, I had begun to make plans for a marriage proposal. *New Seeds,* alas, had failed to cinch the deal, and I had not yet bought my first car, so I couldn't impress her with any phony mechanical skills.

Linda was one of the editors of *Stillpoint,* the UGA student literary magazine. The title was taken from the "Burnt Norton" section of *Four Quartets* by (who else?) T.S. Eliot, and of course the quality of our college magazine varied from quarter to quarter. Linda accepted a number of my poems to publish there, so except for those printed in *The Madisonian,* they were my first pieces of published creative writing.

On February 24, 1972, still living at home in Madison with my parents and Laura Jane, and a senior at UGA, I got a letter in the mail from one Patricia Austin at Agnes Scott College in Decatur. Agnes Scott is a well-known private college for women, and that year it had started a writer's conference—the first in what would become an annual literary gathering. To encourage creative writing at Georgia's colleges and universities, it included a contest for student poetry and prose. Winners would be invited to Agnes Scott in the spring where they would give readings, and lights from the literary world would discuss their work. I had submitted a number of poems a few weeks before and expected nothing. Patricia was editor of *Aurora,* Agnes Scott's student literary magazine, so as I opened the letter, I took a deep, hopeful breath. She told me that four of my poems had been accepted for the conference, would be published in *Aurora,* and then be discussed by a panel of writers. She asked for biographical information and told me that I would be expected to read my "prizewinning material" at the meeting, which would be held on Friday, April 14. After the readings, there would be a luncheon, followed by the panel discussion. Fame! Fortune! Something that might tip the scales with Linda other than rebuilding her carburetor! I thought I'd won the contest and maybe the girl.

That winter of 1972, Linda moved into an apartment in a rambling, rat-infested house on Hancock Street right behind the crumbling remains of the old St. Mary's Hospital—where I had been born in 1950. (Kathy had graduated, and for a quarter, still at the trailer, Linda roomed with a girl named Sharon and her white German shepherd.) Desperate to stay close to her with our undergraduate years ending, I rented a room upstairs, despite a frightening lack of cash. Fortunately, I managed to land a job in the produce section of the Foodland grocery store on Baxter Street, just a few blocks from the house, and so I allegedly moved into my tiny room upstairs from my beloved. Actually, of course, I was living with her. And in a way, the place *was* romantic, since we were living together for the first time. The double bed we inherited was so shot that we had to find a huge unused door from another floor in the house and jam it between the mattress and the saggy slats. And I'm not kidding about rats. The house was *filled* with them, ghastly puppy-sized refugees from the abandoned hospital behind us. At night they clawed, danced, and hummed enough for a Broadway musical. The "hospital" was filled with vermin from basement to eaves, and so was our house. Once I went in our kitchen in the morning and saw a loaf of bread on the kitchen table begin to mambo between the salt and pepper shakers. I grabbed the broom and leaped into what I took to be a Samuri posture. The well-fed rat, which had eaten a tunnel from one heel to the other, poked his nose out of the loaf, and sniffed at me. I shouted and aimed my "sword" at the filthy creature, but it shot out of the bread and hit the linoleum with a sound like a poodle being dropped from a third-floor window. There were holes in our bathroom walls and floor, and sometimes a rat would peek out to say hi and ask what was for dinner. I cut up plastic milk jugs and nailed them over the holes. Screw with *me*. (Right after we graduated that June, the city condemned the house and demolished it. It should have been torn down while we were still in it.)

That quarter, Linda and I got into a mammoth running argument. She wanted to go straight into graduate school, working on a master's degree in English. (Her undergraduate degree in English had taught her a lot, but for getting a job it was nearly useless.) I wanted to graduate and work for awhile before even thinking about grad school. My senior project was a laughable waste of time, though I got to know Beckett's work quite well. But I had no intention of actually working in a commercial television station. Poets don't work in TV. Besides, I knew by then that I wanted to try and make some kind of living—any kind—as a writer. On lovely winter days I would drop by the Hobbit Habit and find that, so far, the sales of *New Seeds* had leveled off at zero. (They were priced at $1.25, which was far too steep, I guess.) When Linda asked what they said at the store, I made up shameless lies.

"It's moving," I said, smiling. "They say it's moving. Overall, it's moving, for poetry." Notice I never actually said anything about sales. I could have been talking about theft.

In April, I dressed in my one suit, borrowed the family car, picked up Linda at our apartment, and headed off to Decatur for the Agnes Scott conference and my first step on the road to fame. The authors who would discuss my prizewinning work were well-known poet and novelist May Sarton, who was writer in residence at Agnes Scott that quarter; poet Michael Mott, writer in residence at nearby Emory University; and my own professor (and a published novelist, poet, and critic), Marion Montgomery. In later years, the conference would host some of America's finest writers, including (as its website now says) Eudora Welty, Reynolds Price, Richard Wilbur, Margaret Atwood, Rita Dove, Jane Smiley, Tim O'Brien, John Updike, Anita Desai, Junot Diaz, and many more. But 1972 was the first conference, and I was the first winner. Or so I thought. When I got a copy of *Aurora*, I found, to my shock, that all I'd won was an honorable mention in poetry. The winner was a guy named Gary Kerley, who was a graduate student in English at UGA. I felt as if the wind had been knocked out of me, but after a few minutes, I realized it didn't matter. Linda was with me, and for the first time in my life, people treated me with literary respect, even deference. (And Gary and I went on to become friends.) The readings and lunch went well enough, but a minor kerfuffle broke out during the panel discussion when Mott, who was a British national, criticized me pretty harshly for one of my one of my poems, "Elegy: The Firing of a Gun," which was about Vietnam and strongly against the war. Mott said that I couldn't use a narrative voice that speaks of events happening in the war if I hadn't actually been there. Sarton flared at this and snapped that I had every right in the world to write about something I had deeply considered, even if I hadn't actually seen it. For a moment, I thought they were going to get into a shouting argument, and Sarton was so upset it seemed she might even take a swing at him. But it all calmed down soon enough. Many years later, she would blurb my first published novel, and I had to remind her of the day she defended me in front of my girlfriend. I owed her one for that defense and also for the blurb. (I would have even been more starstruck if I'd known that Sarton had once loaned her house near Harvard one semester to a fellow professor named Vladimir Nabokov, but like many things, I didn't know that in those days.)

In the meantime, I earned my first national poetry acceptance on May 21, 1972, with an avant-garde piece called "Bhangi" which appeared the next winter in a well-known post-Beat magazine in San Francisco called *Beyond*

Baroque. (Bhangis are a caste of untouchables in India that also include Hindu saints.) The editor, George Drury Smith, was kind to me, and I was thrilled to be in such a handsome magazine. That following year, as we tried to get our own literary magazine off the ground, Linda and I returned to the conference, hoping to get a few words with that year's main speaker, Robert Penn Warren. I was too tongue-tied to try very hard, but he did sign my copy of his book-length poem *Brother to Dragons*, though in my haste and nervousness, I got him to sign it to me alone, something Linda held against me, but only for the next two or three decades.

Early in spring quarter of our senior year, I asked Linda to marry me. And, like the usual response from the magazines I was inundating with poems, she rejected me. But at least it wasn't a form rejection slip. She'd get back to me. I'd managed to outlast Frantz Fanon (well, not Fanon, but Linda's philosophical coterie in Athens) and coat pockets filled with fried catfish. We had walked together on a Cape Cod beach at sunset. I had waged war against a battalion of rats and almost fought them to a draw. I'd written and co-printed my first book, and in sales it was showing signs of climbing into double digits. And I'd gotten two seasoned writers into an argument over one of my poems.

We went to graduation that spring, and while she planned to come right back for graduate school in English, I had by then accepted my first professional job as managing editor of a small newspaper, *The Clayton Tribune*, up in the mountains of northeast Georgia where they'd just finished filming a movie called *Deliverance*.

He has traveled so little. A friend is just back from Prague. Another has spent the summer in Kamchatka. He drives to Atlanta, Memphis maybe. Distance unsettles him, and he knows what others say: He is defining himself. He is parochial, meaning he is self-limited. Travelers seem smug to him, dazzling with Londonderry Airs, with Indian Ocean catamarans. Now, in middle age, he watches travel shows on Public Television and dreams of not being there, of visiting the country of his own hands on the keyboard. That is his land, his sinecure, and he defends it from his singular parapet. He wonders if he will grow old. He wonders what the lifespan might be in Indonesia, where there are volcanoes and 17,508 islands. Only 6,000 are inhabited, and he does not live on one of those.

11

Whole Lotta Shakin' Goin' On

It seems quaint now, but in those days job openings for graduates were put on three-by-five index cards and thumbtacked to a tan cork board in the main hall of the Journalism Building at UGA. With some desperation, I'd been dropping by to see what newspaper jobs were opening around the state and all over the South. I needed to get out of college, but I was also desperate to hold on to Linda. In perhaps the first fully mature act of my life, I knew that if I gave in and went on straight to grad school with her, my odds of keeping her got *worse*. She needed to see that I could be strong and sure, even if I could never rewire her house. One day in spring 1972, I was trawling through jobs on the board and spied an opening for a managing editor at the weekly newspaper in Clayton, Georgia, a rugged and mountainous town snug-up against the North Carolina border. I knew that part of the state well, since my parents had begun taking us as children to a place called the Cowee Valley, across the border in North Carolina, to mine for rubies and sapphires. My mother also had gone to junior college at the Rabun Gap-Nacoochee School, just up the road from Clayton, graduating in 1943.

I wrote a letter to the contact person listed on the card, one James Wallace, who worked for Community Newspapers, Inc., the chain that had bought the Clayton paper from its local owners a few years before. Linda watched all this with glum disbelief. I borrowed the family car and drove up for an interview. I had already mailed him a huge folio of stories and personal columns I'd written during three summers at *The Madisonian*, so he had time to judge my work before we met in person. Mr. Wallace, a nice middle-aged man with thinning hair and a thick, dark mustache, was a bit distant and little formal, but he said he was impressed with me and my work, and he'd be in touch. I have since often thought with amusement that

Community Newspapers might have given serious consideration to John Dillinger as editor, since Clayton was still just a bit out of the way in those days. (Today, it's a resort area where real estate is pricey, and people own second homes.)

My first call was to Adelaide Ponder, editor at *The Madisonian*, and on May 12 she wrote me a recommendation that most twenty-two-year-olds can only dream about. If I had a hundred lifetimes I could never repay Adelaide for what she did for me in these and later years. I was still trying to be a literary person, but I thought I needed some hard, practical work as a journalist to help me along the literary path. And I was right. In those days, the MFA in creative writing was available at only a handful of universities, and I knew I couldn't compete with the students winning slots in those programs anyway. Not long before we graduated, Mr. Wallace called and offered me the job. I accepted immediately, and Linda, rather than ply me with congratulations, was angry almost beyond words. She was going home to spend the summer in Decatur and find a job until grad school started in the fall, so my one concession was that I would drive the hundred miles from Clayton to visit her every weekend. (Linda's summer jobs always scared me to death. One year she worked at a restaurant apparently run by organized crime, but, as she shrugged, the tips were great.) With our future unresolved, Linda and I parted that June, and I drove up U.S. 441 to the mountains in the first car I ever owned, a navy blue 1967 Mustang, scared witless of my first real job, worrying that I'd never amount to anything as a poet or novelist, and that I'd blown my last chance with a beautiful girl.

My job at the weekly *Tribune* was fairly straightforward. I had to sell all the ads for each issue of the paper, write all the stories, take all the photographs, develop and print them, and then design and assist in laying out the paper at a central office twenty-five miles up the road in Franklin, North Carolina, and *then* take the finished product to Murphy (also in North Carolina) for printing. After all that, I had to bring the inky papers back to Clayton for labeling and mailing. The good part was that I was getting $110 a week for this. (Mr. Wallace said any man worth his salt could put out a paper alone in three days; I should have peppered him with questions, but I didn't. I need to add that I found out he was really a nice man who treated me well the whole time I was there.) I was also chain smoking Vantage cigarettes, and my hands had developed an ominous tremble, not unlike

Tom Hanks's character decades later in *Saving Private Ryan*. As I pulled into Clayton, I had no place to live. Other than that, it was my dream job.

Clayton was then and is now a lovely, beautiful little town. I fell in love with it on the first day I got there in June, and it's been a lifelong affair. But in 1972, it was different in some noticeable ways from now. On Saturdays, what we called country people trucked into town out of the mountains to shop, and many of them looked rather like the denizens of *Deliverance*. Fortunately, they were nothing whatever like Dickey's fictional hoodlum rednecks. Some were a bit stand-offish, but most were kind and generous and modest. A few I got to know bore the false shame of poverty with great dignity. I had heard of James Dickey and vaguely knew they'd filmed a movie of his book in the county, but as I've said before, general knowledge was a wildly different thing in the days before the Internet. (Christopher Dickey's marvelous book *Summer of Deliverance* gives a glimpse of what Clayton and Rabun County were like in those days.) The film was released on July 30, but I didn't write about it before I left and frankly knew only a little about the whole thing. I had no remote idea that my literary life would become entangled with James Dickey's eleven years down the road.

I checked want ads in the *Tribune* to find a room or apartment for rent and located a room at a boarding ranch north of town run by a nice woman named Eula Parker. I still have the receipt for the two weeks I spent there. Cost: forty bucks. The place was clean and well-lighted, but I wanted something different, and so by mid-month had moved into a single room in a huge rambling boarding house just down Main Street from the *Tribune* office in downtown Clayton. I wasn't there long before I split for a basement apartment owned by an old man named Duvall. While I worked myself almost to death at the *Tribune*, I did manage to make friends—an outdoorsy bunch of guys who worked for the U.S. Forest Service in town. I was young and stupid, and so when they suggested we start taking long night-time hikes to little-known waterfalls around Rabun County, I was cautious as always.

"I'm in!" I cried. "Who's bringing the beer?"

We got lost a number of times doing this, but we were always so toasted that being lost seemed manifestly hilarious. Once on a moonless night our sole flashlight went out, and after spending a couple of hours at a dramatic hidden waterfall with a glowing palisade of bioluminescent foxfire around it, we started walking generally west. We decided we'd each hold on to the back of the trousers of the man or woman in front, and there we were, wandering like a drunken caterpillar through the crickety woods. After an hour of raucous laughter, falling into holes and slamming into trees and through diaphanous spiderwebs, we stumbled out right by our cars in the parking lot. God does occasionally save poets and fools. One of the people at the Forest Service was a guy whose name I remember as John Lambert, though it could have been anything. He was a grad student in forestry at UGA as I remember and getting some practical experience for the summer. He rented a tin-roofed cabin up the road in the tiny town of Mountain City, three miles north of Clayton at the foot of Black Rock Mountain. John was going to be leaving in a couple of weeks to go back to Athens, and he said I could move in with him and take the place when he left. I called the guy who owned it, and he seemed pleased enough with the agreement. I did all this, you understand, without seeing the cabin. So one day after work I drove up to Mountain City to take a gander.

"Holy shit," I said as I stepped out of the Mustang. Or rather I said that when I saw where I assumed the house probably was. I had called John and told him I was on my way, so he was standing next to the road when I arrived. "John, don't you ever mow the grass?

"Why would I want to do that?" he asked, grinning. "I like it natural."

"What about snakes?

"What about them?"

John was balding and had a Klondike explorer's rusty-colored beard, and I told him I thought the cabin, which had a den, a kitchen, a cramped bedroom, and a bathroom, and which was buried to its shoulders in a green sea of weeds and vines, would be fine for me. So I moved in, and we lived together for a couple of amiable weeks. He was gone most of the time, so we only had a few good conversations before he left my life forever, and I had the cabin to myself. The first thing I did was hack and mow the jungle back to a safe perimeter.

True to my promise, I left Clayton every Friday after work and drove the two-plus hours to Decatur to visit the love of my life. I got through every week because I knew I would see that lovely face around eight on Friday nights. She would be waiting for me there with a cold Falstaff and a cigar. Then at dawn on Monday morning, I would drive back to Clayton and straight to the *Tribune* office for another week of sales, writing, and laying out the paper. From time to time, I wrote a bit of poetry or prose, but working seventy-five hours a week and more, there was little time for that. Still, a magazine named *Cardinal Poetry Quarterly* in Melrose Park, Ill., accepted a poem called "Morgue" on September 5. I also placed another poem, "The Instruments" in the *DeKalb Literary Arts Quarterly* in the Atlanta area. In a fit of desperation, I also wrote the fabled *Saturday Review* in Manhattan and told them they'd be crazy not to hire me. I got a letter back dated August 13 from John Poppy, managing editor for the arts, telling me that the magazine was in the process of moving to San Francisco. He also startled me by revealing that his wife's family was from Atlanta, and he had recently spent time with family and friends in *Athens*! I had told him what I had done so far in music and poetry, and he was impressed enough to ask me to freelance for *SR*. There was only one problem. I didn't know what "freelance" meant (!), and there was no way to find out in Clayton. Ashamed of my ignorance, I never responded, throwing away a possible chance to write for the *Saturday Review* at age twenty-two. As a small solace, a journal called *Patterns* in New Jersey accepted my poem "Sunshine Silver Mine" late in the year.

Back at *The Clayton Tribune*, it was me, a pleasant but very young office manager named Judy, and, in the back, a salty ancient fellow named Jake who ran the old-fashioned, hot-metal Linotype machine for job printing like Van Cliburn playing Tchaikovsky. (He looked startlingly like Burgess Meredith who was a Linotype operator in a 1963 episode of *Twilight Zone* called "Printer's Devil.") Jake interested me greatly, and fifteen years later I would name a character in my novel *All the Western Stars* in memory of him. There was also a crew at the paper's central office in Franklin, and I nearly got into a fistfight with one of them, a heavyset man with a Prince Valiant haircut, after he refused to help me as I thought he should. As the summer dragged on, exhaustion began its inevitable grind. I got to know a family that lived up the mountain slope behind me. I was never quite sure what was wrong with them, but they were slow, quiet, happy, naïve, and awkwardly friendly. The placid sway-backed horse they kept in a large pen between our houses was about the same, and by early fall I brought him sweet-smelling but bruised apples I got for next to nothing at a roadside stand. Their small house wasn't much larger than the cabin I rented. I liked them all enormously and was touched by their closeness to each other and their clear affection for me, even though I barely knew them.

One firefly Friday night that summer in Decatur, Linda and I sat up after everyone else had gone to bed. I slept in the bedroom with her small brother Brian, and I was so in love I could hardly stand not seeing her until Saturday morning.

"I've been thinking of something," she said, holding a sweating can of beer and looking down.

"And what have you been thinking of?"

"Getting married."

"Really." I sat up and tried to breathe, couldn't.

"Yes."

"And what have you decided?"

"That I want to."

"All right then."

So, months after I'd asked her, in her own time and her own way, Linda said she'd have me, even though she knew for now it would be for poorer, not richer, since there was no way in hell I'd be rich any time soon. We got married on September 30, 1972, at her parents church, Central Congregational in Atlanta. Our wedding was small and intimate, and she was absolutely gorgeous in her gown. We spent a honeymoon week at Jekyll Island on the Georgia coast, and most of the time I felt sure I'd wake up from what must be a dream, perhaps having fallen in a hole and banged my head while hiking the north Georgia woods in darkness. Since it was early October, the beach was almost empty, and so we had a long strip of a beautiful barrier island almost to ourselves. Linda brought her black cat, Africa, when we moved in to our cabin in Mountain City, and we settled down as a newly married couple while the peaks shimmered into a spectacular crimson-and-golden autumn. Linda tried to find a job, applying everywhere and not even getting an interview. And with graduate school on hold now for both of us, our future was unclear. She made even better friends with the family up the mountain slope behind us, and when we went to the grocery store, she began buying nicer apples for us to feed to their horse. We also took occasional small gifts—canned food and the like—to our friends. They knew we were very poor and accepted our small gifts with joy. They gave us home-canned fruit and so forth, too. I still remember the golden glow of a late October afternoon and the cropping sound of that horse as he gently ate winesap apples from our hands.

That fall Richard Nixon ran for re-election against George McGovern, the liberal senator from South Dakota and Democratic presidential nominee. Because I'd written a few personal columns in the *Tribune* with a progressive slant, the McGovern Georgia Campaign got in touch with me and asked if I'd be a county McGovern campaign coordinator right in the heart of *Deliverance* country! I accepted immediately. Linda and I campaigned, but no one paid much attention to us. Mr. Wallace even let me endorse McGovern on the *Tribune's* editorial page. I got more than one threatening phone call, though, and one whiskey-soaked right-winger threatened to kill me. I ignored the threat and didn't tell Linda, but nothing happened. McGovern got just under twenty percent of the vote in Rabun County. I also wrote a "house" or unsigned "institutional" editorial when Ezra Pound died in November. The fact that we were no doubt one of the few weekly papers in North American to do so is a point of pride with me. I had also picked up, as a damaged book, Noel Stock's *The Life of Ezra Pound*, and it became another of my totemic volumes, though I had to find out later, on my own, how dark the darker parts of Pound's life were. Then, around Thanksgiving, my office phone rang one morning, and it was Bob Chambers, the wunderkind publisher of Athens Newspapers, the company back in our college town that owned the morning-afternoon combo of the *Daily News* and the *Athens Banner-Herald*.

"Got an opening for a copy editor on the *Daily News* and wanted to see if you were still interested," he said in his mile-a-minute, rat-a-tat-tat way of speaking. Linda was itching to return to Athens and start graduate school, and I was getting almost no personal writing done because of the volume of my journalistic work. I had applied to Athens Newspapers about the same time I applied for the job at the *Tribune*.

"Can I talk it over with my wife and call you back tomorrow?"

"Yeah, sure, sure. But I need to know right away."

"Yes sir, I will."

And so, by mid-December 1972, we packed our few belongings and headed back south toward Athens. But first, we had to say goodbye to our friends up the mountain. Linda and I walked up one Saturday around noon with a bag of polished apples for the horse, and the whole family, a man, his wife, their small son, and daughter, came out to tell us goodbye. I don't know if others in the area hadn't spoken to them much, or if they were just touched by us and the apples we brought to their horse. But as we told them goodbye, they began to sob, even the father. We hugged them, but their grief was so genuine I could only look at Linda with damp eyes and amazement as she held on to the mother.

So my first job had lasted all of six months. We found a basement apartment in Athens on a wide shady street simply called Boulevard, and I started work at the *Daily News* with a crew of brilliant, hilarious, and relentlessly tough journalists. Linda had already applied for graduate school in English literature and been immediately accepted. And, except for the publication in *Aurora*, and a few other little magazines, I had gotten no further down the road toward being a published creative writer. I didn't know that while I would soon begin to publish poems steadily, my first *real* published book was still twelve years in the future.

Today is his last day at The Athens Observer, *and these frames will be left on the cutting-room floor: He is thirty-eight years old, and he walks through the offices, knowing what has changed and what cannot. The work was exhausting, at times exhilarating, but now it is gone; it is over and gone. He shakes hands with his friends, bids them farewell. He photographs himself in memory so he can misplace the images later. They are putting the next week's paper together. None of us is missed much when we leave for a new job. For a week, less, we're waking shadows, moved-on conversations. We are the work someone else has to do and does. But he sees himself as indispensable, necessary. Surely the paper cannot come out without him. Surely all news will cease. But when he is gone, nothing stops, and soon enough he is forgotten, then the paper is gone and forgotten. No one knows a newspaper was ever in this building. One day, not a living soul will remember its name.*

12

Setting the Words on Fire

The old *Daily News/Banner-Herald* building in downtown Athens is now long gone, like the original St. Mary's Hospital where I was born on Milledge Avenue and the rat-infested house in which Linda and I lived as seniors at UGA. (A new building replaced the *Daily News* structure, though years after I worked there.) But it was a daily newspaper operation and light years from *The Madisonian* and *The Clayton Tribune*. It was bigger, faster, and wilder than either of those small weeklies. We rented a basement apartment from a retired warden at the Clarke County work camp and his wife, lovely people. We had my Mustang, and for a wedding gift, Linda's parents had given us their old Ford Fairlane station wagon that Linda named Hardy, after Oliver Hardy, her favorite comic actor. (In a strange coincidence, he had spent part of his childhood in Madison.) To help pay our expenses, Linda got a part-time job in the photocopy room of the Main Library on campus where she worked in between classes.

I began writing again and finished a sketchy, avant-garde novella I'd started in Clayton. I knew I had much to learn as a poet and a writer of prose fiction, but I felt by then as if I knew newspaper journalism reasonably well. It took me about fifteen minutes of my first manic day at the *Daily News* to find out differently. Since it was a morning paper, I had to work from two in the afternoon until about midnight five days a week. This was in the days of AP and UPI machines endlessly clattering in a somewhat-soundproofed cubicle just off the newsroom. I knew I was young (twenty-two) and by the standards of the *Daily News* staff inexperienced, but nothing could have prepared me for Johnny Futch and Plott Brice.

Plott served as city editor of the *DN* and was my immediate boss. Johnny was sports editor, a veteran of the Vietnam War, and, at first, intimidatingly scary. I say at first, because we soon became good friends, and he taught me more in the year I was at the *DN* than anyone else ever did about journalism or writing for the rest of my life. A stringer once brought in a story about Little League or something, and Johnny set *fire* to the poor kid's copy and threw it in the metal trash can. I doubt the stringer ever forgot it—I sure didn't. But the boy went back and rewrote the story, and it was at least acceptable the second time around. I saw little of the publisher who'd hired me, Bob Chambers. He was a walking streak of ambition, in his early thirties and feisty as a bantam cock. Our associate editor was a veteran journalist named Larry Young. Larry hated every political word we ever breathed—for the first time I found myself largely among moderates and liberals, a great relief, and Larry was a rock-ribbed conservative. But for some reason we respected each other, and he was always on our side. He was a great reporter, too. Billy Berryman and Bill Bryant were solid writers and hilarious guys. (Berryman later went to law school and became the county attorney.) Murray Dennis was what was quaintly called in those days "women's editor" (Murray was a woman, and a delightful and highly intelligent one), and another writer and favorite of mine was Gary Spooner. *Nothing* bothered Spooner. He smiled all the time, even under the withering barrage of an editor's lashing. He became a minister later, a decision that didn't surprise me in the least. Cheryl Walton was a young and very bright woman (and one of the first African Americans on the staff of an Athens newspaper) who wrote obits and had a droll attitude we all loved. Bob Perry was a first-rate reporter, and Laura Basan was a staff writer—she and Bob later married and moved on. A truly talented crew.

Plott and I were soon close friends, even though he was my boss. He had a wicked and wide-ranging sense of humor, and we often did strange and reckless things in the newsroom. We had a series of air-pressurized pneumatic tubes to send copy down to typesetting—this was more than a decade before computers. And we often shot strange things down to the production crew in these tubes. (Years later, my friend and famous literary critic Hugh Kenner told me that he used just such a mail delivery system in Paris—a *pneumatique*—to send his first note to Samuel Beckett, setting up a meeting.) Once we sent a tube downstairs full of popcorn. Another time it was a dead mouse. In mid-1973, I got one of the standard purple AP-machine ribbons, put it in my typewriter, and typed up a phony but amazingly realistic F L A S H that Spiro Agnew had resigned as Vice President of the United States. The production crew downstairs exploded in glee until I had to come clean on the hoax. (Agnew *did* resign in October, but I was anticipating that wonderful event by a few months.) Together, Johnny and Plott were the best teachers a young newspaperman could want. While Plott was hilarious, he was also dead serious when it came to the quality of his work—and mine. I didn't make the same mistake twice. I began shyly to ask Johnny for advice, and he patiently taught me. With him I was scared to make the same mistake *once*. (Plott and I once made an agreement that on a certain day we would only communicate all day by singing phrases from pop, rock, or Great American Song Book music. We damn near pulled it off.) We also, while waiting on Friday nights for area prep football scores to come in during the fall of 1973, played "baseball" in the newroom with a wadded and taped hunk of wire-machine paper and a cardboard tube for a bat. This worked until one night when I was batting and turned around to see Chambers standing behind me. The man had little sense of humor and was not amused.

One event that remains whirling in my memory was a tornado outbreak in the spring of 1973. In those days, the weather was pretty much a mystery, even to TV and radio weather reporters. Predictive weather models barely existed, and forecasting was much worse than today—and as we all know, today's models aren't consistently useful, either. That May morning, savage systems strutted across the South. Unlike today, when National Weather Service computers can report rotation in a storm on any street, we only knew of breaking weather news through phone calls from staffers and friends. (I need to point out that Johnny and Plott were only a few years older than I was. But in journalistic experience, light years hummed between us.) We'd actually had a tornado two months earlier, on March 31. Linda and I had gone to the movies (to see *Cabaret*, which we loved), and by the time we got back to our apartment and our cat, Africa, the world seemed close to falling apart. The power went out, and we went inside and played chess by candlelight and drank beer. While there was damage then, the gathering storm two months later seemed even more ominous. It was May 28, and that morning, the sky shaded into an odd greenish-yellow. The air felt sinister, almost refused to let us breathe it. We knew by early afternoon that there had been damage from tornadoes in Alabama, but it was a shock when someone's phone rang—I can't remember who it was now forty years later—and he turned and shouted that there was a tornado at the Hess Station, and it was headed into town. The Hess Station was a familiar landmark, the last bit of commercial property before one headed west out of Athens and into the country. Phones started to ring all over the newsroom. People shouted. Plott began to scream out tentative plans for who could cover what.

"It's coming down Prince Avenue!" someone shouted. I froze. Linda was in our apartment one street over on Boulevard. But our place was in a basement, and our bedroom closet was almost underground. "Everybody to the press room!"

We dashed out of the newsroom and into the stairwells, finding our way down to the vast press room—probably the last place we should have gone with its wide-span trusswork ceiling. But the heavy printing presses made the area *feel* stable. The editors of the *Banner-Herald* still at work began gathering with us, and one of our best reporters, Bob Perry, got the plum assignment to write the lead story. I still remember the look in his eyes: *Trust me, and I will do a great job.* He did. The air outside crackled with lightning just before it became still and quiet and very black. We all doubled down as the storm roared past, but the funnel only glanced us, and after a moment to take a breath, we scrambled back into the newsroom and started work. The first thing I did was call Linda. I got her, but she spoke in a voice shattered with barely controlled panic.

"I got into the bedroom closet with Africa, and we're fine," she said. "But Hardy is destroyed. Trees are down everywhere. I think the house next door is mostly gone."

Relieved she was safe and worried that the house beside ours had been blown to bits, I set to work, and we didn't finish until after one the next morning. The power in Athens would be out for days. After we got the paper printed, I drove home, dodging fallen trees, and managed to get within a block of our apartment before I had to park at the edge of a debris field. The night by then was clear and star-spangled, and sixty-foot oaks lay down across Boulevard from one end to the other, old men who sacrificed themselves to save the younger vegetation. I only guessed at where our apartment house might be and started crawling down the horizontal trunk of a century-old oak tree, calling "Hello?" over and over.

"Phil? Phil?"

The voice was that of Mr. Greenway, our landlord. He and his sweet wife and Linda had waited up for me. (They were older than our parents.) Access to our apartment was a narrow driveway on the right of the house, but it was filled with star-lit trunks, so we had to take an interior staircase down to our apartment. I could barely see, in the darkness, what was left of Hardy—very little.

The cleanup took weeks, but in the following days, a quiet sense of pride could be seen on the faces of everyone who worked getting out the paper that night. We did a superb job, and we knew it. And my grasp on what it took to be a journalist had grown dramatically. Still, journalism was a means for me, not an end. I knew men who had spent their whole lives as newspaper journalists, and most of them were broken down by drink or cigarettes or the pumping adrenaline that sooner or later will kill a person. So in 1973 I took the Graduate Records Examination, got accepted to graduate school, and began the stupidest part of my life.

Just why I thought I could take a full load of classes in grad school and work full time at the *Daily News,* only God (or someone) knows. I think it says something about my desperation to make it in the literary world that I would even contemplate such a nutty notion. I was making $140 a week at the *DN*—better than the *Tribune,* surely, but a sad salary, even for 1973. (After I'd been at the paper for a year, Plott solemnly called me in for a yearly review, told me I'd done a fine job, and announced with restrained sarcasm that management was letting him raise my salary to *$145* a week.) Linda thought I'd lost my marbles. And despite school and work, I was still desperately trying to write, to find time even to scribble down a poem once in a blue moon. But time between those moons grew longer and longer, and I despaired that I would ever be able to be a well-published author.

There was another problem. Getting a master's degree in English literature did absolutely nothing for me, career-wise. Creative writing was still considered an embarrassing hobby in academic circles, and a master's might get me a job teaching in a high school, but I would need a Ph.D. even to become one of the thousands of unemployed college-professor wannabes. If I had been a patient, my prognosis would have been easy to diagnose as terminal. Linda had the same problem. She had always said she would *never* teach public school, but here she was, still going to college after five years at it, unsure where it would lead.

In the summer of 1973, early on a Saturday morning, I awoke, Linda and Africa sleeping soundly at my side. I had been reading and re-reading Stock's biography of Pound, and I couldn't get the idea of a little poetry and art magazine out of my mind. In London and Paris seventy-five years before, the literary world revolved around such tiptoe attempts to overturn the literary establishment. I had enough of the revolutionary spirit in me to feel those men and women were kindred spirits. While the New York poets published in well-known outlets such as *The Paris Review*, their work could also be found in such edgy small magazines as *Angel Hair, "C," City Lights Journal, The Floating Bear,* and *Locus Solus.* Maybe, instead of focusing on getting into those magazines, I should be focusing on something else: *founding and editing my own journal.*

"Linda!" I cried, sitting straight up.

"What happened?" she asked. Africa, lying placidly between us, didn't move.

"We can start our own little magazine, and I can print it on the presses at *The Madisonian*!" I said. "And I even know what we can call it."

"That's nice," she said, lying back down.

"*Ataraxia,*" I said. It was one of my favorite words, used by the Epicureans to describe a state of tranquility and bliss. I'd liked it so much I'd gotten my brother Mark's girlfriend (and future first wife) to hand-letter it on a three-by-five card that I kept with my writing stuff. "We can call it *Ataraxia*. I'm sure the Ponders will let us print it there. What do you think?"

"Sounds good to me," she yawned.

Linda's not a morning person. But soon enough she was entirely on board. If I couldn't get into the literary world, I'd bring it to my own door. And my first promise to myself was that *editor* Phil Williams would not turn down any submissions from *writer* Phil Williams. So in addition to graduate school, a full-time job in journalism, and my own writing, I was now going to bring the Paris and London of 1920 to Athens, Georgia. My literary publishing had suffered, though. I was sending out very few poems, and in 1974 I only had one publication, a poem called "Dmitri Shostakovich" in a small magazine named *Stone Country* in Madison, New Jersey. (Linda, who was also writing in those days, and beautifully, had several poems in *Stone Country*, too.) The Shostakovitch poem was from a series on composers I called *Princeps Musicorum* and wrote in 1973, along with another cycle called *Images*, which was about artists. So I *was* writing, though just how I made the time escapes me now. By November of that tornado year, the grind had ground me down. I had to choose between grad school and journalism, and I felt as if I had no real choice. So beneath the glaring fluorescent lights of the newsroom, I told all my friends goodbye and left for the world of English literature and a part-time job in the University of Georgia Bookstore.

I worked in the textbooks section, where my boss was a lovely and decisive woman named Dolores Slay. I also got to know Bill Powell, who was the assistant manager of the bookstore, a wonderful older guy with a riotous laugh and a copper bracelet that he swore cured all manner of ills. There were several other student workers there, including Mike, who had finished everything but his dissertation for a Ph.D. and had then decided things would be easier just working at the bookstore for the rest of his life. (There was one student when my parents started at UGA in 1946 who was still there, taking classes *fifty years later.*) Some people are ready to settle, right from the starting line. I wasn't one of them, or so I thought. One older man who did blue collar work in the back was standing near me once when a song by country singer Tom T. Hall came on the radio whose sound was piped through the store. "I'd just as lief hear a mule braying in a brass barn," the old guy said. The world is filled with poetry, it seems. And needless to say, my path would later cross in a bizarre way with that of Tom T. Hall.

After leaving the *Daily News,* we decided to move and found another apartment in the basement of a boutique, Homeplace, in a section of Athens near campus called Five Points. We added another cat to our little family, too. Brewster was solid black like Africa but fluffy. Since then, we've always had at least two black cats. The apartment was huge and hippieish and featured an enormous hanging bed. My childhood friend Edward Hudson, a student at UGA and improving every day as a marvelous visual artist, rented the adjoining apartment beneath Homeplace, and we had something approaching a cheerful commune. He also signed on as art editor of *Ataraxia.* The job at the bookstore was easy, but I wasn't used to picking up heavy boxes of books, and I often lifted and turned in ways that caused Dolores to cringe and warn me. I made the mistake of letting a few of the workers know that I was a poet and in the planning stages of my own magazine, and Stiles, a languid, long-haired student worker, gave me a free obscene couplet that he said I could publish. After that, I told one guy I was working on a graduate degree in karate.

"No shit," he said, taking a step back. Mess with me.

For a short time, Linda and I balanced our part-time jobs, graduate school, and planning *Ataraxia*. I already knew I wanted to be the next Ford Madox Ford, the famed English writer and editor of the influential *Transatlantic Review*, for which a young Ernest Hemingway once worked as a substitute editor. (My name-dropping of Ford at this point is no accident. Like many of the writers I admired early, later in life my path would cross in a second-hand way with Ford's.) We loved living in Five Points. A beer store called to us from across the street, as did Boxcar Pizza, and up on our side of the street a coin-operated laundromat chugged and churned almost constantly. Bell's grocery store was next to the pizza place. One didn't need much more than that to live happily at twenty-three. Once when Edward badly needed cash, we loaned him sixty dollars. After a couple of months, he came over and said there was no way he'd ever be able to repay the debt. Would we consider taking one of his paintings? And he offered us a gorgeous, *dazzling* backstage-at-the-ballet painting that was a staggering four-by-six feet.

"Yes!" Linda and I cried at the same time. That painting is still on the wall in our den all these decades later. Best deal we ever made. People have been trying to buy it from us for years.

I had been a political liberal for several years, and Linda, Edward, and I were watching TV on our black-and-white set the night of October 20 when CBS broke in with a special bulletin. President Nixon had ordered Attorney General Elliott Richardson to fire special prosecutor Archibald Cox, who was looking into the Watergate horrors. Richardson refused and resigned, as did Deputy Attorney General William Ruckelshaus. I leaped up screaming.

"That bastard! That son of a bitch!" I was talking about Nixon, of course, and at that moment my liberalism turned a more radical hue.

A less intense moment occurred earlier that summer. Edward was a casual housekeeper, and he'd had, on his stove top, a half-full pan of Tuna Helper that had been sitting there beneath a clamped-tight lid for weeks and weeks. God only knew what was growing inside. One night, tipsy and in high hilarity, we decided we would take the atomic Tuna Helper into the back yard and remove its lid. Hee. Whatever was inside was bound to be gaggingly hideous and possibly poisonous. We carried the pan out by the handle and set it on the ground.

"I'm not opening the thing," I said.

"Don't even think about looking at me," Linda said.

Edward looked around a bit in the dark until he found a garden rake. He would then stand five feet from the pan and tug the top off. By this time, I was laughing so hard I was crying. We nudged each other and made *Exorcist* sounds, as if the offensive and now-ancient meal might be rising for the kill. Edward got the tines of the rake on the lid and pulled, and our shield against salmonella came off. We huddled together giggling and pushing each other. Just then, a dopey, smiling dog we'd never seen came loping around the corner of the apartment house, saw the pan, and dove right in.

"Oh my God!" Linda screamed, pointing. "We're going to kill him!"

The dog seemed to think it was delicious though, and he finished it all, licked his lips, and dashed on off into the darkness. I hope he was fine. Whatever twinge of guilt I felt about it has been leavened over the years by the remembered sound of our weeping laughter.

My interest in graduate school in English grew complicated. What had started as a way to engage every day with literature was still a delight. I took Chaucer in Middle English and many other courses I loved. But I could never shake the feeling that I was being self-indulgent and even wasting my time and Linda's. The best I could hope for was another five years in school, life at or below the poverty line, and a job in the very distant future explaining symbolism in *Moby-Dick*. I also wondered if I hadn't made a mistake leaving journalism, since that was at least writing and editing. We had traveled to Madison and met with Adelaide Ponder, and she was delighted to let us use the facilities of *The Madisonian* to print *Ataraxia*. So we had that much to look forward to. If I couldn't decide what to do, I had only to wait. As it usually does, Fate showed up and bit me on the ass.

One morning at the bookstore, I lifted a heavy box of art-history textbooks, turned, and set it on the unpacking table. Unfortunately, I did it without moving my *feet*, and I felt my entire lower back rip out. That's the only verb for it. I cried aloud, fell down in hideous pain, and stayed there until I could move a little about an hour later. People nowadays use a cell phone when something like that happens to make their first call to an accident-and-injury lawyer. That never occurred to me. It was my fault. Dolores had warned me. The Bookstore and UGA, I knew, had *zero* moral or legal liability. And I still feel that way, with my back trouble now passing its fortieth year. I managed to get home, but I was in such agony that the next morning I went to the UGA Infirmary. Indeed, everything was torn in my lower back, and I went into physical therapy with a kind and gentle woman who in addition to being a therapist raised goats. Her favorite goat was named Grace, and I'm embarrassed to say that I can remember the name of that goat but not its owner. I had PT for several weeks into 1974, and it was clear that I could no longer work at the Bookstore or do any kind of casual labor to pay my part of our bills.

"What if I asked Mrs. Ponder if she'd give me a job at *The Madisonian*?" I asked Linda one night.

"I thought she couldn't afford you." (In her recommendation to Mr. Wallace in Clayton she'd said that her only regret was that *The Madisonian* couldn't afford to hire another full-time writer, or she would have offered me a job then.)

"What if I told them I'd work for a really low amount?" I said. "You could get a job, and we might be able to make it on that. And I could do my own writing then."

Our dream in those naïve and younger years was to open our own bookstore. The only writers I knew who ever really did it were Larry McMurtry and Louise Erdrich. Aside from the fact that we had no savings and no assets, we would be perfect as bookstore owners in Madison—a town too small for such a shop anyway. Still, Linda thought she might be a teacher's aide or a substitute teacher. When you're young, nothing seems forever. Maybe we could do that for awhile, and then do something else. Plott and Johnny had given me a Rhodes Scholarship in journalism during my year at the *Daily News*, and their teaching would be valuable at *The Madisonian*. And of course I had a great deal of affection for the paper in Madison, since it had published my first poetry, prose fiction, drama, *and* journalism. (Sadly, it, like the *Daily News*, has vanished from its original incarnation into the history of once-fine newspapers.) It would also make working on *Ataraxia* far easier. I also knew and was friends with the Ponders' three daughters, Anne, Mary Graham, and Douglas. They were intelligent, articulate, and beautiful. I knew their son Bill less well, since he was much younger than I was. Anne was a journalist at *The Madisonian*, too. Writhing in continual pain and doing clerical work with increasing unhappiness at the UGA Bookstore, I wrote Adelaide and asked if we could come talk to them. I wanted to work for *The Madisonian*, and I'd do it for one hundred dollars a week. That was $5,200 a year. Even at that level I was worried, because newspapers, especially back then, made very little profit after giving the owners a living. The company did job printing, too, as I said, and Graham had a rural mail route that he loved and kept for many years. She said they would like to talk to me, and one Sunday afternoon, Linda and I drove to Madison in the car we had then, a 1968 Buick LeSabre. Trading the Mustang was a fit of insanity I've always regretted, but to me it was just a small car, and I wanted something larger, even if it ran like a coffee grinder. Adding me to the payroll must have been an iffy thing for *The Madisonian*. But they hired me, and I promised that I would work hard to repay their trust. What I didn't say was that I was committed to a life in literature, and I would never quit trying to be a published author.

No one remembers the aunts and uncles in their autobiographies. He does. His mother's siblings: Harmon, Laura, Charles, and Mike. His father's: Vivian (nicknamed Ben), Sambo, and Cecil. He barely knew Harmon for decades since he lived in the North. They got to be friends late in Harmon's life. Mike also moved away after college. Sambo's given name was Vincent Astor Williams, named after the businessman and philanthropist for reasons no one knows. Sambo died on his forty-third birthday, as he had predicted decades before. Cecil died tragically young. He thinks of his aunts and uncles here in early mid-life, and he was closest to Aunt Ben, Uncle Charles, and Aunt Laura. He talks with them on the phone from time to time, but no one thinks of a nephew as he stands before the paste-up boards, putting together this week's edition of The Athens Observer.

13

Street Signs and *Moonlight*

The Ponders were members of an Episcopal church on Academy Street in Madison that had few members but a gorgeous sanctuary, and right next door to it was the church's largely unused parish house, a magnificent, blindingly white mansion built in the 1800s. With no place else to live, we accepted when Graham offered us the upstairs of the parish house for a reasonable rent, and we moved there in the summer of 1974. I started full time at the paper on June 10. The house was enormous, and except for an hour on Wednesday evenings when a few members of the church had a meeting downstairs, we had it to ourselves. So in one swoop we'd gone from a hippie apartment in an Athens basement to a mansion with a mahogany four-poster bed the size of Australia. The mattress was so high off the floor we almost needed a ladder or a vault-pole to get on top of it. When no one else is around, huge houses have an odd silence, an imminent and immense sense of expectation. Soft stripes of sunlight from venetian blinds painted still-lifes across every room. At times during the day, a parallelogram of that light spread across a section of the heart-pine floorboards, and I watched as it slowly slipped from wall to wall. While our apartment roamed across four huge rooms and a bath upstairs, the industrial size kitchen was on the first floor, which meant a nightime snack included a trip down the long, wide steps of a creaky old house that felt marginally haunted. I *loved* it. Our cats also adored the place, too, able to get a running start and slip sidewise on the wide, polished hardwood floors.

I had reason to wonder of hauntings because the house was next to the monumental Madison city cemetery. Since boyhood, I've been on a first-name basis with the honored (and otherwise) dead. As a teenager, I'd helped my father visit every cemetery in Oconee County, South Carolina, his home, and write down all the information on tombstones for archival reasons. No one asked him to do it. He just thought it would be a good idea. And of course he and my mother could recite whole chunks from Thomas Gray's "Elegy Written in a Country Churchyard." (And on a trip to England when they were in their sixties, they visited the church at Stokes Poges, the inspiration for Gray's poem.) To this day I love that poem with the intensity of a young man for his young lover:

> The curfew tolls the knell of parting day,
> The lowing herd wind slowly o'er the lea
> The ploughman homeward plods his weary way,
> And leaves the world to darkness and to me.
>
> Now fades the glimm'ring landscape on the sight,
> And all the air a solemn stillness holds,
> Save where the beetle wheels his droning flight,
> And drowsy tinklings lull the distant folds;
>
> Save that from yonder ivy-mantled tow'r
> The moping owl does to the moon complain
> Of such, as wand'ring near her secret bow'r,
> Molest her ancient solitary reign.

As I have said before, I am addicted to that "solemn stillness," and often on quiet rainy Saturdays when I wasn't working at *The Madisonian*, or writing at my home desk, I would go into one of the formal downstairs rooms and sit and read Keats or Shelley or Wordsworth out loud or take a walk in the cemetery. Still, I couldn't ignore the fact that after the foxfire waterfalls of Rabun County and Clayton and the intense year with Plott and Johnny, I had moved back to my home town, only a few blocks from the house where my parents and Laura Jane, by then a first-rate pianist and making all A's in high school, lived. While part of me loved being around what I knew and people I loved, another part was well aware that this was no way to start an international literary career.

The Madisonian was in a two-story redbrick building in downtown Madison, built in the Nineteenth Century and renovated a few years before we moved to town that summer. When the ugly multiple paint jobs of a hundred years were sandblasted, the surface of many bricks went with them, giving the structure an interesting, almost hand-carved and even

Gaudiesque look. The town itself was beginning to change from the typical dusty small southern village into a showplace, in an effort led by Adelaide, a community activist named Chris Lambert, and dozens of other civic-minded folks in town. My job was to write news and feature stories, help lay out the paper on Tuesday and Wednesday, and then take a turn driving the pasted-up pages forty miles to Crawford, Georgia, for printing. Then on Thursday and Friday, I was expected to help out with job printing in the back. I've mentioned Billy and Peggy Arthur, and I never met finer people. The marvelous Monaray Powers was the typesetter (this was still almost a decade before computers) and bookkeeper, and Bob Moore our photographer. Anne Ponder Tamplin was our governmental affairs reporter. And keeping it all together was Adelaide. Graham wasn't there in the mornings, out driving around the county and delivering mail. And of course there were many others who wrote small pieces for the paper in one way or another. If I had taken the job right after Clayton, I'm not sure what I could have brought to it. But after a year of intense work with several of the best journalists in Georgia, I was champing at the bit to do a good job. Surprisingly, though, it took me a couple of months to get my feet under me. Everyone was patient as I learned the pace of things, though, and I soon realized that I *could* be the associate editor of *The Madisonian* and a creative writer. In fact I had already tiptoed back into the paper, starting a personal column there in late April. I was probably trying to use it as a way to get my foot in the door, but I just don't recall. What I do know is that I called the column the same moronic thing I had in high school and college: *Comment*. Why this wasn't a basis for firing, I'll never know. By the time I started full-time in June, I still had a weekly column, but the title "Comment" was mercifully gone.

On the day I started, the paper also added a summer intern from the University of Georgia, Debbie Blum. She was bright, funny, hard-working, and had a pet tarantula. She would also go on, as Deborah Blum, to win the 1992 Pulitzer Prize for Beat Reporting at the *Sacramento Bee* for a series on animal research. And she has also published many superlative books. We're still in touch.

In those days I also taught Linda how to fish. Growing up in the suburbs, she'd never had the chance, and so we began to fish almost every weekend on ponds and several years later at the newly impounded Lake Oconee, only a few miles from Madison. We also camped there on moonlit summer and autumn evenings, and I taught her all the woodscraft I'd learned as a boy. Those were lovely days, fine nights.

Living in a mansion didn't mean we could have its requisite lifestyle—far from it. Linda needed a job, and so we took advantage of the close ties one can find only in a small town. Principal of Morgan County Middle School (there was only one such school in the county) in those days was Bill Corry, formerly head football coach of Morgan County High School. Our football team had been almost ridiculously successful, winning Class B state titles in 1955, 1956, 1958, 1959, and 1962. All but the first title had been directed by Corry. But he knew he could make more money as an administrator and became a principal. And it didn't hurt that the person who'd hired Corry as head coach in the first place was my father, at the time principal of MCHS. So Linda went to the Middle School and applied for a job as a substitute teacher or teacher's aide. We had no idea if she would get a job, since she had taken no education classes. But she *did* have a degree in English and a year's graduate work in it. When Bill looked at Linda's resumé, he took it to the county school superintendent, Thomas Riden, and together they realized that if they could get Linda an emergency teacher's certificate, she could start immediately as an eighth-grade teacher. Mr. Riden had been principal of MCHS when I was a student there, and his family had moved into our house on the edge of the country when we left it in 1960. When Linda found out, she was excited and perplexed at the same time. But this was too good an opportunity to pass up, so she told them she was interested, and Mr. Riden drove to the State Board of Education in Atlanta and got her a temporary certificate. She would have to take summer education classes to get fully qualified. (Later, she would get a master's degree in education the same way.) So by that fall she had a job—and we were suddenly "rich"—making almost $12,000 a year together. Our income more than doubled, and we couldn't believe our fine, good fortune. The best part was that Linda found out quickly that she was a born teacher. Over the following years, Mr. Riden said getting that teacher's certificate for Linda was one of the best things he'd ever done in education. He was truly, truly, one of the finest human beings I ever knew. Linda was also fortunate in that a slightly older teacher, Peggy Carter, became her mentor. Peggy was happy and cheerful and loved teaching and children. She taught Linda so much. And God bless Bill Corry—he saved us right when we most needed saving.

Once my early-days jitters at the paper subsided, I began to get my sea legs as a small-town journalist, though I didn't really hit my stride until the middle of 1975. I wrote poetry and composed music when I could. This is probably a good time to mention that there has never been a day of my life when I haven't listened to classical music. It, far more than anything else, has been the soundtrack of my life. And to be honest, I know more about serious art music than any other single subject. I have lived from 78s to streaming audio, and through it all, I have been an avid fan of classical music. I also knew that at some time in my life, I *would* compose symphonies and concerti, that I would find a way to be the perfect mate for my first love. My father mostly loved Mozart and Haydn and early Beethoven, so by the time I left home my ears were ripe for more contemporary music. (Mother's favorite piece in all the world was Richard Strauss's tone poem *Don Juan*.) So when I wrote very early in the mornings before I left for work, I listened to classical music.

One of the very first things I did when I started at *The Madisonian* was a front-page photo essay about misspelled street signs in town. It was quirky and funny and got the city manager, Charles Young, rightfully mad at me. I quickly lowered my head and began to mix my reporting of Morgan County in 1974 with historical articles about the town and county in the past. These feature stories allowed me to use all the techniques I'd learned in poetry and fiction, and since I was in charge of the paper's content, I could make the stories as long as I pleased. Slowly, I began to mine better verbs, use sparklier adjectives. The mechanics of fine writing intrigued me more and more. And I began to realize that making long, gorgeous sentences and telling stories might not make poetry my art form of choice. So I began to read fiction with increasing joy. I started to see how a writer weaves parts of a novel together. I read *Bleak House* by Dickens, stunned at the richly different narrative voices in it. I had already fallen madly for *Cane* by Jean Toomer, a miscellany born when that scion of the Harlem Renaissance had spent a brief time as a school principal in Sparta, Georgia, just down the road in Hancock County. I had also bought and been dipping into *Ulysses*, but in those days, I couldn't afford any analytical material, and that great novel's wonders lay just out of my grasp.

I read *The Great Gatsby, The Sound and the Fury,* and dozens more. I remained under the spell of *The Journal of Albion Moonlight* and read any experimental or avant-garde fiction I could get my hands on. But I was still as interested in history as fiction, and while I struggled to see around my own literary corner, I kept writing poetry like a man whose burning hands can only be extinguished with verse. My collected papers contain hundreds and hundreds and *hundreds* of unpublished poems. In July I tried to start a local creative writing class to make a few more bucks, but only two people signed up, and I shrugged and forgot about it.

We had one page-turning advantage when it came to books, though: the Bargain Center. Linda and I (and Edward) still lived under Homeplace in Athens when we first discovered this barny store in the nearby small town of Monroe. It largely sold furniture from estates in upstate New York, of all places. They had excellent hutches and marvelous buffets, well-worn rocking chairs, and the kind of dusty, overstuffed sofas that students could afford. And their prices were more than reasonable. It turns out that ballast is a problem when shipping huge truckloads of furniture, just as it has always been in ships. But in breaking up estates, the buyers had a ready solution: *books*. They could buy whole personal libraries and stuff the volumes in the space between pieces of furniture to give the trucks a steady and even ride. The books were in our price range: all paperbacks a dime; hardbacks, a quarter. This sounds like an insanely good deal now, and it was only a little less so in 1974. The best part was that since they had to keep merchandise moving, each week they roared south from the area of Rochester, New York, with a wildly catholic load of books. (The problem with most stores that sell used books is that the merchandise changes so rarely. Skip a Saturday going to the Bargain Center, and you might forfeit a first-edition of a great novel someone else would snatch away for two bits.) Come into the Bargain Center and the first thing you smelled was the rich and pungent aroma of old books—*heaven*. We already owned, then, even in our poverty, nearly a thousand books, many of them rare and desirable as collectibles. We had bought them for next to nothing because in those days bookstore owners rarely knew the value of used books if they sold them. Many of these estate libraries came from people who loved to read or own fine books. When we finally slowed down some years later, we had a personal collection of almost six thousand books. So from the very beginning of our married life, we had the world's great literature.

I need to back up a little to finish the story of the Bargain Center. One Saturday when we were still living in Athens, Linda, Edward, and I drove to Monroe to see what we could scrounge up. We had begun to buy small pieces of furniture, and once Linda and I had even obtained a pretty, burled-walnut secretary from the 1920s, and to this day it's in my study. But on this Saturday, when we came inside the warehouse, we saw that the book aisles had almost been emptied. I felt a sinking sadness, but we decided to ask the woman who managed the store if they'd gotten out of selling books.

"Far from it," she laughed. "In fact we just got a huge load of them in the warehouse back there." She pointed to a brick wall behind us. "It's a *lot* of them this time, too." I glanced hungrily at Linda. An entire *load* of books that no one else had even seen, much less picked through?

"I don't guess you'd let us...." I began.

"I can't," she apologized. "If I let you look at them, then I'd have to let everybody. And they haven't even been sorted or anything." (The sorting was principally into fiction and non-fiction, as I recall.)

"I understand," I said, voice trailing. It was a cold day, and an enormous cigar-shaped heater that blew hot air like a jet across the warehouse roared happily a few feet away. "I mean, it...."

"But I tell you what I will do," she said. She knew us. We were very good customers, often dropping wads of crumpled bills, or piles of quarters and half-dollars on to the check-out counter when we settled up. "If you want the whole new shipment of books, I'd let it go for, oh, fifty dollars."

Fifty dollars! It was crazy. Her price was at the same time ridiculously fair and far more than what we had on us or that we had available for such things in our checking accounts. Not to mention the fact that the three of us had come in one car, and it had no room whatever for what must have been hundreds of books.

"Could we just stand in the warehouse and see what we're talking about without going through them?" I asked.

"I reckon that would be all right."

So she took us back into the cold warehouse area, and I suddenly became Howard Carter peeking into a just-opened tomb in the Valley of the Kings in the fall of 1922. Stretching before us were *dozens* of boxes, and peeking out of the tops were old books—some of them *very* old and gold-leafed—and hardbacks by the cargo-hold-full. I glanced at Linda, and her blue-green eyes grew wide with ecstasy. Edward was about to jump out of his skin.

"What if, ah, what if we went back to Athens and got a truck and looked around to see if we could scrounge up the money?" I asked. "Would you hold it for us for a couple of hours?"

"A couple of hours," she said. "I reckon I could do that."

Hooting and cheering, planning with the glee of mad bibliophiles, we drove back to Athens, got the old brown truck Edward owned, dug in our apartments under sofa cushions and in bureau drawers until we had the fifty bucks. (We may have hit up some friends, too; I just can't remember.) Once back, we paid up and loaded Tutankhamun's treasure into the back of the truck, the three of us crammed and giddy in the cab. We got back home and unloaded it all, and it did indeed contain treasures. A red-leather-bound set of Dickens. Two or three bookshelf-long sets of books—Balzac from the 1930s—and many other lovely discoveries. Edward took what he wanted, and we did the same. Nearing the end of it all, there was, in one cardboard box, a kraft-paper grocery bag, and inside there was a cheap home medical dictionary, a few other undesirable books, and a small jewelry box. I laughingly opened the jewelry box and saw that it was full of costume junk. I clipped on a baubly earring (as Ezra Pound had once done as a joke at a poet's gathering in London) and tossed the box to Linda. She dumped out the rest of the jewelry, and she and Edward put something on. Then, laughing, she gave the empty box a hopeful shake.

It rattled.

She opened it once more, and nothing was inside. She shook it again. I felt myself rising from the floor where we sat, surrounded by books.

"Do that again," I said, almost choking. She did, and it rattled once more. Then, like a deft archaeologist she reached into the top of the box and loosened its cardboard "roof," and when she did, a ring, hidden there for God only knew how long, fell out on to the floor. The laws of physics ceased to operate. We became still as mummies in their horizontal splendor. Slowly, slowly, I reached down and picked up the ring and looked at it, my hand trembling.

"This looks real to me," I said hoarsely. "It's a diamond ring." The idea of a windfall is wildly different when you're poor. We suddenly bristled with delight, fear, and paranoia. I thought police would break down the door any moment to arrest us, even though we'd bought the boxes, which included the ring, legally. For a moment the thought of being a *full-time poet* flashed before me, a sign that paranoia was mixing with delusions of grandeur. We could even see an inscription inside the band—it had been a Christmas Day gift in 1925, long ago hidden inside a box with costume jewelry and then forgotten when its owner died.

We shimmered with the possibilities for a week. Edward visited a friend of ours in Atlanta, a registered gemologist, and he said the stone *was* a diamond, half-karat, and it was set in platinum. Alas, the stone was an old European cut, not the newer "brilliant" cut, which at the time made it worth only a few hundred dollars. Deflated, bemused, we decided to pack the ring away and keep it for a rainy day and to split whatever we got for it with Edward. We never sold it. But the real treasures we mined that day and on many others at the Bargain Center were between the covers. And to this day they line the walls of our home.

After we'd lived in the Episcopal parish house for a few months, the Regional Library in Madison, located in the beautiful old building where I went to first and half of the second grades, began to get ready to move into a new structure across town. When they did, the wooden, handmade bookcases in the library were to be sold. I got wind of it at the paper, and because Linda and I had almost a thousand books by then, I managed to buy for very little a number of huge bookcases that would turn our piled volumes into a library. Alas, I propped them behind the parish house before taking them upstairs to our apartment, and a member of the church saw them there, stormed up to me, and royally chewed me out, presuming I would be nailing them to the floor or the walls. The old man's nastiness was palpable. And with Linda now working, we could afford something larger anyway. When he found out what happened, Graham apologized profusely to me, but by then we were gone. So we took our new bookcases (and a pool table we'd bought on a day of weakness) and moved a couple of miles to a tiny subdivision called Beacon Heights. (The beacon, once used for planes, was long gone, as was the air strip. The area had apparently started as Beacon *Lights* but the name had gotten corrupted somewhere along the way. There are no "heights" in Madison.) There, we had an entire house for the first time, and room for our bookcases. The second bedroom would become a pleasant, snug study for me.

The best event of that summer was the resignation of Richard Nixon. Linda and I were dedicated Watergate junkies, and our Schadenfreude Meters were off the scale for months. It seems odd, but in our toxic 2014 political climate, Nixon would probably be considered almost a liberal.

In between all this craziness, Volume 1, Number 1 of *Ataraxia* finally came out in late 1974. Ezra Pound dedicated his early volume *Personae* "To Mary Moore of Trenton, if she wants it," a smug paen to a former girlfriend. We dedicated the first issue of *Ataraxia* this way: "For Ezra Loomis Pound (1885-1972) *whether he wants it or not*." I seriously doubt anyone knew the origin of that dedication, but I really didn't care. I had the idea of putting a small ad in *The Paris Review* to solicit submissions, and it worked better than we imagined. We received submissions from all over the country. And we printed the best of what we got, though the quality was, I admit, wildly uneven. Still, old friends helped out, too. Marion Montgomery, who stood shoulder to shoulder with May Sarton to defend me at Agnes Scott, gave us a set of five poems called "Four Moon Tunes and One," and we put them in the middle of the first issue of the magazine on different paper from the rest of it. The quality of artwork that Edward obtained was far superior to the poetry Linda and I managed. He also created the drop-dead gorgeous cover. Together, the poetry and art made a more-than-respectable little journal. *Ataraxia* thus became the first independent poetry magazine in modern Georgia and one of the first in the South. I wasn't Ford Madox Ford, and Linda wasn't George Plimpton, but we *were* founders and co-editors of our own literary magazine. And as 1974 turned into 1975, I was thinking more and more about prose fiction, but I lacked a catalyst to make myself try it. That would come in a year or so, and, like all the good things that have happened to me in this life, it would come from Linda.

The sound of small wood falling on to small wood. What is that? Brandon, nine, had come inside after playing in the woods, but he is now out again, taking a walk down the small creek just off Merlin Court where his family has lived since 1982. The man turns to see if he can echolocate the sound. Not a clatter but a clat—singular and registered deep in memory. But nothing moves, not even wings. He walks to the massive tulip poplar and wonders if it's a state champion, if its majestic circumference, hidden here, is a measurement to last. He does not know what will last, but he suspects certain things. Can he make one phrase, one sentence, one paragraph, that will last, that will be measured and written down in books? The idea seems silly, vain. One sound might last if he thinks of it long enough, loves it more dearly than his own life.

14

Waiting for a Sign

Our small house in Beacon Heights fanned the flames of fiction that had been flickering around the edges of my life. I began to read it like a cheetah on speed and yet luxuriate in it at the same time. I finished *Ulysses* for the first time and told Linda that no one could ever write a better novel. I haven't changed my mind. (Though Nabokov's *Pale Fire* comes very close.) I read and loved the rest of Joyce except for the immovable feast called *Finnegans Wake*. Now, nearly forty years later, I have an "altar" on the desk in my study with the works of two writers: Joyce and Nabokov. I dug deeply into Faulkner and especially I recall finishing *As I Lay Dying* on a chilly fall Sunday, saying aloud "Dear God in heaven" and knowing I would never in a thousand lifetimes be remotely that good. I read Flannery O'Connor's short stories and *Wise Blood*. She lived only forty-five miles down the road in Milledgeville and died when I was fourteen, but I never even *heard* of her until I went to college. (Marion Montgomery knew her personally, though, and she blurbed his first book.) Linda and I had discovered Kurt Vonnegut about the same time in college and read virtually all of his books as they came out. Bellow, Pynchon, Gaddis, Barth—I read them as a starving man eats steak.

I also read the biographies and autobiographies of writers ceaselessly. Later, in 1978, I discovered Carlos Baker's biography *Ernest Hemingway: A Life Story*, and it overwhelmed me, too. Until then, I'd only read *The Sun Also Rises*, which I thought splendid, but I didn't know a single one of Hemingway's brilliantly astringent short stories. Later, I would teach them in my classes at the University of Georgia, and I never tired of the astounding talent that he held in his heart and hands at such an early age. At the same time, I read biographies of composers and artists. I was in high school when I discovered *Lust for Life*, not long after *The Agony and the*

Ecstasy, and though no one would call Irving Stone's biographical novels high art, they do come alive on the page and can be a verbal blowtorch to the gasoline of youth.

I had a growing sense of myself, of what life meant for me, and I knew early that I would have to fail sequentially and miserably and yet keep going if I wanted to make a name. I felt a sense of inevitability to my desire for writing, as if someone might have predicted it, saying, *It is written*. Oddly, I was at the same time deeply, profoundly solitary and shy, but in company, almost always (I hope) pleasant and interested. I had already begun to use my quiet and genuine interest in others to help me in my story interviews for *The Madisonian*. I began to know how a sharp and sympathetic interview can get a subject to open up in entirely unexpected ways. But while I worked hard to improve as a reporter and writer, I remained hypersensitive to light, sounds, and noise. A newspaperman with monastic tastes is an odd combination indeed. Sharp light devastated me, very often kicking off migraine auras, though in those years neither I nor the doctors knew what they were. At the same time, I loved the outdoors. So I sought woods and the mottled and moving shade of oaks, pines, and tulip poplars. By my late teens I had begun to suffer terrible headaches that I inherited from Mother, who started having them as a teenager herself. Mark and Laura Jane also agonized with them, and to this day I struggle with pain from constant headaches and my ruined back.

My daily writing habits had by then also become as much of me as breathing. Every day, including Saturday and Sunday, Thanksgiving and Christmas, I rose between four and five, made coffee, and went in to my study and picked up where I'd left off the day before. Of course I was too self-indulgent with my talent. Some days I would do first drafts of five poems before I left for work. But if I did not work in that ecstatic darkness, the rest of my day was misery. Linda, fortunately, was a heavy sleeper, and so the clattering of my Royal manual typewriter never awoke her in the next room. In those years I composed poetry about half on the typewriter and half with a pen. I only wrote one novel manuscript out of more than thirty by hand. I type quickly, and by the early '70s I thought with my fingers dancing on a keyboard. It was also in early 1975 when I began to realize my need for the Big Project. Simply writing a few perfect lines a day as Dylan Thomas did was not enough. I wanted a vast project, such as Pound's *Cantos*. I needed a book that took a very, *very* long time to craft and could impress by its ambition alone. I wanted to leave a body of work. Every young writer seems to have a Haiku period, and mine lasted only a few weeks because "small and perfect" never appealed to me as remotely as much as "ambitious and sprawling." Clearly then, I never found much pleasure in Raymond Carver's work and its packed-down-to-nothing locutions. (Whether that style was created by Carver or his editor seems to be an open question at this writing.) When minimalism almost completely ran MFA-World in this country, I kept hoping we'd get more gloriously expansive metafictions such as those by Pynchon, Barth, Coover, Gaddis, and Gass, and, much later, David Foster Wallace. In a few years, I would find that placing postmodern fiction was devilishly hard, even with the editor who would years later buy Wallace's first book. I also found how wrong I could be when I first read Mary Hood's brilliant short stories.

Even if I did try to write fiction, though, where would I fit? In 1975, I didn't have the remotest idea. Now, careerists want to have their first book out by the age I was then, twenty-five, but I didn't think I was remotely at the point of knowing enough to write a novel. I needed to know those endless find-the-verb sentences of Henry James. Linda gave me *Giovanni's Room* by James Baldwin, the first novel I ever read with a gay protagonist, and I loved it because of the quality of the writing. I found out that I couldn't read most of Steinbeck profitably but would, years later, fall in love with his collected letters and read the covers off them. I loved multiple narrators, complex narratives, and strange, offbeat humor. *Mad* magazine, Monty Python, and the jokes on the back page of *Boys' Life* all influenced me. But how could I become a writer of prose if I didn't know more? And even more? So I kept reading and writing, reading and writing. My love of poetry was the central literary passion of my life. But I hoped to work on a larger canvas. So I kept my head down, worked hard, and waited for a sign.

In late 1974, I was reading a copy of *Newsweek* one day, when Adelaide looked over my shoulder and pointed at an African American artist in the news roundup section.

"He's from Madison, you know," she said, nodding toward the man with a large Afro. I felt disoriented. A nationally known artist in *Newsweek* was from *Madison*? I had no idea, and immediately I wanted to find out more and possibly write a story about him. Clearly, he had moved away years, decades before, and he was enormously successful. His name was

Benny Andrews, and he was a Realist in the day when Abstract Expressionism was King, Queen, and Knave of the art world. In 1969, he'd founded the Black Emergency Cultural Coalition in Manhattan to protest a show called "Harlem on My Mind" at the Metropolitan Museum of Art because none of the show's organizers was black. The same thing had just happened at the Whitney, and that was news, too. That night I told Linda about him.

"Maybe we could do something in *Ataraxia* about him," she said.

"God, I hadn't even thought about that. I'll see if I can get his address and write him."

It seems so quaint now. In those pre-computer, pre-Internet days, when long-distance phone calls were expensive and usually reserved for emergencies, we contacted each other by writing letters. That meant we had to use more than 140 characters. We needed to read more than one could say in an all-lower-case e-mail. Will some author of the future publish his *Collected Texts* one day and not mean his books but his tiny electronic squibbles? I doubted I could contact Benny Andrews. But I was feeling even more parochial as the months passed, and I needed to do more than have one poem in a San Francisco magazine and an advertisement in *The Paris Review*. As it turned out, I did contact him, and Linda and I became good friends with Benny. I didn't know it then, but Benny was one of ten children and grew up in the by-then mostly vanished Morgan County community of Plainview. And one of his brothers, Raymond, wanted to be a novelist. Ray lived in Queens with his then-wife Heidi (her proper name was Adelheid, and Ray usually spelled its diminutive as "Heidy"), a Swiss national, and he'd already published an essay in *Sports Illustrated*. But he was ambitious for greater things and was trying to be a writer.

When we met Ray the following year, his immediate warmth and self-deprecating personality cemented a lifelong friendship. We visited him several times after that in New York, and on publication day of my first novel in 1984, Ray moved to a house near Athens where he would live until his tragic death in 1991. He was a once-in-a-lifetime kind of friend, and his loss crushed us. We also became friends with other members of the Andrews family and felt especially close to Benny and Ray's sister Shirley.

In 1975, a group of far-thinking people including, of course, Adelaide and Graham, finalized their dream of beginning to turn the old Madison graded school on Main Street into the Madison-Morgan Cultural Center. I went to the first grade and half of the second grade there, and the Library came in after the school left. Now, the library was gone, and the massive Romanesque Revival building empty. Just bringing it up to codes would cost a fortune. The highly intelligent and motivated people involved knew how to write grants and obtain money from private foundations, though, and by some time in 1975, it was clear the Center, with art galleries, a history museum, and a gorgeous auditorium for concerts, would open to the public some time the following year.

In January 1975, Benny opened a solo show at the High Museum in Atlanta. (Our daughter Megan would have two photographs in a group show at the High decades later, and I had been to a number of events there, so we knew the space well.) On Thursday, January 16, Benny drove to Madison for his first visit in a long time. His father, George Andrews, was still in town, but his parents had divorced decades before, and his mother lived in Atlanta. Benny dropped by *The Madisonian*, and I was, I admit, star-struck to meet this internationally known African American artist from Morgan County. I immediately asked if we could interview him for *Ataraxia,* and he agreed. That led in short order, to plans for an entire issue on him, the single best one we ever published. Adelaide wrote a huge front-page feature about Benny for *The Madisonian*, and little by little my sense of being narrow began to lift. I also wrote a column on Benny after spending quite a bit of time with him. He was warm and friendly and had just sold a painting for $68,000, which was a flat-out fortune in 1974. He would rate a bylined obituary in *The New York Times* when he died in 2006. Benny and Ray had a white grandfather, and they talked often and openly about being at the intersection of race, a term that now has very little scientific meaning but left the American South in ruins for more than two centuries. That intersection would, in fact, be the central focal point of all Ray's writing. In fact, to get a sense of how difficult race could be, my father years later did some geneaological work for Benny and found out that the Andrews family had a white ancestor who fought for the South in the Civil War.

By the middle of 1975, I began to get my sea legs as an editor and designer. That summer at the Georgia Press Association awards at Jekyll Island off the coast of Georgia, *The Madisonian* cleaned up, winning six first places, including the top award, General Excellence. Unleashed, shot out of the proverbial cannon, I came back mad for journalism and for making each issue of the paper better.

I met one other native Madisonian writer that summer, Buddy Atkinson. Buddy had grown up in town but left early, winding up in California where he became a television writer and producer for "The Beverly Hillbillies," "Green Acres," and "Love Boat." Buddy didn't take himself very seriously, but he was a delight to be around, and we swapped stories of the film industry, something I would soon see up close and personal.

That June, Benny came back to Georgia, and I did a very long interview with him on tape for *Ataraxia*. Linda, Edward, and I spent a great deal of time with Benny, and he clearly was delighted that someone in the South recognized his work. By November, the special issue on Benny was out, and a picture on the front page of *The Madisonian* showed Linda, Benny, Ray, and me looking at the issue of *Ataraxia* that featured him and the entire Andrews family. Though some friction later developed between Benny and Ray, Benny never stopped doing everything he could to help Ray, and he gave us an excerpt from Ray's unpublished novel along with some writing from his mother. So we were the first to publish the prose fiction of Raymond Andrews, later a member of the Georgia Writers Hall of Fame.

That summer, *Jaws* came out, and in order to capitalize on it, I wrote and published (but not until November) a magazine-length story on my close encounter with fins in the Florida Keys. As a journalist, 1976 was my *annus mirabilis*. Everyone buzzed about the country's bicentennial, and later in the year, the Madison-Morgan Cultural Center would open. My poetry career also took off finally, and I published poems in many small magazines around the country, including *Modus Operandi, Front Street Trolley, Green's Magazine, Gray Day*, and the *En Passant Poetry Quarterly*. But one look at the newspapers of that year shows a dramatic change. I was getting better and better as a designer, for one thing. The pages sparkle. And my writing began to soar. Early in the year, I drove to Athens for a meeting of the Georgia Press Association and had lunch with the day's main speaker, nationally syndicated columnist James J. Kilpatrick. Instead of chatting about Nixon or politics, though, I talked to him about meeting Ezra Pound, which he did when Pound was a patient in St. Elizabeths Hospital in D.C. after being found unfit to stand trial for treason at the end of World War II. It didn't hurt my ambitions or my fading sense of the parochial, that Hollywood came to town in February 1975. Linda also found, to her astonishment, that she was not only a fine eighth-grade English teacher but that she loved it.

Georgia had been for some time openly courting film companies, and Madison, with its lovely streets and traditional town square began to be highly sought as a venue. The first production had the slightly hideous title of *Remember Those Poker Playing Monkeys*. Why anyone thought this was a good title for *anything* baffles me, and it would later be changed, with only a little more success, to *The Great Georgia Bank Hoax*. In truth, looking at the film many years later, it's not the hideous mess it could have been by any means. The cast was full of old pros: Richard Basehart, Burgess Meredith, and Arthur Godfrey, along with relative newcomers Ned Beatty and Michael Murphy. (For Beatty, this was only two years after *Deliverance*, so he'd been to Georgia before.) Godfrey was past seventy and kept flubbing his lines, necessitating a considerable number of retakes. Murphy, who would later become a steady and remarkable screen presence and would go on to work with Woody Allen and many other fine directors, was only thirty-five at the time and would score a major hit with the television movie *The Autobiography of Miss Jane Pittman*. I got to meet most of the crew, and Laura Jane and the high school band performed in a scene in the film, shot in downtown Madison. (Laura Jane was also shortly in the news for another reason: being in the top 5 percent in the country for the Pre-Scholastic Aptitude Test.) Linda and I were eating dinner at the local Holiday Inn one cold evening when we ran into Richard Basehart at the checkout counter.

"Mr. Basehart, it's a pleasure to see you again," I said. Linda and I had been around film actors before. We attended a party for the cast of a film called *Poor Pretty Eddie* when I was at the *Daily News* in Athens. There, we had met Shelley Winters, Slim Pickens, and Ted "Lurch" Cassidy. (This was late in Winters's career, a sad comedown from playing Charlotte Haze in the first film version of *Lolita*.) The movie, which was never widely released, was shown at the Atlanta Film Festival, and afterwards the director of the festival apologized to the onlookers and called it "a horrible, disgusting atrocity," a phrase I haven't been able to forget.

"Hi, kids," Basehart said. "Why'd you let it get so cold in Georgia?" One of Linda's favorite movies was *La Strada*, and Basehart had starred in that Fellini masterpiece with Anthony Quinn twenty years before. I remembered Basehart more for *Moby-Dick*, in which he acted with Gregory Peck. So we stood there and talked for awhile, though I stupidly spoke too long about an episode of the TV detective show "Columbo" in which he'd starred a couple of years before. Soon enough, the cast and crew left town, but we found out almost immediately that another movie, *Greased Lightning*, would be filmed in town that July. It too had a strong cast I got to meet, and included Richard Pryor, Pam Grier, Vincent Gardenia, Cleavon Little, Bill Cobbs, and even Ritchie Havens, who Linda and I had heard in concert performance in Athens back in our college days. (Along with Sly and the Family Stone and many others.) By far the most friendly and personable was Gardenia, who would be so wonderful with Cher years later in *Moonstruck*. I tried to talk to Pryor, but he wasn't available.

Despite all the tinsel and glitter from the movies, though, the most important event in town that summer of 1976 was the opening of the Madison-Morgan Cultural Center on Friday, July 9. As part of it, the Center was delighted to get a show of Benny's drawings from his *Bicentennial Series*, several panels of which we had reproduced in *Ataraxia* (though in black-and-white). Young and eager, I agreed personally to take the shipment of Benny's art on arrival. I also volunteered myself and Linda to hang the show. So there we were around midnight the week of the grand opening, eyeballing spots for Benny's work in what was called the Little Gallery, upstairs in the Cultural Center. How we managed to get it done it time (and get it all straight) is beyond me now. We weren't curators, and we'd never hung an art show. But somehow it worked. And that week we finally got to meet Ray and Heidi, along with Viola Andrews, Benny and Ray's mother, and other members of the family. The events were terrific for a small town in north central Georgia, and Linda and I loved both Ray and Heidi and promised to come visit them in New York soon. In fact, we went a month later.

They lived in an apartment in Queens, but Ray and Heidi both worked in Manhattan. We slept on the floor in a spare bedroom of their apartment and went in with them every day and prowled around the city. When we had been undergraduates, we'd fallen in love with lapsang souchong tea, so we decided to take the subway down to Chinatown and see if we could find some real lapsang, not just commercial tea bags. The world we wandered into was like nothing I'd ever seen. There were close streets, unfamiliar spoken languages, and plucked chickens hanging by their feet in shop windows. And the air *was* full of spices. We stopped numerous people on the street trying to make them understand what we wanted, but they mostly smiled and backed away from us. We finally found a shop that sold lapsang, and its rich aroma followed us around the rest of that day. After stops at the Strand Bookstore (which years later would carry a number of my own books) and a few places in the Village, we found ourselves at the World Trade Center's Twin Towers and decided to go inside. Walking through their lobbies and trying to imagine the immensity of what was above us, even Linda, who grew up near Boston, was impressed. When the towers came down on September 11, 2001, the feeling of that collapse was heart-churning to me, since I'd been inside, though of course that fact applied to millions of others, too, I suspect.

We met up with Benny and his then-wife Mary Ellen in the Westbeth Artists Community in the West Village. The now-legendary block had many famous occupants, and Benny and Mary Ellen were friends with many of them, such as actor Moses Gunn. (A photographer, Mary Ellen took a fine portrait of Gunn we published in an issue of *Ataraxia*.) The poet Ed Sanders (who was in the *New York Poets* anthology), legendary photographer Diane Arbus, and Robert De Niro, Sr. (father of the actor and an artist) also lived there. I seem to remember the Andrews apartment had a view of the Hudson River from which they had seen the Bicentennial regatta of tall ships earlier that summer, but I could be wrong. We also went to the historic Scribner's Bookstore on Fifth Avenue, and I pretended I was Ernest coming to visit Max. I forget at which store I bought it, but I came home from New York with another life-changing book, in many ways more important to me than the *Anthology of New York Poets*. It was a thick novel called *Gravity's Rainbow* by Thomas Pynchon, of whom I'd never heard. As I read it for the first of many, *many* times (I later taught it at UGA as well) I began to have an even deeper sense of how insular I was in Madison and how badly I needed to know about the larger world. *Gravity's Rainbow* changed everything for me as a writer and thinker. I would never again look at fiction the same way. It also led to a three-decade-long fight to publish my own version of postmodernism that finally took flight with my novel *The Divine Comics* in 2011.

At the Museum of Modern Art for the first time, we saw Picasso's *Guernica*. I was absolutely staggered. The humanity in its vast spaces (11.5 feet high and 26.6 feet wide) was utterly overwhelming, and I knew then with my heart what my head had told me years earlier about Picasso: genius. The painting was returned to Spain in 1981, so I'm pleased we visited it at the MoMA before it went home. As a sidenote, when Picasso died in 1973 I kept the original AP print-out from the wire room at the *Daily*

News, and it was part of my papers that I donated to the University of Georgia.

Back home, the rest of 1976 after the Bicentennial celebration, the opening of the Cultural Center, and the filming of two movies in town was all anticlimax. Our little house in Beacon Heights was, it seemed to me, really in the middle of nowhere. Already, Linda had suffered there, having spent six weeks in bed after a spinal injury. We had also picked up a neighborhood dog no one else wanted, a beagle we named Andrew and thought was a male until she had puppies.

When are one's best days behind him? I worked every day on my writing—every single day—and I still had little to show for it. And as 1976 turned into a new year, I was beginning to worry if I had already peaked, and the feeling horrified me. I would just have to work harder.

Sitting in the darkness. That moment when the previews end, when the nudge for snacks is over. When the Paramount peak arises, when the lion groans. He loves this anticipation, the salty taste of popcorn or tears to come. He cries at the movies, unashamed, not caring who sees. When he was a boy, it took him weeks to get over Ben-Hur. *But film to him was organic, something harvested in a distant world, not something created by the touch of human hands. In his early forties, by himself for a long weekend, he went to see* Dances with Wolves, *and it was obvious and very nearly unbearable. He wept in the middle rows. To make* <u>*that*</u>*. To be able to make something like that. And gleeful while watching* Sullivan's Travels *for the twentieth time. And, oh dear God,* To Kill a Mockingbird. *To have worked on that.*

15

Between the Lines

In those Madison years, my doctor, Rose Ann Weaver, discovered that the T-waves on my electrocardiogram were inverted. I had no clue what this meant, but since my grandfather Williams had died at forty-three of heart trouble (in 1935 when my father was twelve), I began to imagine all kinds of horrors. Soon enough I would go to the Emory Hospital in Atlanta for tests, but in the meantime, I decided to have a nervous collapse. I'm not going to say much about this episode, since I wrote a whole book, *Crossing Wildcat Ridge*, about it some years ago. But it's worth noting that my collapse could have been foreseen, since I was wound tighter than a silk tapestry. I had also spent all of 1976 with the pedal to the floor on every aspect of my entire life. As it turned out, I had a disorder called in those days Barlow's Syndrome and later mitral valve prolapse. For many years, it was asymptomatic, but my valve finally fell apart in 1994, and I had it replaced with an articifical one. I still tick like a clock. When I went into Adelaide's office and told her I was losing my mind and needed some time off, she gave me exactly three words of advice, possibly the best I ever got:

"Take long walks," she said. I did during the three weeks I took off that winter, slowly putting my head back together and finally, when I got back to work, doing less writing and exacting design work than I did all during the year before. Of course, I wanted to share the collapse with my closest friends. Ray wrote me to commiserate in February:

> Howdy! Got your Christmas card but Heidi [Ray spelled her name both ways] and I spent the holidays, and a few other days, in Switzerland and weren't able to get right back to you through the mail. Nevertheless, we were thinking of you and were more than sorry to hear about your heart condition, Phil. But don't worry, as

you said, having to "live" with it, because as long as you can live with it then everything's fine. Just live with it.

Being crazy cut into my poetry production, too, and I only published two poems in 1977, "Wassily Kandinsky" in *The Kansas Quarterly* and "The Poet Asserts Himself" in *Cat and Moon*. The Kandinsky poem was from the *Images* manuscript that I wrote in Athens several years before. I had already learned one irrevocable truth about the literary life by then: If I wanted to aim for literature rather than commercial fiction, I would never make a living solely as a creative writer. But that was all right, because I wanted to be James Joyce, not James Michener. So I would always have a full-time job. Hemingway said that being a journalist is good training for a serious writer, if he gets out of it soon enough. Hemingway achieved that at first by marrying rich and richer wives. I had a wife so wonderful I didn't remotely deserve her, and she was a public school teacher, changing lives every day but not making much money. So I would have to be a journalist and editor for the rest of my working life while finding time to be an artist. People misunderstand this. I was often asked if I still wrote fiction and poetry in my "spare time," as if it were a hobby like making duck decoys or collecting stamps. The truth is that I was a *journalist* in my spare time. Today, young writers get an MFA, try to publish a book, and then get into the gene pool of writers who are college teachers and have summers off to write. More power to them, but that wasn't possible for most of us forty years ago. I never had "time off" to write *anything* between college graduation in 1972 and my full retirement in 2012. And yet in that period I wrote more than thirty books, composed eighteen numbered symphonies, and did much more besides.

"Are you going to write full time now?" I was asked repeatedly after my novel *All the Western Stars* was a huge success in 1988. I just smiled in the bliss of pretend-Zen. I knew literary history too well by then to believe in the gods of enduring literary good fortune. I knew too many writers who, after a success, got a new car, new house, new wife, and an overpolished ego. And a few years later, they would often be scrambling for love and any paying work they could find.

In the early summer of 1977, though, the idea I could ever live off my literary work was laughably idiotic. And I was beginning to feel as if I needed to leave Madison and find a way into the larger world of poetry and fiction. By then, I was once again getting back on top of my game, and we were still publishing *Ataraxia* and had even received a grant from the National Endowment for the Arts to keep it going. Still, in addition to my own writing, working at *The Madisonian,* and getting over the breakdown, the journal's days were clearly numbered. Edward decided to move on from *Ataraxia,* and our good friend Jane Shook from Athens helped us ably for an issue or two. Bless her. An Atlanta writer named Kay Hagan assisted us with what became the final issue, which we printed on newsprint. I was sad to see it go, but we were just too busy to keep that particular dream alive. Maybe I would never become Ford Madox Ford. It was in the midst of my year of *ennui* that I got two letters that changed everything for me.

I had for many seasons been following the development of an exceptionally fine alternative newspaper called *The Athens Observer,* modeled after *The Boston Phoenix* and run thirty miles up the road where we'd lived before moving to Madison. The paper was an unusual and extremely attractive mix of populism and progressive politics. It had made its name by clear-eyed reporting on the University of Georgia, something the local dailies usually avoided, and a long list of fine columnists. The staff was huge compared to *The Madisonian's,* and it was printed at Greater Georgia Printers in Crawford, Georgia, where we also printed *The Madisonian.* The paper had been started in 1974 by Pete McCommons, Chuck Searcy, and Chatham McCommons (later Murray and by 1978 Pete's ex-wife). Don Nelson, who was a brilliant photographer, later brought some money to the cause when the paper was in danger of foundering and became a part-owner himself. I always picked up a copy from the spoil-pile at the press when it was my turn to take our paper to Crawford for printing. And I knew, as well as I knew anything, that it was where I wanted to work. In Athens again, I would have access to the UGA Libraries and to a town that was just then becoming the mecca of new rock and club music. Madison was a lovely place and my home town, but I knew I needed to get away, and Ray had even told me so in a letter. So I was startled to see in the *Madisonian's* mail a letter to me that I got on June 11. Typed neatly on *Observer* stationary, it said this:

Dear Phil,

Just a note to tell you I saw this week's *Madisonian* at Crawford last night, and I was impressed with the paper—particularly with your feature on Rutledge.

It's a clean-looking, informative paper, one of the better weeklies I've seen.

It was considerate of you also to mention the *Observer* in your column about the University. I wish the *Journal* and *Constitution* people had as much awareness and knowledge about the situation as you do.

Drop by and see us when you're in Athens.

Chuck Searcy

I was delighted and wondered if Chuck's interest in my work was theoretical or if he was feeling me out for a possible job. Then, not long after, I got another letter, also on *Observer* letterhead:

Phil,

This is just to say I admire what you all are doing at *The Madisonian*.

I particularly enjoyed your article on the 1914 confederate veterans' reunion this week, and Chuck and I both liked the recent one on Rutledge.

We would really enjoy getting together with you to drink a beer and talk. Thursday and Friday afternoons are best for us in that department, and we hope you'll give us a ring the next time you're heading for Athens toward the end of a week.

Pete McCommons

The letter almost literally knocked the breath out of me. Pete was already a famous figure in Athens and too cool to believe, with his long graying hair and nonstop-motion intellect. Chuck had been well-known for a long time, a veteran who had worked with Vietnam Veterans Against the War and other progressive causes. Chatham, a terrific visual artist, was also deeply involved with liberal politics. It sounded like heaven to me. Athens, in fact, is a tiny blue island in the big Red Sea of Georgia. That Madison was only thirty miles down the road helped keep it from being quite as conservative as most of the rural South. I had left Athens to get experience on a small paper where I could learn everything. Now could be the time for me to return. I met with Pete and Chuck for a beer or three soon enough that summer, and though they liked me, and I felt they were kindred spirits (though a decade older), they simply weren't yet in a financial position to hire a new editor. They were futurecasting—sizing me up for a job six months or a year down the road. I had all but packed my bags, so I was disappointed, but I knew that summer that I would never quit trying.

At the beginning of 1977, we decided to move again, renting a rambling white-frame house at 291 Pine Street, within walking distance of downtown Madison and the paper, and only a couple of blocks from my parents and Laura Jane. The property was owned by two lovely old ladies in south Georgia, Rachel and Runae O'Dillion, and handled by a nice man who lived on Poplar Street—next door to us when my family lived there for a year in 1960. One of its most attractive features was an enormous backyard, where we planned a summer garden. By then we were also becoming a shelter for homeless animals. When we lived at the parish house, we had added to Africa a fluffy black cat we named Brewster, after the town on Cape Cod where Linda's grandfather owned property and had a retreat they all called The Camp. We brought Andrew the beagle with us (minus the puppies, which we had found homes for) and had her spayed. We were also adopted by an indoors-outdoors cat we named George. He had an enormous head and the single most placid personality of all the cats who would pass through our lives over the next four decades. On Pine Street, I also had a study/library, and in it I made a decision to do something I'd avoided for several years: write my first full-length novel.

I am always amazed at people who try to write a serious novel without having read more than obvious popular fiction. That's like deciding to build a castle when you've only constructed a bird house in Vacation Bible School. And yet having a widespread knowledge of prose fiction somehow makes the challenge of writing a decent novel even worse. A person ignorant of, say, Faulkner, doesn't have to feel the Sage of Oxford peeking over his shoulders. I did. And James Joyce. And dozens of others I had read. I had no idea what style to adopt for my own writing. I knew experimental literature very well by then and was attracted to it as young people often are and for the same reasons: it allows the writer to do virtually anything and call it art without having done the real work of obtaining the tools and learning the craft. But I knew, too, that I had to start somewhere. So I did. In 1977, I began my first full-length novel.

My protagonist would be the young editor of small-town newspaper in the South. His love interest would be his pretty young wife. He would be brilliant, courageous, intelligent, and in possession of story that would knock the socks off the whole world! I know, I know. But with each passing day as I worked on the novel, I was learning both about the novel form and what I wanted to do as a writer. Part of me knew the book was a meretricious mess, but another part wanted to believe that at least the pages were piling up. I *was* writing a "novel." And I decided early on to call it *Let Us Have Madness*, a phrase I found in Kenneth Patchen's *The Journal of Albion Moonlight*. (In addition to the paperback copy I got in South Yarmouth in July 1971, Linda had a month later bought me a gorgeous hardback, a fifth printing from 1946. It is still in pristine condition in my home library.) I didn't find out until later that few critics at that time took Patchen seriously, but I was very young when I discovered him, and the affection I feel for the man and his work continues, even now.

In July, still buzzing from the letters I'd gotten from Pete and Chuck, I got a letter from Ray, late in answering one I'd sent him. He started out by saying he and Heidi were about to leave for a long visit to Heidi's hometown in Switzerland. Ray was always asking me what I was writing so we could compare notes. Even though he was sixteen years older than I was, we had begun to feel the same age. He wrote:

> You sound very busy this summer, which is a good sign...Didn't know you wrote plays. A playwright, poet, journalist, editor, animal lover...and photographer. We've been seeing your photographs of Morgan County's hamlets. [This is what Pete and Chuck also noticed, specifically my story on the small town of Rutledge.]....
>
> Thanks for the invitation to spend some time at your new home. It sounds nice, especially with the garden in the back yard. But lately things have been popping for us somewhat here.

First, Ray noted, Heidi, who was interested in theatre, had gotten a part in the chorus of a play he described as "a Greek tragedy in a modern setting," along with two small speaking parts. Then, as he often did, Ray dropped a bombshell in a casual, almost offbeat way: "Meanwhile, Dial Publishers decided to buy *Appalachee Red*, which I didn't put up much of an objection to, and the contract has been signed. Now it's just a matter of working together over the manuscript."

Linda and I were stunned and overjoyed for our friend. We had begged him earlier for an excerpt to run in *Ataraxia,* and he'd sent us the whole novel, which I immediately devoured. I loved it and had never seen anything remotely similar. Though in places the seams showed, and it often appeared strangely constructed, it had an undeniable power. I had written Ray a letter telling him how much I loved the book and wanted to excerpt a huge chunk for our journal. The sale to Dial meant we'd never get to use it, but as I said, *Ataraxia* was on its way to small-magazine heaven anyway. He continued in his letter:

> I must admit I was flattered by hearing your opinion of *Appalachee Red.* Especially you, being a Southerner, it meant something to me that it made such a favorable impression on you. I suppose I'll always be writing about the South…as I'm truthfully proud of it, black, white, and Indian. Can't get more Southern or even American than that. Anyway, the book I'm on now, *Rosiebelle Lee Wildcat Tennessee Is Dying,* of which you read the introduction, has been slowed considerably due to these last few months. Changing jobs (day from night), celebrating a book sold, and even coming down to Madison for my uncle's funeral, all had their effect upon poor *Rosiebelle Lee* who's fighting for her spot up alongside or above *Applachee Red.* Never below. It's going to be my favorite book. My second book, *The Hairy-Legged Gypsy,* is not Southern. It takes place in New York and is somewhat of a satire. At least, I hope it is.

He was, of course, talking about his own family when he spoke of race in his letter. (We didn't get to see Ray or Benny when they'd come down earlier that year for the funeral.)

Slowly, my work on *The Madisonian* was improving back to its 1976 levels, but with the letters from Pete and Chuck in hand and pages from my first novel piling up on the desk next to my typewriter, I began to feel like myself again. Each night, I fell asleep almost immediately on the king-size water bed we'd had for several years by then. (We had stayed up half the night the year before watching from that bed a flickering black-and-white TV on which we saw a Georgian, Jimmy Carter, elected president of the United States. I had interviewed Carter years before when he was running for governor of Georgia. And Graham had told me, quietly, that Jimmy was going to run for president a couple of years earlier.)

In August, Linda began to feel extremely unwell. It had been a sad few months anyway, since her friend and mentor Peggy Carter had died, shockingly, of breast cancer the year before, only forty years old. Linda had other friends by then, and her principal Bill Corry was always extremely nice and helpful to her, but the loss of Peggy really hit her (and the rest of the community) hard.

"I'm afraid something's really wrong with me," she said quietly one night. This frightened me badly, since Linda never complained (or complains) about anything. (By then she'd suffered, hideously, with endometreosis for several years, in addition to her bad spinal disc.) "I'm going to go see that doctor in Monroe." She was referring here to her gynecologist, and the mention of that doctor unnerved me even more, since women have so many diseases of the reproductive tract. So one afternoon that summer, she drove to her doctor. I got home from work early to clean house and wring my hands. I was too nervous even to put on classical music, which had become the background to our lives. Finally, she pulled up behind the house where we parked and where our huge garden was flourishing. She seemed to have a small smile as she walked toward the house, and I stood on the back steps, holding a wet dish towel and giving her a puzzled look. She got to me and stopped.

"Well," she said, "you're going to be a father."

We celebrated quietly and intensely that night, and we planned how we'd tell our parents and work friends. We didn't know the baby's sex (one couldn't find that out easily or at all in those days), so we almost immediately started picking names for a boy and a girl. But for a little while at least, we kept the secret to ourselves. I was simply ecstatic. I had always loved children, and the idea of having a family was like coming over a hill and finding Brigadoon. Linda had been told for a while by her doctors that getting pregnant would be hard because of her endometriosis, so in a real sense this seemed like a miracle to us.

I had only finished about fifty pages of *Let Us Have Madness*, but already I had a sense that it was going wrong. The problem was that I had, among my many obsessions, an interest in the last days of the Third Reich. Remember, this was 1977 and only a little more than thirty years since the end of World War II, so most of those who fought in it and many who commanded it from both sides were still very much alive. Here's how it started:

Slowly, the sound of keys fills the morning air, and she tugs the sheets up to her smile and thinks, as the backyard birds begin to beg her for seeds: he is writing again. She says I don't know when to stop.

The southern sun has broken across the line from Charles Matthews' house where he lives with his moron son and 52-year-old daughter, Diedra, the one with the Ph.D. in English, who went nuts and now walks around town singing constantly. My dog, a beagle of uncertain ancestry, is still sleeping on the front porch. She rises and happily unwinds from the night's sleep as the teakettle screeches mindlessly louder than even the blue jays.

I pour hot water into the cup over the teabags friends sent us from New York, lapsang souchong, which we looked for all over Chinatown last summer and couldn't find, though we found a teashop where the old Chinese woman could only say "thank you" in English. As I dip the teabag, I hear Mr. Matthews' daughter slamming the door behind her, going downtown to check the mail.

It is Saturday again. Willow, Georgia, is awakening from its great snore, and I hear my next door neighbor coming outside in his underwear, checking his garden with a practiced eye and slapping his thick chest: all's right with the world. I listen for the sounds a woman makes in her sleep, the little wounds that become safe when dreamed in a quiet bed. I hear Asha kicking against the covers like a child in its crib.

That beginning wasn't entirely bad, but it did show a first-person narrator thinking a bit omnisciently, and it didn't explain why someone in a house would be "going downtown to check the mail." Also, as you might have noticed, I was writing straight out of my own life. It also showed an early and lifelong addiction to the present tense. The story began to wobble, though, on the bottom of page two. There, the narrator announces his suspicions that a group of people who have settled in the southeast part of the county might, in fact, be Nazis who fled after the fall of the Third Reich and may be planning the Third Reich II. Just why I thought I could get away with such nonsense escapes me now. My fiction writing *had* improved a bit over the past two years. My plotting and ideas about the world demonstrably had not, though that "little wounds" sentence was reasonably nice. Maybe I was still crazy.

The first trimester of Linda's pregnancy was rough on her, though you'd only know it by the pain written on her face. I never met anyone in this life who complains less than my girl. Part of it was her New England upbringing. Her grandfather Rowley would certainly have agreed with the old adage, "Don't complain, don't explain." But it went more deeply than that, a sense that one's deepest feelings should remain once and forever private. If she ever wrote an autobiography, she would probably do it in the third person and never get around to mentioning herself. Slowly, though, she began to feel better, and by the time football season had returned, she walked through the world in the glow of a happy pregnancy. We settled quickly on names: Jennifer Leigh if it was a girl, and Samuel Brandon for a boy. "Samuel" is a family name on my father's side, and "Leigh" was the name of my mother's father and Linda's maternal grandmother (though they both spelled it "Lee.") And of course my middle name is also Lee, after my grandfather, Lee Sisk. But if it was a boy, we'd call him Brandon. We had no idea that there was about to be an explosion of Jennifers in the U.S., so by the time we got our darling Megan in 1991, we'd long abandoned "Jennifer," though it's a name I still like. (Mark, as an archaeologist years later, once taught a summer field school with no fewer than *six* Jennifers in it.)

In August, Elvis died and, to my knowledge, is still more or less dead.

Through the end of 1977, I worked on my novel, tracking former Nazis across north central Georgia. I had also begun to convince myself that the book was not only good but that it would get a book contract. Soon enough, I'd have my own literary agent and see my book in the window of Scribner's Bookstore on Fifth Avenue in Manhattan. Linda taught school as her stomach grew, and I kept working as hard as I could at *The Madisonian* while courting Pete and Chuck as much as was seemly. Laura Jane had graduated from Morgan County High School the spring of 1977. As pro forma reportorial work, I called the high school to find out that year's valedictorian, only to discover it was my own sister. When I hung up the phone, I immediately called Mother at the Department of Family and Children Services in Madison, where she'd worked for several years as a caseworker. When I told her the news, she burst into tears, and my mother *never* cried. As I said, Laura Jane and Mark were Brains. I wasn't, but I was working as hard as I knew how, to make up for it. That fall Laura Jane started as a freshman at UGA, the family university by now, and Linda and I tried to learn all we could find out about becoming parents. When 1978 came, it would bring a new baby, a new job, and a jolt about how bad my first attempt at writing a novel really was.

He cannot remember a time when history was not his family's avocation. To live in the past is to know the present more keenly. It is to see the frame and the picture, the screen and the film. Native Americans (or Indians as everyone still called them when he was a boy) lived on all this land. Famine and disease drove them away, other warring tribes. But mostly we did, and the idea of it is more than he can bear. He is no tribe's savior. But history blows past one patch of one land. He remembers his high school social studies books, the giddy joy of paintings from Medieval days. He knew the past to know the past. Now he cannot see himself fit in any shape of history to come. He can see himself past, folded in, gone.

16

Pronoun Antecedents

My family were all South Carolinians for generations past. Georgia has an endless number of famous people I admire without restraint: Dr. Martin Luther King, Jr., President Jimmy Carter, Flannery O'Connor, James Dickey, Michael Stipe, and hundreds more. But my mother and father were South Carolina natives, and our family has lived there since the Eighteenth Century. Except for our branch. My father has always been a man apart. Ninety-one years old and flourishing as I write this, he is a good-hearted voyager who often believes in the past more than the present or future. My mother had a quick sense of humor, beautiful eyes, and a love of children and opera. She earned her college degree in English literature and especially loved the Romantic poets and Shakespeare. She was social and cheerful while our father can be solitary and strong-willed.

His name is Marshall Woodson Williams, and hers was Ruth Valentine Sisk Williams.

Born on February 14, 1924, in the tiny mill town of Newry, South Carolina, Mother was named by her grandfather, and being saddled with the name "Valentine" was something she didn't always appreciate. She always wished she'd been named Ruth Ellen. But she was a bright-hearted and loving woman, though late in life, plagued with ill health, she would need intensive treatment to recalculate her health and joy. She also suffered from terrible headaches, starting in her adolescence, and as I've said here, Mark and Laura Jane and I all inherited that tendency. (Our father swears he's never had a headache in his entire life.) He was born October 1, 1922, and earned a degree in chemistry at UGA. We were in a distinct minority in Madison growing up—kids whose parents had both been in the war *and* graduated from college. But we were trained early not to act as if that made us different from anyone. (Incidentally, our father has compiled the most thorough family tree imaginable. He started at it in the mid-50s and by the time Ancestry.com came along, he already knew our family back generations.)

Of grandparents, I only knew my mother's side as a boy. Lee Oliver Sisk, my grandfather, was a hearty man with a big laugh and a love of baseball. On many lightning-bug summer nights, Mark and I would sleep in his bedroom, which had his single bed and a vacant saggy old double bed with iron head- and endboards. He lived from 1898 until 1969. We called him Papa as my mother did. Our grandmother we called Mama, though her name was Lillie. Before marriage, she had been a Kirby. Mama was quiet and gentle and loved crossword puzzles and songbirds. She was a homemaker her entire life while Papa worked in the company store at Newry. As I noted earlier, my father's father, Arthur Samuel Williams, died young in 1935. After that, my father, the youngest of four children, was raised by his mother and his aunt Elmyra Luis Williams, whom he called Aunt Ellie. My father's mother was named Isabel Jaynes Williams, and she lived from 1890 until 1947. So both grandparents on my father's side died before I was born.

Solomon Smith, Papa Sisk's grandfather, fought in the Civil War with the 38th Georgia. One of my great-great-grandfathers on my father's side, Joseph Bearden, was a riflemaker who crafted copies of the original British Enfields at the Cook & Brother Armory in Athens during the Civil War. After Sherman's troops broke through Atlanta and headed to the sea, the Athens Home Guard, including Joseph, was pulled out and sent south, intercepting part of the Union Army near Griswoldville. The battle there was a resounding Union victory, and the South's casualties included fifty-one dead, four hundred wounded, and six hundred captured. My great-great-grandfather was wounded in the leg, and after he had healed, having had enough of war, he walked home, twenty years old and tired of it all.

Our most famous ancestor by far was Daniel Sisk, one of the Patriots who helped defeat the Loyalists led by British Major Patrick Ferguson at the Battle of King's Mountain on Oct. 7, 1780. This battle was a turning point in the American Revolution and slowed the northern advance of British troops. Daniel was one of nine hundred patriots who attacked the Loyalists at King's Mountain in rural York County, South Carolina. (Ferguson was the only Brit on the field that day; the "Loyalists" were Americans who had chosen to fight for the British.) The battle was an overwhelming victory for the Patriots and a mere twenty-nine died in combat. Alas, poor Daniel. He was killed that day, and now his name (spelled *Siske*) is on the monument atop King's Mountain as a hero of the American Revolution. I am proud to be his great-great-great grandson.

There is no tradition of any writers on either side of my family, though our father wrote poetry in his youth. But music is, to mix metaphors, a different story. On my father's side, almost everyone, it seems, loved music and played an instrument. My father's father played the fiddle in a mountain string band. His brothers were also musicians. (He was one of three Williams brothers who married three Jaynes sisters, not as uncommon then as it would be now.) My father remembers his father and friends sitting in the parlor in the evening playing favorites such as "Chinese Breakdown." My father, his brother Sambo, and their sister Vivian were all musicians. Of the Williams siblings, Cecil alone did not play an instrument, but he was learning to play the fiddle when he grew up, and life interfered. He did love music, though.

Newry and Seneca, where my father grew up, are only a few miles apart. In 1939, Papa Sisk bought a house on South Fourth Street in Seneca and moved his brood from Newry. The house, as it turned out, was only a few blocks from my father's house. My father met and became good friends with Mother's older brother Harmon, and so Daddy knew a different member of the Sisk family before he knew Mother.

In World War II, my father joined the Army Air Force and trained as a glider pilot before (thank God) being transferred to a photo reconnaisance unit. Mother in 1941 went to the Rabun-Gap Nacoochee school and earned a junior college diploma there in May 1943. Early in the war, Daddy suffered a hernia and came home for a short time on furlough, and while there, he and Mother came together at the right moment for them both. Before, she had just been the kid sister of his friend Harmon, hanging around in the background. During that week they dated, sparks flew for them both, and for the rest of the war, Daddy wrote her, and she wrote him. Mother was restless as the war went on, and she joined the WAVES, riding the train all the way to New York City, quite a brave thing for a girl who'd been almost nowhere. As the war in Europe ended, he came home from two years in England, principally at the Mount Farm airfield near Oxford, and was mustered out of service, but with the war in the Far East still churning hideously onward, she was transferred from New York to San Francisco.

Arriving back home in South Carolina, he got a bus ticket for California and set off across the country for the woman he loved. On November 17, 1945, they married in the First Baptist Church of San Francisco. The war had ended in August, and so she was mustered out, and together they moved back to Seneca to start their new life, living for a time in the upstairs of Mama and Papa's house on South Fourth Street in Seneca. They awoke there on the morning of December 25 to see a white Christmas, the loveliest of wedding gifts in the American South.

For all the people out there who say they hate the federal government and want it drowned in a bathtub, I have one thing to say: *G.I. Bill of Rights*. This government program allowed an entire generation of soldiers, men and women, to go to college, and Ruth and Woody weren't going to pass up the chance. Their first choice would have been Clemson College, only nine miles up the road from Seneca, but it didn't allow women, and the next closest university was in Athens, Georgia. So they applied and were accepted as students, moving to 297 South Hull Street in January 1946. They were both excellent students. Mother loved her classes in English and was able to get credit for some of her work at Rabun Gap. My father was the kind of student who loved organic chemistry and made an A+ in it. They graduated in only two years, and mother wasn't able to attend her college graduation because she was pregnant with my brother Mark. By late 1948, my parents had moved back to Seneca and lived in a house owned by Papa Sisk's Aunt Lou. That fall, Daddy took a job as a chemistry teacher at Calhoun-Clemson High School while mother took care of Mark, who had been born on August 1, 1948. Daddy taught there a year and would have stayed longer, but a bureacratic snafu with his South Carolina teacher's license led him, in frustration, to leave the school in 1949 and with his pregnant wife, head back to Georgia. They moved to 1023 Oconee Street, a small lane on Carr's Hill just above the Oconee River. While there, Daddy worked repairing radios and televisons to make ends meet. I was born on January 30, 1950, in the old St. Mary's Hospital on Milledge Avenue.

I still have the bill for my birth time in the hospital with Mother. We were there from January 29 until February 4, and the total cost was $69.45. The hospital room and care were $7 a day, and we got charged $10 for the delivery room fee. Anesthetic, whatever they gave her, was $5, and "medicines" came to a grand total of $1.45. They charged me $3 for my part of the "operating room" for some reason, too. There was a $5 lab fee and $10 for "care of baby." My father wrote a check for that care to Dr. Tom Dover, who delivered me, on the First National Bank of Athens. I still have that canceled check.

In the early fall of 1950, the principal of Calhoun-Clemson high school got in touch with Daddy and said they badly needed a chemistry teacher—and they would be glad to solve the problem with his teacher's license if he'd come back. (South Carolina was claiming he needed to take one more undergraduate course to qualify, something that angered Woody, since he *was* a college graduate and was fully qualified to teach in Georgia. Not to mention being a veteran of World War II!) With two kids, he relented, and in the fall of 1950, we moved to a small brick house in Clemson, and Daddy began his second year there as a chemistry teacher. By the end of that school year in June 1951, he'd had enough of the whole situation, and he gathered his family and took us back, yet again, to Athens. He once again worked repairing electronic equipment, but this time he also began to work on his master's degree in education, something he was sure would help him get a better job than he'd had in Clemson. (Master's degrees for high school teachers were far less common in those years than they are now.) In the spring of 1953, he got a call from the placement office at UGA: there was a job opening for a chemistry and physics teacher in the small town of Madison, thirty miles south of Athens. Neither he nor Mother had ever been there before, so they packed us boys into the car and took a drive. It was a pleasant small town, and Daddy met with the high school's principal, Jack Padgett. And just like that, he had a job, starting in the fall. So around the last of July 1953, we packed our few belongings and moved from our house on Sylvia Circle in Athens into the old Madison A&M principal's house, only a few hundred yards from Morgan County High School and on a dirt road at the edge of the country.

And that's where I grew up, learning to love what my parents loved—classical music, poetry, visual art, and the quiet life. We also grew to love science, since Daddy taught physics and chemistry, and he had a small electronics "shop" in a small room just off our back porch. I also learned on my own to know the solitude of country. Daddy became assistant principal almost immediately and then principal when Padgett left at Christmas 1955. That same year, he finished his master's degree in education from UGA. Laura Jane was born on September 24, 1959, and our family was complete. We stayed there until Daddy left the teaching profession in 1960 and then moved into Madison on a shady lane called Poplar Street. By 1962, we had moved around the corner to 301 (now 613) Foster Street, and it was there that I lived from age 12 until I graduated from college a decade later.

All their lives, my parents were intellectually curious and full of energy for life. In his nineties, my father decided to get his DNA tested to find our family origins, and one May evening in 2013, he sent Mark, Laura Jane, and me this email:

"I'm only 1.7% Neanderthal (they say that about 2% is normal). Northern European, 42%; Mediterranean, 39%; Southwest Asian, 18%. Both male and female lines originated in east Africa, they say, and went to the Arabian peninsula, then north to northern Asia, then west to northern Europe (Denmark and Germany), then southward to France, England, and SPAIN. That's the male (my father's) line. My mother's line did a similar path from Africa, but never did the France and Spain trip."

He capitalized "Spain" because he's always had a theory that the dark hair and black eyes of the Williams clan may have come from shipwrecked sailors from the Spanish Armada after they were rescued and lived out their lives in Wales.

If my family were all South Carolinians, I never felt like one. I was a Georgia boy, and with that I took a healthy joy in the good parts of the state and the American South, along with a lifelong sorrow at the darker parts of the state's history. But Madison was a lovely town, all my friends came from there, and to me it was then, and forever will be, home.

He's drunk. He has been sampling a tableful of beer and whiskies, and now his head is roaming, his face acceptable in the mirror over the throw-up sink. He is ebullient. He sings and dances, tells mirthless jokes at which everyone howls. Has he always been this strong, this handsome? Yet? The way they look at him, as if it were a parlor game, as if they're in on it from the start. He intuits all this, doesn't care. His foot hits someone who's passed out under the table, and it's his friend Phil Sanderlin, roundly curled into a snore. Husbands hang on their wives, on others' wives. Gossip flares, flames, goes out when the wrong person approaches. It takes him awhile to know it, but he's the wrong person. They are parting for him, Red Sea in his unreliable approach. He decides to ignore them. Hooray for me! Hooray for the man I never was!

17

Of Kindness and of Love

It's easy for a man to say his wife's pregnancy "went smoothly." More than once when I have said that about Linda's time with Brandon and Megan, she's shot me an amused look across the room, as if she were Albert Einstein, and I was a scoutmaster trying to explain the General Theory of Relativity to a group of twelve-year-old boys. I think women have a pretty fair understanding of men. I think most men don't know the remotest thing about what it means to be a woman. Still, I've tried. I really have. I was in the front lines during the fight for the Equal Rights Amendment. Okay, not the *front* lines, but at least I reported for duty. I have said many times in public venues that we should give the entire government of the United States to women permanently. It would take them *centuries* for them to do as bad a job as the men have. I have marched, signed petitions, donated money. Linda and I even subscribed to *Ms.* for years. Still, as my wife's first pregnancy neared term, I was scared witless. Linda, as always, was calm as a flat line from here to eternity. She decided to take time off from teaching after the turn of the new year in 1978, thank God. It's stressful enough teaching seventh and eighth graders without an alien wandering around in your innards. Except for the first trimester, Linda's pregancy went smoothly.

I kept typing away at *Let Us Have Madness*, and I had the oddest sensation that the manuscript was being hijacked by the former Nazis I was writing about. Many days, I found myself trying desperately to believe it was good while fearing it would be laughed at by one and all. (The Edward Bulwer-Lytton Fiction Contest wouldn't begin until 1982, thank God. It is for the worst opening sentence in the worst imaginary novel. The 2010 contest winner, Molly Ringle of Seattle, submitted this shudderingly brilliant entry: "For the first month of Ricardo and Felicity's affair, they greeted one another at every stolen rendezvous with a kiss—a lengthy, ravenous kiss, Ricardo lapping and sucking at Felicity's mouth as if she were a giant cage-mounted water bottle, and he were the world's thirstiest gerbil." Well done, Ms. Ringle!)

I stayed in touch with Pete and Chuck and read every word of every single issue of *The Athens Observer* and very nearly memorized them all, just in case I ran into Chuck or Pete on the sidewalk in front of their office in Athens, where I sometimes wandered, as if I just happened to be there. (A trick I learned, remember, by stalking Linda in college.) I knew every name in their staff box, including all the freelancers, and there must have been forty. I found out that if there was a financial profit at the end of each working week, management gave it to their employees, great for staff morale, probably less good for staying in business until they could hire me. (This ended shortly after I started to work there, but I'm reasonably sure it had nothing to do with me.)

I love Nineteenth Century books that talk about women about to give birth as "entering their confinement." I love it because it shows the idiocy of the patriarchy in determining what is proper and safe for women. Linda enjoyed her days off as her stomach grew. And she is a small woman, so that baby really showed. From about mid-term, we both felt sure it was a boy. One night in March, Linda began to have contractions. We took it seriously because I had to drive her twenty-eight miles to Athens for the baby's birth. Madison had a hospital, but it was mostly a way station for emergencies and a final destination for the very old and very sick. (My own beloved mother would pass away there thirty years after our baby came into the world.) I got a watch and started timing the contractions.

"Oh my God, that was like three minutes," I said, leaping up and pacing, something I have a tendency to do under stress.

"For God's sake, get a grip," said Linda. She laughed at me and had a contraction at the same time, and it came out as half-giggle and half-groan, and I started pacing again. Finally we drove to Athens, and Linda was doing just fine. Though that was only three-and-a-half decades before the time I'm writing this, it could have been the late 19th century as far as childbirth protocols went. No huddling in the birthing rooms. No casual friends and relatives wandering in and out. No father cutting the cord. Like an episode of "The Dick Van Dyke Show," I was downstairs, pacing, while Linda was upstairs with a baby playing jump-rope with its umbilical cord in her abdomen. This went on for several weeks, or it seemed to. By the next afternoon, I was sitting glumly downstairs by the proverbial telephone with my parents and Linda's parents and others—to this day I have no idea who else was there.

"That phone's *never* going to ring," I whispered. As if going *bleeagh,* it suddenly rang savagely, and I jumped halfway to Charleston. When I finally scrambled back to the phone, the entire family contingent rose and huddled around me.

"This is Phil Williams," I choked.

"Want to come up and see your wife and baby?" the doctor said. (His name is Leon Smith, and as it turned out, in a nice bit of karma, he also delivered Brandon's future wife, Laura Boyd.)

"What is it?" I asked, meaning which sex, relieved and a little confused at the same time.

"I'll let her tell you. Come on up." And with that, he hung up on me, probably ready for a meal or for bed. I dropped the phone back into its cradle, and my mother all but leaped on my back.

"What is it, a boy or a girl?" the entire contingent asked, in unison and *a capella.*

"He said I'd have to go upstairs to find out," I said, feeling already as if there had been a major political shift in my marriage. Everyone there was thrilled and disappointed at the same time. I dashed to the elevator and probably looked like a giraffe during a zoo break-out. They led me to Linda, who was lying on a bed in the hall. She looked exhausted, but since I knew I looked like utter hell, I'm sure she was the more attractive of us.

"Are you okay?" I choked. "What is it?"

"I'm fine. It's a boy," she said, lifting the cover and showing me the baby in all his naked glory. "And I'm fine."

And that's how Samuel Brandon Williams came into the world. We loved him with complete devotion, and Linda's mother came to stay with us and help out, a job she knew only too well, having raised five children of her own. I had planned, months before, to ritually read Brandon his first poem and to play for him a first piece of classical music. The poem was easy: "Lines Composed a Few Miles Above Tintern Abbey" by William Wordsworth, a lifelong favorite of my parents, and one of mine, too:

Though absent long,
These forms of beauty have not been to me,
As is a landscape to a blind man's eye:
But oft, in lonely rooms, and mid the din
Of towns and cities, I have owed to them,
In hours of weariness and sensation sweet,
Felt in the blood, and felt along the heart,
And passing even into my purer mind
With tranquil restoration:—feelings too
Of unremembered pleasure; such, perhaps,
As may have had no trivial influence
On that best portion of a good man's life;
His little, nameless, unremembered acts
Of kindness and of love....

I struggled about what to play Brandon as his first experience in the world of classical music, but Linda solved that one.

"Play him one of the Brandenburg Concertos," she said, and I grinned from ear to ear. Of *course*. So I put on Bach's Brandenburg Number One and walked around the room holding my son close to me. The following week I wrote a "Letter to My Son" as my column in *The Madisonian*, sentimental but perhaps forgivably so. Brandon was healthy and happy, and soon our little family was doing things together. I have a photo I took of Linda and Brandon when he was still very small as workers came to move a historic home called the Parks Mill House, saving it from the rising floodwaters of the newly impounded and slowly rising Lake Oconee.

It was in 1978, too, that Linda, my sister Laura Jane, and I attended a session of the Georgia Press Institute in Athens because one of the speakers was Susan Myrick, who had been a close friend of Margaret Mitchell's, and at Mitchell's behest was hired as a dialect coach when *Gone with the Wind* was filmed. Linda was still pregnant at the time. We loved hearing Ms. Myrick's stories of working on the sets of the film in Hollywood. We went up and chatted with her afterward, and she told us, to our shock, that she had no way to get home to Macon.

"We'll take you," I said without asking the others.

"Would you?" she asked, putting her hand on my arm. "Oh would you?"

We would. And all the way home to Macon, Susan Myrick, 85, regaled us with tales of working on one of the greatest Hollywood films ever made. Sue had been a newspaper woman in Macon for decades—that's why she was at the Institute.

"Clark Gable?" she said, in response to a question. "He was everything a girl wanted Gable to be. He was shy and modest—just like the boy next door. Now Leslie Howard was a different matter. It's funny. I went to Hollywood expecting to like Howard and dislike Gable, but I never did like Howard much. He thought he was the greatest actor in the world, and he acted like it. Teaching Vivien [Leigh] to speak with a Southern accent was easy. She worked very hard and, after all, the English 'R' isn't that much different from ours. Leslie Howard was a different matter."

She also got into a titanic argument with producer David O. Selznick over the design of Tara, the family home of patriarch Gerald O'Hara and his family.

"When I first saw the model, I said, 'You can't do this'," she said. "It had huge round columns, and I told them Tara was a country house. You might have columns like that in Columbia, Mississippi, where there had been wealthy planters for years, but Atlanta at the time was pioneer country."

As she talked it became clear that she was still madly in love with Clark Gable and told of going to parties "over at Vivien Leigh and Larry Olivier's place." *Larry Olivier*? This was far beyond *Remember Those Poker Playing Monkeys*. She told us story after story, wonderful things. We asked her what Margaret Mitchell was like, and she recalled many tales and then said: "People were always telling her that her book was nothing more than a melodrama. She would just say, `Well, they were melodramatic times.'" When we got to her house in Macon, I went to the bathroom, and on the inside back of the bathroom door was her nightgown—hanging from a coathanger made from the head and shoulders of Clark Gable as Rhett Butler. I finished and came back out and whispered to Linda.

"Go to the bathroom," I said.

"Excuse me?"

"Just go to the bathroom."

She and Laura Jane did one after the other and came back with a story none of us would ever forget. Sue Myrick lived alone and died that September and was buried in Milledgeville. As her entry in the *New Georgia Encyclopedia* said, "She never married nor had any children."

Early in April, I dropped Pete a letter just in case he'd forgotten me in the three or four days since we'd last talked:

> Hello Pete,
>
> Things have really been jumping around here, but I did want to write you and tell you what a grand job I think you guys continue to do. It's nice that Athens at long last has a real newspaper.
>
> Our son, Samuel Brandon, was born in Athens General March 18 and it's been quite a jolt learning how to be a parent. I suppose my normal routine hasn't changed much, but learning to expand your life in this way is challenging to say the least. Linda and Brandon are doing fine, though his penchant for three a.m. feedings has started to leave me somnambulistic through much of the day. I'm told that will change. I hope.
>
> Our magazine has been shelved for the time being for several reasons Mainly, I just can't handle the work load. We have quietly folded our tents and stolen away probably for at least a year, or until I can find somebody willing to take an active part in both the editing and business of the magazine. Still, we got very encouraging comments from all over the country about our most recent issue, so I suppose we gained something from it all.
>
> I mainly want to write to remind you all that I still want to work for the *Observer*, and am patiently and comfortably waiting. Madison is a nice town, but I still feel like I left part of me in Athens when we left in 1974 and getting back would be marvelous. Over the past year I have been made a few offers for jobs here and there, but in all honesty, I like this area of the state and no sum could make me put myself into a situation I would despise....Things at *The Madisonian* are going well, though this week proved to be one hell of a lot of work. Our typesetter has been in the hospital with pneumonia, and in her absence, I had to set most of the type on the Compugraphic as well as making up the paper, writing stories and my column, and writing headlines. Tuesday afternoon our shop dinosaur, a Varityper headliner died and we spent a lot of time blowing up [enlarging] the headlines, etc. All in all, a bitch of a week, but I guess I'm lucky they don't come more often.
>
> My own writing is progressing. I finished two plays and two books of poems in the last year and am now starting my third play. I

also have two unfinished novels which glare at me through the dust every once in a while.

My garden is planted and thank god winter is finally over. Our house has been brutally cold this winter, and now we are able to open the house back up.

Needless to say, I will be glad to talk with you guys any time and remain interested in being part of the most vital and interesting newspaper in NE Georgia.

If my own writing was slowly progressing, this letter was close to a masterpiece. If I had patted myself on the back more times, I might have dislocated my shoulder. But everything I said about my work at the paper and my creative work was true. The plays were so-so piffle in large part, but they were honest efforts informed by intense reading of dramas I knew to be good. By June, though, a sense of now-or-never had begun to strangle me. *The Observer* was becoming more and more successful and one of the best newspapers in the state and, to be truthful, in the Southeast. The time seemed perfect for me. It had never had a college-trained editor or one with remotely as much experience as I'd gained in five years as a professional and three or four before that working summers. So barely two months after my last letter, I wrote Pete again:

Dear Pete,

Perhaps nothing is so continually grating as the clarion call of one's own ego, but then again, nothing is as "second-grating" as expecting the world to beat a path to your door.

That's why I'd like to point out something of which I'm proud—my feature writing award at the GPA [Georgia Press Association] convention last week. In all, *The Madisonian* won eight awards, including four first places at the convention. This brings to 34 the number of state and national awards we've won since I've been here, including 15 first place awards in the state contests.

The award to me was for that series on the small town in Morgan Co. (The sheet with judges comments are enclosed.) It was really gratifying because I worked pretty damn hard on it.

As far as my column was concerned, the judges said they would have given me an honorable mention if the "GPA had such an

> award" and said my work "rates high in effectiveness, style and subject matter." That's a nice way of saying I didn't place.
>
> At any rate, I send you all this nonsense because I continue to be interested in working for *The Observer*....
>
> Mayhap you might even consider hiring me part time.
>
> Incidentally, everybody I talk to here loves the *Observer*. That idea about expansion would work, I'm sure. After all, who this far out from Athens gives a shit about Athens's alleged dailies?
>
> We have been understaffed here for three months due to pregnancies, and yours truly is worn to a frazzle. So we're going to take our four days' vacation (we couldn't afford to go to the GPA thing at Jekyll) and go to Savannah from July 4-7.
>
> Sometime after that, my longwinded novel should be finished, and I hope to get my life a little more in order.
>
> As usual, thanks for your time reading all this, and extend my cordialities etc. to the comrades on Lumpkin St.

We had stayed in touch with Ray and Benny, of course, and that June we had pictures of them side by side in *The Madisonian*. Benny was opening a solo show in Atlanta while Ray was, for some reason, signing what appeared to be galley proofs of his novel with Dial, *Appalachee Red*, which wasn't out yet. But it was a precursor of the competition that would make life occasionally complicated for the brothers. On June 26, I finished *Let Us Have Madness*. Below the finishing date on the manuscript, I wrote "Finished edit, July 28." Now, decades and many published books later, I find the idea of a month for editing and polishing laughable. Now I can spend a year and often much more on that part of the process. But as I didn't really know how to write a novel, I surely had no idea how to *re*write one. As the years passed, I grew to love writing subsequent drafts far more than first ones.

Ray's novel, when it came out, was awarded, by his publisher, Dial, the James Baldwin Prize for Fiction. Baldwin himself was there for the presentation at the Dial offices in Manhattan high above the noisy streets, and Ray was of course delighted. (And thus my tiny connection, mentioned earlier, to Baldwin.) In later years, Ray was a bit dismissive of the award, since it was created by Dial, also Baldwin's publisher, at a time when Baldwin was in low spirits, apparently, as a way to boost him. It was never given again, so Ray had the distinction of being the first and *only* winner of the award. Still, Baldwin was an important and often magnificent writer, and if it had been me, I would have been thrilled to be associated with the man and his work.

As I was completing the manuscript of my first novel, Pete and Chuck called me to Athens for what I hoped would be an important meeting. It was. They offered me a job as managing editor of *The Athens Observer* for $200 a week, more than I was making at *The Madisonian*. I was ecstatic, and I agreed to start in two weeks' time, but it immediately presented us with problems. Where would we live, for example? Linda still had a job she loved teaching at the Morgan County Middle School. Brandon was only five months old, and we would need to make plans for child care if we moved. In Madison he was kept during the day by a wonderful young woman named Penny, who lived up the street from my parents. I only knew that I had worked for a year to get this job, and I wasn't about to pass it up. In the end, I decided to commute from Madison to Athens and did it for nearly a year before we moved back to our beloved college town.

I had had my ups and downs with Adelaide and Graham, though all the downs were my fault. They treated me with patience and kindness and allowed me the sort of freedom in my work that very few people in their early twenties ever get. I would miss Peggy and Billy, Monaray and Bob Moore. I would miss Anne, who had also just had a baby. A couple of years before, when I had been criticizing someone for something in a typical office harangue, Monaray leaned back from her typesetting machine and gave me an amused look.

"You can find a lot of things wrong with somebody you don't like," she said simply. I never forgot her axiomatic proclamation, and more than once it's informed my life. In the paper for July 20, I wrote the story of my own departure: Williams resigns position. The piece noted that after four years I was leaving *The Madisonian* for a new job as managing editor of *The Athens Observer*. It didn't say that I was suddenly terrified of what I'd done, leaping from the frying pan of Madison into the fire of Athens. I wrote a goodbye column on July 27, essentially reassuring the good people of Madison that they could live without me. Months later, I would run into people who didn't even know I'd left. Ah, fame. But if small-town journalism offered little hope for that, I *had* finished a novel, was ambitious, and I knew I would never give up. I didn't even publish another poem until 1981, for heaven's sake. Failure may have been the only real option immediately before me, but I had failed before, and it didn't kill me. I was young and filled with hope both for my new job and the novel. Surely things would work out. I had leaped, but in truth I had no real idea where I was landing.

The job at the *Observer* would be extremely challenging every hour of the seven years I spent there. But without it, I doubt I ever would have become a published novelist, poet, and essayist.

Box Turtle in the Driveway

This shelter moves with her. The sky has turned cantaloupe
In the evening west, paints fruiting flesh across her dome.

I want to tell my daughter one thing quite specific.
That our lives are a slow going, that when we become

Impenetrable, seasons change, do not hold their color.
I lift the wiggling tortoise by the shellac of her shell

And say, Look, this is the ancient one, whose box gleams
In my midlife light. She bears bugs into their sleeping.

My daughter, thirteen, leans to look upon the crow's-foot
Eye of her kin. She asks one specific thing of me now.

Boy, I caught them in our woods to watch them swim
The waves of air. I turned and let them feel it, liquid

As birth in the forest afternoon. I want to tell my daughter
That moving slowly, going nowhere, is also grace.

I want to tell her that this curved hull will sail away
Tonight, going nowhere in particular, then arriving.

I have hidden things from you against my own will.
Stand on my shelled back and look for the curvature

Of love, the very thing that saves us from ourselves.
Cast a small shadow. Move against time with your life.

18

Bit on the Neck

In its heyday, which I wandered into, *The Athens Observer* was a superb newspaper. A tabloid, as I said, founded along the lines of legendary *Boston Phoenix*, it was a polyglot mix of many personalities, but especially of Pete, Chuck, Don, and Chatham. Started as a free weekly in January 1974, it was smart, lively, and moderate-to-liberal politically. But it was so much more than that.

The state of Georgia has always had a progressive strain amid the generally conservative (and sometimes violently racist) tapestry of history and life. I published a novel with St. Martin's in 2004 and set in Georgia, about southerners who were against the South's position in the American Civil War. Barack Obama got 47 percent of the vote in the 2008 presidential election in my state and just under 45 percent in 2012. Atlanta, of course, is the thriving center of progressive politics in the state, but Athens isn't far behind. So starting a liberal newspaper there made good political sense, even if it was unclear how it would work as a business. By the time I came aboard in the summer of 1978, *TAO*, as it was known, was cranking. The papers were larger and larger, and one issue that fall would be an astounding one-hundred-and-twenty pages. If you want to know what working at the *Observer* was like when I started there, buy or rent the film called *Between the Lines*. It came out in 1977, was based on the *Phoenix*, and featured a raft of future stars, including Jeff Goldblum, John Heard, Lindsay Crouse, Bruno Kirby, and many others. *The Observer* was very much like the crew of that film's *Back Bay Mainline*, though we had a much larger staff than the paper in the film did. Most of the *TAO* employees were in their twenties and exceptionally talented at their jobs. Pete was the grand old man at thirty-eight. There was a lot of drinking, a great deal of smoking, and an almost endless supply of personal crises, high spirits, and political dialogue. I *loved* it.

The paper had started in controversy. Pete was working at UGA's Institute of Government when a protest broke out at the UGA President's Office. Drawn to controversy like a fly to honey, Pete went over, along with Chuck and a number of other Athens activists and managed to get himself arrested and then fired. The trial (and retrial) of the so-called Athens Eight was in the news for months, and all those (like me) in the progressive cadre admired them. Pete and Chuck began to cast about for something else to do, and the idea of a newspaper began to circulate among them and Pete's wife Chatham. (She and Pete were separated at the time the paper started, but they would not divorce until 1977.) She was an exceptionally fine visual artist and is still working wonderfully well now, thirty-six years later. Don was a student at UGA when he came aboard, bringing some badly needed cash and obvious talent as a photographer. Chuck was something of a visionary and had a strong interest in the business side of the *Observer*. Pete loved to leap into any issue headlong and brought a sense of plausible recklessness that attracted many readers. He could also charm the socks off a snake. He was the public face of the paper, and he wrote (and still writes) extremely well. Chatham each week illustrated numerous stories with her highly original line drawings. (Her superb paintings were and are quite different from those drawings, but she did what was necessary for the paper. They all did.)

I should note at the outset that although some people believe I was a central figure in part of the paper's history, that's only true to a point. The paper would have done just as well without me from 1978-85, but it would have done it a lot less effectively. As it turned out, my gift was not in journalistic writing—I didn't write much news or feature copy for the *Observer* in my years there. What I *could* do was organize that huge group of disparate souls into a well-oiled machine, design an attractive newspaper each week, and paste most of it up. I kept the trains running. The quality of my columns was inconsistent, and I have been amused over the years at some publishers suggesting a book compiling my best columns. All I can say is that it would be a damn short book.

When I arrived, the paper was in transition. In fact, I had been there for quite a while before I realized my hiring was done to make those transitions easier. I had a real sense that Pete and Chuck were both absolutely exhausted. And after being there a few weeks myself, I couldn't understand how they rose each morning. The sheer volume of work was brutal. And the production crew had developed a schedule of working all night Wednesdays, getting the paper to press, and then mostly taking Thursday off and showing up around noon on Friday looking like hell but itching to start it over again. A few months later, I was startled when Chuck and his wife Anne Marchand left for Washington where he'd get a job in the Carter Administration.

My first week on the job, a production department employee named Wayne bit me on the neck.

The incident started innocently enough. There I was in my nice shirt and wide, 1970s tie, my long brown hair down over the ears, rubbing my droopy mustache, standing in the production room and looking over the paste-up pages for that week's edition. One of the women who worked in production came breezing by me, took an assessing glance, and said, "We need a floater on twelve." I didn't have the vaguest idea what she meant. I went to the paste-up boards and found page twelve. After desperately looking at the page for a moment, I realized that one story had been designed with room for a pull-quote—a line from the story in larger type for design purposes alone—to break up masses of gray type that happen when a story is long and there isn't enough art. It's hard to imagine now, but in those days, one couldn't simply download another image from the Web—either you had a useful photograph in hand or you didn't. I scanned the story, found a line that could be used as a "floater," as I found out they called pull-quotes, and gave it to a woman walking by.

Earlier, when Pete was trying to find a desk at which I could sit (no office for the managing editor—it reeked of a hierarchy if not patriarchy) he looked around and asked me out of the blue if I liked Willie Nelson. I did.

"Then you're sitting right here," he said, pointing to a desk in a large room with four of them. Right across from me was Jimmy Cornelison, the paper's sports editor and next-great-southern novelist. He was counting money and smoking a cigarette, and a loaded pistol lay on his desk pointing my way.

"What's happening," he said to me, still counting money. He was in charge of circulation for the paper, too, and I presumed the pistol was a precaution for when he was out collecting cash from coin boxes and stores that sold the paper. This wasn't Madison. Jimmy also liked country music, and so Pete figured we might get along. As it turned out, our ideas for the future of the paper weren't exactly in synch. He wanted to stay a tabloid, but with the size of the paper that fall and the need to stay current with our advertising and reader base, there had been some talk already about going to the standard broadsheet size. Jimmy was a slender, laughing man with more self-confidence and ambition in one glance than I'd earned in my whole life up to that point. Above all, Jimmy wanted the paper to be crackerjack smart, edgy, and alive with energy. In the end, he may well have been right. The only thing I knew was that I felt very inferior around Jimmy and almost everyone else in the building.

I was getting to know the production crew by mid-week, and it was obvious I was working with a group of graphic artists who knew their business. As it turned out, thank god, my years of drawing miniature versions of each page ("dummying") and then doing the full-size paste-up from that, served me well. I had a good sense of the current look of the paper, too, from studying it for the past year. Someone in the production room asked me a question of some ilk, needing a yes or no answer.

"I assume so," I said. There was a pause in the general noise, and I saw a tall, bearded and grinning young man coming toward me. Others stopped what they were doing with watch-this expressions all around.

"*Whaaaat* did you say?" the young man asked. I'm not tall, so he seemed about seven feet high as he stopped in front of me. He smiled at me, and I smiled back.

"I'm Phil," I said, stretching out my hand. He didn't take it.

"*Whaaaaaatttttt* did you say?" he asked.

"I said, `I assume so,'" I said.

"NEVER," he shouted, rising on his tiptoes and threatening to break through the old pressed-metal ceiling, "assume *anything*!" Then he leaped on to me. A few people in the production department kept on working as if it was nothing special. And then Wayne bit me on the neck, a firm vampirish snap. Having bitten me, he backed off, clapped me on both shoulders with his hands, and went away. Frozen with confusion, I looked up to see that Pete had been watching from the doorway.

"It's okay," Pete said. "That means he likes you."

What hath God wrought.

The paper was on two floors of a building in downtown Athens on North Lumpkin Street. The space was well-lit by tall, arched windows. I had known that area of Athens well since my childhood, and had even gone to movies at the Georgia Theatre just across the street. By then, though, the *Observer's* ad manager Hap Harris and his business partner Sam Smartt were turning it into a live music venue. All of Athens, it seems, was going that way. Downtown, once the home of middle-class clothing stores and a couple of restaurants, was rapidly tuning into an avatar of the youth culture. The air crackled with possibility. New bands formed in garages and houses almost every day. That October, the 40 Watt Club would open. There was no community for serious writers, though. My old mentor, Marion Montgomery, had published a big, serious novel with Harper & Row four years before, but beyond that, it was Coleman Barks on campus. He had done a volume of poetry (also with Harper & Row) in 1972. Other than that, I had no one to ask about the writing life. I was driving as fast as I could in a place with no roads and no real destination. (By the time Marion passed away in 2011, he had more than 30 exceptionally fine books to his credit. Coleman became world famous for his translations of the mystic 13th century Persian poet Rumi. On the night before he died, Leonard Bernstein had a friend read him some of Coleman's translations—that is how deeply Coleman's work had dug into the general culture.) But I already knew them both, and they were also insanely busy academics, and so I would have to write, dream, and learn about it all by myself.

Aside from being bitten my first day on the job, I found that I had so much to learn that I was working all the time. In addition to the sprawling staff of writers, graphic artists, and advertising people, the offices were filled with freelancers, the interested, and the plain weird from the community who would simply wander in because they knew one of the *Observer's* employees. Angelheaded hipsters (to use Allen Ginsburg's term) with Medusa hair would suddenly appear next to the coffee pot, asking me what in the *hell* I thought I was doing. I just walked past them. Everyone seemed to do that. While Chuck was more businesslike than most of the upstairs crew, Pete loved to stir the pot into chaos, just as he loved to print things written by the woman (or man) on the street. Chatham had a separate studio from the *Observer* offices so she would be in and out. Don was always moving quickly up and down the stairs with an ever-present camera on a shoulder strap.

Every Monday afternoon, one of our regular columnists, Bill Tate, came into my office with his handwritten piece for the week. This was William Tate who had first come to UGA as a student in 1920 and spent decades as Dean of Men at the University. He was beloved and a little feared, and when he died in 1979, UGA would name the student center after him. Every time I go into the Tate Center now, I remember the man himself. He was then and always called "Dean Tate" by everyone—the title was for life, even though he'd been forced to retire a while back at UGA for what he called "statutory senility." He was a tall, potbellied, white-haired man who wore carpet slippers all the time and loved to tell, with great glee, off-color stories about early administrators at the University. Dean Tate's columns had no shape or form, and I would rewrite, cut, and shorten them each week. He never said a word, but the following week, his column would have every word I'd cut out the week before.

I also got to know Ed Tant, a longhaired liberal firebrand who was a regular columnist for the paper almost from its first issue in 1974 until the *Observer* was in its death throes decades later. Ed was (and is) a strong voice for the right things. While I was completely unknown in Athens then, *everyone* knew Ed Tant. His voice was one of the most important of our generation in the American South and even nationally. In almost everything he wrote, he spoke for me and so many others.

I felt guilty leaving Linda, Brandon, and our home every day to drive to Athens. And I felt guilty leaving a little earlier than I should from the *Observer* to drive the thirty miles back every day. The stress of it all was a killer. After having been on the job for a few months, I woke up once in the middle of the night standing in the back yard of our house on Pine Street in Madison in my underwear, screaming. I had been dreaming and sleepwalked, possibly to keep from having my neck bitten again. So I asked Pete and Chuck and Don if I could tinker with the production schedule, and with grave doubt, they said I could try.

As you might recall, I had in my letters stupidly told Pete I was writing a novel. Newspaper reporters are always writing novels, but you're not supposed to *talk* about it. In trying to impress him into hiring me, I'd mentioned that I'd finished *Let Us Have Madness*. He pressed me to read it, and I finally relented, regretting it from the moment I put the thing in his hands. I waited several weeks until one day I saw Pete walking toward me with my manuscript. He handed it to me with a knowing grin, and I wanted to crawl into the wide floorboards of the *Observer* office and hide. Deep down I knew it was weak, but it's hard to admit that something you've worked on so hard and for so long is rotten to the core.

"I don't think it's any good," he said, folding his arms. "All that stuff you have about people driving down the road and then suddenly thinking of *Mahler*? To me that stuff is just *funny*." He and I both knew it wasn't supposed to be amusing. The brilliant man I saw every day at the paper had just bitten me in a far more personal way than Wayne ever had. I nodded, took the manuscript, and put it in my briefcase. We never mentioned it again. As it turned out, Pete's verdict was the single greatest favor anyone ever did for me as a writer. I realized then I had two choices: quit or get much, *much* better. With duties as a father and husband, with things popping at the *Observer* and my commute, I had little time to write anyway. But on those drives I *did* have time to think, and I knew Pete was right. Of course he was right. I had been in an echo chamber, and it's a slayer of both talent and ambition. So I took a deep breath and decided to start over from scratch. I was only twenty-eight years old, and I had time. When I got home, I held the manuscript of my novel over a trashcan for a long time and then backed away. Maybe I needed to keep it around, like a carpenter revisiting his collapsing first house to see how far he's come with the new mansion. I put it in the drawer of my desk, and there it stayed until I began to donate my papers to the Hargrett Rare Book and Manuscript Library at UGA in 2013. Whenever things were going literarily bad for me (and they would go sour many, many times over the years), I would take out *Let Us Have Madness* and remember Pete's gift. (He never stopped getting better as a writer himself; decades later as editor of *Flagpole* magazine in Athens he was writing the best personal columns in the history of the State of Georgia. I rank him with Ralph McGill.)

He could have pretended to read it and just lied. But he told me the truth, and, as Frost's narrator says in "The Road Less Traveled," that "has made all the difference."

Why would he not love sports? In his younger days, he was around the mighty Morgan County Bulldogs. Around but not playing, being small and slow. But he did play Little League, was on the golf and tennis teams in high school, just better than mediocre but playing anyway. He loved college football more than anything as he became an adult. When he grew old, his loves were golf and baseball. More than anything, he loved the esthetics of golf, the quietness, the slow pace, the manners, the punctuated roar of winning. Nothing could surpass the sound of the ball hitting the bottom of the cup on a perfect green. He and Linda got to see a round of the Masters in person. It was a huge letdown after seeing it on television. Too many people. Too much movement. Far too much noise.

19

Finding an Agent Named Molly

Stars aligned just before *TAO* hired me. First, in April 1978, the paper was named the county legal organ after a court fight, for the first time taking that title, and all the cash from legal notices, out of the hands of Athens Newspapers, Inc., down the street. Second, Chuck had decided, restless and ambitious as always, to move to D.C. and see if he could get a job in the Carter Adminstration. Finally, Pete and Don were a bit worn down from the never-ending pressure of newspaper work. And though I never had a more demanding job on any level you could name, working for the next seven years at the *Observer* changed my life for the better. It put me into the maelstrom of the most exciting alternative newspaper in the Southeast and allowed me to meet new people and earn more confidence in my work. Pete's honesty had thrown me back down the ladder to the first rung on my fiction, but if he hadn't, I would have never published a word between hard covers.

The main reporters were John Toon and Phil Sanderlin, and you couldn't imagine two more different humans. John was a tall, thin, and vanishingly quiet family man, meticulous to a fault. Instead of writing stories directly from his notes, he first typed all his story materials and then arranged them before writing, something I've never done once in my life. He was interested in science, as I was, and he also broke numerous important environmental stories. (John would later go on to be an outstanding science writer and editor at Georgia Tech, while I held a similar job at the University of Georgia.) He was a simply brilliant reporter. Phil was a born comedian, but he was also obese and drank far too much, a giddily cheerful volcano who could write nine perfectly fine stories in a single day if he had to. I felt sad for Phil from the day I met him. Two years older than me, he lived alone in a small apartment, but spent much of his life at bars and parties, of which there was one almost every night of the week in Athens. He was kind, gentle, warm, and deeply melancholy. Lee Shearer was the best all-around reporter we ever had, though he wouldn't come on board for a couple of years. (When I was in the hospital recuperating from heart surgery, years after I'd left the *Observer*, Lee brought me a paper grocery bag filled with detective novels, one of the most touching gifts I ever got in my life.) He was still a newspaper reporter thirty-five years later. Some time later, I hired Merrill Morris, and she became an award-winning feature writer, though she could cover and write anything beautifully.

The talented production crew when I started there, Joe, Janet, Jennifer, Allyn, Connie, Julie, Bud, and Sigrid, could be edgy and eager at the beginning of each new production cycle, but soon the whole group gained cheerful torque, and, with Crosby, Stills, Nash, and Young on the office record player, they would start to crank with the enormous talent they all had, and each week the paper made it to Crawford pretty much on time. And of course Chatham was there much of the time, too, and her presence helped—a lot. Their work was dazzling. It was the days of bell-bottoms, long hair (men and women), being on a first-name status with barkeeps, and endless cigarettes, even in the office. Downstairs, our more-formal advertising staff worked roughly normal hours. Hap, Phyllis, Catherine, Emory, Tina, Bob, and Val dressed nicely and felt the constant need to sell more. The tensions between editorial and advertising at the *Observer* were the same that they've been since newsprint "tattlers" wallpapered London in the 18th century. When someone was going out of the office, he might say if anyone was looking for him, he'd be "between City Hall and the Courthouse." That sounds innocent enough, but it was actually the location of Friends bar, and you could find some staff member there by late morning every day, knocking out a hangover with a couple of beers.

Change at the *Observer* was more constant than anything else. Chuck left early in 1979, and by April was assistant administrator for public communications at the Small Business Administration. Jimmy Cornelison jumped ship in March to work for the *Charleston News & Courier*. I hired a bright young man named Michael Booth as sports editor to replace him. Hap Harris was gone by that May. The staff in production and advertising changed all the time.

I wrote many personal columns in those years and an occasional feature story. One memorable piece I did in the spring of 1980 was about the

Metropolitan Opera's touring performance of Giuseppi Verdi's opera *Aida* in Atlanta. I found a flyer in UGA's school of music asking for "supers"—extras—for the famous grand triumphal scene in the Met's production. Anyone volunteering would get five bucks and the memory of a lifetime. So I signed up and drove to Atlanta and became a torch bearer.

"Where is my torch *bearies*? Where is my torch *bearies*?" cried the Italian in charge of getting extras into the scene at the right time. We rehearsed in street clothes that afternoon, but when show time came, we had to wear slatted skirts that are familiar from film epics of the 1950s. We were only thirty minutes from our scene when an assistant something or other came in and started screaming at us about jewelry. I ran out in the parking lot to my car and hid my wedding ring under the driver's side seat, where it stayed lost for the next six months. The scene came off flawlessly, and we torch "bearies" held our own (as well as our *faux* torches). I wrote a backstage-at-the-opera piece about it that was published on May 23, 1980.

Within three months of joining the *Observer*, the new production schedule I designed began to click into place. The only problem was that it required me to be at my desk dummying the front section of the paper by 4 a.m. each Wednesday. But I did it. We all did whatever it took. Along the way my title changed from managing editor to editor, and I was more or less in charge of everybody's work insofar as it touched on getting the paper to press. When Carter lost the presidency to Ronald Reagan, Chuck returned from D.C., and took the title of president and general manager in July 1981, and everything changed. He did a thorough analysis of the *Observer's* finances, and it was clear that it couldn't keep going with the staffing levels it had then, nearly thirty full-time employees. For reasons that seem vague to me now, the management of *TAO* decided that the only thing that could save us was to publish the paper twice a week. I wanted no part of it. So I told Pete and Chuck and Don and Chatham that if I was required to do twice as much work for the same salary, I would be looking for another job. One came more quickly that I might have imagined. By April 1982, we began Observer Communications as a wholly owned subsidiary of The Athens Observer, Inc. Toon was gone by then, and over the next few years we were lucky enough to have Merrill Morris and Lee Shearer join Phil Sanderlin as reporters. Observer Communications would be run largely by Chuck and me. After all, I had a degree in television directing.

In January 1982, Chuck and I, along with a young man named Bart Reynolds whom Chuck had hired to work for OC, drove to D.C. for a conference of what was being called low-power television. It was thought there could be a spot in the broadcast band for tiny media companies that might have city-sized broadcast areas. Chuck badly wanted into the supposed new field (it never happened), and so we stayed in Washington with our friend Buck Pennington. (I had known him from college.) It snowed heavily while we were there, and Chuck and I visited the Jefferson Memorial at night in the snow without another living soul anywhere in sight. It was one of the single most moving and magnificent sights I have ever enjoyed. The conference, however, broke down in chaos when it was clear no one knew anything.

The twice-a-week *Observer* nearly killed Pete in 1982. It nearly killed everyone. It was a crazy idea from the beginning, for everyone to work twice as hard for the same pay. By fall, Observer Communications was wobbly, and I was gone, back as editor of the paper when Pete realized he couldn't keep doing it and stay alive. I smoothed the transition back to weekly, and the company limped along, bruised and unsure of what future lay before it.

I would hang on as editor until the summer of 1985, but by then my life had changed. I had become a published author.

By 1980, I knew once thing certain: I could not write a commercial novel. I could only write what flowed from my head and hands, from a deep connection to who I was and dreamed I could be. I still passionately loved postmodern fiction, but I assumed (rightly, as it turned out) that the market for it had already begun to wane from the high early days of Barth and Pynchon. That dip in interest was brief but real. It would come back with a vengeance when Little, Brown published *Infinite Jest* by David Foster Wallace in 1996. But in 1980, I knew only that my voice had to lie somewhere in the place between poetry and prose. In order to make sure that I would not create some cockamamie plot as I had in *Let Us Have Madness*, I deliberately set out to write on the smallest possible canvas (to mix metaphors right out of the, er, gate). I first made a list of a few things I truly loved in this life: old people, fishing, American Indian history, the natural world, teaching. There was much more, of course, but this would do for a start.

I loved old folks because I drove around with my father to visit his elderly relatives when I was a boy, just checking on them. This was in Oconee County, South Carolina, and many of these people had been born as far back as the 1870s—they were adults *before electricity and cars came along.* And I found they loved to talk to me, and I adored listening to them. Great aunts, great uncles, distant second cousins: we would sit with sweet tea on hot summer afternoons and chat.

Linda and I fished almost every weekend, as I said earlier, on Lake Oconee when it was first impounded. I taught her how to bait a hook, how to take a fish off a line, and release it or put it on a stringer to eat later. I showed her how to find good cover in a lake, to be able, almost, to *smell* a spot where a hand-sized bream or a thick bass might be lurking. That came to a stop when she left her job at Morgan County Middle School and was hired by the middle school in Oconee County, just south of Athens and within easy commuting distance for her. My year of burning up the thirty miles between Madison and Athens was finally over. By the fall of 1979, we had moved into a large rental house on Pineview Drive on the south side of Athens. Brandon was a smart, giggly, tow-headed boy, and we loved him dearly. We found a sweet old woman named Sue Woods to keep him during the work day, and together Linda and I managed to make enough to keep food on the table, though until 1983, we had less than three hundred dollars in savings.

Like many Americans, I was fascinated with Native American history from boyhood, and during my *Observer* years, I was in the middle of a decade-long glut of study and reflection on Indians and Anglo-created genocide. I read dozens of books and was obsessed by them. About this time I read, for the first time, Dee Brown's opinionated masterpiece, *Bury My Heart at Wounded Knee*. It shattered me. Incidents surrounding a frontier outpost in Wyoming, Fort Phil Kearny, came to be an obsession. Dee Brown also wrote a wonderful book about this place and its time at the center of prairie conflict.

I've been an outdoorsman my whole life, but not in the sense that you see in magazines today of insanely fit superheroes running the entire Applachian Trail and then swimming to Europe without stopping. (I did envy them, though.) I never hunted and dislike guns. I *have* hiked and camped and fished aplenty, but here I am speaking of simply being out in the natural world in as sentient a way as I could manage. I drank color, bathed in light, inhaled and tasted a conifer wind.

My wife, father, mother, brother, sister, and I were all teachers. I came to it late in life as an adjunct professor of creative writing at UGA, but once there, I leaped into it with my whole heart. Daddy was a high school teacher and principal when I was young, and I still remember the power I felt prowling through the empty school in the afternoons when the students had gone home.

But how could these things add up to a *plot*? I simply said to myself: *A retired junior college history professor with a terminal disease, who taught American history and specialized in the history of the frontier, spends his final year at a cabin on a pond in north Georgia where he grew up.* That wasn't a plot, but it was a situation. What, I wondered, was the difference between situation and plot? Characters and actions. So I began to create a set of characters to surround this old man: an almost feral boy who lives nearby, unschooled and needful; a wife who has passed away and a local woman who had been his girlfriend years before and is now a widow herself; a former student who has stayed in touch with the old teacher. And many others. The first thing I did was give my protagonist a name: Andrew Lachlan. When I did, a story began to flow immediately.

The setting of the pond was a gift I already had in my literary tackle box. For a number of years after we moved to Athens, I went every Sunday by myself just before dawn to the Sandy Creek Nature Center north of Athens, and its central wetlands: Clay Pit Pond. It helped me decompress from the stress of the *Observer*. I got permission to do this, and I arrived at the parking lot of the Nature Center just before first light. The place was silent except for animal noises and wind gentling the leaves. I knew the trails as if they were inside our house. The area was deeply wooded for many acres. So I would take my fishing gear and set off in moonlight, arriving after a walk through the woods of several hundred yards at the pond's edge just as dawn turned the eastern sky a smudgy rose. This was *heaven*. Fish and beaver filled the pond, and often, rather than casting, I would simply stand in complete but complex silence and wait for the natural world to accept and ignore me. I knew every blade, every rich aroma, each fold and bend of geography. I knew the sound of a beaver tail as it hit the surface of the still pond with a tremendous **slap!**

At first I wrote a number of pages that I tore up and threw away as soon as I pulled them from my typewriter's platen. Finally one day, in a sweat of desperation, I closed my eyes and tried to assume the breath and pain of Andrew. And when I did, I began a fictional journal. I wrote this:

> May 1
>
> Morning is rising in silence. Nothing will happen along the green edge of the pond for several minutes more. I rest among a tangle of ferns. At the far edge of the water's mirror are *Typha latifolia*, common cattails, erect and masculine, stalk-straight as the light edges from the east. I would like to crush their roots for flour. My pen makes noises like a frog, scratching, creaking. But there is no symbolism in this.

I felt the hair stand up on the back of my neck. I had no idea if it was good or not. But I knew that I had suddenly leaped inside another man's skin, that I was a young husband and father, thirty years old, *and* a dying old man hoping for the grace of one final truth before death found him beside the still waters.

"Please, *please*," I said out loud as I began to type quickly and then even faster. My *please* was addressed to the writing gods, and to Andrew: Let me wear you until this story ends. And I promise it won't be long. Every morning I brewed a cup of strong coffee and began to write. Years later when the Internet came along, I'd give myself thirty minutes to check e-mail and the day's headlines before I started to write. What had begun as a possible need, a glimpsed desire, became a roaring necessity. Every morning when I got to the *Observer*, I had already written three unedited pages on my novel. I maintained that routine until I retired in 2010, and I still do it now, even though I am growing old and have few places to go.

I became more and more proficient at the *Observer* as I began to live in a different world in my mind. I would be shouting an order over yet another crisis or chasing out the door some savage and malevolent freelancer who was threatening me. In the mansion in my head, though, I was walking slowly around Willie Sullivan, the boy who lived near Andrew and who became part of his life. I was imagining *nothing*. I became an invisible visitor in a world that seemed to me very much alive, hearts beating, legs walking around the edge of what I called Shadow Pond.

Pause for a little explanation:

Why in heaven's name was I pretending, at age thirty, that I was a dying old man living alone in the middle of nowhere?

We are told from our writing infancy to write what we know. I knew about being a small-town journalist, but I knew nothing about Nazis. I couldn't even read or write German. (Well, a little.) *Let Us Have Madness* was no more than a pose. It was pure pretense, and the book's first reader saw through it (and me) as if we were plate glass. The only thing about the new book I had to imagine entirely was what it felt like to be old. But I *had* spent years talking to old people, being with them, and I had an intuitive bond with the solitude of age. I realized after a few weeks that I could not only make this book real. I could make it *true*. That still doesn't explain a young man choosing to write in the first person about old age and dying. To this day, all I can say is that Andrew and the story chose me. It was a gift for which I remain grateful. As I was to find out, though, such gifts often come at a price. And, for the record: I don't believe in "write what you know." Young writers? Write what you *dream*. Just be sure there's a firm foundation of facts beneath your castles in the air.

As 1980 passed, I saw myself more and more as a novelist and less as a poet or composer. Still, I wrote poetry when I could, and I knew that some day I would at least have a body of work as a composer, even if no one else ever heard it. I also realized that my creative life wasn't a choice for me; it was essential, necessary, just as I had tried to write when I was sixteen. I created part of the novel on my Royal manual typewriter and, as I recall, part on the IBM Selectric at the *Observer* office that Chuck still had from his days in the Viet Nam Veterans Against the War. Some days the urge to get back to the novel was as strong as sex. Page after page would go straight into the finished and printed book with scarcely an edit. Though the date Andrew begins his journal is May 1, I actually began the book in August, finished it early the next year, 1981, and I let Linda read it, terrified that she would repeat Pete's opinion of my first full novel. How does a writer know a book is good or bad? The answer is that we rarely do, and often a writer's editor is wrong, his agent is wrong, the *world* is wrong. Those cautionary tales about novels that were rejected multiple times and then went on to become famous are all over the Internet, the sanctuary of every rejected would-be author on Planet Earth. Still, I was as sure as I could be that the book had quality.

Before I handed it to Linda, I gave it a title: *The Heart of a Distant Forest*. That's from James Dickey's poem "The Lifeguard," and Dickey was touched that I used a line from his poem for my title (or told me he was, a few years later). The lines I chose, about a lifeguard failing to save the life of a boy in his care, directly reflects how Andrew feels about the lost and wayward Willie Sullivan. More, it was a poem that seemed to catch the breeze across a pond and through the Georgia pines. It made the pond a place of happiness, sanctuary, and menace. Thirty years later, my first literary agent said it was still her favorite title of all the fiction she'd sold over a long and illustrious career.

"This is not bad," Linda said finally, high praise from someone born and raised in Boston. I knew she wouldn't lie, and she knew I knew it. So I thanked her, took the manuscript, and put it in the drawer of my desk, not planning to do anything else with it.

Athens in 1980 had an even stronger reason to celebrate than its booming music scene: a freshman running back at UGA named Herschel Walker, who was supposed to be something special. By the time I finally finished my novel, Walker *was* famous, and the only person to read my novel was still my wife. The pages began to gather dust in my desk. And there the novel stayed for two years.

On April 28, 1981, Ray wrote in response to my note that we were planning another trip to New York City that summer:

> Sorry it has taken this long to get back to you, but I've just gotten back from Virginia where I did some reading from my books and ran a workshop at George Mason University in Fairfax. Now it's back to the typewriter where I'm months and months behind in book number three. How do you write so fast? I envy you. My goal is to finish ten books, or twelve, in my lifetime, but at the rate I'm going I'll have to live another century to do so. Maybe I will.
>
> I don't remember what I said in that letter but whatever it was that got you back to writing, I'm glad I said it. Maybe you should send the letter back to me to get me back to work. Anyhow, I'm glad to hear you've rejoined the world of damned if you do and damned if you don't. Welcome back!

He told us that he and Heidi had been divorced since June 1980 and that their split was amicable. She wanted to move home to Switzerland, and Ray felt he could not write there.

> We are friends and correspond. But when one has the curse, writing, as I do, he's possessed and it's difficult for wives, friends, children, cats, dogs, family, old folks, police, politicians, relatives, football teams, the moral majority, God, neighbors, publishers, editors, agents, baseball free agents, landlords, apple pie and mom to dig. The novel was invented to keep lunatics like me off the streets.
>
> Yes, do come up this summer and you can stay with me. I'm yet at the same place minus the cats (Heidi won them) and a wife. Just let me know well enough ahead of time so I can pick up the dirty sox (they seem to grow everywhere) sober up the mice and hose down the sink.

In the summer, Linda and I took that road trip with her sister Gail and Gail's husband Dave Tarpley, both wonderful people, intelligent, accomplished, and extremely bright. We had a fine time in New York City seeing Ray and shopping before heading to the Cape for a week. It was a memorable trip, and we brought home gleeful stories we were still telling thirty years later.

One day, in October 1982, I opened the mail that the people downstairs thought should go to Editorial, and inside one envelope was a flyer from a small publishing house in Atlanta called Peachtree Publishers. The flyer said that Peachtree had published more books by Georgia journalists than any other firm—as a way of doing a little apple-polishing during National Newspaper Week. I tried to check on them, but in pre-Internet days, finding out anything was slow and difficult. Finally, feeling the itch of desperation about *The Heart of a Distant Forest*, I asked my friend and fellow journalist Vinnie Williams, a generation older than I was but still active as she would be for decades more, to read the manuscript and tell me if it was any good. If she said yes, I might just send it to Peachtree. At this point I knew absolutely nothing about literary agents or how to get one. But Vinnie had published several well-received novels with a major New York publisher, and I thought that if anyone could tell me the truth, she would. By this time, she was editor of *The Oconee Enterprise,* in which the *Observer* had a financial interest—the weekly paper in nearby Watkinsville. (At this writing, she is still working as a journalist at age 92.)

She dropped me a letter a couple of weeks later that left me more hopeful than I'd ever been. She said wonderful things about my novel, about the quality of the writing, about my possible future as a novelist. So I thanked her and bundled up my manuscript and mailed it to the Peachtree's executive editor, Bill Emerson. He had been *Newsweek's* southern bureau chief during the Civil Rights Era, not to mention editor of *The Saturday Evening Post.* His friend Willie Morris once said Bill had "a gargantuan disposition," and that's as close as one might get to describing an endlessly interesting guy. Peachtree not long before had made its first foray into publishing original fiction, a tale by a doctor in Fayetteville, Georgia, named Ferrol Sams called *Run with the Horsemen.* It had done well for Peachtree, and against all hope and knowing no better, I thought Peachtree might have an interest in my book. I stood around looking at my watch as I performed the routine chores of assigning stories to Phil and John, or, more often, taking the stories they had found and written. They were professionals and acted like it. We had the usual daily life dramas of a small business, magnified because we were young, and a lot of drinking went on. But when it came time to put out a paper, everyone worked at the top of her or his game. Finally, one day Valerie Winfrey from downstairs, who sometimes handled phone calls (as well as being in charge of classified ads) told me I had a call on line two. I punched the button. It was Bill Emerson, and the sheer knowledge that he had read my novel all but left me faint.

"Philip!" he shouted into the phone. "I got your novel, and good *God,* son!" He paused. I was sitting at my desk, and I wanted, desperately, to talk to Linda. "Look here, you find me right now in the twilight of a failed career!" That, obviously, was ludicrous, but as I would find out later, writers always, right to the end, consider themselves failures in one way or another. Maybe Bill knew how he'd failed, but I sure didn't.

"Thank you," I squeaked doubtfully. Years later *The New York Times* in his obituary called him "loud, boisterous, tall (he stood 6 foot 3) and perpetually amused," and that, too, was the man calling me. (Well, he sounded tall.) He began to tell me that he thought my novel was very fine indeed, but I was ahead of things a bit for Peachtree. They *had* published a novel, but the future of long-form fiction at the house wasn't really clear yet. He did have a suggestion, though.

"I have a good writer friend, Otto Friedrich, and his daughter Molly is starting out as a literary agent in New York!" he shouted. "Would you mind if I sent it on to her?!"

"That would be great," I said. Bill paused for a moment.

"Son, how old are you?!" he asked.

"I'm thirty-three," I said. There was a pause on the other end.

"Good *God,* you're young!" he boomed. "Let me give you the information about Molly!" And he did.

Molly Friedrich, now known as one of the finest literary agents of her time in Manhattan, was young in those days as I was. Of course I knew absolutely nothing about her. I would find out many years later that her parents were ex-pats who met in Europe after WWII when her father was writing and her mother painting. They married and had three kids over there, with Molly born in London. They moved back to the States settling, penniless, on Long Island. At first, Molly says in an interview she gave to *Poets & Writers* in 2008, they lived with the mother of revered postmodernist author William Gaddis. Indeed there is a scene early in Gaddis's most famous book *The Recognitions,* that involves a naked two-year-old gamboling on a lawn in summer, and that character was supposedly based on Molly. *The Recognitions* is about art and forgery, and almost as if preordained, Molly grew up and went to Barnard where she majored in art history. While in college, she rented a room from one Tom Congdon and his wife Connie. Congdon had been the editor of Peter Benchley's ultra-successful novel *Jaws,* and he told Molly that she should go into publishing. (In yet another bizarre, six-degrees-from-Kevin Bacon kind of thing, the novel that Molly and I ultimately broke over, several years later, was bought for film by Richard Zanuck and David Brown, who produced—*Jaws.* And I need to say now that while I regret that Molly and I couldn't keep working together, I have always thought she was right when she stopped repping that book. If I had been her, I would have done the same thing. But I was me and not about to give up on it. No person in the literary business was ever kinder to me—she's one in a million.) After a time working in book publicity, Molly had started working in the Aaron Priest Agency at 344 East 51st Street. When Bill Emerson sent my book to Molly, the agency consisted of Molly and Aaron. But small agencies are often tremendously influential, though—I hate to keep saying this—I didn't know it then. Molly would ultimately go on to be the agent for such literary superstars as Pulitzer Prize winner Jane Smiley and bestsellers like Sue Grafton and Terry McMillan. Grafton sells more books on any Tuesday than I have in my whole career. She was also the agent for the biography *De Kooning: An American Master*, by Mark Stevens and Annalyn Swan, also a Pulitzer winner.

Among the million things I didn't know about publishing, I *did* know two things. First, *The Heart of a Distant Forest* was a solid, well-written, and very moving novel. And second, it was the most uncommercial book imaginable, as popular as a feed-store catalog in a Fifth Avenue boutique. I would later become accustomed to rejection and to taking it with a smile and a *thank-you*. That seems disingenuous, but it's true. Ask any seasoned writer. But in those days, I feared it worse than contracting Ebola.

In November of that year, 1982, my phone rang at the *Observer* office one day, and it was Molly Friedrich. I was extremely nervous. In less than the time it took her to identify herself, I had mentally composed her entire speech telling me, as Pierce Arant, my voice teacher at UGA, once had, to go into motel management, that I couldn't write my way out of a kraft lunch bag. Instead, her voice was strong and lively, assured and clear. She liked the book very much and would give it a try. She didn't give me much hope that it might sell, and I've never known (and never asked her) if she took it on just as a favor to Bill Emerson and thus her father. It wouldn't have bothered me if she had.

"And I'll call or write when I hear from someone," she said.

And like that, I'd gone from the editorship of an alternative weekly paper in Athens, Georgia, to writer with a literary agent in Manhattan. Pete was impressed, though I hadn't let him read the new manuscript because I knew he was a busy man. I was also frightened of what he would say. I knew that whatever happened, I wasn't writing to get out of my eight-to-five job.

I had also started writing the book I really wanted to write, a postmodern comedy based on Dante's *Inferno*. I had been obsessed with *The Divine Comedy* since my undergraduate days—and I mean really, every-waking-*moment* obsessed, as I have noted before. Ultimately, I would go on to write the *Purgatorio* and *Paradiso* sections of it, finishing with a thousand-page postmodern novel called *The Divine Comics* that was finally published in 2010. If I had known it would take that long to see it into print, I still would have done it. That was wallpaper, though, to the work that took all my real energy as a writer: waiting to hear from Molly.

In yet another analog from film, the scene in the fine film *Sideways*, when Paul Giamatti's character Miles finally talks to his agent is so true to life it made me cringe. Waiting to hear from an agent is agonizing, and the dance around bad news when the call comes is *exactly* like it is in the movie.

I have always been one of those scribblers who writes long and longer letters to agent and editor just to thank her or him for giving me the time of day. Molly in the *P&W* interview said that one of things she likes about being an agent is that writers all love her. If a publisher turns a manuscript down, that of course isn't her fault. On the other hand, if she sells something, the writer adores only her. Not a bad place to be. True to form, I wrote Molly a long letter. Twice. I should go ahead and prove how little faith I had in my "career" by noting the fact that I rarely kept copies of the letters I wrote during my years as a novelist and poet. So I can only occasionally quote from my own words while I can quote endlessly (with permission) from anyone who ever wrote me more than a syllable. I have kept everything. *Everything*. From my first colorings in the early 1950s as a toddler, I have it. It's not quite as bad as you think, though. I simply like to rummage around in the past, and I thought I'd enjoy, years later, poking around in the attic of my own mind.

On December 1, Molly wrote me for the first time on what was known as "airmail stationery" in those days—onionskin paper.

> Anyway, many thanks for your two nice letters—publishing is in such rotten shape these days it's becoming increasingly rare to make a writer feel a bit better by the simple act of agreeing to try and sell his book. Toward that end, I've sent the book to Larry Kessenich of Houghton Mifflin and here's hoping. Just as long as you realize that this is the far side of a long shot....

At that time her agency's client list was already impressive and included humorist Erma Bombeck, novelist Philip Caputo, and famed southern author and Civil Rights activist Will Campbell. The idea that I might see myself in that list seemed a little crazy to me. If I wasn't clear how commercial she thought my novel was, she left no room for misunderstanding in her letter:

> I am always looking for solid commercial fiction and non-fiction for the adult trade audience—*The Heart of a Distant Forest* is the exception, not the rule to my list.

At this distance, my incessant letters to Molly look like bad manners. But since I doubt anyone in Athens had ever *had* a literary agent, I had no way of knowing how to act. Still, every writer had heard of Houghton Mifflin, one of the best-known publishing houses in the business. But who was this Larry Kessenich? As it turned out, he was my age and like many people in publishing had started somewhere else. Still, his star was rising. He had read a one-line description of a story in an anthology of Canadian writers and wondered if it could be turned into a novel. The writer was named W.P. Kinsella. The novel that Kessenich and a senior editor urged Kinsella to write was published as *Shoeless Joe*. The film made out of it a few years later? *Field of Dreams*.

All that autumn, playing with Brandon, who would turn five in '83, was a joy. He, Linda, and I had, in 1982, moved from our rented house to the first place we owned (or had a mortgage on): a tiny modified A-frame west of Athens off the Jefferson Road. It was at the end of a dead-end street and abutted many acres of woods that in those days was almost wilderness. I was sure it would look like wilderness to a growing boy. And oh, it did. Those were *his* woods as he grew.

I settled in for a very long wait, months perhaps. As it turned out, I only had to wait a few days. Around Christmas, Molly called: Larry Kessenich had read my novel and was simply mad for it. My heart began to drum wildly. But first he would need to get more in-house support before he took it to the whole editorial board. I dropped Molly a note toward the end of the month and asked if I could write Kessenich while the drama unfolded. She answered:

> By all means, write to Larry...Just two points: Don't mention money, not even the fact that you could survive with no advance, for the pleasures of being published. You are a humble newspaperman surviving in a terrible recession. Also don't tell him you finished this four years ago—it's just better not to, on general principle.

I knew about the recession, alas. The mortage lending rate was more than 17 percent at the time, and we'd bought our new house on a 13¾ percent five-year balloon loan. That meant in five years the whole note would be due. I was gambling that the rate would go down, and we could refinance, and I'm not remotely the gambling type. But I wanted a home as much as I wanted to be a published novelist. I wrote Larry immediately, and he wrote me back, on Houghton Mifflin letterhead.

I remember the afternoon when I got home from the *Observer*, found the letter in our mailbox, and opened it. No e-mail ever received can match the thrill of a postal letter bearing wonderful news. Larry told me it was one of the most moving novels he had ever read. He promised that he would do his best to get the novel accepted at HM. To that end, he had asked senior editor Robie Macauley to read it, and *he* was definitely in favor of publishing it. Larry promised that he wouldn't keep me in suspense any longer than he had to. Here's hoping, he ended, that we will one day be working together on the publication of *The Heart of a Distant Forest*. Before coming to Houghton Mifflin, Macauley had for some years been fiction editor of *Playboy*, and he knew everyone in the literary world, including the great Vladimir Nabokov. In college he had studied under Ford Madox Ford (thus the connection mentioned earlier), and at Kenyon College he'd roomed with Peter Taylor, Robert Lowell, and Randall Jarrell. While a master's student at the Iowa Writers' Workshop, he *dated* Flannery O'Connor. He had succeeded John Crowe Ransom as editor of the *Kenyon Review*. He had known *Gertrude Stein*, for God's sake. And he was in favor of publishing my novel!

I froze the moment, to remember it for all my life. I was standing in a rhombus of light from one of the two large windows high on the front of the house. The chocolate brown wall-to-wall carpet felt warm on my sock feet. Linda and Brandon hadn't gotten home yet, and a cat hummed on my ankle for food. All my dreams going back to adolescence were about to come true. I had done it. I was going to be an author.

My literary ship would come in soon enough, but not then and not from Houghton Mifflin.

The sound of falling water. He sits at the edge of movement and stares at the foxfire on the damp rocky wall. It glows greenly, no, blue-green, as cicadas symphony the forest darkness. Rivers, seas. Taking off from the Orange County airport in southern California and making a sweet arc out over the Pacific Ocean before turning back toward America. Horse Branch as it trickles along the edge of Madison, and remembered sunlight from his boyish delight. The Mississippi at New Orleans, impossibly wide, monumental, draining half a continent. Dry Falls near Highlands, North Carolina, the lip and the plummet, the icy spray as you walk behind it. The Oconee near Park's Mill, not impressive, not large, but indelible, redolent of fish. He goes there sometimes, and to the Keowee, rivers destroyed by greed and power. Water does not fall there any more.

20

Three Manhattans

In the trendy, lit-saturated world of Manhattan and MFA grads, my excitement probably looks quaint at this distance. When twenty-three-year-olds have agents and even published books, my giddiness at age thirty-three over a *possible* book contract would likely amuse any student in the Iowa Writer's Workshop. But for a young man in the American South in 1983, it was a miracle. By then, Athens was slamming on all cylinders, a twenty-four-hour roving party to the background beat of bands like R.E.M., Pylon, the B-52s, and Love Tractor. Fatherhood and my fanatical interest in writing had somewhat tempered my worst excesses. I didn't wake up leaning on a wall in a strange house only to remember the party I'd launched myself into hours before. But we all still partied hard and often enough. I wasn't going to tell people I had a literary agent in Manhattan or that a major literary publishing house in Boston was interested in my novel. Then I did. That was a mistake I learned not to repeat, because one sunny winter afternoon, my phone rang at the *Observer*, and it was Molly. I came halfway out of my seat. By then, in the endless musical chairs of office shuffling at *TAO*, Pete and I were sharing a huge office just across the hall from production. Fortunately he was out of the room. Someone across the hall was yelling at someone else—the usual.

"I've got bad news," Molly began, not waiting to let me have a breath of hope. Bless her, she knew how to deliver all kinds of news. "Larry Kessenich just called, and this isn't going to happen."

I sat down abruptly in my chair. There had even been talk of submitting *The Heart of a Distant Forest* for the famed Houghton Mifflin Literary Fellowship, which meant a huge launch and a $10,000 advance, a great deal for a first novel in 1983. Instead, the head of the editorial department had, as I understood it, killed the book by an act of Olympian intercession.

"Crushed" doesn't begin to describe how I felt. I could barely hear the rest of what Molly told me, but little by little I began to move past her tone—which was warm and protective and sad and hopeful at the same time—and understand what she was saying. She wouldn't quit. She loved the book and didn't want me to worry. Even coming this close on the first submission for a literary novel from an unknown writer had a kind of glory that shook down quiet glitter if one knew how to look for it. I thanked her, hung up, and took a walk around Athens. Two drunks were arguing under a stop sign. A woman who had green hair and a chihuahua peeking out of her backpack came long-striding past me, as if she was in a hurry on Tim Burton's version of the Appalachian Trail. Telling my friends at the paper was a nightmare, but I did it. Telling Linda when we got home that afternoon was worse. I went to my study and closed the door and wept. But soon enough, I was over it. That was the last time I ever became seriously upset by rejection. In that sense, it was a usefully astringent moment. But what I remember most is Molly Friedrich's warmth. God love her, she made rejection something almost worth going through. Anyway, The Aaron M. Priest Literary Agency, Inc. was not sitting still with my book. They had already sent the book to their film subagents and had begun to shop it around Hollywood. Most production companies passed on it quickly as non-cinematic, and I knew they were right. Still, dreams die hard. I was back to waiting.

In the meantime, I had finished *The Inner Kingdom,* the postmodern retelling of the *Inferno* section of Dante's *Divine Comedy*. It was absolutely nothing like *Heart,* but it was where *my* heart lay. I had also finished a more commercial novel started a year or so before that I was calling *Asphodel.* Molly said I could go ahead and send it to her, so I did. In addition to the movie people, Molly had sent the manuscript of *THOADF* to several other editors. Soon enough, their responses came tumbling in. Pat Strachan at Farrar, Straus, & Giroux found the book enormously satisfying but wished it had been non-fiction instead of a novel. Even after the book came out in 1984, many people looked at its young author suspiciously since I'd managed to write in the voice of an old man with some authority. Jon Galassi at Random House thought the novel was extremely good, but he wasn't going to make an offer because of a book called *Autumn* (of which I'd never heard) that came out the year before, and he felt they were apparently similar enough that he didn't want to go down that road. Molly sent it next to Jim Landis at William Morrow. He found it quite lovely but turned it down. Molly quickly declined to represent *Asphodel,* and I wasn't surprised or especially disappointed. It was a mistake to put her in that position, one I regretted. She did say she didn't mind if I sent it myself to small literary or university presses, and I thanked her for that.

Spring came and went without a sale, and the brief excitement I saw in my friends' eyes when I walked by faded into a he-coulda-been-a-contender commiseration. Then in midsummer 1983, Molly called me one afternoon. Pete was sitting at his desk working on that week's column. I had been editing copy, expecting nothing. She began by telling me that Doubleday couldn't quite decide, but that an editor there named Allen Peacock loved it. I nodded, having heard it all before. Then she dropped the proverbial bombshell.

"But we do have a small offer from Norton, from an editor there named Tom Wallace," she said. I sat straight up and waved my hand to get Pete to shut up. The only sound he was making was the clack of his keyboard, but he immediately knew Something Was Up. He froze.

"Would you say that again?" I asked hoarsely.

"Tom Wallace at Norton has made a small offer on *Heart,*" she said. Norton. Half the music books I had in high school when I *knew* music would be my life's work had been published by that venerable New York house. I sometimes lay on my stomach on my bed as a teenager and read the titles and the publishers off the spines of my small home library. Molly told me the amount of the advance Norton offered. It could have been fifty cents for all I cared. In fact, it was $2,500—small even for 1983 but far more than it is now. Linda and I had almost no savings, and we could hear the wolf howling in the woods for us on days when big expenses came up. We maxed out charge cards, tried hard to pay them off.

"That sounds really great to me, Molly," I said. Seeing Pete look at me, I broke my rule about not speaking of my writing at work again. "I've always admired that house as a publisher. Do you know when it would come out?" She thought probably late the following spring. "Well, let's do it then."

"You want to do it? Great. I'll call Tom and let him know. He will be pleased. And I'm so happy for you, Phil." And she was. She had made absolutely no money from me so far, but she knew well enough how I must feel, and she was right there, in the moment, with me.

"Bless you, Molly." I hung up, and Pete was already standing and taking a couple of steps toward me. I did not remember rising from my old squeaky chair, but I was standing in the warm office in sudden shock and disbelief. A well-known New York publishing house had just bought my novel.

"It…they…." Pete tried.

"Norton," I said. "W.W. Norton. They just bought my novel, Pete."

He seemed as shocked as I was, since the only fiction of mine he'd read was *Let Us Have Madness.* How could I have gone from *that* to *this*?

"Then you're coming with me," he said, leading me to the door of our office, down the stairs, and out into the hot sunshine of Athens, Georgia. Linda was still teaching, so I couldn't tell her until we got home. I knew where Pete was taking me: to a bar to celebrate. We walked up Washington Street on a hot, still afternoon and went to Friends, our usual hangout. It was a little too classy for the pierced and dyed-hair denizens of downtown Athens, but it had a good mix of different types, and we often met movers and shakers there for drinks and serious talk. We came in out of the heat, and I felt like I was walking into Rick's Place in *Casablanca,* through a great deal of marble and potted plants. We sat at a table, and a bright-eyed waitress came over, bringing a hint of tip-inducing perfume with her in the cooled air.

"Bring this boy a Manhattan!" Pete shouted. "Make that two!"

I drank three, I think, and I'd never even had a Manhattan, a mixture of bourbon, sweet vermouth, bitters, a cherry, and an orange peel. I was a bourbon-and-water man, Evan Williams most of the time, Black Jack when I could afford a pint. I found the drink rather ghastly, but it could have been nectar poured straight from the thermos of Max Perkins. It was the single happiest drink of my life, and one of the kindest gestures a friend ever offered me. Pete was one of the few people I ever knew who was instantanously capable of such intelligent generosity. A couple of years later, when a group of us went to see the film *Between the Lines* at a small theater on campus, there was a lot of giggling about how familiar the movie seemed, with its alternative-paper scenario. But it was only when Michael, the character played by Stephen Collins, announces to the group that he's sold his book and is going to New York for the rewrites that we all realized just *how* true-to-life the movie was.

That night, Linda and I did some serious partying. Around midnight, I remember dancing and singing around the great room then falling to the floor and laughing hysterically while the ceiling, two stories above us, opened, and the stars came pouring in. The next day I would have a world-class tympani-tantrum of a hangover, but that night I didn't care.

Tom Wallace told me that *The Heart of a Distant Forest* was very tight and well constructed, if I am reading my notes of that phone call from the next day correctly. I had a monstrous headache. He said they would try hard to get good blurbs, and he was hopeful because "serious writers tend to be pretty generous." He said it was a wonderful novel and needed "no work at all" and that I was "absolutely a writer to be published."

Gaw. I asked him to tell me more about Norton, and he did, and on August 9 sent me a copy of their fall catalog. My book would be coming late spring of 1984. I filled out my first author questionnaire for Norton's marketing people—the first of dozens in years to come. Then came another shock. Since my protagonist Andrew Lachlan in *Heart* specializes in the history of the American West, he mentions how much he loves Dee Brown's *Bury My Heart at Wounded Knee*. I had no idea, but when Tom Wallace was an editor at Holt, he had been Brown's editor on that book and four others. And he was a close friend of Brown's and couldn't wait to send him a copy of my book when it came out. Holy mother of—this couldn't be happening.

By August 19 I had received, signed, and mailed the contracts with Norton back to Molly. I couldn't stop praising Molly, so I wrote to her:

> Again, I think you're just a goddamn miracle worker. I feel light as a feather these days, except for today, as I have a wicked hangover, but what the hell. I'm just so happy that you represent me I can't convey it. Maybe I'll come to NY in the fall to say hello to you and the folks at Norton.

Not content with a contract from Norton, I sent *The Inner Kingdom* to Indiana University Press, which had a modest fiction publishing program. I just thought they might be interested in me as a postmodernist. And I did have a contract with a New York publishing house as a minor bit of leverage. In the meantime, I had written to James Dickey at the University of South Carolina to ask permission to use the line from "The Lifeguard" as the title of my book. I hadn't heard from him until one afternoon our reporter Phil Sanderlin came into my office at the *Observer* with a stricken look on his face.

"What happened?" I asked.

"*James Dickey* is on the phone for you," he said in disbelief. In the literary world in those years, this was like getting a call from Hemingway at his height. Dickey's fame would plummet long before his death fifteen years later, but then it still soared. That often happens, but Dickey was a great poet, and his fame and influence *will* return soon enough. He was kind and gentle with me, granting me permission but saying I'd have to write Wesleyan University Press to get legal permission. (I did, and they gave it.)

"It was such a sweet letter you wrote to me," he said. "I'm really touched you'd want to use one of my lines as a title for your book. I think that's the first time it's happened." We chatted amiably about literature and a few other things, and I noticed that several *Observer* staffers had crowded into the doorway and were looking at me with baffled respect.

"I'm so grateful to talk to you," I said. "I studied your work in college." There was a pause from the other end.

"Son, how old are you?" he asked.

"I'm thirty-three," I said. This time, there was a longer pause.

"Well, good Lord," he said.

Dickey promised me a jacket quote and said he'd help promote my book, but of course he did neither. I didn't really expect it, but he was nice even to say it. By mid-September Tom Wallace had sent me some sample pages of *Heart*, and they were gorgeous, in a font called Janson Alternate. I was to expect galleys by November. My friend Don Nelson from the *Observer* took my first jacket photo in the creek next to our house. The dust jacket of my first novel was another matter entirely. I will let one reviewer speak for many: It looked like the first watercolor your grandmother ever attempted and should immediately be torn off and thrown in the trash. A waterfowl the artist thought at one point of using wasn't even entirely erased, and even now you can see its embarrassed ghost on the cover. When I first saw the finished book, I almost threw up, but I soon got over it. In the end, maybe it was the fault of someone besides the artist. One never knew. Beneath that jacket, though, the physical book was gorgeous.

Feeling a little desperate and having no clue that I didn't need to rush *another* manuscript to Molly, I sent her a novel I'd finished in the summer called *Edge of the Current*. It was about another old man, this one being forced off his land because of a hydroelectric project. It had its strengths, but not many of them, and I knew it. It did have a major postmodern trope—a novel within the novel—but it meshed poorly. She got it just before Thanksgiving. In the meantime, Linda and I decided on another trip to the Big Apple, this time for meetings with Tom and Molly. At first, we thought we might stay with Ray again, but Tom had another idea. He was an old Yalie, and the Yale Club is right smack in the middle of things in Manhattan at 50 Vanderbilt Avenue, just across from Grand Central Station. So I wrote to Ray to see if we could get together while we were in town:

> We'll be in New York on Dec. 8-10, but we've arranged to stay in town at the Yale Club....
>
> Anyhow, could you meet us for dinner on Friday night, Dec. 9? We'll get to the Yale Club on Thurs., but I've got meetings set up with my agent and editor on Thurs. and for lunch on Fri. We'll also have a little time on Sat. morning.
>
> We're coming up on the train just for the hell of it...If you don't have any other ideas, Linda and I would like to eat dinner and then go to O'Reilly's.

As I said, Ray and Heidi had gotten divorced in June 1980, and he was living alone in the same apartment in Queens. He had visited us in March 1982 in Athens, and he spent the night with us, the first of dozens of such visits. (Starting in 1984 when Ray moved to Athens, I'd lay in a case of beer on Friday, pick him up at his house, and then take him home Monday morning. Brandon grew up with "Crazy Uncle Ray," as Ray called himself, sleeping on the sofa every weekend for years.) Ray answered my letter and said he was looking forward to seeing us:

> You and Linda just think of yourselves as Scott and Zelda coming by Pullman to the Big Apple.

We arrived at the Yale Club, having no idea that it was unbelievably stuffy and required that women, at all times, wear dresses on their premises, something that made Linda laugh. She had no intention of being ordered to wear a dress by anyone, but since it was winter she wore a long coat over her blouse and slacks, almost daring their *maitre d'resscode* to throw us out. They didn't toss us, but I almost wished they had—seeing Linda go toe-to-toe over being told what to wear would have been worth the price of admission. Our room was pleasant, though, and if we *did* feel a little like

Scott and Zelda, we could be forgiven. Only fifteen years later did the Yale Club became the first of the New York City Ivy League clubs to go "business casual" as a dress code, a shift "received with polite scorn by other clubs," according to an article in *The New York Times*. Among the Club's members are Hillary Rodham Clinton, Bill Clinton, John Kerry, and David McCullough. If I'd known that, *I* probably would have worn a dress if they'd told me to. And by the way, my mention of Scott Fitzgerald isn't just fanciful. In chapter three of *The Great Gatsby*, Nick Carraway mentions that he "took dinner usually at the Yale Club." It has also shown up over and over in popular culture.

The first day we were there, we walked around a corner on a cold Manhattan street, and I ran—physically ran—right into a friend from Athens, John English, a professor in the UGA journalism school and a fine writer himself. We got a good laugh and a decent small-world story. (My best one would come on a visit to D.C. some years later.)

Linda and I lit up the town, had a ball. We went to the Strand as usual and bought too many books. Molly told me she liked *Edge of the Current* and that she had sent the manuscript over to Tom. But I felt sick about the possibilities, since I had a strong sense that Molly might not have really liked it. Tom was nice during my meeting with him, and Molly was lovely and wonderful when we met for lunch at the Algonquin. (We got to see, sitting alone at a table nearby, legendary *New Yorker* editor William Shawn.) Linda and I trolled the festive Christmas windows of all the midtown stores, hung out with the skaters at Rockefeller Center, bought lunch from a sidewalk vendor. I won't keep comparing my life to movies, I promise, but if you watch a film called *Falling in Love* with Meryl Streep and Robert De Niro, you will see the Manhattan we saw on that trip in 1983. Heading down the escalator in Penn Station for our train back, someone refused to step off at the bottom, and Linda and I, along with about thirty other people, all tumbled down the steps, hard. But we only had scrapes and hurried to catch our ride south.

It was only after we got back to Athens that I began to realize how stupid I was to force another novel on Molly and Tom before my first novel had even been published. I think I was trying to make up for lost time, not really realizing that thirty-four is a good age for a first novel and that rushing things in publishing is almost always a mistake. It's a glacial business by design, or was in those days. With new media now, people are beginning to bypass traditional publishers. Someone can post a manuscript as an e-book on Amazon and make more than they ever would going through traditional routes. But back then, and even now, I argue, if you want to be taken seriously as a writer, you must go the traditional route. And since, as I have said, I wasn't writing for money, it wouldn't have mattered to me anyway.

I wrote Molly immediately:

> I want to thank you very deeply for our fine time in NY. I hope you did not come away from our lunch thinking I was a hopeless rube. I felt like I acted somewhat stiffly, but I honestly did not know how to act. But I was so delighted with it all that I probably acted like a dimwit. If so, I promise that I am usually a little more sociable.
>
> I felt very happy with Tom Wallace, Norton and everything. The people there were nice to me and I felt strongly that it is the publisher for me. Also, as I told you, please forget what I wrote about money, etc. That letter came at the end of a period of massive overwork, frayed nerves, and shaky finances....
>
> Anyway, I suppose now we wait on EDGE OF THE CURRENT. I must be honest and tell you I was scared to death you wouldn't like it because I knew it wasn't as commercial as it started out to be.... Hemingway once said that anyone who knew him personally must have been convinced his books were shit. I hope my visit did not have the same effect on Tom....
>
> I always love hearing from you, even a couple of lines. It's kind of a confirmation to me that I am going to be published. It is all still unbelievable to me.

By January 1984, media in the South and elsewhere had gotten wind of the new boy novelist about to be hatched in Athens. *Library Journal* wrote me and asked me to write a short statement of two hundred words or less about how I became a writer. They dutifully published my answer in an issue that went to libraries all over the country. Tom Wallace turned down *Edge of the Current,* and while I was embarrassed and ashamed, thank God you did, Tom. Sometimes I look at my unpublished work, and it makes me feel a case of Ebola coming on. He had made some rewriting and restructuring suggestions, but I knew that was hopeless and told him so. By February, he'd sent the manuscript back to Molly. She commiserated. Then she shared some fairly good news:

> I did get a response from Cheryl Peterson of CAA (Creative Artists Agency) on the West Coast. She loved the book (*THOADF*) and would be willing to show it to six directors. What this means is that she thinks it's a fine book but is extremely doubtful of her ability to find either a director or a producer to option it.

This was "fairly good" because it put my name before CAA, the agency that would wind up selling my novel *All the Western Stars* to MGM for a great deal of money a few years down the road. Other good news for *Heart* continued to pile up. I had forgotten until I saw Norton's catalog that they did have one author I knew personally: May Sarton. I told them this, and they sent her galleys, and she responded with generosity beyond what I imagined:

"I found *The Heart of a Distant Forest* a deeply satisfying experience," she wrote. "The journal as a device works perfectly here as we are carried through it into the center of an old man's consciousness, an old man who has decided to die in his own way, in a cabin by a lake, communing with nature. Of course human life breaks in, and, without sentimentality, with great poignance and truth, Williams illuminates both the hazards and the necessity of discovering new ways of loving even in the last months of life. A notable first novel indeed." Ms. Sarton and I swapped a few warm letters about this time, too.

Norton printed that on the inside flap and another quote from Eugenia Price on the back flap. (To be honest, I wasn't too enthusiastic about the Price quote. Though she was a Georgia author, her audience would be nothing whatever like mine.) In April 1984, a package came for me at the *Observer* office, and I unwrapped it, hands shaking. Pete was looking over my shoulder. I wanted to crawl under my desk. The dust jacket was *ghastly*. Then again, maybe I was being too serious about the whole thing. What the hell. Bizarrely, I was at the same time invited to a writers' conference on Georgia's St. Simons Island. And one of the other panelists would be—Aaron Priest, who owned and ran Molly's agency. I'm not sure if he came—I just can't remember—but Molly did think it would have been a little pointless for him "to go there to find authors since the only good writer is someone we already have." What joy to get something like *that* in the U.S. Mail.

On pub day in April, Raymond Andrews moved to the new summer studio Benny had built in the country just outside Athens. He wrote us a letter at Easter to let us know he was coming:

> Come May 19th, Benny and I will be borrowing the truck used in the film *The Grapes of Wrath*, load up and head out of the Big Apple, bound for the Big Peach. A reverse migration. After 35 years of city life (Atlanta, San Antonio, San Angelo, San Francisco, Seoul, Tokyo, Washington, Lansing, Chicago, New York, Amsterdam, Hamburg, Copenhagen, Zurich and Bergdittikon [Heidi's hometown in Switzerland]), I'm going "country." Got to get myself a pickup, shotgun and a dawg. God still drives a pickup, I hope. Anyway, watch your henhouse, pigpen, watermelon patch and pecan trees because there will be a hungry writer on the loose in the Athens vicinity. Lookout!
>
> Never got around to thanking you and Linda for the dinner you bought me while here last December (?) It was great seeing the two of you again and I was honored to be part of the occasion. That night you two looked so happy I thought you were newlyweds. Your second honeymoon. How is the book coming? I'm looking forward to reading it. Let me know when it's out. How is the rest of your writing coming? Remember, rather than a culmination of something, your first book just opens a can of worms. Remember, also, to enjoy each moment of each book.
>
> This past March 30 I left this job of mine after 11 and a half years, determined to work now solely for myself. Come June, BIG 50 will descend upon my youth and 45 of these years have been spent working for others (having picked my first cotton boll at five), putting me a bit farther behind schedule than the average writer. Having published only three books, I've got to spend more time accumulating a body of work. I have five more novels in mind and these I cannot write while working full time and putting in only 1-3 hours of work per day writing. I just don't have that energy anyone [sic]...despite my youth. Anyway, I want to spend the next coupla of [sic] years concentrating solely on writing. Also, I need to get out of New York for awhile, out of the fast lane, and specifically, high rents. When I moved out here in Queens 10 years ago this place cost me $200.00 per month. The next lease will be $565.00 per month. My paycheck hasn't risen at that rate. I know going to the backwoods will be a change and after a few hours back there I'll be screaming

for a dirty subway and a derelict or two. But I'll keep counting to ten...and writing.

This letter is just to say that you and Linda (and Brandon, friends and relatives) are invited to come out anytime you want to. For awhile, it will be a bit primitive (despite electric and an indoor outhouse) so you will have to look over that...plus bring your own beer. But come anytime...and bring Linda's sister [Gail] and her husband [Dave Tarpley] (the two who were with you here in '81) whom I'll have to ask about buying a mule, perhaps, instead of a pickup.

Take care of yourselves and am looking forward to seeing y'all. Lord, Lord!

Selah,

Ray

I began to get nice reviews all over the country, even in *The New York Times* and *The Los Angeles Times*. *Nashville* magazine said it was almost flawless. A great review in *The Dallas Morning News*. And on and on. The reviewer from the Atlanta daily paper wrote a smug, condescending, dismissive review that stung, but the paper also ran a cover story on me and the book in its Sunday magazine that was sent to almost a million people. I got wonderful letters of praise from people like Will Campbell (see earlier) and the novelist Nicholas Proffitt. Columbia Pictures turned it down. Hee. I began doing autographings and speeches everywhere. Just about this time, mass-market paperback rights were sold to Ballantine for ten times the advance I got from Norton. The literary world was at my feet.

Alas, those feet were about as elegant as a jazz dancer with one leg shorter than the other. I had gotten a home computer for the first time (as we had at the *Observer*), and it sped up my writing unbelievably. Buoyed with my contract, I finished several novels I'd started and quit in the past few years, and with her consent, I mailed several to Molly. She tried to weed out their narrative lines and to be helpful and honest, but she was far nicer than I deserved.

Fortunately *Heart* sold well, more than fifteen thousand copies in paperback alone. I still to this day have people stop me on the street and tell me they liked "that first novel of yours" best. (Rather like Woody Allen's character in *Stardust Memories*, whose fans like his "earlier, funnier" movies better than his later, more serious ones.) We also sold the novel to Sweden, and in translation it would do very well there. Smart people, the Swedes. And a large-print edition in the United Kingdom. All through 1984 and into 1985, I was busy with *Heart* in one way or another. Only years later did I realize that *Heart* was a true gift to me from the literary gods. If I wanted to publish more than one book, I would have to learn much, *much* more about writing. God save the mark, I would have to start over again.

I finally got to meet James Dickey in the summer of 1985 when Stan Lindberg, editor of *The Georgia Review*, put together a conference at UGA called Roots In Georgia. Dickey was sober and magnificent in his reading, modest and delightful. (Harry Crews was reeling and toasted from the start and left at one point, he told me, to "go get drunk for the faculty." God love Harry's ghost.) After Dickey finished his reading, Linda and I went to the front of the hall to meet him. I wasn't sure what to call him, because the departmental secretary at the University of South Carolina had to call him "Dr. Dickey," even though his doctorates were honorary. (On the other hand, he *did* have a degree in English, Phi Beta Kappa, from Vanderbilt, along with a master's, which was plenty for me.) I told him who I was and thanked him.

"My goodness," he said, shaking his head. "Well my goodness. It's a very special book." I still doubt he ever read it, but I didn't care.

Ray stayed at our house for the three full days of Roots, and after two days I was utterly exhausted. But he loved being an author, and as a panel participant, he wanted to be around writers such as Dickey, Erskine Caldwell, Mary Hood, Terry Kay, Judson Mitcham, Toni Cade Bambara, and Coleman Barks until the last minute. (Ray never in his life learned to drive and so, of course, never had a car.)

In the meantime, I had found myself the author of yet another book to send Molly, a not-bad mystery called *Slow Dance in Autumn*. It had originated when I injured my back again and spent a whole day self-medicating with liquor and writing. The first sentence was this: "Evan Williams Black Label sour mash bourbon whiskey is the best in the world, and I should know." That was me, Phil Williams, talking, but as days passed I morphed into a detective named Hank Prince through a dandy little plot set in Atlanta. I even spent a day on patrol with the Atlanta cops to find out a few facts I needed to know. The hunger for publication knows no shame, but even in retrospect, it's a good little genre book, I think.

The greatest change in my life during 1985 came as a shock to everyone. I decided to leave *The Athens Observer*, where I'd been since 1978. After the failure of going twice a week and of Observer Communications, the blossom had begun to fade from the *Observer's* rose. And the quality of my work there, which had ebbed and flowed, had a wider ebb tide by 1985 than the Righteous Brothers. (If you don't know the reference, look it up. Sorry.) *The Heart of a Distant Forest* had been out for more than a year by then, and nothing was in the works for me as a novelist. The *Observer* could eat a person alive. Just one example will stand for many. One weekend, our reporter Lee Shearer, who worked part time at a small bookstore nearby on weekends, called me and told me I'd better get the hell downtown—someone had just shot a cop at the police station right across the street from our office. I leaped into my car and drove like hell, flashers burning, and pulled up with a theatrical screech in front of the *Observer*, ran up the stairs to the editorial offices and found a camera, loaded it. I then dashed back to the northeast corner of the building and opened the window to see chaos below—ambulances and police cars amid the squawk of walkie-talkies. I leaned far out the second floor window and snapped off the only pictures taken of the wounded police officer being taken out on a gurney. The officer lived. They tracked the shooter down and killed him. And that was my life too often. One day, I had just had enough, and I walked to the Human Resources office on the UGA campus and was startled to see a posting for a science writing job in the College of Agriculture. It would be an eight-to-five job. I would be a writer again instead of an editor. I would have time for my books. It made sense from a hundred different directions. It even paid more and had superb health insurance and retirement benefits. So I applied for the job, went to the interview, and got hired over about twenty-five other applicants. This coincided with Pete taking back over as editor—we exchanged jobs so often at the *Observer* one would need a diary to keep up with it all. And of course he had every right to do it—he was one of the owners. But it was the push I needed to move on.

"I know you all have heard that Pete is taking back over as editor of the *Observer*," I told the writing staff in our weekly editorial meeting. "What you may *not* know is that I am leaving the *Observer*." Stone silence. Even the words sounded odd. I had been around for seven years, since that day Wayne bit me on the neck. After thirteen years, I was out of the newspaper business, and I would never come back. For the next twenty-seven years I would be happily hidden on the University of Georgia campus as a science writer, for which I had a great passion. But I was thirty-five years old by then, and it was time. I had just begun to feel what the years in newspapers had done to my body and mind. I needed peace and quiet, or I'd never write another novel. Unfortunately, it would be another three years before a book of mine saw print.

Pain: the organizing principle of his life. A thing no one else can see or feel or take on faith. Worst are the headaches which began when he was a boy and developed into hideous migraines by the time he was in his teens. Tests: MRI, MRA, CAT scan, X-ray. Medicines: every one made. And finally control, but no more. And his back, torn apart in graduate school. And his right rotator cuff, ripped completely off in a fall when he was in the late fifties. And the big toe of his right foot, jammed savagely against a door-frame. Nothing can be done for it. He guesses most people hide pain, fearful to be culled and cut out from the herd. He is expert in biofeedback, but that is not enough, not nearly so. He has suffered only a fraction of what his mother endured. She did not bring her pain to others. He struggles to be half the person she was.

21

Turning Ritzy at the Ritz

Molly decided to handle *Slow Dance in Autumn* for me. It was an odd, quirky manuscript, but she, being Molly, was ever supportive and kind. (It would later be the only book of mine to be reviewed in *The Washington Post*). By August 1985 as I started a new job, she was already sending it around. That month, Rachel Christmas at Holt turned the book down, and though she liked the plot and my protagonist Hank Prince's dry wit, she was turned off by his excessive drinking. So Molly sent it over to Paul DeAngelis at E.P. Dutton.

> I am delighted to hear about your new job [Molly wrote to me]. I hope you'll continue to be a good spy and find me some low-down biographer who has been working on some highly original manuscript for the last years....

DeAngelis didn't like *Slow Dance*, either. So Molly sent it to Arbor House, which was publishing Elmore Leonard. I had also begun to think again of Peachtree Publishers as a possible outlet. What if we just sent them *Slow Dance*? Molly wasn't terribly interested in a southern publisher yet, and of course at that time she was right. This was her *business*, for heaven's sake, not a hobby. And it didn't make sense that she would make more money from Peachtree than a New York publisher.

That September, I got a great letter from Michelle Rapkin, my editor at Ballantine, who told me that over the summer she'd been walking past a high-end bookstore in New York City called Endicotts. And the paperback edition of *The Heart of a Distant Forest* was in the front window. She went in and there was a whole table with the book for sale. What lovely news. But I was having to scratch hard to find it. I suppose at the time I was just crazy, but in the fall I finished yet another novel, and it was finally one that I felt came together narratively. I called it *All the Western Stars*, and it was about two old men who escape from a nursing home in Georgia and hitchhike to West Texas to be cowboys but wind up in the film business. The title was from "Ulysses" by Tennyson, an old worn-out chestnut for sure, but it was a poem I'd known since boyhood and had a great deal of affection for. The genesis of the novel was actually rather odd. When *Heart* came out, I got asked incessantly at readings and autographings what I was working on next. I didn't want to mention the series of train wrecks I'd inflicted on Molly, so I made up a standard line about two old guys escaping from a nursing home and running off to be cowboys. People always laughed, *always*. One woman actually began *clapping*. The novel is light and amusing, narrated by Jake, a retired steelworker, but it also evolves into a quiet depth with a serious purpose. His friend, Lucas Kraft is a former National Book Award winner in poetry and marginally crazy. But they both desperately want one last adventure. I know, I know. It sounds like a bucket list. I won't point any fingers, but similar movies began to flood out of Hollywood after my book became a hot property at MGM. But I was sanguine enough not to slit my throat or anything. I thought my novel was funny and poignant, narratively interesting, and filled with attractive characters. Molly liked it enough to try and send it out, but almost immediately we ran into trouble. We had given up on *Slow Dance in Autumn*—good book, wrong place in my career. New York wasn't unaware of my first novel, and this was no way to build on the career I'd started with *The Heart of a Distant Forest*, and, for that matter, neither was *Slow Dance in Autumn*. Tom Wallace at Norton liked parts of *Western Stars* but not enough to make an offer. My career was going nowhere, and it wasn't even going nowhere fast. It was stuck in park. I was depressed and didn't know what to do next. In late January 1986, Molly wrote me:

> I did receive your letter of the 2nd and decided to ignore it because I figured you were just feeling more bummed than usual about the publishing business. I am truly sorry that this New York scene has caused you such pain and and aggravation and I don't honestly have much to say by way of its defense.

She was still fighting for me, though, and had sent *All the Western Stars* to Marian Wood at Holt. Derek Johns at Random House had turned the book down without a blink. Molly responded to my incessant hectoring:

I won't forget about Peachtree, I promise—I just want to go to a greater length with New York's version of publishing before I talk to Chuck Perry.

The great Bill Emerson had retired from Peachtree, and Chuck, whom I'd known for years, had taken over as editor awhile back. Chuck was an Athens native who was working at the *Banner-Herald* while I was at the *Daily News* in 1972-73. He'd then gone to the Atlanta papers, and he'd left *them* for Peachtree when the job for an editor came open on Bill Emerson's retirement. Chuck and I weren't close friends, but we certainly knew each other.

Meanwhile, I was learning how to be a science writer and settling into the office of Agricultural Communications in Conner Hall on UGA's South Campus. The job of our office was to work for the State's Agricultural Experiment Stations, a system forever confused with the Cooperative Extension Service. Far from dealing with troubles on the farm or the proper way to prune azaleas (something I'm not demeaning—I love farms and azaleas) I was to be the lead writer, covering the research underway in a huge college filled with very bright scientists in a number of fields touching on agriculture. Working with me would be Helen Fosgate, sharp, funny, young, and extremely intelligent. She was already a solid writer but would develop into a first-rate reporter and magazine editor and spend her entire career at UGA. We also had graphic artists, proofreaders, and other editors whose main job wasn't news. Head of our office was Randall Cofer, a lean, taciturn and suntanned man somewhat older than I was, a man who loved getting outdoors and could often be found with a cigar stuck in the corner of his mouth. In general it was a very pleasant place to be, and I found out that I loved writing stories about science and getting them out to the media.

This is as good a place as any to explain that my job writing about science wasn't a fall-back position or something merely to make money while I wrote novels. I loved it, and I was very good at it. I spent every working day for the next twenty-seven years in laboratories and offices talking to scientists of all kinds about their work and then writing stories that we sent to the national and international media. I had to read and study constantly and with great concentration even to keep up in numerous fields of the physical and biological sciences. I liked writing about science because it was by far the hardest writing job on the University of Georgia campus. I realize some people see such work as public relations, but I never did. In fact, we called it public information, and that is what it was, more than anything. My stories were scientifically solid, well written, and interesting. I'm proud of the thousands of stories I wrote between 1985 and 2011. But in the end, they were ephemera. I never felt as if what I did in that position was a profession. I had no choice but to perform my job (science writing) at the same time as my vocation (novelist, poet, and essayist). I think I did well in both of them, but in the end it was a bargain with the devil that several times threatened to drag me down.

On May 1, 1986, not too long after I'd changed jobs, I went to an awards banquet for the Townsend Prize for Fiction. Given only every other year, it was for the best work of fiction published by a Georgian in the past two years. Publishers must nominate books for the award, and I was pleased that Norton had submitted *The Heart of a Distant Forest*. Ten books were nominated in all, including Charlie Smith's *Canaan, How Far She Went* by the great short story writer Mary Hood, *A World Made of Fire* by Mark Childress, *Dark Thirty* by Terry Kay, and *Cold Sassy Tree* by Olive Ann Burns.

Virtually everyone thought Olive Ann would win. She was almost sixty-two, and her novel, which came out in 1984 like mine, had been selected by the Book of the Month Club and made into a fine TV movie starring Faye Dunaway and Richard Widmark. The book had been inspired by Olive Ann's battle with lymphoma in the not-too-distant past. She and her husband, Atlanta newspaperman Andrew Sparks, were two of the finest people anyone ever met. I loved them both instantly on meeting them during the Roots in Georgia conference in 1985 and again that day at the Ritz-Carlton in the Atlanta neighborhood of Buckhead. I was startled to find that Linda would be taking a day off from school to go with me, as would my parents *and* Linda's. But they all loved my book, and I figured they were just being supportive. In a diary she briefly kept around this time, my mother said that the publication of my book was about the most exciting thing that had ever happened to our family. Nothing that ever happened to me in my career meant more to me than those words. Linda kept asking me what I'd say if I won, and I looked at her like she'd lost her mind. Surely Olive Ann would win. And Charlie Smith's national profile was rising strongly, as was my dear friend Terry Kay's. It turned out that Linda had some inside knowledge that I didn't. Worried that I wouldn't show, the people with the Prize committee had called my old friend Pete McCommons at *The Athens Observer*, not knowing I had changed jobs, and Pete had secretly called Linda. No wonder she was acting nervous. But I was as dense as osmium and expecting nothing. Linda told Pete to tell them I'd be there.

The event that May was certainly ritzy. The people in my office, whom I barely knew yet, were cheering for me. The prize was named after influential *Atlanta Magazine* editor Jim Townsend, who had been mentor to many writers who had gone on to publish books. The luncheon speaker was Pat Conroy, who I only knew by reputation at the time, though I would get to know him better later. His speech was riotous. He'd used the line before, but he defined Southern literature to the huge ballroom crowd this way: *On the night the hogs ate Willie, Mama died when she heard what Daddy did to Sister.* The place was crazy for Pat, who was at the height of his fame, too. Atlanta newspaper woman and author Celestine Sibley had won the award the first year it was given, 1982, and Alice Walker had won it in 1984 for *The Color Purple.* Walker wasn't there, so it fell to Celestine to deliver the news of the latest winner. She said the winning book was a lovely thing, and she wanted to read from its opening lines. My mother was smiling widely, beautifully. And for the first time it began to dawn on me. Celestine began to read the opening of *The Heart of a Distant Forest.* Oh my God in heaven. Aside from the giddiness, I felt sick for Olive Ann. I really believe she was as prepared to win as I was to lose. And I was cheering for her myself.

I stumbled up to the podium to a deafening standing ovation by the literary movers and shakers in Atlanta and from many other places across the South. Celestine handed me a silver tray and a check for $500. I even got a Western Union Mailgram:

> PHIL, ALL OF US AT W W NORTON ARE PROUD AND DELIGHTED TO HEAR THAT YOU ARE THE 1986 WINNER OF THE TOWNSEND PRIZE FOR FICTION. WE RAISE A COLLECTIVE GLASS TO YOU, CHEERS, TOM WALLACE.

A nice, old-fashioned touch, that. While this prize might not be terribly well known nationally, it *had* been won by Alice Walker, and the effect of it was to blast me into a high position among southern writers. The next day my picture and a story about the award appeared on a section front of *The Atlanta Constitution*, somewhat easing the nastiness of their review of my book a year earlier. With the $500, my father, brother Mark, and I bought lumber and designed, built, and wired a writing cabin for me behind our house on Merlin Court west of Athens. When the Atlanta papers came to do a major spread on me following the success of *All the Western Stars* in 1988, the pictures of me would be taken in my cabin. (Though we moved from Merlin Court in 1991, my cabin is still there.)

By that September, though, Molly hadn't been able to sell any of my projects, and I was deeply depressed about any future I had in publishing. She was a great agent, so I had to believe it was my fault. She wrote to me:

> God, Phil. You sound so awful! I'm so sorry I couldn't have sent better news. I don't think anything happened to you after the writing of HEART, except that the publishing houses in New York turned the tables on a lot of good writers....
>
> Please stay in touch. Please don't give up. Please give me at least a chance to read whatever novel you can bring yourself to write.
>
> I'm just sorry it's been so long between books. That's what you are: between books, because you *will* publish again.

If there were a Nobel Prize for literary agents, I would nominate Molly Friedrich in a New York minute. Still, my despair had been over Molly's decision, which she sent to me in a letter on September 8, not to submit *All the Western Stars* anymore. It had been turned down by G.P. Putnam's Sons, St. Martin's, Doubleday, Scribner's, Delacorte, Crown, and Harper and Row. Molly was honest:

> I'm sorry Phil—I just don't want to drag this on further. The practical side of me is winning out.

I knew that I had to leave Molly and find another way into publishing. So, with great reluctance I told her I was going to approach Peachtree on my own and that I wished her well. Nearly three years had passed since the publication of *The Heart of a Distant Forest*. If something was going to happen, I'd have to be my own agent. On September 16, I wrote a letter to Chuck Perry, whose title was executive editor. By then, *The Heart of a Distant Forest* had sold six thousand copies in hardback and nineteen thousand in softcover. I asked if he'd like to see four or five finished novels I had. He wrote me back a couple of weeks later and said "Of course I want to see your work." So I did something quite nutty: I sent four novels at the same time to Chuck: *All the Western Stars, Slow Dance in Autumn,* a new novel called *The Song of Daniel,* and my orphan postmodern novel, *The Inner Kingdom.* Chuck told me he'd read them in a month and get back to me. I don't think Superman on speed could have read all those novels in a month and done anything else.

The Song of Daniel was the new kid on the block. I have always been interested in innocence and experience, since my father loved British poet William Blake's *Songs,* and I enjoyed hearing him read them aloud when I was a kid. Not long after my Uncle Sambo (Vincent Astor Williams) died tragically young in 1958, my father adapted Blake's poem "The Lamb" into a transcendently beautiful song for piano and voice. I also love cemeteries for their peace and tranquility. So I created a narrative about a mentally challenged young man, who works in the very real Oconee Hill Cemetery in Athens, and his relationship with a cynical English professor at the University of Georgia, which adjoins the cemetery. It's a very quiet book that comes uncomfortably close to sentimentality in a couple of places. It also throws into the mix a Georgia mountain poet based on a real ballad-poet and novelist named Byron Herbert Reece. Sick (with tuberculosis) and despairing, Reece had shot and killed himself in 1958 a few months before my uncle died. It was a book that eventually sold well and touched a great many people, though I now consider it a minor novel. By the time I got to sending the four manuscripts to Chuck, a career as a freelance writer that I had worked hard to cultivate crashed and burned, too. I took an assignment for *Southern* magazine, now long gone. It was a lifestyle magazine but also had some pretenses to serious journalism, and the editor wanted me to write a story about the alleged lifelong underground influence of the Kappa Alpha fraternity on those who belonged to it in college. Taking time off from work (stupidly) I interviewed dozens of people, including John F. Kennedy's Secretary of State Dean Rusk, who was a law professor in those years at UGA. Rusk had been a KA, and well remembered its fondness for the Old South and things related to the Confederacy. (All of which sickened me.) I made a million calls, worked late into the night, and found there was no underground railroad for old KAs. Or at least not one I could find in those pre-Internet days. I wrote a long piece anyway, and the editor turned it down flat, paying me a kill fee and saying that the rejection in no way affected his desire to work with me. It affected my desire to work with him, though. We never spoke again. So by the time I sent the four novels to Chuck in January 1987, I was scratchy, to say the least. Losing Molly had been stupid of me. It was good for her, though, because she was soon representing more clients that actually made a living for her. I really didn't know what to expect from Chuck. I didn't know him very well, and I knew next to nothing about Peachtree Publishers except that they weren't in New York.

This might be a good place to puncture a myth. Young writers always seem to believe that the only goal in life is to be published in New York City. And in a sense, they're right. It *is* the red hot center of the publishing world and has been since just after World War II. But in a greater sense, they're flat wrong. I have published books with major New York houses (a lot of them), smaller regional operations, and even two different university presses. And being with a New York press isn't always better—not in terms of the books you sell or the money you make, the publicity you gain, or the happiness you find. I didn't know it, but I was about to leap headlong into the big leagues through a small publishing house in Atlanta, Georgia.

Chuck Perry was a dark-haired man with a mustache (I had one, too—seems like most men in the country did in those days). He spoke quickly, had a wicked sense of humor, and knew books. I was genuinely glad to see him when we met at the History Village restaurant (and hotel complex) in downtown Athens on Friday, March 6, 1987. I kept telling myself that he must be willing to publish at least one of the books, or he wouldn't have set up the meeting. He seemed relaxed and cheerful. I was about one step from jumping off the Chrysler Building.

"I think you're going to write a lot of very good books in the coming years," he said when we finally got shed of the small talk. "And Peachtree wants to publish them." I tried to hide the complete ecstasy I felt, and I am sure I failed. "And we're ready to make you an offer on three of these here today." I slid my chair back and tried to speak. Nothing came out. I sipped my water and wondered how Ernest would handle this situation with Max at the Algonquin.

"I see," I said finally. *Idiot.*

Since I couldn't talk, at least for a time, Chuck did. They wanted *All the Western Stars, Slow Dance in Autumn*, and *The Song of Daniel*. As I suspected, my orphan postmodern novel *The Inner Kingdom* would remain lost and wandering. It was simply too strange and uncommercial for Peachtree. It had been turned down by Indiana University Press and LSU in 1984, and in 1985, I tried hard to locate an editor who might be open to that kind of fiction and found Gerald Howard at Viking Penguin. He had worked his way up at that venerable house and was there when Thomas Pynchon's great novel *Gravity's Rainbow* was published. The fact that Howard agreed to read it (this was in February 1985, and I did it with Molly's permission) startled me. I expected little, and I only got a little more. He told me I had a lot of talent and that the characters were funny and tragic at the same time, but he thought it was talent gone unchecked. That was a fair assessment, but since *The Inner Kingdom* was only a third of the book I fully intended to write, he couldn't see the whole arc of my story. As Kurt Vonnegut would have said, So it goes. I never forgot Howard's kindness, though.

The publishing schedule Chuck and I agreed on was no doubt a mistake for everyone involved, and to this day I can't say I'm sure why we did it. Peachtree would publish all three novels in an eighteen-month span, starting in the spring of 1988 with *All the Western Stars. Slow Dance in Autumn* would come out (naturally) in the fall of that year, and *The Song of Daniel* in the spring of 1989. The advance for *All the Western Stars* would be a very good $4,000 (for a small house in Atlanta and for someone with my small and spotty track record). The largest advance Peachtree had ever paid for fiction was $5,000, and I wanted to undershoot that a bit. I promised in a March 9 letter that I'd hold up my end of the deal:

> I'll do everything in my power to help you sell books. I'll do autographings, book clubs, bar mitzvahs, and Tupperware parties if it will sell the books. I did that as much as I could for my first book, but I promise you I'll work as hard as I can to make sure the books sell.

Chuck also mentioned that he knew of another possible project that might interest me.

"I hope it doesn't involve the KAs," I said. He looked at me like I *should* jump off the Chrysler Building. I told him what had happened with *Southern* magazine, and he laughed. As it turned out, it involved country music. A well-known country singer and songwriter named Whisperin' Bill Anderson was already working with Chuck on his autobiography, and Bill was also looking for a writer to help him develop a proposed network television drama set in Nashville and about the country music industry. Bill had some general outlines of what he wanted do, but he needed a professional writer to help. I was young and hungry, and Chuck knew it. Would I be interested in working with Bill on spec? Yep.

A few weeks later on April 23 I signed a contract for *All the Western Stars* and *Slow Dance in Autumn*. I walked out of that meeting dazzled and stunned. I had no idea that things were changing rapidly at Peachtree and that soon Chuck would be gone. I got back to the office and told Helen Fosgate I'd just sold three books, and soon enough all the others in the office were stopping by my office with congratulations and genuine happiness. That night, when I told Linda, she was happy that I wasn't going to jump off the Chrysler Building. I don't think Chuck or I stopped to think of the work involved in publishing three of my books in eighteen months. Or whether it was good for me or Peachtree. *The Heart of a Distant Forest* had come out in 1984, and time was passing. I was thirty-seven when I met with Chuck, and I could see my career drifting away. I knew too many one-hit wonders and was determined not to be one of them.

Brandon was by this time taking cello lessons and becoming quite good. Since I played the piano, when his recital took place on January 30, 1987, I accompanied him. This was in the classy UGA Chapel, and I'm sure the moment meant more to me than to Brandon. He was a very good cellist, but like me he loved the woods and outdoors, and he would grow to be a first-rate navigator of the natural world.

While Chuck was the editor-in-chief at Peachtree, the publisher (and owner) was a tall, genial man named Wayne Elliott. His mother had actually founded the house some years before, and Wayne was always kind to me. The following spring, he would call me with news that would, finally, put my family on sound financial footing. But I couldn't have guessed it then. My entire *life* was still more or less on spec. (That's the film industry term for a project done "on speculation" and with no guarantee of any profit.)

Whisperin' Bill Anderson and I finally introduced ourselves to each other in May of that year. Chuck had told him of my interest, and we talked on the phone, and I wrote him one of my endless letters. Bill was still a young forty-nine and had had an astounding seven number-ones on the country charts, the most recent one in 1976. Almost thirty more of his singles reached the Top Ten. His songs were recorded by everyone, and in 2001 he would be elected to the Country Music Hall of Fame. As you may know, he was called Whisperin' Bill because of his soft voice and frequent use of spoken-word passages in his songs. As it turned out, Bill's interest in working together coincided with a rising interest of my own in country music. I still loved (and knew) classical music best and wanted to write my own symphonies, but to relax, Willie Nelson was my man.

Bill first wrote me on May 4:

> Several years ago, I came up with an idea for a television soap opera based on the City of Nashville. At the time, I was working part-time on an ABC drama called "One Life to Live," and I got to know a lot of people involved in that end of the business at the network level. I was able to interest one of the top executives there in my concept but by the time we were able to get it off paper and on to videotape, the soap opera concept in television...was on the wane. The networks turned a deaf ear toward us and I did nothing for a long while.
>
> A few months ago, some of the same people who had been interested in the idea for a television series approached me about revising my idea...[This] is very much alive and I think within the next six to eight months there will be a big-budget pilot done on the concept.

It turns out the television people had suggested that one way to kindle interest in the project would be for someone to write a novel about it—a sort of reverse novelization. I was also interested in writing scripts, and Bill held out that as a possibility, too. (The advance and royalties on *The Heart of a Distant Forest* had long ago been spent on bills, and we were almost back to where we started. We needed the money.) He also seemed like a really nice guy. Maybe this could lead somewhere. While Chuck Perry and I worked on the manuscript of *All the Western Stars*, Bill and I decided we needed to meet, so on July 9, Linda, Brandon, and I drove north to Nashville. We both liked Bill immediately. An extremely talented, big-hearted man with an unguarded laugh, he had ambition exploding in about a hundred directions at once, something I understood all too well. His son Jamey was about Brandon's age, too, so they got to hang out when we visited Bill and his then-wife Becky. More than anything, I needed to know more about the music business in Nashville, so late one morning Bill and I started out at Tootsie's Orchid Lounge in downtown Nashville behind the Ryman Auditorium. This was the legendary honky tonk bar where everyone but God had played over the years. Willie Nelson (see my *Observer* years) got his first songwriting gig after singing in Tootsie's, according to an enthusiastic article in Wikipedia. Even before we got inside, a wild-eyed man, downtown looking for country music, saw us and came shouting over.

"My God! My God!" he cried "It's Whisperin' Bill Anderson!" He pawed at Bill a bit as we went inside. It was around ten, and a few serious drinkers were getting their shaking hands calmed down for the day, living the troubled life of a country song. The house band broke into one of Bill's songs, and the orchid loungers raised a glass. We went all over town after that, meeting producers and session musicians.

In one of the most eerie moments of my life, he managed to get us in the old Ryman Auditorium. The Mother Church of Country Music, where Hank Williams (the real one, not his unfortunate son) once sang alongside every other star who ever strapped on glitter-boots, was in sad shape in those days. The Grand Ole Opry had moved to Opryland, and now the Ryman was falling apart, abandoned. No one knew quite what to do with her. She was like a nerdy girl with cat-eyed glasses at the high school prom, left alone and behind. Bill took us up on stage, and we stood right where Hank had sung. The place was a tomb, silent and sorrowful. A man who couldn't be inspired there, then, didn't have a pulse. It was happier over at the Nashville Network, and we were wandering down some hall when we ran into country singer Vern Gosdin. Vern was fifty-two by then, and as someone once said, the only three things he could do were sing, write songs, and work on the tour bus. He had started in the business as a young man and then quit to run a glass company in Atlanta when things went bad. But he was in the midst of a major comeback, and I loved his voice. The following year, he would join the ranks of country immortals with one of the greatest crying-in-your-beer songs ever recorded, "Chiseled in Stone." Its directness and simplicity and its understanding of the deep grief of a person just trying to get by make it one of the necessary bar stools in country music. (The greatest country song, and one that cannot be equaled, much less bettered, is "He Stopped Loving Her Today" by George Jones.)

"Vern Gosdin," Bill said, laughing and shaking hands. We were in a dimly lit corridor just outside a studio auditorium that was empty at the moment.

"Bill Anderson," Vern said, also laughing.

"Vern, I'd like you to meet a fan from Athens, Georgia, Philip Lee Williams. Phil and I are working on a project together, and he's in town for that. I'm showing him Music City." I shook hands with Vern.

"Athens, Georgia," he said, thinking and looking up. "Athens, Georgia. I got married at a little town outside Athens, Georgia, one time."

"Really," I said. "What was the name of the town?"

"*Hell*, son," he said, leaning over and grinning conspiratorially. "I don't even remember the name of the *wife*." Now *that* was a country song.

That night, we went to the Grand Ole Opry, and Bill arranged for us to hang around backstage, where we met and talked to some of the stars of that era along with singers whose heyday had been decades in the past. (Brandon, who was nine, was at Bill's house with Jamey and Becky and a babysitter.) Bill even arranged for us to sit on stage during the show, which was a lovely touch. The curtains were still drawn when I looked up and saw Bill standing, oh my God, next to Roy Acuff. Roy Acuff! They stood talking in the wings, just offstage, and Mr. Acuff had his fiddle in one hand and looked like a man precisely where he felt most comfortable. He was eighty-three years old at the time and fresh as a spring flower, bouncing on his toes. The fourth person to be inducted into the Country Music Hall of Fame (after Hank, Jimmie Rodgers, and Fred Rose, who had all passed away before they were inducted), to say he was legendary in Nashville is to somehow mock the word *legendary*. He had co-founded Acuff-Rose Music, which had signed Hank Williams, Roy Orbison, the Everly Brothers, and dozens more. Bill caught my eye. He was standing right behind Mr. Acuff and pointing down at his head.

"Do you want to meet him?" Bill mouthed. Before he finished the sentence, Linda and I were halfway out of our seats. My eyes began to water. I was nodding so hard it was a wonder my head didn't fall off. We dashed down from the stage seating area and got to Bill and Mr. Acuff. I don't really remember what we talked about—mortals kneeling before Mount Olympus probably all suffer from amnesia. But I do remember shaking his hand, looking closely at his fiddle, and wondering what my grandfather would have thought. Arthur Williams, who parlor-fiddled with his friends and died in 1935, fifteen years before I was born, surely would have been impressed with how far his grandson had come. Bill was emceeing the show that night, and it was on the radio as well as before a packed house, and when it came time to wrap things up, he had a custom of saying goodnight to his son over the airwaves. This night, though, he ended the show by saying, "Goodnight, Jaybird! Goodnight, Brandon!"

Back home in Athens, my excitement began to grow both over *All the Western Stars* and my project with Bill. I was working madly on a full treatment for Bill's story—the characters and much of the plot lines were his, but my job was to write it all. I was also working on rewrites of the novel and enjoying my family. And oh yeah, there was that full-time job thing. Bill wrote me in early August saying he'd gotten the first-draft treatment I'd sent up. He'd issued a standing invitation for me to go on tour with his band, too. He also dealt with some of the business issues between us which were, to say the least, foggy. The idea by that point was that I would write a novel based on Bill's ideas, that we would try to publish it (under a pen name), and that we would then use that as leverage with network TV in pitching a series set around the country music industry in Nashville. Maybe it wasn't the best way to go about things, but it was an idea anyway. The only real problem was that we didn't really have a central business plan or anyone to carry it out. I didn't even have an agent at the time, and letting Bill's business people handle things wasn't exactly right, either. For a time, we thought Chuck Perry might somehow help us through Peachtree, since he'd brought Bill and me together. But then it started to become clear that there was only one person to coordinate our project.

I was about to leave the eye of a hurricane and get walloped by the winds. I was about to meet Harvey Klinger.

The mountains when he first moves to Clayton: deep June green, sudden, gorgeous at sunset, more beautiful at dawn. He loves the shape of them, the way sound shudders down to silence in respect. Outside Aspen in mid-July, driving up one of the fourteeners, snow on the ground, an icy breath of amazement. Scargo Tower in a duny high spot on Cape Cod. But mostly Rabun Gap, where his mother went to junior college in the early forties, a place of such transfixing beauty that the words alone take him there. He is not who he is without mountains. Circumstance placed him seven hundred feet above sea level, not atop a Mahlerian monument in Colorado. He thinks: This is what was given to me. I take it, raise it high enough to be my own.

My mother's parents, Lillie and Lee Sisk

My father in uniform, 1943.

My mother looking like a movie star, late 1930s.

My parents on their wedding day, November 17, 1945, in San Francisco. Daddy had been mustered out of service, but Mother was still in the WAVES. Photo taken on request by a passerby.

297 South Hull Street, Athens, Ga., where my parents moved into a room to attend the University of Georgia in 1946. Demolished decades ago.

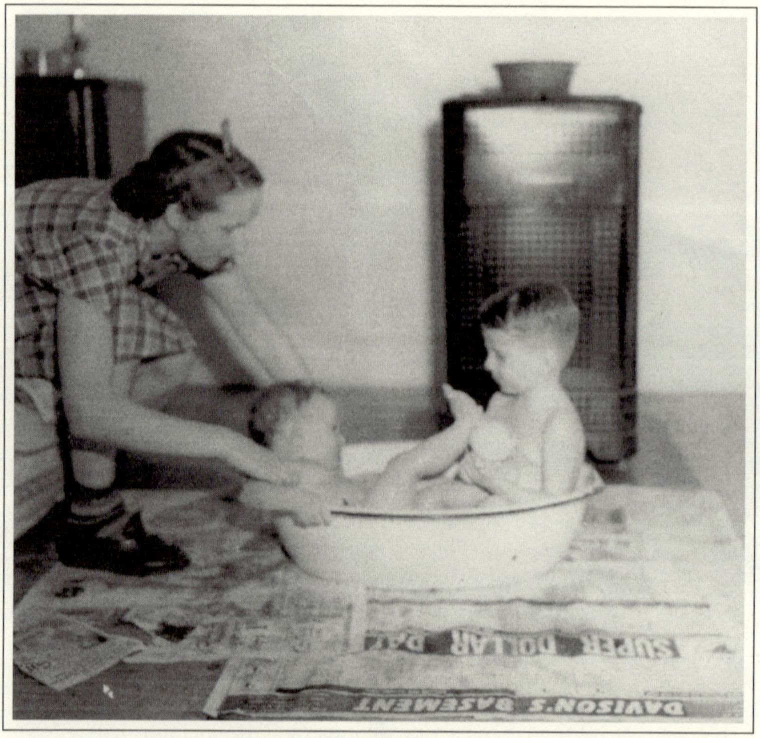

Mother bathing Mark and me in 1950.

Mark (R) and me on Christmas morning, 1955.

Linda as a toddler by the fountain on the Boston Common, about 1953.

House on the Old Buckhead Road outside Madison, Ga., where I grew up in the 1950s. Photo taken years later when the house was in disrepair.

Mother, Mark (L), and me with a case of the giggles.

My third grade picture. That's me on the far left in the back row next to Mrs. Frances Biggers, one of my favorite teachers.

Mark, Laura Jane, and me, fall, 1959.

American Legion Little League team in Madison, about 1961. I am in the back row, sixth from the left. Our coach, just off my right shoulder, was named Oscar Hanson and was a Marine hero on Iwo Jima.

Me in 1964, about the time I decided to become a composer.

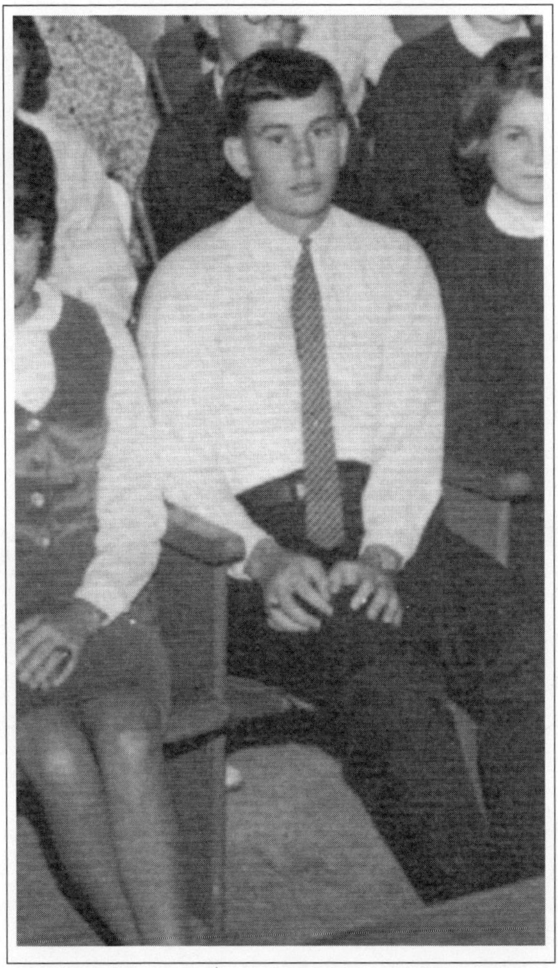

From my senior annual, a picture of me as part of the Student Council.

Buster Hudson (L) and his brother and my good friend Edward Hudson, with the remains of a tarpon bit in half by a shark that almost caught me. Off Key Largo, summer, 1970.

Linda sitting on the hearth at her parents' house in 1970, showing the attitude that made me fall for her at UGA.

Cover of my first book, the self-published volume of poetry, *New Seeds.*

I took this picture of Linda in the trailer she and her roommate Kathy shared on the south side of Athens during our college years.

Linda pretending to catch a fish on a trip we took the the north Georgia mountains after we started dating. That fishing pole is a stick.

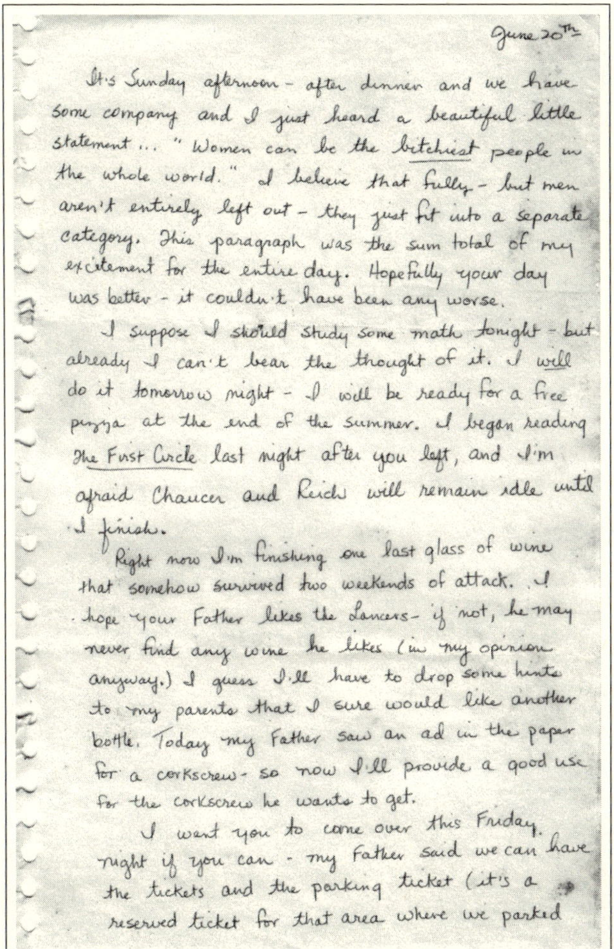

June 20th

It's Sunday afternoon - after dinner and we have some company and I just heard a beautiful little statement ... "Women can be the *bitchiest* people in the whole world." I believe that fully - but men aren't entirely left out - they just fit into a separate category. This paragraph was the sum total of my excitement for the entire day. Hopefully your day was better - it couldn't have been any worse.

I suppose I should study some math tonight - but already I can't bear the thought of it. I *will* do it tomorrow night - I will be ready for a free pizza at the end of the summer. I began reading *The First Circle* last night after you left, and I'm afraid Chaucer and Reich will remain idle until I finish.

Right now I'm finishing one last glass of wine that somehow survived two weekends of attack. I hope your Father likes the Lancers - if not, he may never find any wine he likes (in my opinion anyway.) I guess I'll have to drop some hints to my parents that I sure would like another bottle. Today my Father saw an ad in the paper for a corkscrew - so now I'll provide a good use for the corkscrew he wants to get.

I want you to come over this Friday night if you can - my Father said we can have the tickets and the parking ticket (it's a reserved ticket for that area where we parked

Page of a letter from Linda to me. Summer, 1971.

Newly married, coming out of Central Congregational Church in Atlanta on September 30, 1972.

In graduate school with animals and really long hair. In our basement apartment in the Athens neighborhood called Five Points.

By the time I was a senior in college, I was something of a hippie.

Visiting friends in Kentucky. I grew my first mustache as my political views began to change strongly.

During my years as editor of *The Athens Observer.*

The wonderful Molly Friedrich, my first literary agent. We were both young when we worked together. She's gone on to represent Pulitzer winners and bestsellers. *(Photo by Brandon Shulman)*

Sitting in a hay barn at the UGA dairy about the time *All the Western Stars* came out. *(Photo by Helen Fosgate)*

Cover of my breakout novel, which was published in 1988.

Country star Bill Anderson with whom I had a project in the late 1980s.
(Photo by Dennis Carney)

On the set of *Driving Miss Daisy:* famed producer Richard Zanuck, me, and Dick's assistant, Judy Schefke. *(Photo by Sam Emerson, courtesy of Lili Zanuck)*

Linda, me, and our dear friend Raymond Andrews. His suicide was one of the hardest things that ever happened to us.

Me about the time the movie of *All the Western Stars* crashed and burned. This was on stage at the Madison-Morgan Cultural Center in Madison, Ga.

Then-Governor Joe Frank Haris of Georgia presents me with a plaque as Georgia Author of the Year in Fiction in the fall of 1990.

Cover of *Coup de Chaud,* the French translation of my novel *Final Heat.*

My beautiful mother in later life, always ready to laugh.

Linda and Megan as a little girl having fun at the beach.

Megan's graduation picture from Oconee County High School in Watkinsville, Ga., in the spring of 2009.

Our son Brandon and daughter Mollie. We love spending time with Mollie and her wonderful brothers Caleb and Elliott.

Part of Philip Juras's gorgeous painting of the Keowee Valley in South Carolina graced the cover of my book-length poem, *The Flower Seeker: An Epic Poem of William Bartram.*

Laura Jane and our father in the dining room of his house in Madison, some time after our mother passed away. That's her picture in the background on the piano. She will always be a part of us.

Mark's portrait from the website of the Department of Anthropology at the University of Georgia

One of my favorite pictures from my life. This was taken about 1955 in the backyard of our house on the Old Buckhead Road outside Madison, Ga. I have my arm around the neck of our dog, Flipsy, and Mark is holding our cat, Gym.

22

Breakout at Age Thirty-Eight

I don't precisely remember the first time I talked to Harvey, another Manhattan literary agent, on the phone. But soon enough I knew the sound of his voice—when he could slow it down enough for me to understand it. He was a walking fireball of verbs, nouns, and pure energy. He ate rubes like me for breakfast. He was sarcastic and funny, a man who could see plot failures or character weaknesses in novels almost before he read them. And, as I was to find out, he was one *hell* of a fine literary agent. We argued a lot in the ensuing years, but I couldn't in a hundred years repay half of what the man did for me.

The way Harvey Klinger got into the middle of all this was that he represented Peachtree's entire list, handling reprint rights, overseeing film and foreign rights, and generally keeping their name in the middle of all-things Manhattan. Thus Harvey would shortly get a copy of *All the Western Stars* and send it to his West Coast sub-agent, Bob Bookman at Creative Artists Agency, to try and sell film rights. And Harvey had strong contacts in Europe and Asia, too, so there was a hope for foreign rights. I couldn't know it then, but when I finally left Peachtree four years later, Harvey would for a time become my own personal literary agent as well. The fact that Harvey would handle the whole project with Bill Anderson put me in a rather odd position. Nominally, I wouldn't have had any contact with Peachtree's sub-rights agent, but as always seems to be the case, something was going on in the background at Peachtree. I didn't know it, of course, but Cox Commucations, which owns the Atlanta daily papers, had decided to get into the burgeoning book publishing business, too. And they'd decided to hire Chuck Perry as their editor in chief, taking him back after he'd been at Peachtree a few years. But this wouldn't unfurl until early in 1988. And after Chuck left, Peachtree would hire a new editor named Margaret

Quinlin, and she would become my champion and dear friend. Margaret is a great human being, one of the best I ever met, and she did more for me than I ever deserved. But that transition was still a bit down the road.

By that fall of 1987, I was working on a new novel, editing and rewriting *All the Western Stars,* and talking constantly with Harvey, who had gotten into the middle of things when I asked him for ideas about the plot Bill and I were working on so far. I had never met anyone like Harvey. He spoke faster than my mind could process his words, and while I worked hard and was not unsophisticated about New York publishing, we might have been talking in different languages. He wanted Bill to work on a large-scale canvas with dozens of characters. I wanted to focus on a single strong lead with a good supporting cast. And the more I talked to Harvey and Bill, the larger the project became. I started with the idea that I could write the novel in six to nine months, get to know the country music business, hang out with Bill Anderson and others in Music City, and in general have a good time. Knowing Bill had been a joy. But the book seemed out of control by the middle of October. I wrote a letter to Bill on October 12 more or less pulling out of the project, but I couldn't force myself to mail it. We both knew it was in a rut, though, and we both had huge commitments otherwise.

Still, I had given my word to Bill and to Chuck, and I could see no way to back out, even with *All the Western Stars* coming out in a few months. So I took Harvey's advice the best I could and rewrote and rewrote until I had a couple of hundred pages of the spec Nashville novel and a tight outline of the rest of it. It wasn't what I thought it could be, but we had enough pages to try and move forward. By the end of 1987, I sent Bill what I'd written so far, and he generally liked it and said he thought we were off to "a heckuva start!"

By February 1988, I was beginning to feel a growing excitement over *All the Western Stars*. Every time I spoke with anyone at Peachtree, it was clear they thought this would be my breakout book. Harvey had loved it. In fact every one who'd read it so far had loved it. Bill and I had begun to talk about clarifying our relationship legally—just who was doing what in the project was a bit murky. Bill suggested we work with his attorney-friend Dean Booth, who was with Kilpatrick & Cody, a top firm in Atlanta, but things never got that far for us. In the meantime, inspired by my trip and the strong place country music had in the popular culture in those days, I decided *I* wanted to get in on things. So my brother Mark and I drove to a guitar store in Atlanta and bought me a Peavy T-60 guitar and amp. The Peavy is a solid body guitar with a sweet sound, and it weighed about eighteen pounds, but it was in my price range, and I loved it. Also, Mark was a seasoned guitarist and bandsman by then, and he thought it would be right for me. I also began to write songs and was even stupid enough to show some of my lyrics to Bill Anderson. He told me I had some good ideas, but he couldn't bring himself to actually lie. I *did* have a lot of musical talent, and I knew it. Just not for writing country songs. I had lived the wrong life for it. I had been raised on Beethoven and Toscanini. Still, I loved much of the country music coming out in the early 1980s, and I had known bluegrass since childhood. By early in the year, Harvey had begun to send out the spec pages of what we were calling *A Death in the Country*, but no one was interested. It was promptly rejected by eleven publishers. Only Harvey Ginsberg, vice-president and senior editor at William Morrow, had any real interest, and he thought it would have to be completely rewritten before he'd even seriously consider it again. Months of work seemed to be swirling down the proverbial drain. And neither Bill nor I had made one cent from the project.

By April, as *Western Stars* was set to come out, I wrote Bill more or less withdrawing from our project. My tone must have been dark, since at the time things seemed to be falling apart with Peachtree. Bill, wise and filled with perspective of a man thirteen years my senior, wrote me:

> I certainly understand your not wanting to jump back into this project again right now and I wouldn't try to push you in that direction for anything in the world. I know you've got another career apart from being co-writer with me and you've got things to write other than murder mysteries dreamed up by some hillbilly singer. [Bill had graduated from college and was one of the most intelligent men and sharpest business minds in Nashville.]
>
> At the same time...friend to friend...I want to tell you this. The tone of your letter and the tone of your voice the last time we talked sounds a bit angry and a bit bitter. Take it from an ole fogey that's been around a few more years than you have: There's no reason to be angry *or* bitter....

> You're still a great writer...and I like to think you and I formed a friendship out of this that will last beyond anything we might have composed together.

In the meantime, Chuck Perry dropped his bombshell. He would be leaving to become executive editor at the new Longstreet Press, also located in Atlanta. And he wanted me to go with him. Even though I'd signed contracts for two books with Peachtree, I had a sense that great things might be aborning at Longstreet, so I decided to break my contract with Peachtree and its president Wayne Elliott. It was the single stupidest mistake I made in my entire literary career. I wrote Wayne and told him, and he called me up, extremely unhappy with me, as he had every right to be. But as I pointed out to him, I had a book coming out shortly with Peachtree and, by then, three more in the pipe, and *he* didn't have an editor. While granting that point, he talked to me at length about doing the right thing. I would be breaching a legal contract, but I felt I had good cause, and I doubted Wayne really wanted to sue me. Still, by the time I hung up, I felt absolutely sick to my stomach.

What *was* the right thing to do? I *knew* what it was. It was to fulfill my promise to Peachtree. I often wonder what might have happened if I'd followed Chuck to Longstreet, but I knew that day I couldn't. (As of this writing, Longstreet is long out of business, and Peachtree is still humming along.) So I called Wayne back, apologized, and told him I'd stay and see who he hired as editor. He was relieved. And it was a good thing I did. A cannon was about to fire, and I was in the barrel, about to be lauched from Atlanta to New York and then on to California.

In early spring, *All the Western Stars* hit the pre-pubs—the trade magazines that publish reviews of books before they actually come out. And a review in what was in those days the bible of the industry, *Publishers Weekly*, was my first flat-out rave. My novel, *PW* said, had "a heart as wide as a sky full of stars." My phone began ringing almost immediately. I've often wondered how different my career track might have been if the Internet had existed in those days. As it was, the phone and the U.S. Mail were the only ways to contact someone.

In late February, the *Atlanta Journal-Constitution* magazine had decided to do another cover story on me, this one a feature by my friend Don

O'Briant, along with a lengthy excerpt from the novel. When that came out, my life began to spin cheerfully out of control. Requests for me to speak and do autographings poured in. Reviews began to appear across the country, almost all of them strongly positive. Harvey Klinger, meanwhile, was working in New York on movie and foreign rights. It may seem odd, but I didn't have a clue what was going on with that, because Harvey was *Peachtree's* agent at that point, not mine. I had, with full knowledge of what I was doing, given Peachtree a cut of any movie sales I made on *Western Stars*, because I knew Harvey would be handling the sale. And by God, he *was* good. Wayne let me know, in a few cryptic calls, that there was already huge interest in my book from Hollywood. But I didn't know how huge for a while longer. In short order, Harvey sold mass-market paperback rights to Ballantine for $25,000. For the first time in my life, I was starting to earn my keep as a writer. (I only got half that, minus agent's fees, but it was still a lot of money when you had been essentially broke your whole life. Half went to Peachtree, and I was happy for them.) Linda, Brandon, and I were still living in that tiny modified A-frame on Merlin Court, though we were about to add a room, since interest rates had plummeted. Harvey sold rights for a German translation to the publisher Bastei Lubbe. A woman named Sonja Schleicher would translate it—my second book in Europe. Without consulting me, Bastei Lubbe changed the title to *Das Letzte Abenteuer: Zwei Männer auf grossen Treck* (*The Last Adventure: Two Men on a Long Hike*). I got a huge laugh out of that. In between readings and interviews and work and family, I had begun to sense something big about to break. Harvey never called me because he wasn't supposed to. But when we did talk about my project with Bill Anderson, Harvey dropped enough vague clues to make me wonder.

Finally, on May 10, I came back to my office in Conner Hall to find a phone message slip: Wayne Elliott had contacted me at 11:25, a few minutes before, and he wanted me to call him right back. My hands literally trembled as I punched up Peachtree's number. When I got Wayne on the phone, he said my name in greeting, but it came out oddly, almost weak or excited beyond words. I closed my eyes.

"We have our movie deal on *All the Western Stars*," he said. *That* much I understood. The world suddenly seemed very different to me.

"Wayne!" I shouted.

"It's Sam Brown for MGM, 25 against 250, plus two-and-half percent of the net profits," he said, reading from his notes. I suddenly felt completely confused. I *thought* he'd said *Sam Brown* but wasn't sure, and I had no idea what "25 against 250" meant.

"And this Sam Brown is…."

"No, *Zanuck-Brown,*" he said slowly. "Richard Zanuck and David Brown. Their production deal is with MGM." Oh, *that* Zanuck-Brown. As in the producers for *The Sting*. For *Jaws*. And most recently, for *Cocoon* (directed by Ron Howard, with whom I would later have a business deal). Holy mother of *God*. I suddenly remembered nearly being eaten by a large shark off Key Largo and allowed myself a wry smile at the pleasure of coincidence.

"And that 25 against 250 thing…." Wayne shuffled some papers and took a deep breath.

"It's $25,000 for a one year option," he said, still excited. "And if they make the movie, we get $250,000. Plus two-and-a-half percent of the net profits. And Zanuck-Brown have their production deal with MGM. So the contracts you will get will be with them."

"Son of a *bitch,*" I said. "Wayne, man, you wouldn't, you wouldn't, I mean, you wouldn't…."

"Kid you?"

"Um."

"No, no," he said, laughing. I heard a commotion in the background at Peachtree's Atlanta office. "I just got off the phone with Harvey. It's true. It's real, Phil. Congratulations to you and to us. I couldn't be happier."

And he couldn't have been. Wayne was such an easy, quiet man, and to hear his voice so filled with pleasure gave me a jolt of the deepest joy. I had no idea then that "net profits" was an accounting joke in Hollywood, that no film had ever, by Tinseltown's calculations, *ever* reached net profits. So that in essence was two-and-half percent of nothing. But I couldn't have cared less. Selling a book to W.W. Norton and winning the Townsend Prize for Fiction were nice, as was being translated into Swedish. Getting great advance reviews on *All the Western Stars* and terrific ones after it was published? Marvelous. But selling the film rights on my book to Metro-Fricking-Goldwyn-*Mayer*? Beyond comprehension.

MGM: *The Wizard of Oz, Singin' in the Rain, An American in Paris, Bad Day at Black Rock* (one of the films Linda and I have watched a thousand times), *Lust for Life, Friendly Persuasion, Gigi, Cat on a Hot Tin Roof, Ben-Hur,* and even the movie that made me want to be a writer, *Dr. Zhivago*. By 1988, of course, MGM only cast a thin shadow; its glory days were long gone. And they would only distribute what would be a Zanuck-Brown production. But that kind of thing had been done before. In 1939, MGM distributed a film produced by Selznick International Pictures called *Gone with the Wind*.

I asked Wayne if I could call Harvey and talk to him, since we had already been working together on the project with Bill Anderson, and Wayne said sure, it would be fine. He also said that we needed to meet, and soon, about future book contracts. He would do it any way I wanted—a series of contracts or maybe a multi-book deal. He was ready to work on it. And I didn't even have a literary agent. Maybe, I thought, I didn't need one, though. Why give fifteen percent to an agent for a deal I'd made myself? After I hung up with Wayne, I called Linda and got her out of class. Linda may have thought I'd taken the day off and gotten drunk at a bar in Athens. Then I called my mother. She was thrilled, as was my father. Laura Jane, who knew and loved films as much as I did, was delighted. Mark even raised a glass or two.

Then I called the man himself, Harvey Klinger. If our work on *A Death in the Country* had been difficult, there weren't two sides here. Harvey and Bob Bookman at CAA had done a magnificent job, and frankly if I'd have been in New York I might have kissed Harvey on the lips. Good thing I was in Georgia. I got him on the phone, and he was still humming with cheerful energy. Closing a major deal to Harvey is almost more fun (but not quite) than making money. And no one was better at the art of the deal than he was. The promise of financial security (after being poor so long) and being in the major leagues left me spinning.

"All along, Zanuck-Brown was the number-one choice because of *Cocoon*," he said, referring to the 1985 film that starred Jessica Tandy, Hume Cronyn, Don Ameche, Wilford Brimley, Maureen Stapleton, and many more. That wonderful film was about a group of old people who find the secret to eternal life and health and who have to choose whether to take it or not. Dick Zanuck's success with *Cocoon* made him more than ripe for another story about old guys. A number of companies wanted *All the Western Stars*, it turned out, and some of them wanted it badly. But Harvey's eye (and that of Bob Bookman for CAA who was actually working on the deal in Hollywood) never wavered from Zanuck-Brown. They had already shown they could make a great film about senior citizens. A deal with them would be a natural. And while their early offers were not the highest, they kept coming back into the bidding.

"The whole process was just crazy," Harvey said, this from the man who nearly invented crazy. "Calls were going from coast to coast nonstop as it all unwound. They absolutely love the book, and I think they fully intend to make it."

That night, Linda and I got seriously wasted. Leonardo DiCaprio's Jack Dawson, claiming in *Titanic* that he was king of the world? An amateur. (Okay, *Titanic* was nine years *after* our giddy moment, but anyway.) We danced and sang, imagined me winning an Oscar, a Golden Globe, a Screenwriter's Guild award, a Tony (for the musical), hell, even maybe a *Grammy*. I shadow boxed, shouted, cursed everyone who had ever done me wrong. I toasted Wayne Elliott and Harvey Klinger and Bob Bookman. I even found a moment of quiet wistfulness for Molly Friedrich. Linda and I had been poor for a very long time. No more.

Then I passed out on the couch.

One other thing happened at Peachtree that week. Two days earlier, Wayne had announced the hiring of an executive editor, Margaret Quinlin. From the press release announcing her appointment:

> Quinlin will bring fifteen years of experience to the Peachtree position, having held several editorial positions in a variety of publishing areas, including college and scholarly publishing and having consulted with several trade publishers. [Quinlin], who holds an MBA from Emory University, leaves her post as Editorial Director at Aspen Publishers to assume the position with Peachtree.

In the press release, Wayne described Margaret as an "author-oriented editor." No truer words, as they say. It would be awhile before I got to know Margaret, but when I did, she was the editor I'd always dreamed of having, intelligent, articulate, modest, and warm.

In late May, Bill Anderson wrote me again, and, with better news coming my way almost every day, I was so glad to see his name.

> I can't pick up hardly any publication these days without seeing some mention of your newest book. People who know that you and I know each other keep sending me clippings, and I've run across a few on my own.

In the meantime, in a surprising turn, The Nashville Network had suddenly once more gotten hot on Bill's original idea for a drama about the country music business. A producer at the network had even been meeting with Bristol Meyers in New York to seek funding. They weren't going to use much (if any) of the ideas Bill and I had developed, but I was glad for Bill that the project had life again. He wrote again in mid-June when news of the movie sale hit the Atlanta (and national) media:

> Don't forget when you get to be a big superstar it was us little people who made you what you are. Keep tearin' it up!

I never became a superstar, and it was for the best that I didn't. I had started out wanting literary glory, not fame or money. And here I was rolling in dough and working seventeen hours a day at what I assumed I was the height of my career. I wish Biting-Wayne from the *Observer* days had been around to remind me never to assume anything.

He is leaving Madison for the second time. He has been working at the Observer *for nearly a year, and he is no longer afraid to go to the office. He is earning the respect of his colleagues. Linda's job in Oconee County is a perfect choice for her. Brandon stays during the day with a wonderful woman named Sue Woods. When he first moved to Athens and then to Clayton, he felt wayward, unmoored, without direction. Now he sees roads ahead, directions. He will have more time for his own writing without the commute from Madison. And yet he is always awakening, in imagination, in the field behind the house where he grew up, and it is Saturday, and he is alone, and there is no motion anywhere and no sound, and he cannot imagine loving anything this much ever again.*

23

Toasted in La-La Land

On Friday, May 27, 1988, I found myself on a jet heading across the country to Anaheim and the American Booksellers Association annual meeting. A number of Peachtree staffers were going, and I was on the plane with Margaret and sales manager Jill Smith. I would be meeting Bob Bookman, the super-agent from Creative Artists Agency (CAA), one of the top talent firms in Hollywood, and a number of people from MGM. Oh my God. Jill was filled with happiness, and her blue eyes seemed to shine all the time. She was absolutely first rate at her job, too. A lovely lady. Margaret was complex, quiet, and extremely intelligent, and we immediately began to talk. I liked her a great deal, and only after we had chatted for awhile did I realize how big her challenge was. Before stopping for a layover at DFW, we were friends, and I trusted her. I owe her a lot.

I had never been to California. Hell, until a few weeks before, I'd been only two tiny dance steps from the wolf at my door. The day after the sale to MGM was announced in the media, investment bankers from all over the country began to track me down, apparently hoping I'd just give them the money I hadn't even gotten yet. So it was appropriate that we were staying at the pleasant Holiday Inn in Anaheim, right across the street from—Disneyland. Not quite the Hotel California but close enough. As kids in the country right outside Madison, Mark and I had watched "The Mickey Mouse Club," and here I was, right across the street from the risible rodent's fantasy kingdom.

While part of me reacted with giddy glee and wanted to see, feel, and touch every square inch of southern California, another part was terrified, crushed with anxiety. So as soon as I got to my room, I took my medicine that came in a quart bottle with a screw-off top. Once I got my nerves settled underneath me, I realized how much I liked the taste of bourbon and took another dose. In fact, my medicine was so effective that large chunks of that trip were fried away and forgotten forever. I drank in the morning. I drank around noon. But I made up for it by drinking at night. Any anxiety I felt fled to Pleasure Island with Pinocchio. (See Disney, Walt, above.) The sad thing is that like any Real Boy, I was from time to time acting like a jackass and didn't know it. Most of the time, though, I exuded enough bonhomie to make an Optimist's Club feel like the scum of the Earth.

At dinner that night with the Peachtree staff, we were all happy and laughing. After a light breakfast the next morning (Saturday) I had exactly five minutes to speak to national sales representatives on *All the Western Stars* (just out) and my upcoming fall book *Slow Dance in Autumn*. I'm a morning person, even after drinking the night before, and the Peachtree people told me later that I'd wowed 'em. I had the rest of the morning free and wandered around Anaheim trying to look like a writer—this in an area where every other bellhop is trying to sell a screenplay. I worked the Peachtree booth that afternoon and had only been there a few minutes when I saw a well-dressed man coming toward me with the force of a thrown hatchet. He seemed insanely glad to see me, and I'm always attracted to anyone who likes me at all, much less that strongly. He came straight for me, cannon-fired, grabbed my arm, and proceed to dislocate my elbow. Almost, anyway.

It was Bob Bookman. Bob would still be at CAA as I started writing this book, only leaving in March 2013 for the Paradigm agency. To say he has been successful understates the facts almost laughably. According to the story in *Deadline Hollywood* about his move to Paradigm, while he was at CAA " [Bob] Bookman was in the center of such projects as *A Beautiful Mind, The Silence of the Lambs, In the Name of the Father, Jurassic Park, The Cider House Rules, Jerry Maguire, Apollo 13, and United 93....*" and on and on. Bob couldn't have been happier to see me if I was a winning lottery ticket. Alas, as a lottery ticket I turned out to be a match-the-numbers scratch off. But he didn't know that. I never felt more important in my life.

After hanging out with Peachtree (booths 4033 and 4035), I dashed back to the Holiday Inn to take my medicine and then came back to the convention center where I did an autographing at Area 2, Table B. I signed as fast as I could. These were booksellers who would use the signed books they gathered as store displays or to give away as gifts or to sell. A surprising number of them knew of me.

That night I was supposed to have dinner with the Peachtree staff. Instead, I was hijacked and taken off by people from MGM. I think. Everything I remember from this point on shudders into a tale whose focal point keeps shifting in and out of the light. We made it to a bar somewhere—I remember that much. And there were four or five of them, and they immediately began to ply me with drinks. Much later, when reading about William Faulkner's drinking in Hollywood, I understood a little better why he did it. The only way I could have been more full of myself was if I'd eaten my arm. Like a kidnapping victim being tossed from a moving car, I stumbled out of their bibulous vehicle when they finally took me back to Disneyland. As I awoke Sunday morning, needing a cab to the airport, I felt like a hand grenade had exploded on my tongue. Hooray for Hollywood! After another layover in Dallas-Fort Worth on the way back, our pilot flew us almost directly into a massive thunderstorm and had to push the throttle to forty thousand miles an hour while at the entry angle of an Olympic high diver. Passengers crossed themselves and confessed sins. I had on dark sunglasses and was singing "I'm in the Mood for Love," having taken another dose of medicine just before we left southern California. A few days later, Karen Humphries from Peachtree wrote me and said I'd been a big hit with the sales reps, booksellers, and "the many people who flocked to our booth to meet you." Karen enclosed copies of *ATWS* to be signed for the people at MGM and a number of others. (I vaguely remembered signing something for the MGM people; maybe it was their hands.)

Around this time Peachtree threw a huge party for me at an Atlanta venue called the Waterworks. Nothing was spared—a barbecue, live music, invited local celebrities. My publisher had even had "*All the Western Stars*" bandanas made as gifts for those who came. (We gave these away in Anaheim, too.)

That year wasn't entirely filled with the nonsense of fame. As winner of the 1986 Townsend Prize, I had the good fortune to present the prize to the 1988 winner that year—Mary Hood. Mary is a great short story writer, and she had been my friend since Roots in Georgia in 1985. Giving her the prize was pure joy.

Since Peachtree had been between Chuck leaving and Margaret arriving early that year, they hired a sharp freelance editor named Melinda Boyer to edit *Slow Dance in Autumn*, and I found working with her a delight. I have been asked more than once how I came to write what is essentially a detective novel—and why. A friend once told me she'd figured it out: I was doing a sort of cook's tour of the genre world, and writing one book in each genre, and *Slow Dance* was my mystery. There is a slight bit of truth to this. But the main reason is that I had a good time writing the book and thought I might be able to make money with a series that would subsidize the books I *really* wanted to write—like *The Divine Comics*. The hero is a former Triple A baseball player named Hank Prince, and he is a private detective in Atlanta. The book was obviously based on the Chandler-Hammett tradition though Hank Prince was much less in control than Philip Marlowe. In the end, it was simply a lark that I didn't expect to be published. But it was, and it immediately drew a huge number of fans, to my astonishment and worry. From the start, people started to ask me about the next one, assuming I'd be writing one or two of them a year. I even went so far as to write another one I called *Declared Dead*, but in the end, I didn't want to be known as a mystery writer—even a part-time one. So I never published it. One thing that *Slow Dance* does point out is the length to which writers will go to get manuscripts they really love in print. But I was making it all up as I went along, and even if I had had someone to ask for advice, I probably would have been too stupid to take it. Still, worrying about each misstep one makes in a life or a writing career is surely folly. The best one can hope for is a book (or two) that has the power to cut through the background noise of an age and, for whatever reason, last.

By mid-June, Jack Lemmon and Walter Matthau were both pushing hard for the roles of Lucas and Jake in the film version of *All the Western Stars*. I knew this because Dick Zanuck had called me and told me so. I had always been a huge fan of Lemmon, less so of Matthau, but they were the eternal odd couple of American cinema and would be superb in our film (Lemmon would, in the end, be the one who single-handledly sank the whole project, but that's years down the road.)

Wayne Elliott had been pushing me for a new book contract, in light of our suceess so far with *Western Stars*. I wrote him on June 14:

> One of my main considerations in staying with Peachtree is, frankly, Margaret. In the short time we have worked together, I have really grown fond of her, professionally and personally. She seems to

care about my work and is working hard to let me know it. You did good in hiring her, Wayne.

In fact, everyone at Peachtree treated me like a king. What a wonderful gang they were! I have in the years since published with many, many publishing houses, and some have been marvelous and others less so, but no staff ever treated me with more kindness than Peachtree did in those lovely early days. So on July 7, I signed contracts for *The Song of Daniel* and a new novel on which I was still working, *Perfect Timing*. (And these books have been in print ever since. In fact, I signed new versions of my contracts in June 2013 so they would all come out as e-books.)

Bill Anderson and I stayed in touch, and he followed my escapades in the newspapers. Alas, when I was back in Nashville for an event in September, he was in Atlanta for the Georgia Music Hall of Fame Awards and Show. I was there for the Southeast Booksellers Association meeting and on a panel with Lee Smith, Elizabeth Spencer, and Ellen Douglas. Once, when a group of us were going somewhere, I got to sit in a back seat with Ms. Douglas (a pen name—her real name was Jo Haxton) and had a great talk, mostly about her new book, *Can't Quit You, Baby*, which was just out, and which I'd already read and loved. In the front of my copy, she signed it "To Phil Williams, With many thanks for his kinds words and appreciation of my book. Ellen Douglas." Then, at the bottom of this, she wrote "Jo" and circled it. We also had a get-together at Will Campbell's house. Among those present was country singer Tom T. Hall. He was a good friend of Billy Carter (President Carter's brother), who was terminally ill with cancer. Tom T. was clearly upset, and I was touched by his sorrow. I mentioned that moment to a friend years later and wound up, to my shock, at an event honoring Tom T. and was even asked to speak. Standing before a gigantic dinner crowd, I had to admit I didn't know the man at all. Ah, life.

After getting settled in Athens, my pal Ray Andrews dropped me a postcard that rather summed up the craziness of the past few months:

> Howdy!
>
> I've checked with all of the local movie house owners and they are erasing their marquees in anticipation. They didn't believe I know you, of course. The book is great! In a few years, you and I can play the parts. I'm old enough now. Drop your new telephone

number in the mail to Morton Road so I can call and find out how to write an Academy Award book.

Ray

The postcard was a picture of 42nd Street in Manhattan on a busy night. We had changed our phone number to an unlisted one because sudden fame was leading all kinds of crazy people to our door. Twenty-five years later we're still unlisted, if there even is a list anymore.

Also that September, Peachtree sent me to Palm Beach, Florida, to the national sales meeting for a book chain called Waldenbooks. Once well known and powerful, Waldenbooks faded off into liquidation in 2011. But in 1989, it was at its height. It was on that trip that I met novelist Anne Rivers Siddons, who became a friend and blurbed a book of mine the following year. We were even on the same plane down and didn't know it until we landed.

While my publishing schedule was set through *Slow Dance in Autumn* that fall of 1988, we hadn't completely decided on the book to come out in the spring of 1989. The plan had always been to publish *The Song of Daniel* (which at that point was called *Timothy*), but Margaret had it in hand and had looked at other manuscripts of mine, and so the question remained open. Harvey loved a manuscript called *Darkness*, a short, taut, and very dark story set in a southern town based on Madison just after the end of the First World War. I wrote and rewrote it for *years*, but it simply never satisfied me.

That November, with *Slow Dance* in production, Harvey called me one day with some shocking news. I may have heard a bit of this from Margaret or Wayne, though I just can't recall. MGM, as it turned out, was in total disarray. I still have my notes from that phone call, and it was clear Harvey was furious at how complex things had gotten with MGM. I need to say one thing again: MGM was by this time a film *distributor*, and its great days as a production company were long behind it. What it did do was work with independent producers such as Richard Zanuck and David Brown. But it was becoming clear that even as a distributor MGM was teetering on financial ruin. One of the contractual sticking points for us was what is called a single-frame credit. Harvey insisted that, on screen, my name not be combined with anyone else's. It took a while, but MGM finally gave in on that point. (Thank you, Harvey.) But it was much more complicated than that. Even a summary of what happened to MGM in those days would take forty pages. So if you're interested, look it up online. Suffice it to say that I was in the middle of a mess. I never got to know David Brown. By the time MGM was finally sold a couple of years later, he and Dick had dissolved their producing partnership. I got to know Dick Zanuck very well, though, and if one-tenth of the people in Hollywood were one-hundredth as nice as Dick, the place would be heaven on Earth. Dick died unexpectedly in the summer of 2012. God rest his soul. What a fine man he was.

When I talked to Harvey, I also mentioned that I had written a screenplay or two (this going back a couple of years by then) and asked if he'd be interested in taking a look. He would, and nothing about it seemed unethical or illegal, since my contract with Peachtree said nothing about independent film projects. I've always felt a little guilty, though, because after that Harvey and I talked often. He was scrupulously careful not to do anything Peachtree wouldn't have wanted him to do. But he was a great help as I began to understand more about Hollywood and the New York publishing world.

By late October, Margaret and I had decided to do the "Timothy" novel after *Slow Dance in Autumn*. After that one, we thought, we might do another book I'd written that year. Though it's never seen the light, it was called *Speak Again, Bright Angel*, and it was about a down-at-heels Shakespearean actor who had developed a show that he performed at high schools in the South in the 1960s. I had seen something similar at Morgan County High School and imagined what it must be like to be trying to sell *Hamlet* to three hundred laughing and spitball-throwing nitwits. The manuscript was in tone very similar to what would be my last (and I think, best) Peachtree book, *Perfect Timing*—nutty, light, and very funny, but with a serious underpinning.

I wrote Wayne Elliott a letter full of misplaced dudgeon. Years later, I feel nothing but shame in reading it. The reason was that *Slow Dance in Autumn* came out of the gate like a plowhorse after a day on the south forty. We'd made one mistake with the lead blurb on the back cover. It was strong: "A classy, fast-paced page turner with the kind of irony and hard-edged sentimentality that Raymond Chandler fans will adore." It was given to us by the novelist William Diehl, at that time most famous for *Sharkey's Machine*, which had been made into a film with Burt Reynolds. A few years later, Diehl's book *Primal Fear*, turned into a terrific picture starring Richard

Gere, Laura Linney, and Edward Norton, would shoot him into the mystery stratosphere. (I would down the road meet Linney in my hometown of Madison, of all places.) But for reasons I can't recall, we identified him in the blurb as *Bill* Diehl, a name under which he never published. The other blurb was from a man named Mark Stevens, who ran the Science Fiction and Mystery Bookstore in the Virginia-Highland area of Atlanta where much of *Slow Dance* was set. We had had the break party there, but it was a shop with little parking, and only a small crowd came. The main problem had nothing to do with all that, though. It was simply too soon to publish another book. And I'm sure I was pushing like the maniac I was in those days. Mark Stevens was wonderfully kind to me.

Being slathered over by MGM had apparently made me believe everyone on planet Earth owed me more, starting with Peachtree Publishers. All I can say, twenty-five years later (to Peachtree) is I'm sorry. I was an ass. But a man who has been starving for decades is going to try and eat every scrap of food in the house the first chance he has. Maybe in a sense my fit helped a little. All my life, I've been the nice one in the crowd. People can count on me to be sunny and even-tempered. (Stop glaring at me, Linda. I mean in public.) But I was almost thirty-nine years old, and to me it was then or never, and I was scared. To their credit, my friends at Peachtree didn't have me kidnapped or beaten up and instead came up with a strong plan for what was now being called *The Song of Daniel*, which would be out in the spring of 1989. I had really wanted to call the book *Timothy*, but when someone from Peachtree called me and said there was an Australian actor named Mel Gibson who had been in a 1979 movie called *Tim*, about a developmentally challenged gardener and his relationship with an older woman, I was stunned and shocked, since I had never heard of the film. Its plot was very vaguely similar to my novel's, though, so it would be suicide to call my book *Timothy*. So I changed the main character's name to Daniel and called the book *The Song of Daniel*. It's a decent book but certainly not my best.

We did manage two good blurbs. Anne Rivers Siddons said it "is a lovely and valuable book. I don't know of anyone writing today with such perfect pitch when it comes to the music of the New South; Williams catches its style, substance and import perfectly. I think his will be one of the defining voices of our generation."

That, I knew, was worth a dozen MGM contracts. My friend Raymond Andrews also gave us a good blurb for this book. (As I noted some time earlier, Ray had moved to Athens in 1984, and by this time we were extremely close. He was one of the best friends I ever had, and he adored Linda, and she loved him.) I had even introduced Ray to Margaret, and she would publish his superb memoir *The Last Radio Baby* in 1990.

In February 1990, Wayne Elliott called to tell me there was pre-publication movie interest in *The Song of Daniel*. This was encouraging since *Slow Dance* had sold poorly, though we had gotten a decent paperback deal with Dell. I thanked Wayne and crossed my fingers. In the meantime, the sales figures on *Slow Dance* changed my plans completely. I had envisioned it as a commercial series that might prop up more serious books. But by this time, it was clear the whole thing was a misfire. So I told Margaret we should forget my detective Hank Prince. That decision brought me a lot of heat later, because mystery fans are fanatics (bless them!), and a great many hounded me for years to produce the next in the series. More than once I've offered to send *Declared Dead* to a mystery fan as a Word attachment to an email if they would just stop bothering me. But letting Hank Prince "die" back then was the right decision. (I didn't know until some years later that *Slow Dance* had been a finalist for best "First P.I. Novel" prize in the 1989 Shamus Awards, the national honors given to detective novels. Just as well I didn't know.) At the ABA in New York City in 1991, the owner of a huge mystery bookshop in London backed me into a corner and more or less accused me of letting his customers down. But I stuck to my, ah, guns.

The Song of Daniel came out in the spring of 1989 to mixed reviews. The reviewing service Kirkus, as it loves to do, savaged the book. *Publishers Weekly* was lukewarm. I started to understand that I was in trouble with my publisher, and I wasn't sure what to do. In March, Margaret sent me two unbelievably gorgeous spec cover designs for *Speak Again, Bright Angel*. If we had published that book, it would have been the best cover of my career. It still makes me ache that we never did. It's hard for me to remember that we were, at the time, planning to publish my next book after *The Song of Daniel* in the fall of 1989. I'm sure I was the one pushing this, and all I can say is that I must have been insane. Poor Margaret. So gentle and so kind and having to deal with a nut case like me. This would have been *four books in the space of two calendar years*. Harvey clearly thought I was crazy. Bob Wyatt at Ballantine, a champion of mine (Ballantine had done the paperbacks of *The Heart of a Distant Forest* and would do a drop-dead gorgeous mass market softcover edition of *The Song of Daniel*) thought I was moving far too fast. (He may have also thought I was crazy; I never asked.) Margaret did her best, but it's philosophically invariant that one can't argue with a lunatic.

So I backed off. I didn't have a choice. But I also began to think seriously of the wrong turns I'd made so far as a writer. I had been pushing *The Inner Kingdom* since 1983 with no success, and *that* was the writer I really wanted to be. In my core, I wasn't a writer of so-called popular fiction. That's why I couldn't think of what I was doing as a career. I was still working full-time at the University of Georgia. I had gone quite a distance from being a poet in love with Ezra Pound's poetry and small magazines.

Trying to regain my bearings, that summer I sent Margaret a huge collection of my poems. It was a motley lot, without design or an overall theme (and no rhyme and little reason). That she treated the whole idea seriously humbles me, even now. She responded to the poetry on July 11:

> I have been reading *Night Wings* and I am incredibly impressed. First by the power of your expressive ability and then by the diversity of your subjects.

In the meantime, Bill Anderson had published his superb autobiography, *Whisperin' Bill,* with Chuck Perry over at Longstreet. It was one of the best books I'd ever read about country music, and I told Bill so. He wrote me back that June:

> If nobody else on this whole planet says anything nice about my book it won't matter. I'll just take out the beautiful letter you wrote me and read it over again....

The new head of all daytime programming at NBC-TV was a friend of Bill's and someone who'd known about all our efforts. She had just called Bill out of the blue and asked for another copy of all our "Nashville" stuff. I didn't expect anything, but it was a pleasant reminder of some happy days.

By summer's end, Margaret was working hard on the poetry collection. She had told me the obvious. It would need to be edited down to something like sixty-four or eighty pages. And we would need to go through them and cull out the weaker ones. To that end, she had asked several experienced poets to go through the mess I sent and mark ones they thought were keepers and ones that should be used to start fires. For some reason, this amazing support struck me as dispiriting.

I haven't spoken much about newspaper and magazine stories about me, and I haven't reprinted reviews. (*Western Stars,* for example, was reviewed well by Carolyn See in *The Los Angeles Times.*) In his autobiography, Anthony Burgess took great glee in reprinting every bad review he ever got. But I can't imagine readers being terribly interested in all that. I will mention one to stand for many. That summer, a huge feature story about me by Jeanne M. McGlinn came out in a magazine called *The Arts Journal.* It was a his-life-to-that-point kind of story and a midcareer assessment of my work. I was touched and warmed by the piece.

My speaking schedule in 1989 was as insane as I might have been. I was everywhere at once. But the event I will remember most was my time on the set of a film that nobody at the time had yet heard of: *Driving Miss Daisy.*

Fishing at Grayson White's

I cast the line far out, away from reel
And hand, the configurations of delight
Apparent in musculature, the whispering
Horizon, one small splash out there.
I grieve for water. Clouds spread east
Across the surface, green and patient
For a breeze. Bream come up toward me.
I lay across the delicacies of that surface
And drift out into the lake with birds
Low and skimming small familiar ripples.
I could sink toward hydrilla and childhood.
I could spread my fins like wet sails,
Get caught by eddies, pushed on south
Toward the dam. I could exhale geese.
At the end of discovery is the fair beginning
Of another cast. I make that old motion
With its splendid spell, its dying arch.
I find that I am caught on this edge
Of sand and water, taut against the lines.
I find consolation. I rise to the light.

24

Free to Wander Around

I keep several career mementoes on a shelf in my study, awards and so forth, out of public view but close enough to remind me of well-traveled roads. One of my favorites is a photograph of Richard Zanuck, me, and Dick's assistant Judy Schefke, arm in arm on the set of *Driving Miss Daisy*. Dick had told me in a phone call that they would be filming near me, at several locations in Atlanta. Would I like to come up and hang around? You bet I would. Judy called me on June 8 with details for the following week—where they would be shooting, what I should do. I had been in touch with the screenwriter that Dick and David Brown had hired for *All the Western Stars*, Mick Garris. This was early in Mick's career, but I knew him from his script for a children's TV movie called *Fuzzbucket* that our son Brandon had seen several years before and liked. Mick was a delightful guy, self-effacing and eager to make a good impression on Dick and on me.

It feels a little strange now when I type "Dick," as if he were just another cog in the Hollywood gears. He wasn't. The son of the legendary producer Darryl F. Zanuck, Dick had made his own way, being the nice guy in a very tough town. When he died in 2012, believe me, those tears were real. (Mine, too.) He and David Brown, as I said, took a chance on a young director named Steven Spielberg when they hired him to direct *Jaws*. Less well remembered now, *The Sting* was a great movie, too, and they produced it. He produced *The Verdict*, the superb picture for which Paul Newman should have won an Oscar as best actor. And later, after our association, Dick would produce six films in the 2000s for director Tim Burton. In 1989, he had also optioned for film the novel *Rich in Love* by South Carolina writer Josephine Humphreys. (I knew Jo slightly from an autographing we did together in Atlanta a year before.) In short, Richard Zanuck was as accomplished in Hollywood as he was beloved. By the time of *Driving Miss*

Daisy, though, Dick and David Brown had dissolved their partnership, so I would be working with The Zanuck Company (though I had no idea how deeply). Lili Fini Zanuck directed their film *Rush* in 1991, doing a fine job in a day when women directors were few and far between.

I located the house in one of Atlanta's tonier neighborhoods where filming was underway. I had been on film sets many times before, so I knew the etiquette, and I knew I wasn't going to be tripping over cables in the middle of a take. The cast was a dream: Jessica Tandy, Morgan Freeman, Dan Aykroyd, Patti Lupone, and Esther Rolle. The director was Australian Bruce Beresford, who had helmed *Tender Mercies*. I can barely type the name of that 1983 film without tearing up. It is, in my judgment, one of the great masterpieces of American cinema. It had, to use a Southernism, "tore me out [of] the frame" when I first saw it. I was terrified of meeting Beresford, but he turned out to be sweet and easy, though at the same time extremely intense. I parked my car on the street and wandered down to the property where filming was underway and just stood there. Finally I saw Dick and Lili over near the house, in which a scene, set at a nursing home where Miss Daisy has gone near the end of her life, was about to be filmed. Lili saw me before Dick did and whispered in his ear and nodded to me. Dick smiled and waved and came walking over. He was a small man, half a head shorter than I, with white hair and not an ounce of fat on him. He was fifty-three and looked about my age (thirty-eight).

"So you found us all right," he said, taking my hand. "It's great to meet you, Phil. We're so excited about *All the Western Stars*. I'm going to be busy, but I've told people you're here, so feel free to wander around. I guess you know about being on sets and such." I got my hang-tag credentials and looped them around my neck, officially a big shot.

He introduced me to Lili and then headed inside the house, me right behind him. I almost walked right into Dan Aykroyd, and I managed not to say anything out loud. I started to say hello, but he was holding a script and walking around, studying his part, and I didn't even make eye contact. Beresford was just about to begin a take with Jessica Tandy in the "nursing home," quietly shuffling across the room, lost and old, her snowy hair in the disarray of far old age. She had just turned seventy-nine, and with makeup, she looked about a hundred and twenty in the scene. Without movie makeup (as I saw her at the Oscars on TV the next winter), she looked about fifty. Beresford called the scene, and I held my breath and didn't move as they did take after take of that one small bit. We spent a good part of the morning on that and another scene set in the same home. When I went outside for awhile, Morgan Freeman came walking over to me. He had been nominated for an Oscar for Best Supporting Actor the year before, but his most famous work (including *Driving Miss Daisy*) was still ahead of him.

"Can you loan me a few dollars?" he asked, smiling. I thought he was kidding, and maybe he was, but it's hard to tell where great actors are coming from sometimes. I must have looked like one of the film's employees. I think I had maybe three dollars in cash.

"I'm so sorry, Mr. Freeman," I said. "I don't have it."

"It's okay," he said, grinning and patting me on the shoulder. "I don't either." We both laughed again, and he went off to find it somewhere else. Nominated five times, he finally won a well-deserved Oscar for *Million Dollar Baby* in 2005. Some time that afternoon, I got to meet Dan Aykroyd briefly, but I didn't meet Patti Lupone or Esther Rolle. I don't think they were on set that day. When we broke for lunch, I found myself sitting at a table right across from Jessica Tandy. She was still in makeup and the consummate pro, careful not to mess anything up but eating a good meal, too. I wish I could repeat verbatim all we talked about, but I simply can't. Ms. Tandy was a complete delight. She knew well that this was a plum part, and she was going to make the most of it. (Bette Davis had apparently hounded Dick for days trying to get him to cast her. She would have been utterly and disastrously wrong, and he knew it.) I did ask Ms. Tandy what it was like to work with Alfred Hitchcock, and she launched into a delightful story, filled with anecdotes and fond reminiscences. (She was in *The Birds* and had appeared on "Alfred Hitchcock Presents" on TV.) What I do remember is how stunningly beautiful a seventy-nine-year-old woman can be, even in "old-face."

Judy Schefke and I hung around that afternoon during filming, and she was a delight, telling me that Dick really was as warm and wonderful as he seemed. What a day that was, one of the best of my professional life.

By year's end, Mick Garris and I had talked several times, but I would not read his first draft of the screenplay for *All the Western Stars* until May. Still, I felt we were headed in the right direction. *Driving Miss Daisy* came out on December 15, just in time to be considered for Oscars to be given out in 1990. I went to see it by myself and found it very moving. Even Dan Aykroyd, whose casting seemed iffy to me, was marvelous. And when the

Oscar nominations were announced early in 1990, the film got nine and won four: Best Picture, Best Actress (Tandy), Best Makeup, and Best Adapted Screenplay (Alfred Uhry, based on his own play). My friend Dick Zanuck accepted the Best Picture Oscar in front of a billion people around the globe. I was on my feet screaming. (Weirdly and wrongly, Bruce Beresford wasn't nominated for Best Director.) The next morning, I sent a huge bouquet of flowers to The Zanuck Company in Beverly Hills. Dick wrote me and said the flowers filled their "hearts with happiness and post-Oscar joy."

While I was still struggling with Peachtree on what to do next, Bob Bookman had sent me the first draft of Mick Garris's screenplay back on May 4. Bob liked it, and so did I. But the higher ups, I found out later, weren't so sure. Mick and I talked on the phone frequently, and he was working with Dick on rewrites. Casting had slowly began to take shape, too. After seeing *The Freshman*, which had come out on July 20, Dick had gotten interested in the idea of casting Marlon Brando.

That summer, Wayne Elliott wrote me that the manager for alternative country singer k.d. lang had sent us some of her CDs in hopes we'd use her music in the movie. Why the manager thought we had any say in that puzzled me, but I did enjoy Ms. lang's music. I was mainly getting nervous because the first year's option on *All the Western Stars* would be up in November. That option was $25,000, and under the contract, future options would be the same amount. In October Mick told me that he'd heard that The Zanuck Company was definitely going to extend the option and that they'd sent the script to Sean Connery, but his people didn't want him "playing an old man." Mick said Brando was afraid that they just wanted him as a lure to sign other people. In mid-October Bob Bookman (and Harvey) signed the Zanucks to another year's option, and Dick wrote me a lovely letter, thanking *me* for giving *them* an extension. He said it was unclear how much longer they could wait on the "Brando situation," but they thought it was worth a try. Obviously, I did, too. (More than once I sat and laughed about the improbability of me, a boy from a small town in the South, waiting out "the Brando situation.")

As a side note, Dick's assistant, Judy Schefke wanted to try her hand at representing books for film in Hollywood, and since no one was handling *The Heart of a Distant Forest* at the moment and by then I had the rights back, I let her give it a try. She had no luck, and the following year, she moved back home to Michigan. (In my case, it certainly wasn't her fault—my novel would be difficult to make into a film, and it *had* been shopped several years before.) Judy was a lovely lady and so kind to me. I also went back to Nashville in October for the Southern Festival of Books.

Stupidly, unconscionably, I wrote a long letter to Margaret laying out the professional problems I felt lingered between us. (I never felt we had any genuinely personal issues, and if we did, I was to blame.) We had met somewhere along the way, and she had told me that she thought the manuscript of *Speak Again, Bright Angel* was undercooked and needed a great deal more work. She was right. Margaret dove right into the heart of the matter in a letter to me on October 21:

> We all bought into the strategy of publishing three of your books in three seasons for various reasons. There have been pluses and minuses as a result. On the plus side, your name is more widely known now than three books ago. (Despite what you think.) You are known by readers, media, other publishers, and booksellers. Your work has created some solid supporters in bookstores and among readers. This is very important. Reviewers have by and large been very supportive of your work. These are the pluses.
>
> On the minus side, we have raised some eyebrows for "churning out books...." Secondly, your books have been very different—each with its own set of supporters, but by being so different I think you have fractured your audience. As a result there is no cumulative effect of increasing numbers of readers after the publication of three books.

All this was absolutely correct. And I knew she was right. But, slathering like a literary doberman, I wanted more without being able to articulate why. I had succeeded more than most writers could dream about, but I felt like a failure. *Daniel* had sold badly, too, and I wasn't sure which way to turn. The fact that all my books were different was because in my literary house there were many mansions. If my postmodern books could not find a publisher, I would *publish* postmodernly—with different themes, plots, voices, and narrators butting against each other from book to book. Linda and I had been poor, and the taste of money was addictive. But it was more about the fact that I couldn't publish the books I really wanted to write. As I said earlier, I wanted to be James Joyce, not James Michener.

In November, I had written Margaret a long letter begging that we shift to my postmodern voice, starting in the fall of 1990 with *The Inner Kingdom*.

Tentatively agreeing, Margaret asked an external editor and writer to read the manuscript, and that editor hated it. I wasn't surprised. But by then, all the fight was out of me, and I had no idea which way to turn.

In the midst of this, I wrote the most savage, brutal book of my career, *Final Heat,* a hellish, violent, and bloody novel set in an endless Mississippi summer. It was a book I came to loathe, but the anger I felt leaked on to every page. I finished it that summer with my blood boiling, unsure what, if anything I would do with it.

When 1989 ended, I had no book planned from Peachtree because we simply couldn't decide what to do next, or when. I had finally listened to Margaret and quit pushing so hard for a pub date on the next book. We thought maybe spring 1991, but even that might have been too fast. I had a tiger by the tail and was just afraid to let go.

His mother loves her job at the Department of Family and Children Services. She is the first one there each morning, the one to make the coffee. In a journal she keeps, she notes that being early or on time is something her whole family does. She does not say her younger son is quite insane on the matter, will arrive an hour early for a reading in a distant town and then have to drive around or go to a coffee shop to await his time. He has never seen anyone love children as much as she does. At Magic Land, her face appeared to be made of light. She taught the children to sing in Sunday School. She takes meals and books to people in nursing homes. He does not want to look too far down the road for her. They both know what will come, and it is fine. It will in time come for them both. And it is fine.

25

Good Reviews, Strong Sales

Late in fall 1989, I picked up a project I had started a couple of years before and finished it late in the year in a joyful rush. I felt the darkness of that year begin to lift a bit as I put the finishing touches on *Perfect Timing*, one of my favorites of my own novels. This book was already under contract to Peachtree, even though we hadn't decided quite when to publish it. It's a midlife crisis book dealing with homelessness, classical music, and a bizarre, just-released-from-prison, born-again Christian. It turned out be almost everyone's cup of tea, and coming after *The Song of Daniel*, it even threatened to put me back on top.

After two straight years of pedal to the floor and my picture in the papers regularly, I settled back to just *live*. Of course, I couldn't stop writing. My life was framed around that blissful hour or two every morning when I made coffee and walked in the dark down to my writing cabin behind the house. In the winter, it could be knuckle-cracking cold until my small space heater warmed the place up. I had had a computer since the early '80s, and its speed and utility made it possible for me to work until about 6:30 and then head off to my job at UGA. From 1985-92, I enjoyed my work as a science writer in the Agricultural Experiment Stations. Within a year of starting there, I had been promoted to take over the whole office. So between my salary and my literary earnings and Linda's teaching job, we had gone from being near the poverty line to quite comfortable.

Early in 1990, I sent Margaret the manuscript of *Perfect Timing*, knowing the earliest it could possibly be out would be spring 1991. I was no longer foaming at the mouth, and I felt the world calming down around me. I liked it. In later years a break of two, three, or four years between books became bliss. But after being lit like an anarchist's bomb and rolled into the literary world when *All the Western Stars* came out in 1988, the change of pace was necessary. I had only a fraction of the appearances in 1990 that I'd had in the past two years. I felt as if *Perfect Timing* was closer to what I wanted to write than *The Song of Daniel* had been, so I had hopes for it. In March, Mick Garris called from Los Angeles and said he'd heard rumors that Sean Connery (again) and Paul Newman were being talked up for the film. I had learned to nod and smile and forget about it half a minute later. The chatter around a film project can be deafening, but too often it's just hopeful chatter.

Finally I heard from Margaret in April:

> This is just a brief note to let you know I'm here and still breathing, and I've now read about a third of *Perfect Timing*. I like it—the writing is very strong. I expect to finish the manuscript this weekend, so I'll talk with you about it next week.
>
> Ray's coming down at the end of this week and we'll get together on Friday. I hope to be finished editing his manuscript then, but I have a ways to go....
>
> I'm looking forward to finishing *Perfect Timing*. (You really are very remarkable.)

This seemed promising, and I'd put Margaret through more than any decent person would. Yet I still had the nagging feeling that I wanted to write more artful books, ones I was fully capable of producing. So in my quiet hours, I plotted and planned—avant-garde novels, epic poems, postmodern multimedia farces.

I hadn't heard from Wayne Elliott in a while, and in June I found out why. Margaret had purchased a majority interest in the company. From then on, I would be working with the management side of the business as well as editorial. I think Margaret had always dreamed of owning her own press, and so I felt nothing but joy for her. As part of her planning, she asked me (and, I assumed, others) for any ideas they might have for the future of the house. Margaret responded on July 1 with a lovely, five-page handwritten letter, thanking me for my thoughts and laying out where she wanted to take Peachtree.

We also had new movie interest that summer from Churchill Entertainment, a small company in Los Angeles. Their vice president for production, Richard David, was a fan of mine, and we tried, without luck, to wangle an option from him on *The Song of Daniel* and other of my titles. For a brief time I also corresponded with Harpo Entertainment, Oprah Winfrey's company, but even plowing through all my letters I can't quite figure out what the project was. I believe they contacted me, but at this distance I'm simply not sure. In the fall, Dick and Lili also extended their option on *All the Western Stars* another year, for another $25,000. We heard little of where things stood except that the project was still at MGM, and we were fully expecting for it to be greenlighted some time in the coming year. I was also named Georgia Author of the Year and got my picture taken with Joe Frank Harris, the governor at the time. I would be named Author of the Year three more times in three different categories (fiction, poetry and essay) over the years.

I had turned forty in January 1990, and with four books now to my credit, I felt as if I had made a good start on a body of work. Margaret liked *Perfect Timing*, and I was writing well. But the national economy had begun to go to hell, and home mortage rates were through the roof. Linda and I had begun to think of buying a newer and larger house, and that was now within our grasp because of my literary success. Still, we dawdled about it. Brandon loved our little house at the end of Merlin Court and the creek and the woods beyond. It would always be the house where he grew up.

Frankly, I was exhausted, too. The nonstop motion of 1988-89 had taken its toll on me, and I needed time to recalibrate. Years later, I would finally realize that the joy in being a writer isn't in the literary life; it's those moments of quiet joy with the page and a trunkful of verbs and nouns. Since *The Heart of a Distant Forest* came out in 1984, I had become a far better writer though, in some ways, that book was still my best so far. I worked as hard as I always had at my art, and the result was an increasing stack of finished and partial novels. Sometimes I would do research for months and then never get around to writing any fiction about it. (I did research for *years* on Fort Phil Kearny but never got around to writing that, either.) I was also terrible about not dating things, and so I have many manuscripts whose provenance is shaky at best. But with *Heart, All the Western Stars, Slow Dance in Autumn*, and *The Song of Daniel* in print, I had a growing national presence. I had won a fine literary award with the Townsend Prize, and by the middle of 1990, we had definitely settled on *Perfect Timing* being my next book in the spring of 1991. That meant *Speak Again, Bright Angel, Darkness*, the poetry collection *Night Wings*, and several other projects I'd considered with Margaret were probably gone with the wind.

Early in 1991, though, life suddenly turned frightening for us when Linda got extremely sick. She was always thin and healthy so we were both worried about what might be wrong. Then, after a visit to the doctor, she called me at work one day toward the end of February.

"Well, the impossible has happened," she said, in her usual low, soft voice.

"What's wrong?"

"I'm pregnant. You're going to be a father again."

I don't know how far one can go in describing the word *shock,* but we were both fairly close to the most extravagant definition of it at that point. I had turned forty-one in January, and Linda would be forty-one in April. A new *baby*. It was hard to believe because Linda's continuing and hideously painful problems with endometriosis had left her more or less sterile, or so her doctors said. Our friends and family were beside themselves with happiness and glee, and I was thrilled myself. Even Brandon was happy, and he'd been an only child for nearly thirteen years. Though Linda felt ghastly for the first trimester, after that her health was great, and it showed. She moved with the grace women have when the "good" hormones start to kick in. But if, before, we had idly thought about a new house, it now became essential. Our tiny modified A-frame on Merlin Court might hold three, but it certainly could not hold four.

Late that spring, *Perfect Timing* came out to quite good reviews and strong sales. It hit the national UPI bestseller list on June 2 in ninth place, among books by such writers as Jeffrey Archer, Sue Grafton, John Grisham, and Mary Higgins Clark. I was really proud of the book, and though it had its weaknesses, I felt it was light years better than *The Song of Daniel.* And even before *PT* came out, Harvey and our friends on the West Coast, Bob Bookman and Kate Edwards at CAA, were pushing it for a film deal. There was a considerable amount of interest, but we finally sold rights to Ron Howard and Brian Grazer at Imagine Entertainment. Ron, of course, had directed *Cocoon,* which had been produced by Richard Zanuck and David Brown. He was still relatively early in his career, but no one doubted his talent. He would win the Oscar for Best Director with *A Beautiful Mind* (2001). Thus by mid-1991 I had projects underway with one Oscar winner and another man who would be one. Peachtree had also picked up rights to publish *The Heart of a Distant Forest* from W.W. Norton, which had let it go out of print.

With my career suddenly clicking once more, it was becoming clear to me that I needed to move on from Peachtree, and I knew Margaret well enough to know she wouldn't stand in my way. During my years there, I had gone from the author of one respected novel to a writer with a national name. I was in the media quite a bit. To that end, I began to talk, quietly, with Harvey Klinger about becoming my personal literary agent. Since Harvey had made us both a decent amount of money with sales and subsidiary rights, he absolutely wanted to see what manuscripts I had. When he didn't like something he was blunt. But I was asking to play in a different league, and he was right: I needed to know how tough it was going to be. While I was considering what to send him, I remembered, early in 1991, the angry, bitter, vicious novel called *Final Heat* that I'd drafted a while back. I took it out, polished it over a few months, and sent it to Harvey.

He was wild for it. He called me, quite excited, and all but said we could use it to start printing money. He felt certain we could sell it, and he was amused by my naivete in not knowing what a commercial book it was. I was deeply unsure I even wanted to publish it, but by that time, needing to leave Peachtree, and with a new baby on the way, I said he could try to sell it. By early April, he had gotten a strong offer from Joni Evans at Random House's new Turtle Bay Books imprint (see the beginning of this book), and he called me with the news. The advance would be $67,500, a figure I could only have dreamed of before. And we would definitely be moving, since we had found, on February 16, a huge house on seven acres of land in the woods on a dirt road in nearby Oconee County. I felt sick with guilt about leaving Peachtree with *Perfect Timing* just coming out, but the right thing to do would be to call Margaret and just tell her straight. So I did. She wrote me on April 4:

> "...the more I think about this Random House development, the more pleased I am. I put it in a class with the feature film in the sense that it validates you in the media and the marketplace, and this is just something we don't (yet) have the clout to do at Peachtree.
>
> Thank you for calling to tell me about this yourself. It really made a difference to me hearing the news from you, and I know it took personal courage to do it. I love you for that.
>
> I'm excited about the news, Phil, for what it means for your career. I'm anxious about it, too, because it means potentially losing you altogether and that saddens and discourages me. It's similar to

> my having to face the possibility of letting others work on your books. Working with you has been so personally rewarding for me that I am selfish about sharing you.
>
> I hope with all my heart that there will be a way to share you with Random House—not by way of a bidding war. Obviously I'm not in their league and can't match their offer. If there were some way to differentiate your works so that we could each continue to publish you along two tracks, I would be a very happy person.

Alas, alas, it was not to be. My life was changing in many ways, and I needed to move on. Peachtree, too, would reinvent itself in the coming years, and today, many years later, is happily in business as one of the top publishers of children's books in the country, having left new adult fiction behind years ago. I made so many good friends there along with Margaret and Wayne Elliott, especially the marvelous Kathy Landwehr, who started as a publicist and is now vice president and associate publisher.

On June 1, I was in New York City yet again for the American Booksellers Association meeting, staying at the Penta Hotel, there to promote *Perfect Timing* for Peachtree and to meet Joni Evans and Harvey Klinger for the first time. I left the Big Apple with stars (and dollar signs) in my eyes. In July, Random House came through with a check of $27,500 for delivery of the corrected manuscript of *Final Heat*. Harvey appended a note, referring to Truly, the vicious little vixen who is a front-and-center character in my new novel:

> Had a good chat with Joni making yours truly's (no pun intended) changes in the catalog copy.
>
> Off to Maine, but I'll give you a holler if anything excitin' happens in August.
>
> Type away!

Perfect Timing continued to do well for us and had gone into a second printing by July and was picked as a Literary Guild selection. Harvey had also sold paperback rights to Penguin in an auction for $20,000. When the Penguin edition came out the following year in their Contemporary American Fiction edition, the ads in the back would be for books in the same series by Don DeLillo, William Kennedy, Thomas Pynchon, Philip Roth, Saul Bellow, and others in whose company I trembled.

I was beginning to worry about the film version of *All the Western Stars*. Dick said little had happened since we had last talked and that he'd offered Mick Garris's script to several directors, who passed. Dick also shared his delight that I was now also working with Ron Howard, whom he described as a wonderful person and close friend. If Dick Zanuck said that about you, it was true.

I need to explain that even though I'd sold a book to Random House, my business arrangement with Peachtree was still in force. Summoning the kind of moral thunder that only stupidity can explain, I wrote a letter to Margaret, telling her that I was severing my relationship with the house that had done so much good for me. Someone should have hit me with a stick, but I did write it, and there's no use trying to forgive myself now. Margaret wrote me back on July 6, and it was clear that I had deeply hurt and offended her, and I felt literally nauseous. She was totally in the right, and I was completely in the wrong. If I had had any sense at all, I would have continued publishing certain books with Peachtree *and* Random House, but in my manic-manic world, I simply couldn't see that far. I will always regret the way I handled that situation.

I did a great many appearances in 1991, and even did an an hour-long phone interview with KNUS radio in Denver on September 10. That same month, an excerpt from *Perfect Timing* came out in a gigantic spread in a magazine called *The World & I*, a publication of, oh my God, the *Washington Times*, which was owned by the Rev. Sun Myung Moon. It came with very good original artwork and a thoughtful essay on me and my work by Gail Regier of the University of Central Florida and a frequent contributor to *Harper's* and *The Atlantic*. It also had an absolutely savage review of the book by Monroe K. Spears, James Dickey's major professor at Vanderbilt, former editor of *The Sewanee Review*, and by then a starchy professor emeritus from Rice. I painted a dismal and mildly insulting (though comic) picture of academia in the book, and I think he, a lifelong academic, took it personally. The final line of Spears's pissy dismissal is this: "This novel is good entertainment for the beach."

In the meantime, anxious to have something new to show Joni Evans about the time *Final Heat* came out in 1992, I had spent much of 1991 writing a novel called *Blue Crystal*. (For the longest time, the manuscript had no title;

Harvey came up with *BC*.) This may be one of the weakest things I ever wrote, and when it came out in 1992, people reacted strongly, either for or furiously against. It was a taut thriller set in the Kentucky cave country and ended up with a group of thugs chasing the good guys through a commercial declivity called Blue Crystal Cave. The book did have some good work in places, but I was never happy with it. All my books are still in print as of 2013 except for *Final Heat* and *Blue Crystal*, which I have not allowed to be reprinted, though it's easy enough to buy a used copy online.

In our new three-story house in the woods, we got things ready for the arrival of our daughter—we'd had the sex-determination test done, and so we knew. We had already picked out a name, Megan Leigh Williams, and we got her bedroom, next to ours, ready, along with the family bassinet and her first toys. As Linda came to term that fall, we dawdled, far more mature and knowledgeable about things than we had been when Brandon was born in 1978. Finally, on the night of October 24, Linda said her contractions were getting strong. I got my watch, and we began to time them, and it was soon clear that we needed to pack up and head to Athens Regional Hospital. I was moving a hundred directions at once, but ever-calm Linda was laughing at me and shaking her head. When our son had come into the world, it had seemed like an old black-and-white TV sitcom, with me pacing downstairs. The changes in childbirth procedures since then surprised me. We checked in, and the doctor found that Linda was not too far from delivering. He broke her water, and we went into the birthing room to wait. Linda had already planned an epidural, and so within a few minutes, she was in no pain at all. The Atlanta Braves were in the World Series that year, and the game that night went into extra innings. We watched it until the Braves won, well after midnight.

"You about ready to have this baby?" the doctor asked genially, coming into the room.

"I am," Linda said, shifting a little higher on the birthing table. I was sitting right next to her, and I stood, ready for our new child.

At 1:11 a.m. on October 25, 1991, Megan Leigh Williams came crying into the world. I had the chance to cut the cord, and of course I did. Within a few minutes, I was holding my swaddled daughter in my arms, trying to fight off tears of joy. She would be our late-life gift, a beautiful girl and then a gorgeous woman, with many talents and an absolutely enormous capacity for loving others. She and Brandon were our True North, the real joy that we made. A writing career compared to *fatherhood*? Nothing. *Nothing*. Rocking my daughter, I was wholly, utterly content.

He first saw Journey to the Center of the Earth *not long after it came out in 1959. Even then he knew the center of the Earth was a molten ball of metal, but he didn't care. Over the years, he visited as many commercial caves as he could, and in each one, he was James Mason (not Pat Boone), heading downward into the darkness. He also loved caves because of an Uncle Scrooge comic book called "The Fabulous Philosopher's Stone," which came out in June 1955, written and drawn by the great Carl Barks. In it, Uncle Scrooge and his nephews descend into the Earth in search of the stone that will turn anything it touches into gold. His brother Mark bought him a pristine copy many years later, and he treasures it, keeps it out where he can see it at all times. Now, in his house on Pine Street in Madison, with a new baby on the way, he dreams of wombs, of caves.*

26

A Good Life Gone

On the morning of November 26, 1991, the phone rang in my Conner Hall office on the University of Georgia campus. Someone sobbed uncontrollably on the other end, and I stood up, very worried. It was a woman's voice, and at first I couldn't tell whose. But then I knew it was Margaret Quinlin's.

"Did you hear about *Ray*?" she managed to ask between choking sobs. She meant, of course, our friend Raymond Andrews. I had not seen him after returning from New York that summer, though we had talked on the phone several times.

"No, no," I managed, feeling sick.

"He *killed* himself," she cried, her voice filled with more utter agony than I ever heard from another human being in my life. I must have turned parchment-pale. I sat down involuntarily in my desk chair. "He shot himself down by the gazebo." A bookseller in Athens we both knew had heard about it and called her. This was before the Internet, and no one had called me. After talking with Margaret for awhile, both of us shattered, I called Linda at home and told her, and she began to cry, and Linda *never* cries. Not sure what to do, I called Ray's house, and the phone rang several times before a tear-roughened voice came on the other line: Benny. He had been coming down to talk with Ray and was in town, though I didn't know that. According to Jesse Freeman's biographical film, Benny had let Ray know that Ray needed to start helping support himself more. I suspected that Benny was largely supporting his brother, and I often wondered how Raymond made ends meet. I knew that he believed he had to be a full-time writer or nothing. As it turned out, Benny and Ray had apparently quarreled over the situation some time before, and Ray had told several friends around Athens he was going to be moving, though he wasn't sure where. He told some people Nebraska, others California. Even before Ray died, I thought the notion that any *serious* writer must support himself by writing alone was a bad idea that had wormed its way into America's consciousness. The idea was that if one didn't have the courage to write full time, he didn't have the courage to be a True Artist. I loved Raymond Andrews as much as any friend I ever had, but that notion is pure bullshit, and it still saddens me, decades later, that Ray (and many others) gambled everything on it. There is not one goddamn thing romantic or advantageous about being poor and thereby somehow "pure." But some very bright people disagree with me on that, and I know it. What I do believe with all my soul is that being a serious artist requires every ounce of energy a person owns and then some. A true artist must have true dedication and never give up and *never* give in.

"Benny, it's [I began to cry] Phil," I said. "It's Phil. Oh my God, Benny. Oh my God. Is it true?"

"I...I don't cry," Benny said, weeping. "Phil, he did this for me. He did this for me."

I never forgot his words. Ray had gone around the house and left notes on all his belongings, saying what he wanted to happen to them. He also left Benny a letter telling him that he, Ray, had lived a good life in his fifty-seven years. Then he went out in the yard and shot himself in the head. Ray had a huge group of friends in Athens and around the country, and everyone was sickened and shocked. I spent weeks wandering in the woods, absolutely sure I'd let my good friend down. But in the end, suicides can't be understood. I had an uncle who killed himself some years before I was born, and no one in the family even tried to explain why. There would be no funeral for Ray, but Peachtree would host a memorial service at the Atlanta Public Library some time after Christmas. That he was southern and African American somehow made it all worse for many of us, considering the history of endemic racism in the South, but in the end, it was just Ray. We loved him, and he left us far too soon.

I am fascinated by writers who seem to make no real literary mistakes in their careers, either in the books they publish or the ones they don't. Harper Lee and Margaret Mitchell each wrote one gloriously successful book that was made into an even more successful film, and then they quit. Isaac Asimov wrote or edited more than five hundred books and penned some ninety thousand letters and postcards. In between Lee and Asimov lie the rest of us, and with luck we publish a handful of works that will last. Few people leap out of their seats and shout with joy when hearing Beethoven's Eighth Symphony. Few people *don't* leap up at the end of his Seventh or Ninth. To me, James Joyce did very little wrong in his literary life—just enough, and the right books, too. I will never forget how I felt reading his great short story "The Dead" for the first time when I was eighteen. Even with a large *oeuvre* in Russian and English, Vladimir Nabokov's books seem to flow logically and with staggering genius, one after another to the end. Most of us who publish more than five books in a lifetime have at least one book that is substantially weaker than the others. And as the list of titles goes up, so does the chance of lobbing more clunkers. Some writers put forth nothing but bad books when they find out a person is almost certain to make less money with literarily challenging titles than with those written for people who move their lips when they read. And so it goes, onward and unendingly onward. Raymond's best books, to me, were the novel *Appalachee Red* and the memoir *The Last Radio Baby*. There was something about the man, and his body of work, that hints to me that these two will endure. I can tell you, with every ounce of truth I bear, that you would have never met a finer man than Raymond Andrews. I know I never did. The Atlanta memorial service for Ray in early 1992 was tremendously sad. I read a couple of letters he had written me many years earlier when neither of us had published anything but wanted to be published authors more than anything else in this world.

Late in the year, Dick and Lili Zanuck re-upped on their option of *All the Western Stars* for another twenty-five grand. And I waited to see what happened when my first book from Random House came out in 1992. I was nervous that things would not go well, and when the book came out, it would be far worse than even I could imagine, making me feel even more like a fool for leaving Peachtree Publishers.

As 1992 dawned, I had a new book coming out, a number in print in both hardback and softcover, and three foreign translations, *Slow Dance in Autumn* having come out in Japanese. Margaret wrote me in January to explain her long absence off my radar. Business was tough for all publishers in those days, and Peachtree had the same kind of problems everyone else did. So she was putting out fires while still moving ahead publishing books, too.

When *Final Heat* came out, the prepubs were terrible. Joni was completely baffled. She had also turned down *Blue Crystal* and said that she just thought it was the wrong book for me. Even though there *were* a few good reviews, including a terrific one in the *Atlanta Journal-Constitution,* I felt more dispirited than I ever had in my creative life. A mildly well-known writer, in a deliberately mean review in the *Philadelphia Inquirer,* all but accused me (absolutely wrongly) of plagiarism. I had read a couple of his books, though, and saw nothing in them of particular distinction, so it stung less than it could have. But there *was* a lot of attention, and *Entertainment Weekly* even gave it decent coverage. Bill Starr at *The State* newspaper in Columbia, S.C., penned a strong review. Bill became a friend in later years and has been a supporter of mine since 1984. He is a fine writer and a wonderful man.

Despite the joy of having a new baby, I was depressed by the general reception of *Final Heat,* by Joni turning down *Blue Crystal,* by the continued lack of progress on the film of *All the Western Stars,* and by the little information I was getting from Imagine on Ron Howard's film of *Perfect Timing*. So I did the time-honored thing: I unloaded on my agent. On March 25, Harvey wrote me a letter I've always treasured. It's worth quoting largely in full, I think:

> Having digested your thoughts from last week and thinking through my own, I have basically one thought: you shouldn't think of yourself as having a "career."
>
> What I believe you do have is talent and plenty of it. A talent as important as yours does not automatically become a career. What it is, at any stage of development, is a vocation. I mean that in the Catholic sense; the sense of a calling, like a nun experiences before taking the veil.
>
> The gift that makes an individual an artist is something Flannery O'Connor said was a mystery and a social responsibility. She felt that she wrote, and anyone with genuine talent writes, essentially by virtue of being good at it. The ability becomes the destiny.
>
> As sure as I can be of anything, Phil, I'm sure you will publish again and again and you will see a magnificent advance again because your native ability is not going to let you rest until these things happen. Try and hang it up if you think you want to. Your talent will be there no matter what, sitting in your head, squirming.

> From everything I've seen, the easiest way for a born writer to do his work is to write something that doesn't feel like work. The only thing you can force, in the end, is the truth out of your self.

It was the single finest letter and piece of advice I got in my publishing days, and it saved my life. Of *course*, I didn't have a publishing "career." But for the past few years I'd been fooled into thinking I did. But even though I was making a substantial amount of money, I'd never even remotely considered writing full time. (People who knew of my success and dreamed of their own were absolutely *offended* that I was never going to write full time before retirement. My response was always the same: I've done all this with a full-time job that I like. Why would I quit either?) I think Molly Friedrich sensed the same things about me. I would never be able to write essentially the same book over and over. I wasn't a Catholic, but Harvey chose the right word, though I'd have used it with a little "c." Sales and money were fine. I certainly wasn't allergic to financial security, since we'd been so poor for so long. But money alone has never made me happy.

So, for the first time, I saw a way out. I had already written *Blue Crystal*, which I thought was a lesser book, designed largely, though not completely, to make money, along with many other books that I never had passion for. But beyond that, I could take my time and wait to see where things went. For the time being, they seemed to be going nowhere. I drove back to Nashville for the millionth time on March 20 for an autographing at a large bookstore, and one bored and indifferent employee set me up at a small table far from book-buyers and then went away forever. I was supposed to be there for two hours, but after ninety minutes, not a single person had come, and in a fit, I got in my car and drove straight home, five hours, in the middle of the night, absolutely enraged. This was the bottom of the pit.

It turned out that I would have a much shorter wait than I thought. After Joni turned down *Blue Crystal*, Harvey sent it on to many places, and soon enough, early in 1992, he got a call from an editor named Jim Moser at Grove Press, who *loved* the book. Things had started to look up over the summer when Harvey had sent me a check for a little more than $10,000 for Imagine's second option on *Perfect Timing*. Still, I had heard nothing from Ron Howard or his partner Brian Grazer, and to this day I don't know how far development went. I think it would have made a wonderful film, and Ron Howard would have been, well, "perfect" to direct it.

The thick, gummy, clouded angst I felt over my failure with *Final Heat* and failing Joni Evans began to lift. Grove Press! Founded in 1951, it had published many of the edgiest literary writers around in mid-century, a hefty number of them in translation, including Samuel Beckett, Jean Genet, Alain Robbe-Grillet, Frantz Fanon, and Eugène Ionesco. (By then, some of these authors seemed to have been following me around for years!) Allen Ginsberg, Jack Kerouac, and William Burroughs also published books with Grove Press. But my tie to it was far deeper than any of those. They had also published, in 1957, Frank O'Hara's volume of poetry, *Meditations in an Emergency*. And O'Hara, of course, was the writer who was so central to *An Anthology of New York Poets* that I had bought in 1970. This was much more personal than six degrees of separation. It was *synchrony*. The advance Harvey and Jim agreed upon was small, after *Final Heat*: $10,000. But with a new baby, a new house, and a new idea about my writing, I was delighted to get it.

Then the roof fell in. I had had several delightful phone conversations with Jim Moser, who was a pure pleasure. He was also a musician who had studied in Paris with Nadia Boulanger ("When she was very old, and I was very young") probably the single most famous music teacher of the 20th century and whose other pupils included Aaron Copland, Elliott Carter, David Diamond, and Philip Glass. Born in 1887, she had even attended the premiere of Igor Stravinsky's *Firebird,* for crying out loud. (She and Stravinsky were lifelong friends.) Jim was enthusiastic about *Blue Crystal* and its labyrinthine plot and layers of storyline about fathers and sons. Then out of the blue (apt) on February 18, he called with some stunning news: Grove Press was combining with Atlantic Monthly Press, and the entire staff of Grove Press was being fired.

"Holy crap," I said. "Jim, I'm so, so sorry but...."

"What's going to happen to your book?"

"Well, I was sort of...."

"To be honest, I just can't say at this point," he said. He seemed more worried about what would happen to *me* than to himself. But in the fairly brief time I knew Jim, he always seemed that way. What a fine man. When I hung up, I immediately called Harvey, and he'd already heard rumors that morning. He told me to sit tight, and he'd try to see what was up. But I found out from Jim before Harvey knew. The next morning, Jim was on the phone with more hopeful news: He had been hired as editor-in-chief of the new combined publishing house, Grove/Atlantic. While I was thrilled with this, I couldn't shake the feeling that more chaos lay just beneath the surface of things. It usually did. Before anything else could happen, Harvey and Jim got contracts together, and Harvey sent them to me on September 10. I signed and returned them immediately. Soon enough, my latest book was in production. I was pleased to know that the Grove Press imprint would continue, and *Blue Crystal* would come out under it.

That summer of 1992, Hollywood came calling for me again. Word had filtered to me (from whom I cannot recall) that MGM and Dick Zanuck were not happy, in the end, with Mick Garris's screenplay for *All the Western Stars*. I wasn't surprised. I knew something had stalled the project. I liked Mick and felt his screenplay was solid, and so I was sorry for him. And one day that summer, Dick called me and confirmed my suspicions. I kept notes of his call.

"I have been having some interesting discussions with a Scottish director named Gillies MacKinnon," Dick said. "He did a fine picture with Albert Finney called *The Playboys*. And when I was in London I sent him over the script, and he responded favorably. Then I met him over there a few weeks ago, and he faxed additional notes."

"G-i-l-l-i-s...." I said, writing.

"It's spelled *G-i-l-l-i-e-s* but it's pronounced like *Gillis*," Dick said. "Anyway he's going to be coming over soon to do post-production at George Lucas's ranch in northern California in October or November. And he strongly feels that we should go back to the book to a large extent. He thinks the women in the story should play a much larger part than they do [in the Garris screenplay]."

"I see." Where was he going with this?

"He thinks the current script wastes a lot of time at Fieldstone." That was the nursing home that Jake and Lucas escape from when they head west. "He's suggesting that only Jake go to Fieldstone, and we quickly get them both out on the road and through the road section we learn about them."

This was precisely what had happened with James Dickey and *Deliverance*. Although Dickey's screenplay of his own novel gives the story a shape by showing the men at home in Atlanta before going to the wilds of north Georgia, the director John Boorman insisted that the movie start with the men on the road, heading up there. Boorman made a great movie, but he was wrong about that part, and James Dickey was right. And I felt, at least on this score, MacKinnon was wrong. But he certainly seemed passionate about my book. (His best-known film may be *Hideous Kinky*, which he directed in 1998, starring Kate Winslet.)

"What it all boils down to," said Dick, finally getting to the point, "is that I think we're going to have to put on another writer. And I was thinking of you."

My hand froze to the telephone.

"Me," I said.

"I know it's hard for an author to pull himself away from certain things," Dick said, pushing me to consider MacKinnon's new idea. "Look, I'm off on Tuesday again to be chairman of the jury at the Tokyo Film Festival. Between now and when I get back, I'd like to send you the two notes I received from MacKinnon. And I'd like for you to take a look at those and give some thought to what he said. When I get back, we can talk some about it. And if we see eye to eye, at the end of his stay at the Lucas Ranch, I'll see if he can come out here for a couple of days."

This could mean some serious money for me. I'd written a couple of spec film scripts already and studied the format for years. I felt, working with Dick and Gillies, I could write a screenplay of my own book. Plus, I would be cheaper than almost anyone else Dick could get. (In the end, my contract with MGM was for Screen Writers Guild minimum, but that was still $75,000, no small potatoes, at least not to me.) Harvey and I talked, and soon enough, my depression began to lift. One side note: Since MGM hired me in 1993, I was on Screen Writers Guild health insurance in 1994, the year I had open heart surgery. After my UGA insurance paid its part, my Guild insurance paid most of the rest. It was a hard time, but that was certainly serendipity.

Some time in these years (I can't nail down the date with anything in my archives), I was invited along with a number of writer friends to a conference at the public library in Brunswick, Georgia, on the coast. A number of us stayed on nearby St. Simons Island in an old-fashioned motel and the evening before drank too much as one does at these things. Early the next morning, to clear my head, I took a long walk and wound up at the pier in the village area on St. Simons. I was standing at the top of millions of tons of breakwater rocks when my feet slipped, and I tumbled down fifty or sixty feet, bouncing from rock to rock, head to foot. I didn't break anything, but my face was wrecked. I mean *wrecked*. When we got to the venue that morning, my pal Stanley Lindberg, editor of *The Georgia Review*, was to introduce me. A number of people had seen my face and backed away in horror.

"I'd like to introduce Philip Lee Williams now," Stan said. "As you can see, last night he slipped away from our group and got worked over by a bunch of shrimpers."

After a huge laugh, I didn't bother to correct Stan. The attendees got just what they paid for—a writer who'd done something insane and still showed up. One of my finest hours.

In keeping with my promise to myself to publish only things I believed were solidly artful, I sent Harvey in September a manuscript I'd been working on for quite some time. Called *Almost Light*, it was the story of a junk dealer whose soul is fought over by love (personified by Venus) and Death (ditto, by a traveling tonic salesman). I think it's an inventive, oddball, sweetheart of a novel, filled with sharp humor and deeply structured philosophy. I had worked on it for a couple of years and just loved it. Of course, I knew it wasn't nominally commercial and told Harvey so. He liked much of the novel, but he felt it needed work. He had some good points in his response:

> Let me give you an example of an instance where the central conceit of the novel works perfectly: when Victor the dog is eyeing Death's bones. The daunting task you have before you is to make it work that well every time, lest you stall the narrative with a joke that simply hasn't gone over with the reader.

Point taken, but I could tell already that I liked this manuscript far more than he did, and I didn't want to wander back into *Death in the Country* territory again. I wasn't sure I wanted to take Harvey's advice, but I wasn't in any huge hurry. To ease my pain, late in October Harvey sent me my cut of the sale of *Final Heat's* German rights to the publisher Goldmann. (A funny footnote: *Final Heat* has a vicious Doberman wandering around, wanting to kill something, and it finally gets the chance in the book's last sentence. When the Goldmann translation appeared, the dog on the cover was—a *chihuahua*! I laughed so hard when I first saw the book, I wept with unrestrained glee.)

My life at the University of Georgia moved on, and in October, I took a new job as senior science writer for the whole university, and I moved to the

Office of Public Information in an old building next to the Coliseum, UGA's basketball arena. I would stay there for five years, not always happily.

I was more and more convinced that none of my writing life was working any longer. I began to have serious doubts about *Blue Crystal* even before it came out, and though Harvey was clearly a great literary agent, I wasn't much of a client. So as 1993 came on to the calendar, I was thinking of leaving him. But by then the endlessly nimble Harvey had gotten my contract with MGM settled, I got yet another huge check, and I was deep into writing the screenplay of my own novel. No time to leave Hurricane Harvey. But often the storms of a literary career wash one away no matter what he does.

ଊ

He remembers the first time he saw her walking into the biology lab. She wore blue jeans with anti-war patches and dangly, gold peace-symbol earrings. (This was when that symbol was edgy and deliberately provocative.) Later, he would conflate that moment with one of his favorite Kenneth Koch poems from An Anthology of New York Poets,*"You Were Wearing":*

> You were wearing your Edgar Allen Poe printed cotton blouse.
> In each divided up square was a picture of Edgar Allen Poe.

He remembers her eyes, narrowing with some hidden but possibly superior glee. He was too clean-cut for her, writhed in his seat as she approached. She was too beautiful for him. Probably too smart, too. For a brief hopeful moment, he wondered what she would be like outside class. He gave up before she sat down. Then he didn't.

27

Hiring Agent X

I had almost finished reading proof on *Blue Crystal* and was through with the first draft of my *All the Western Stars* screenplay for MGM. They had renewed their option yet again in the fall, but everyone was nervous that it had gone on for a long time. Gillies MacKinnon and I were talking almost daily on the phone, and I'd even bought a fax machine for my home, something that at the time was expensive but necessary. If the Internet had been cranking yet, there's no telling how much smoother the process would have been. Fax was a baby step toward it, but it was clunky and awkward, especially when working with a one-hundred-and-twenty page manuscript. Gillies liked a great deal of my screenplay, which was far less like the novel than Mick Garris's had been. But since I wrote the novel, I felt as if I had the right. On January 23, I sent a note to Mr. Klinger:

> I just wanted you to know I have a FAX machine at my house. I had to get one to work on the screenplay. I've been FAXing back and forth between here, London, and Beverly Hills for days (regular phone calls, too)....
>
> The screenplay seems to be going okay, though Gillies is a little antsy about what exactly Dick's plans are. I don't see any huge problems in rewriting the screenplay at all. Gillies and I are talking and FAXing a lot about it now.
>
> I've finished galleys on *Blue Crystal*. Linda is reading them this weekend, and I'll be sending them back to Jim this next week. Looks fine.
>
> I've also finished the Indian book....

The *Indian book*? Turns out I'd written a quite good historical novel set during the French and Indian War in northwestern South Carolina at the

British colonial fort that my father, Mark, and I had helped excavate in 1967-68. Mentioned earlier, this is the book I (much later) privately published under the name of Samuel Leigh as a gift for my father after we couldn't sell it anywhere else. It is called *Beyond the River*.

Since Grove/Atlantic had been in such a mess when it bought *Blue Crystal*, they hired an insanely good freelance copy editor named Ed Sedarbaum to copy edit the manuscript. When I got it back from Ed late in 1992, my book looked as if it had been worked over by Hannnibal Lecter. He beat it to a fricking bloody pulp. And did a job bordering on genius. But even Ed couldn't pump real life into a story that never really jelled. The book came out in late spring 1993, and the reviews were generally good, especially in *The Los Angeles Times*.

Jim Moser came to Atlanta in June to meet me and talk about the future. When it comes to meetings, I'm always early. *Always*. And I try to be so personable I'll make Howard Hughes look like president of the local Rotary Club. And yet that day, I cut our meeting time at a restaurant in Atlanta close, and I was twenty minutes late, the only time in my entire career I was late for a meeting of any kind. And of course this was long before cell phones. I finally found the place and did a U-turn in the middle of a busy street in downtown Atlanta and pulled into a parking space. I recognized Jim immediately. He was the one who looked extremely worried and was pacing out near the street and looking both ways. I waved at him as I got out of the car, and I never saw a man's expression change so dramatically in such a short time. Jim and I liked each enormously and immediately. I had never really left Harvey, and I told Jim about *Almost Light*, and he wanted to see it immediately. At the time I thought Grove was going to do *Almost Light*, a book-to-be-named, and then the old post-World War I novel, *Darkness*. If my own literary life was confusing, it seemed worse at Grove/Atlantic. My novel ultimately didn't do well enough for them to make me an offer on another book, so I was left hanging. But for only a few days.

Other things had gone on anon. Demi Moore's "people" were interested in *The Song of Daniel*, but not interested enough, finally, to option it. We were "hearing" an ominous silence from Grove on paperback rights for *Blue Crystal*. In the end, there wouldn't be any, despite the fact that it was perfect for soft cover. I was still pushing *Almost Light* on everyone in sight.

In early June, Gillies MacKinnon called me from L.A. He'd had dinner with Dick and said Dick was very low and depressed about the whole thing. He had reason to be unhappy: after so much work, MGM had put *All the Western Stars* in turnaround. Anyone familiar with the film business knows that term. For others, it's simple: MGM had kicked us to the curb, and our project was finished there. Fortunately, I had already been paid for the screenplay. But no more $25,000 options at the end of the year.

Here's how I described it to Harvey in a Tolstoyan fax:

> Gillies and I had a warm conversation with a valedictory feel—perhaps our last. I can't say for sure, but my best guess now is that *ATWS* is dead. I suspect Dick will let it go upon option in December. Whether it's worth flogging more is something I can't answer, but I don't have much hope for the project any longer.

In the nonce, we'd sold French translation rights on *Final Heat* to Gallimard, and they would publish it in two different editions over the next decade. Linda, Brandon, and I flew to New Orleans in June so I could appear at the annual meeting of the American Library Association. There, I was on a panel with Pulitzer Prize winner Robert Olen Butler, and years later he would graciously give me a lovely blurb on my novel *The Campfire Boys*.

Some time in the first half of 1993, there was a two-hour long conference call between me, Dick Zanuck, Gillies MacKinnon and, I believe, another person or two from Dick's office. We talked forever about structural issues with the screenplay, but I was beginning to worry that we were in an endless, hopeless loop. And when MGM let the whole project go, I could not imagine that all this work would get anywhere. Soon enough, *MGM* was let go—the studio was sold, and a huge number of projects it had been supporting went down the drain. Dick said in late July that when the dust settled, he would bring our project back to the new management. Gillies also landed a plum assignment as director of a new Steve Martin movie, *A Simple Twist of Fate*, part of which would be filmed in the county courthouse in my hometown of Madison, Georgia, and about two hundred feet from the *Madisonian* where I had worked from 1974-1978. Weirdness has no bounds. So with Gillies leaving for another project, MGM sold, and Dick moving on to other things, our movie was going down for the third time.

Gillies and I had already met in Atlanta once to talk about *ATWS*, and we spent an entire weekend at the Ritz-Carlton in Buckhead, a fair amount of it in the bar. We did work hard on the screenplay, though. With the new movie filming in our area, though, he came through in October and visited Linda and me at our house in the country, and we talked about might-have beens. I found it amusing that, growing up in Glasgow, he and his friends played "Rebels and Yankees," and he was quite interested in the American Civil War. During November, Linda and I visited several sets during the filming of *A Simple Twist of Fate*, and I got to meet Laura Linney, Gabriel Byrne, and Catherine O'Hara. Gillies introduced me to Steve Martin between takes in the courthouse.

"It's a pleasure to meet you," I said. "I think I've seen almost all of your films and really respect your work."

"You *doooooo*? *Reeeaaaallly*?" he mugged in the voice of one of the swinging Czech playboys he'd played on "Saturday Night Live" years before. "Well then, let's talk about every single one of them! In order! *Rrrrright* now!"

I would have laughed harder than I did, but I was sick. *Very* sick. And shortly I would undergo open heart surgery and recalibrate my life and the career that Harvey still insisted I didn't have.

Harvey Klinger hated the "Indian" book, *Beyond the River*. Absolutely *hated* it. So on January 3, 1994, I wrote Harvey a note:

> Harvey, I've really enjoyed working with you, but it's clear to me that it's time for a change for both of us. I honestly don't think you've changed since we began to work together, but I certainly have.
>
> I will be looking for another agent. I have many reasons, but mainly I need a fresh pair of eyes to look at my accumulated work. I don't doubt your talent or literary expertise. That's not the problem. It's just that I need to rethink many things about what I'm doing, and I need a new approach that I think our history together precludes.
>
> I know I will always be a kind of fringe client for any agent, but I think I can find a better match, and I know you don't need to waste your time any more on work you find insupportable. This is not a passing irritation at your condemnation of *Beyond the River* but something I've been considering for at least a year. Our most recent conversation simply confirmed my resolve that a change is necessary.
>
> As of now, I don't know another agent, so I'll be muddling my way along trying to see what's out there. In the meantime, I will

> continue to write, as I seem to have no real choice in the matter if I want to maintain my sanity. Anyway, we will, I'm sure, continue to work on the residue of my old books for some time to come. I still get statements from Molly Friedrich on my *first* book, and I haven't been with her for seven years!
>
> Sorry I couldn't help you get the Duesenberg, but I'm sure you're not far away from it anyway. At my pace, I'll be lucky to help an agent get a Yugo.

I wish I could say that within a couple of weeks I had a new agent, publishers were clamoring for my postmodern works, and that I was refusing to take an urgent call from Robert Redford. The truth is that I had just worked myself into a fit and was being dramatic. I'm sure Harvey had seen worse. But it was salubrious in several ways. First, it allowed me to take off the table manuscripts I knew would never fly with Harvey or in New York. It also let me blow off steam about my frustrations with having "talent" and no "career." And finally, it gave me a clear view of what I would do in pursuit of my art and what I would not. But of course, a long business association can't be stopped cold turkey, and Harvey and I would continue to work together, off and on, for some time.

In February 1994, the mitral valve in my heart tore loose. I had known since the late Seventies about that floppy valve, but I was one of the very few people who have to have surgery to correct it. My surgeon wanted to repair it, but when he got into my chest on February 22, he found that the valve was more or less hanging by a bloody thread, and he had to replace it with a St. Jude artificial valve. I came through it all right, but I was so weak that I couldn't even walk upstairs to my study for nearly a month after they cut me open. I would have to take heavy doses of a blood thinner for the rest of my life. My book *Crossing Wildcat Ridge* talks at length about this time in my life, so I won't go back through it here.

When I healed, I had no book coming out for the first time since 1987 and no immediate plans for one. In fact, three years would pass before my next novel hit the bookstores. People wondered where I had gone, but in truth, I was sick of the treadmill and just wanted peace and quiet. In the meantime, independent producers hounded me and Harvey about film rights to my books. Dick tried to pitch *ATWS* to Castle Rock after MGM put us in turnaround, but they turned it down. Jack Lemmon, who had been interested since the beginning, was staying in touch with Dick and still wanted to play Jake. I wasn't very interested in any of it. A deep depression had overcome me after my heart surgery. I had been under anesthesia for more than four hours, and they had stopped my heart and put me on a heart-lung machine while they put in the new valve. Either the anesthesia, the stopping of my heart, or the physical fragility I felt after surgery left me emotionally drained. I would be tethered for the rest of my life to a daily dose of a pill called Coumadin; without it, I would die. I would need a blood test every month, or more often, to see if the pill was working. But while my mind was berserk, my body, within a few months, was dramatically better than it had been just before surgery. I didn't know how sick I had been. Six weeks after surgery, I was back at my desk at UGA. By then the Internet was creeping into human consciousness, and the world began to shift from letters to e-mails. But it wouldn't have mattered. For most of 1994, I was absent without leave on the literary front. I was forty-four, and I was wondering, for the first time, if I would ever get to write, much less publish the fine books I knew I was capable of writing. We were financially stable, but we didn't have so much money that one illness couldn't have wiped us out, even though we had very good health insurance. Although Harvey would continue to handle all the old business between us, I was without an agent or a publisher or much of a future. I tentatively tried to contact Margaret Quinlin at Peachtree in May, while I was still healing, but that didn't work. Peachtree was moving in different directions, and I had abandoned them, not the other way around.

But my dark period turned out to last only six months. As early as a couple of weeks before my surgery, producers were contacting Harvey and asking about the film rights to *All the Western Stars*. In fact, I'm told there was a great deal of interest in reviving the project after MGM put it in turnaround, and the great Richard Zanuck had to move on to other things. But fastest on the draw was an unlikely young writer and director in Los Angeles named Kevin Meyer.

Kevin had been a fan of *All the Western Stars* since the late 1980s and had carefully kept track of what was happening with MGM. Checking on it periodically, he was startled to find in early 1994 that it was once again available. So he took the book and a ton of enthusiasm to Keith Samples, head of Rysher Entertainment, whose film unit was already at its height. Kevin wrote and directed *Perfect Alibi*, which would come out in 1995 with

Teri Garr, Hector Elizondo, and Kathleen Quinlan. Kevin also wrote the script for *A Smile Like Yours* with Greg Kinnear which Keith Samples directed and which was released later, in 1997. At first a producer of television shows, Rysher, in the Nineties, when the economy was strongly growing and before the dot.com bubble burst, had seen an opening for film production, too, and Kevin thought that this was a good place to set up *All the Western Stars*. He was right. Samples liked the story and, I'm sure, loved Kevin's enthusiasm. This would be Kevin's step up into the big time, and he wasn't about to blow it. Unfortunately for me, he wanted to write a new screenplay himself. Clearly, it was a once-in-a-lifetime chance, and he was going to take all of it he could. I couldn't blame him for that; I would have done exactly the same thing. Harvey was once again up to his elbows in my business, and I was tremendously relieved he hadn't just thrown me off the side of the boat after my fax in January. In August, I signed a one-year option with Rysher, and Kevin set to work writing the *third* version of the screenplay. Mine would never see the light of day, alas, and I don't even own the property anymore. (I will explain that later.) The option wasn't gigantic, but it was nice, $12,500 for the year, and I was delighted to give Peachtree the cut they had coming from my original contract with them. They would make a lot more money off of it in the next couple of years. While this part of the option was deliberately modest, the pressure was on Rysher for the rest of it. An additional six months' option in 1995 would cost them $25,000. And the full purchase price of the book for film would be $150,000, payable upon the exercise of the option but not later than the beginning of principal photography. If Rysher released the picture theatrically on more than five hundred screens in the U.S., I was entitled to a one-time additional payment of $50,000. I would also get 5 percent of net profits (hah) and a single-card credit in the film's titles. Unfortunately, if the film got that far, I would no longer own the book or even the characters, having sold them outright. During 1994, I heard occasional drum beats from the West Coast but not much else. I knew about sitting tight, and I was ready to do it again.

That August, the University of Georgia Press hired me as a writer on *The New Georgia Guide*, which would be the story of the state along the patterns of the original *Georgia Guide* from the WPA days. A group of exceptionally talented writers got together, and the Press paid us well, but I wound up spending most of my spare time for a year on this essay, traveling and interviewing people, and so I managed to come in well under minimum wage. But the whole project was a delight.

A small press called Maypop, run in Athens by my old friend, the poet and Rumi translator Coleman Barks, in 1994 brought out as a chapbook a story I'd written back in the *Observer* days for our annual Christmas supplement called Wrap-Up. Coleman had loved the story and often read it out loud to his classes at UGA over the years. It was called *A Gift from Boonie, Seymour, and Dog,* and over the years, a great many people have told me how much they like this tiny book.

Until Bill Contardi of Brandt & Hochman became my agent in 2002, I am sorry to say that I tried several agents who didn't work out, for one reason or another. But writing fiction for me had become like building birdhouses. I might have an idea, and instead of doing an outline, I would write a four-hundred-page novel. Some of these are quite good and should be published. (See a more or less complete list at the end of this book.) I also began to move forward on the rest of my postmodern Dante book. I had written the first part, as you might remember, back in the early Eighties. In the Nineties, I wrote part two, paralleling the *Purgatorio* section of Dante's masterwork. I wouldn't finish the entire book until the mid-2000s, a 1,500-page manuscript that I felt then and now is my masterwork to date. I don't want to speculate what might have happened to my career if Gerry Howard had liked it thirty years ago. Probably nothing different. But I wonder, nonetheless.

By early 1995, I had heard little from Rysher, but I was taking tentative steps toward getting back into the publishing game. Because one agent I worked with in those years refused permission to quote from letters, and because we sold only one project over the next few years, I am going to lump several agents together under the name Agent X.

I had always been interested in the intersection between history and human action, and because I'd helped excavate a British colonial fort whose height was during the French and Indian War era, I decided to write a huge novel with a strong female lead, set in Charleston. It would feature two nouveau-riche warring families against the backgrounds of the French and Indian War and the coming American Revolution. Written in a mock-Fielding postmodern style, it contained poetry and songs (the latter fully scored for piano and voice), written by the characters, not to mention journal entries and tons of letters from one set of characters to another. I called it *The True and Authentic History of Jenny Dorset,* and it was the first book I published since *The Heart of a Distant Forest* that felt like me at the deepest level. In fact, the entire title is *The True and Authentic History of Jenny Dorset consisting of A Narrative by a Retainer, Mr. Henry Hawthorne, Along with the History of Two Households, that of Dorset and Smythe, and How They Came to their Great Battle and How it Finally Ended &tc. And Various Songs, Journal Excerpts, and Letters Such as Seem Pertinent.* Gaw, how I love this book.

Agent X loved it, too, and we sent it many places and got good readings, but the place that loved it best and bought it—symmetry again—was Longstreet Press in Atlanta, where my old friend Chuck Perry had gone after leaving Peachtree. It is an absolutely hilarious and ultimately heartbreaking book. Longstreet's hardback edition, which came out in 1997, was in all ways a work of art. I'm proud to say that most of the ideas for design and even the kind of paper used (super white, like 18th century rag paper, deckle edges) were mine. That version can still be purchased on used book websites, of course, but at this writing it's fully in print in a lovely softcover edition from the University of Georgia Press. Go buy it now. I'll take a break while you do.

Around Christmas 1994, I took Brandon to New York City. I had literary business, meeting with Agent X in a midtown office with a view. But Brandon and I went all over the city. We visited the Strand Bookstore, of course, stayed at the Algonquin, and visited the White Horse Tavern in the Village, where Dylan Thomas supposedly drank his last whiskey. It was also a gathering place for New York poets like Frank O'Hara, John Ashbery, and Allen Ginsberg, as well as other writers such as Norman Mailer and James Baldwin. We met with Harvey. When we got together, I apparently confused one set of literary facts with another and led him to believe I was going to cut him out of dealings on the movie of *All the Western Stars* in the future. It sounds stupid enough to have been something I would have done. Harvey dropped me a letter on February 1, banging my head against the wall and telling me to get in line. I did. Considering the number of projects and facts I had been juggling since 1988, it's a wonder I had gotten anything right.

I think it's worth pausing at the point to clarify something. How much of this book have I written from memory alone? Virtually none. I have talked for hours to Linda, and we can't remember specific details within two *years* of when things happened sometimes. And this isn't just age. I've spoken to many others in these pages who didn't have a clue when things happened, either. No, I have records—letters, faxes, calendar leaves, notes from phone calls, and e-mails. And I kept *everything*. The Hargrett Rare Book and Manuscript Library at the University of Georgia had been asking for my papers for years, and only after I spent a year digging them out of the attic did I realize they contained my whole literary life without me remembering it. You want sources? I've got them.

That June, with option time for the Rysher production of *All the Western Stars* nearing, we began to get extremely good signs from the West Coast. Kevin Meyer finally wrote me with the details on June 21, and what I heard knocked me flat:

> When I found out Zanuck let the option expire, I brought the book to Keith Samples at Rysher. Needless to say, he loved it and from that point on the project began developing a life of its own. Keith brought in David Valdes to produce from Warner Bros. A few of David's credits include *Unforgiven, A Perfect World*, and *In the Line of Fire*.
>
> We are in negotiations with Freddie Francis to be the D.P. [director of photography]. He's British and has won two Academy Awards (most recently for *Glory*) and four British Academy Awards. We want to shoot in Cinemascope and having a man with such a grand, visual eye is very important to me. [Francis did commit.]
>
> Henry Bumstead will handle the production design duties, He's won Oscars for *Unforgiven, The Sting*, and *Vertigo*. A few of his other credits include *Cape Fear, The World According to Garp*, and *To Kill a Mockingbird*.

Jack Lemmon committed to the film. He had wanted to be in it for a long time, and that time was now.

> In closing, I'll leave you with a final thought. When David and I first sat down with Jack to listen to his "script comments" he had only one thing to say: "Don't change a thing." Based on his taste and caliber of talent already surrounding this project, your mind should be at ease. We are dedicated not just to make a film but an "exceptional film" that we will all be proud of.

I'm a film freak and constantly study the credits beneath the title. When I watch a movie, I look at, and listen to *everything*. *David Valdes, Freddie Francis,* and *Henry Bumstead*? This was beyond belief.

As if to seal an increasingly good year with a kiss, I was invited to be a featured author at a festival called The Writer's Sojourn in Steamboat Springs, Colorado. Linda and I flew to Denver and rented an obscenely large SUV for the drive up to Steamboat, destroying the planet while having the time of our lives. Founded in 1993 by the Bud Werner Memorial Library, the festival was in its full glory by the time they invited me in 1995. Other writers that year were Carolyn See (a fine novelist who had given *All the Western Stars* and *The Heart of a Distant Forest* great reviews in the *Los Angeles Times*), William Kittredge, James Galvin, and Elinor Lipman. We had a spectacular visit. For the first time in years I felt well, even at an altitude of 6,732 feet, almost exactly six thousand feet higher than where I lived. We hung out with Galvin and Ellie Lipman most, and the event was the finest at which I was ever a featured author, with absolutely enormous crowds. A group of public school teachers from the area all but adopted Linda when they found out she was one of them. One morning we discovered, leaning against the door of our hotel room, an empty plastic water bottle with an appended note that saying it contained Colorado air, a gift from the teachers of the area to Linda! We thought it a lovely gesture.

Ellie had to fly to Boston. We had a car and gave her a ride back to the airport in Denver after the event was over, and I was very nearly late for the second time in my life after turning in the rental car. All three of us had to run like madmen (and women) down the concourse to get our planes. Linda and I dashed down the loading ramp and straight into our jet just as the flight crew was about to close the door. Alas, that scenario would vanish after 9/11.

I also wrote and co-produced a documentary film that fall on the great ecologist Eugene Odum. Gene had founded the Institute of Ecology at the University of Georgia and was a legendary figure in the field. He and his brother Howard Odum had shared the Craaford Prize in 1986—the equivalent of a Nobel, which is not awarded in ecology. Directed and co-produced at UGA by my colleague David Silvian, the film aired on Georgia Public Television numerous times and won awards from the New York Film Festival, the Telly Awards, and the Columbus (Ohio) Film Festival. It was done on a shoestring, but no one else ever did a full documentary on Gene's life, and I'm proud I was the one to do it. Gene died in 2002 at the age of 88.

Kevin Meyer was busier than I was that fall, and by then producer David Valdes was working on cast, too. On October 5, the team dropped a note to Jack Lemmon saying that it had been more than eight weeks since Rysher had sent the script to—déjà vu all over again—Marlon Brando. Since it was clear Brando wasn't going to respond, their next choice was Alec Guinness to play Jake. Obi-Wan Kenobi apparently liked my story and the screenplay, but his wife had recently broken a hip, and anyway he couldn't understand why they were interested in an "old Brit" to play such an American role. By the time Kevin wrote Albert Finney to inquire about his possible interest in the film, things had moved much further than even I knew: Filming would take place on the road in Richmond, Memphis, Guthrie and Norman (Oklahoma), and, in Texas: Dallas, Fort Worth, San Antonio, and Del Rio. And it would begin March 2, 1996. I didn't find out that the film had been greenlighted until after Christmas, but James Garner knew in early December when Kevin wrote him and asked him to play Jake opposite Jack Lemmon's Lucas. (Note: My novel starts in Georgia and doesn't catch up to Kevin's scenario until Dallas, but it seemed like a small enough change, and Kevin had longtime associations with a route from the East to the West that was farther north than mine.)

I kept my eye on art writing and *had* managed to get a poem into fabled *Poetry* (Chicago) in August 1995, so my eye was still on the prize. Clearly, 1996 was going to be the greatest year of my writing life. *Jenny Dorset* was by then in the capable hands of Longstreet Press, and I felt it would a huge step forward for me when it came out in 1997. And in March, filming would begin on what could be a potentially fine filmed version of *All the Western Stars*. I had read Kevin's version of the screenplay, and he'd done a superb job. It amused me no end that his screenplay was more like the book than Mick Garris's and far more faithful to it than my own. I wasn't sure I could survive another Hindenburgish crash-and-burn, but everyone was so giddy, I knew I wouldn't have to.

At some point during these years, I attended a conference in D.C. for science writers. In a near-empty hall while waiting for the opening event, trying to be friendly, I saw a woman with a tag noting that she was a science writer at the Wood's Hole Oceanographic Institute. I sat down next to her. We talked for a time about why we liked science writing.

"Actually, I know that area of Massachusetts pretty well," I said. "My wife's family is from Cape Cod."

"What town?" she asked.

"Harwich Port," I answered.

"*I'm* from Harwich Port," she said, smiling. "Who is her family there?"

"Her grandfather was Dr. Harold F. Rowley," I said. She leaned back in her chair and shook her head in disbelief.

"He *delivered* me," she said. What in heaven's name are the odds of that—a person you sit down next to at a conference in Washington was *delivered* by your wife's grandfather? My own personal favorite small-world story.

After the first of the year, we were so close to filming that the studio approved paying me, just to get it out of the way. And so I got a check that was, after agent's fees and a cut for Peachtree, the single largest payment I ever got as a creative writer: a bit more than $87,000. I have often said that it's hard to get to the left of me politically or to the right of me when it comes to handling my own money. Linda and I invested wisely, and since both of us had state teacher retirement, it boded well for hanging up our jobs early. (Something we both managed. She retired in 2009, and I retired at the age of sixty in 2010, though I continued to work a couple of days a week until early in 2012.)

Finally, my ship had come in. If I had looked more closely, though, I could have seen that the name stencilled on its bow was *Titanic*.

An LP with excerpts from Wagner's music dramas, and he is gone. He is fourteen, and he goes to the Regional Library up Foster Street from his house. On the second floor is a collection of classical records one can check out but no one does. Each time he visits, the same records are in place, untouched. He checks out a five-record set of the full Die Meistersinger von Nurnberg *by Wagner. He listens, absolutely overwhelmed. From the beginning, all he thinks is: I can do this. I can be a great composer, too. He does not entirely believe it, but at age fourteen, there is nothing to lose. He wants to do something great and be loved for it. He may have some kind of talent. Since the day of his musical epiphany and the overture to* Fra Diavolo, *he has felt it. He reads about Wagner. He studies whatever scores he can afford and buy through the mail. He checks out* Tristan und Isolde *from the library and has to lie down with a cold washcloth on his forehead.*

28

Drinking the Lemmonade

On my birthday, January 30, 1996, I celebrated all day, feet barely touching the ground as I moved around campus. Then, when I got to our P.O. box that afternoon to check the mail, the hideous, savage, *disastrous* side of real life crashed down upon me. I got a letter from Kevin Meyer. Only five weeks from the start of filming, Jack Lemmon had pulled out of *All the Western Stars* to take a larger payday in another film. I opened the letter there in the Post Office and very nearly fainted on the tile floor. On my *birthday*. I didn't know until much later how badly Kevin was shattered. He had been *this* close to directing the film of his dreams, only to have it ruined by what was, in my mind, the callous act of an aging prima donna. I never forgave Jack Lemmon, even after he was dead. While this was terrible for me, the fact that the studio had paid me softened the blow. Kevin had no such cushion. Although there would be a few feeble attempts to keep the picture going, Lemmon had just killed it dead, and I'm sure he knew it. I will always think it was a dishonorable thing to do. The letter Kevin wrote (and which he shared with me and allowed me to quote from) to Jack on January 23 was wrung from a place of deep pain:

> You're my hero. I grew up watching your special magic. I'm crushed things didn't work out for you to make *All the Western Stars*. I spent the last year and a half preparing for this picture and now with production scheduled to begin in five weeks I've been told you are taking something else for a much larger pay day. I'm sure you know this has ended the life of my picture. I have worked without pay the entire time this movie was being put together. David Valdes removed his entire producing fee so that costs could be kept in line. Freddie Francis came from London and brought his Oscar-winning team. Henry Bumstead began building incredible sets with the crew from *Forrest Gump*. Yesterday, I had to stop everything. It was unbelievably

emotional for everyone. Many had been working for much less than they normally would because this picture had become something larger than life. It wasn't about money. It was about being associated with something that would stand for the ages. The dedication was overwhelming. Nine months ago you told me this was the first version of the script that "got it right." You told me not to "change a word." We put our dream cast on hold to wait for your schedule to clear…. We got James Garner to commit and we began preparing the movie. What happened? In the end, I suppose it's just another lesson on how cruel Hollywood can be.

Years later, Kevin elaborated in an online interview:

No doubt the biggest one that got away was a picture titled *All the Western Stars,* based on the novel of the same name by Philip Lee Williams. The story centers around two 75-year-old guys who meet in a retirement home, where they are surrounded by death and dying. Rather than accept their fate, they escape in the middle of the night without a penny to their name and hitchhike across the country to Texas. Along the way they meet odd characters, find adventure, and a reason to live. It's also a movie about finding love at any age. It is one of the most heart-felt stories I have ever read or adapted….

We opened offices in 5 states, from Virginia to South Texas. James Garner came on-board to star opposite Jack Lemmon. We started building sets and had 40 people on the payroll. Then, about 5 weeks from production, I was called into David Valdes' office—he had some bad news. Jack Lemmon had asked that the project be postponed while he did the sequel to *Grumpy Old Men.* It was devastating, as we had waited a year for him and spent more than million bucks in pre-production. The studio put everything on hold. Then, Rysher began to have financial problems and the picture was shelved. It was devastating to me. I wanted to make that movie more than all the others combined. And I intend to still make it one day. It's an incredibly heart-felt and inspirational movie.

Jack Lemmon wrote Kevin back the next day, January 24, and said he understood Kevin's disappointment. He also said, according to Kevin, that he didn't understand why it couldn't be made down the road. Now, many years later, I turn the channel every time a Jack Lemmon film comes on. I know I shouldn't be bitter, but it's hard not to be. As late as 2012, Kevin was still trying, and a production company in Texas got quite interested in *All the Western Stars*. But when Rysher's movie arm went out of business, it sold all its unproduced projects to Paramount. And I was told that Paramount sold them later to Qualia Capital, a firm that, among other things, apparently specializes in buying up started-but-not-made film projects and then reselling them. Reportedly unable to get Qualia to budge on the get-out-of-jail fee, the Texas company finally gave up. I certainly don't blame Rysher, Paramount, or Qualia. That's just business. I do blame Jack Lemmon. Maybe in the end it was no more real than the film-within-the-film in Ben Affleck's movie *Argo*. But of course there are a million behind-the-scenes chapters in the book of every made or almost-made film. And of course the picture could have been the clunker of all time. But with the level of talent committed, I just don't believe that. I think it was *this* close to being made and being a great film. Kevin and I have commiserated often over the years.

No one ever worked harder or longer to try and bring one of my projects to the screen. God love Kevin Meyer. Jack Lemmon died in 2001. Henry Bumstead made it to ninety-one in 2006. Freddie Francis left us in 2007 at eighty-nine. What a film it would have been! At this writing James Garner, the steadfast hero of the whole story, is still alive and eighty-five years old. For a time, Kevin and Rysher kept trying, since so much had already been invested in the film. David Valdes also was a hero to me in his efforts to get the film made. Paul Newman said no. Danny Devito's Jersey Films loved it, but nothing came of that. For a time, it looked as if something might happen with Miramax, but that didn't pan out, either. In a bit of desperation I certainly understood, Rysher went to HBO, but that didn't work, either. (This was some years before HBO began to do outstanding original programming.)

By fall 1996, with my new novel *Jenny Dorset* in production, we tentatively thought about its film rights. It would make a great movie, but it would be expensive to do. Kevin asked me to send him a copy of *Jenny*, and he submitted it to Rysher, where it was read as a potential film and given what Kevin called "a rave," but Rysher's movie unit was already winding down. Turner Pictures, which had scored a hit with the magnificent *Gettysburg* in 1993, passed on *Jenny Dorset*. Turner did love *All the Western Stars* and told Kevin it was exactly the kind of film they wanted to make "just not now." By Thanksgiving, Gaylord Productions was seriously considering handling *ATWS*, but nothing came of that, either.

About this time, I also linked up with Steven Fisher, a West Coast book-to-film agent. We talked about various projects, especially a television film for Meg Ryan's Prufrock Pictures. Meg had a development deal with Paramount Television, and so I thought of a manuscript I'd worked on for a long time. It was about three sisters, one of whom contracts a potentially life-threatening illness. The summer she gets sick, she and her sisters decide to return to the summer camp they loved as young girls. It's still in business, but, unknown to them, it has become a camp for terminally ill children. The story is extremely funny, poignant, and near-tragic. Meg loved it, and Prufrock optioned it for a year. But that deal also finally evaporated, the rule in Hollywood, not the exception. I was grateful for the small option money and to be linked with an actress whose talent I admired. In early 1997 there was a brief and bizzare twist in the tale when Dreamworks might have produced *ATWS*, but that never made it past the stage of possibility. Also, early in 1997, a producer named Susan Rose optioned *The Song of Daniel*. For a time, the possibilities seemed good on this project, and there was even talk of me writing the screenplay. In the end, it all simply faded into past tense. Kevin Meyer couldn't just walk away, and all during 1997 we e-mailed each other as new possibilities flared and then burned out, dying meteorites among the western stars.

The True and Authentic History of Jenny Dorset came out in April 29, 1997, to very good reviews and poor sales. People who read it loved it, but it *is* a five-hundred-page mock 18th century epic with multiple narrative strategies, and it came in the heyday of Raymond Carver and his twelve-word short stories. A huge ad that Longstreet ran in the book section of the Sunday *Atlanta Journal-Constitution* didn't even have my name on it as author of the book (!) and said that "Before there was Scarlett O'Hara, there was Jenny Dorset!" a comparison that utterly horrified me. I was very upset with Longstreet, but it *was* publicity. I was so sure that it would do well that I wrote a sequel of equal length, *The Travels and Adventures of Anthony Clark, Viscount*. It has never been published.

Amid desultory talks with Agent X, I knew it was time to turn the page on my literary career and start thinking of books with value that might help my name but not my bank account. It was time for *The Silent Stars Go By* and *Crossing Wildcat Ridge*.

First were the fields and the night sky. The green of pine and cedar filled us, and brown furrows folded back with spring's enduring promise protected us. Autumn in north Georgia was a treasure of drifting wind, the sharp smell of burning leaves. Lucky children often retreat to the beauty and solitude of childhood images, and I was among the luckiest in north Georgia in the late fall and early winter of 1959, as much for what I did not know as what I did.

The leaves had released their summer hold on the tree limbs. They lay in bronze and yellow piles or simply drifted with the wind currents. We burned great mounds of water oak leaves in our yard, and I imagine my mother, still as a painting, leaning on her rake and watching flames turn those flakes of leaf into an aroma rich enough to taste.

—*From* The Silent Stars Go By

29

The Silent Stars Go By

In January 1997, on the day I got Kevin Meyer's terrible letter, I turned forty-seven years old. My health was fine except for my bad back and the excruciating headaches I'd had all my life. Before my heart surgery, I had kept them at bay with Excedrin, but I could no longer use aspirin because of the heavy duty blood thinners I had to take because of my artificial heart valve. Many days were extremely tough until I found a medicine that helped, and I could tolerate. The great joys of our lives were Brandon and Megan. Most parents would say this about their children, but in our case, it was true in many unexpected ways. Brandon was extremely bright and very liberal politically. At thirteen, he became close friends with the girl he would date through high school and college and whom he would marry in 2003, Laura Boyd. He had also met his other lifelong best friend, Butch Spence. We adored Laura, who is a spectacularly gifted violinist and joyously funny and highly intelligent. She is also a great mother. Megan kept us busy as a bright young girl in love with animals, books, and music.

The pressure of having a book every other year or so had long vanished. Nominally, I had a body of work already, but while it was solid, I knew I could write better books. Maybe I might have time to turn back to 1970 and the excitement I felt when I bought *An Anthology of New York Poets*. I could investigate small and university presses. And with one significant exception that's what I have done since.

That year I also left my position as senior science writer in the Office of Public Information at UGA and took a job as a writer in the Franklin College of Arts and Sciences. It was perfect for me. As always, I got to find my own stories, and in addition to science, I now wrote about history, philosophy, German literature—anything that interested me. And I was well-paid.

On May 19, I had a lunch date with Karen Orchard, then director of the University of Georgia Press. I had long been deeply involved with the natural world, both from my own house in the woods and the trail system I'd built so we could enjoy the land. But I had studied Emerson and Thoreau since I was a teenager, and I was thinking about natural process—the life story of all living things from conception until death. I spent many hours on our land listening, watching, going slowly. One summer I spent whole days watching fire ants. Another time I studied for a very long time how water builds and erases dunes beneath the clear water of Wildcat Creek at the foot of our property. So I began to write a book that combined two stories: the natural history of our land (and other land like it in the South) and a narrative of my own heart surgery. I would be the stand-in for human experience in the book. Our property begins on a high ridge and plummets down to the creek, so I called the book *Crossing Wildcat Ridge*. Karen loved the idea and wanted to see a completed manuscript, so I set to work, hoping to finish it later in the year. This was surely a step in the direction of art.

I did a regional tour with *Jenny Dorset*, and on May 28 I was back at one of my favorite venues, Quail Ridge Books & Music in Raleigh, North Carolina. I did a reading and autographing on a lovely evening, and one bearded man stayed after the crowd had dwindled. He really wanted to talk with me. As any author knows, this isn't unusual, and most of the time the stay-behinds are nice enough, though often it's a middle-aged person who has been trying to break into print for decades without luck. I always did my best to talk to them and give them hope, even though I knew the odds are bleak. This bearded man, though, was introduced to me by the store's owner, the wonderful Nancy Olson. It turned out he wasn't a wannabe. In fact, he had a book coming out with Atlantic Monthly Press, and its pub day was imminent. He was a fan of mine, his name was Charles Frazier, and his book was *Cold Mountain*. Since Nancy always let visiting authors pick out any book in the store as a gift for coming, I got *Cold Mountain*, and Chuck (as he told me to call him) wrote in the front: "For Philip—Thanks for all for all the good books. I look forward to many more—Charles Frazier." Since this was before the official publication date, and it was a first printing, the book would grow to be worth hundreds of dollars after it and Chuck became famous.

He was modest and congenial, and I suggested we go out for a beer, and he was pleased to unwind with me for a bit. The kind of questions he asked me about how to be an author were, in retrospect, amusing. If someone asked him to do an interview on the radio, was that a good idea? I gave the best answers I could, and in a few weeks he was a multi-millionaire and on the cover of magazines all over the country. I was thrilled for him, especially after I read the book and found it brilliant. I have often laughed at Charles Frazier asking the likes of me for advice. His success has always warmed me. I should clarify something here. When I say "go out for a beer," I mean that as a general term only. I did sip at one beer, but I think I had a coffee, too. After my surgery, in order to keep my blood at a certain level of "thinning," I had to quit drinking. And I enjoyed drinking and did enough of it to be something of an expert. But I had no choice, and as I write this I haven't had more than a sip of beer in nearly twenty years.

There was also a "Jenny Dorset" event one evening in Charleston at some downtown venue, and I was interviewed during the live noon news on a local TV station about it. There were "soldiers" in Revolutionary garb at the event that night, but to my embarrassment, the crowd was small. After it became clear that *Jenny Dorset* wasn't going to sell, I sighed at my stupidity in going ahead and writing a sequel, but that wasn't unusual for me. I had written a sequel to *Slow Dance in Autumn* as you might remember, and never published it, either. Most of 1997 after my speeches and autographings for *Jenny* ended was taken up with the quiet life I was growing to love more and more. I wrote long before first light every morning as I had since the early 1970s, now on *Crossing Wildcat Ridge*. But instead of working like my hands were on fire, I went more slowly. I tinkered, moved chapters, wrote new ones, discarded whole sections, started over. I also took a lot of wrong turns. The chapters about natural process were a delight. I had been a member of the National Association of Science Writers for many years, and I was qualified to write about science. But there was much to know, and learning new things still took a while in 1997. I was in no hurry to finish.

As the year ended I was learning a new tempo in my writing life. I was also beginning to think about the single joy of my teenage years: music. I still wanted to compose symphonies and concerti. I had collected full scores for years and studied them intensely. I knew my favorite opera, *Die Meistersinger von Nurnburg* by Richard Wagner, from the inside out, not just because I had a fine recording but because I owned the huge full score, which I'd bought at Schirmer's bookstore in Manhattan on one of my trips to town. One of my favorite personal essays about music is also about

Wagner: "On Watching *Parsifal* with Molly" by Otto Friedrich. It had been published in *Esquire* in 1970 and then collected in the book called *The Grave of Alice B. Toklas And Other Reports from the Past*. The "Molly" in the essay is, of course, my former literary agent. I had already tinkered with a computer-based music scoring system called Music Printer Plus, and by the late nineties I was starting to compose a little. In the early 2000s, my time as a composer would finally come. But that was around a corner I hadn't even quite reached yet.

The Nineties' prosperity had tempted others to begin presses, too. The Internet in the late 1990s was there, but it was more a proto-World Wide Web than what it would become a decade later. A dear friend in Athens, Judy Long, had, with a business partner, begun a small publishing business called Hill Street Press. I had known Judy since the *Observer* days when she helped us in many ways, an exceptionally bright and accomplished woman. As they got ready to kick off the business in early 1998, Judy came to me with a proposal. She had the idea of publishing, each year, a small Christmas memoir by a southern writer, following in the footsteps of Truman Capote's famous story *A Christmas Memory*. The idea was to focus on one Christmas and dig deeply into the heart of memory and love. Would I be interested in writing something like that? And oh yeah, they wanted to have it published for Christmas *that year*. I would. I had written hundreds and hundreds of pages on drafts of *Crossing Wildcat Ridge*, and though it wasn't a mess, it was inchoate, and shaping it had become difficult. Writing the sections about my own struggles with a bad heart had become a nightmare. I couldn't stand coming back to that part of the story, so I wrote more and more and *more* about the natural world. Most of it would never see print. So I was glad to set it all aside for a time.

For Judy's book, I decided to write about Christmas 1959 when all I asked of Santa was a red football uniform. It was an eventful time for our family, since Laura Jane was born that September. She wouldn't recall anything about that year, but Mother, Daddy, and Mark would, so I interviewed all three of them and also went to the UGA Library and looked at microfilm of the 1959 issues of *The Madisonian*. When I started writing what would, when printed, would be a small-format, slender eighty-three-page book, I couldn't stop. I wrote the first draft in a month, and had done three drafts in eight weeks. I like to think it's a generous, lovely little book.

It can be read at a single sitting. And more than anything else I would ever write, it tells the story of my family when I was a boy.

Early in 1998, though, my second documentary aired for the first time on Georgia Public television, the one about ecologist Eugene Odum. (The first was about archaeology in the Oconee River Valley and focused on the work of my brother Mark. My good friend, novelist Terry Kay narrated it, and the business he then worked for, Oglethorpe Power, gave us the small budget to videotape and edit it. It aired in 1987.) It was good but not great, and I'm proud of my part in putting Gene on tape. He was and will always remain important to the history of science, and I'm proud to say he was my friend.

I got the finished manuscript of my little Christmas book, which I named *The Silent Stars Go By*, to Judy, and she absolutely loved it. Terry Kay gave me the most generous of blurbs: "This is simply one of the most sensitive and joyful stories of Christmas that I have ever read. This beautiful memoir of family and of dreams goes to the core of what Christmas should be, and demonstrates, once again, that Williams is one of the most gifted writers in America. Read it. It will make you exceedingly happy." This is a good place to say Terry has been like another brother to me for decades. He's the best.

Production on the book unwound like a sudden, delightful explosion. For the cover we used a picture I loved, taken in March 1960, of me, Mark, and some neighbors in a heavy snow we had that year. Behind us in the distance you can see the old silos and barns that had originally been part of Madison A&M decades before and had been left when Morgan County High School grew on the site. (Terry Kay's father had gone to Madison A&M, and it's in Terry's magnificent book *To Dance with the White Dog*, which Peachtree had published back in 1991, and which had been on TV as a superb movie in 1993 with Hume Cronyn and—symmetry again—Jessica Tandy.)

I saw the first copy on September 12 at the Southeast Booksellers Association annual meeting on Jekyll Island off the Georgia coast. It is a gorgeous little book with a matte finish. I was very proud and was sure it would sell about fifty copies. Linda rarely went with me on literary trips, but she came on that one. The weather was spectacular, and we had a marvelous time. I got to meet Christopher Dickey, son of James, who was there to promote his book *Summer of Deliverance*, a beautifully written memoir of father and son and of the making of John Boorman's film of James Dickey's book. We also met Judy Collins who was there with her new book, *Singing Lessons*. I only said hello in passing, but Linda, normally shy, went straight to Judy's table as we were waiting for a dinner to start one evening and talked to her for quite awhile. Linda and I both found this a crazy delight; we had been listening to her songs since our undergraduate days, and we both knew many by heart.

In October I was considering another documentary, and it occurred to me that one of the major figures of Twentieth Century American literary history lived right in Athens: the literary critic Hugh Kenner. So I approached him, hat in hand, meeting with him and his lovely wife Mary Anne in their home not far from the UGA campus. I was absolutely terrified. This was the man who knew Pound and Eliot and Marianne Moore and Samuel Beckett, and—hell, he knew *everybody*. And in his basement he had a huge archive of letters to prove it. His book *The Pound Era* had been one of the single most influential books of my own life. I'd had no trouble dealing with Hollywood and was only a little starstruck having lunch with Jessica Tandy. But in Hugh Kenner's presence, I felt like a supplicant and an idiot. Fortunately, he was the sweetest of men, and we liked each other immediately. So I began an insanely happy time of research into his life. Once again, David Silvian came on to direct the documentary. I would write the script and co-produce. I consider just knowing Hugh Kenner one of the happiest events of my life.

In November, I began a tour with *The Silent Stars Go By*. From the time it hit the bookstores, I knew this was going to be something special. People stopped me on the street in tears, simply wanting to thank me. I did seven or eight events, and all of them were filled with happy people. Lines of readers began to form at my office door on the UGA campus, wanting me to sign copies as Christmas gifts. Judy asked me to go to an important independent shop called That Bookstore in Blytheville, up in Arkansas, so she paid for my flight to Memphis and for an escort to drive me across the Mississippi River to the bookstore. She (my escort) was standing in the Memphis airport with a sign that said PHILIP LEE WILLIAMS, and after we said our hellos, we set out.

"Is there any place you want to go in Memphis before we hit the road?" she asked. I had a couple of stops before Blytheville, including a (taped) interview at a TV station whose call letters I can no longer remember.

"Yes," I said. "Take me to the Lorraine Motel."

"I can do that," she said.

It was just before Thanksgiving. I was thinking of what gifts I'd get for Brandon and Megan. I had not been thinking of Dr. King at all or the fact that he had been killed in Memphis. Even saying "the Lorraine Motel" startled me. My escort, a nice middle-aged woman, must have been asked to drive visiting authors there before because she didn't blink an eye. In 1988, of course, it was no longer a motel, having closed down a decade before. But in 1991 it was dedicated as the National Civil Rights Museum. In its heyday, though, before that night in April 1968 when James Earl Ray shot Dr. King it had been the place where black musicians stayed when they were in town to record at legendary Stax Records. Otis Redding, Aretha Franklin, "Wicked" Wilson Pickett—the list of artists who had been in residence went on and on. My driver pulled into the parking lot, and right away I could see the second-floor balcony where Dr. King died.

"Just wait for a minute," I said.

"I understand," my escort said. I climbed out of the front seat next to her and walked near the former motel but didn't go inside. Funny, I thought. I expected to feel more. And then I began sobbing uncontrollably. The entire weight of being a white Southerner who grew up in the Civil Rights era landed on me like a burning cross. I had never in my life felt more ashamed. I sensed someone near me, and I turned to see an elderly black lady, looking at me with understanding and pity.

"It's okay, honey," she said, touching my elbow and holding it for just a moment. "It's all right, it's all right." Then she was gone. Some days I wonder if she was really there, or if I conjured her from sorrow we all feel about that place. I recomposed myself and got back in the car.

"Ready?" my escort asked. I nodded. We crossed the Mississipi River and drove into the fertile fields of Arkansas, and that land, flooded for hundreds of thousands of years by the Father of Waters, was black with fertility, unlike the ruined (for most crops) red clay of north Georgia. The event in Blytheville at the bookshop of the warm and lovely Mary Gay Shipley was one of the best I ever attended. The crowd was solid and the streets outside decorated for Christmas. After partying in LA with the crowd from MGM, being in a small town with home folks was beyond joy to me.

I did a number of other events for *Silent Stars* in South Carolina and Georgia, and I very much looked forward to the meeting of a book club at my friend Peggy Galis's house in Athens on December 16. Peggy is one of those people that women, men, children, and animals all adore instantly. Hysterically funny and with a huge laugh that she wouldn't dream of making ladylike, Peggy is a tonic, and people simply love her. By that time, though, something amazing had happened.

Rheta Grimsley Johnson was a columnist for the *Atlanta Journal-Constitution,* and her column was syndicated, so she had enormous reach. She had read *The Silent Stars Go By* and was bowled over by it. So she wrote a column that was nothing short of a rave: "Not since Truman Capote wrote about a boyhood Christmas has there been a book as fine as *The Silent Stars Go By*." Wow. And that was just the first sentence. "I have read it twice, and I can't say enough good about it. If you lack a gift, or if you're having trouble getting your mind right for the holidays, this is the first-class ticket." And it just got better from there. When the column came out, the world seemed to explode around me. Hill Street was not expecting it but nimbly kept up with sales demand. On Amazon, whose sales rankings were new at the time, the book soared into the low 400s within a day of Rheta's column coming out. I knew she was going to write something because she'd called me and chatted about it the week before, but her heartfelt rave was utterly unexpected. I became a celebrity in the weeks before Christmas. People chased me, waving copies of *The Silent Stars,* wanting me to sign them for Christmas gifts. I signed every one.

The lovely women in Peggy's book club teased me about suddenly being famous *again,* but this time I was mature enough to enjoy the ride without worrying about the future. As I recall, it sold something like six thousand copies in only a few weeks before Christmas in 1998. I was still signing copies into February 1999. Amazing.

Ten months earlier, even the idea of that little book didn't exist. It was one of the sweetest gifts I ever got.

He cannot believe they are leaving the only home he has ever known. They are just moving a couple of miles into town, but he finds leaving the fields and the woods almost unbearable. He takes walks by himself, ten years old and already too sensitive for his own good, trying to unravel sensations. He can taste burning leaves in the fall. He hears the wind breathing through pine boughs where he pads along in the undercanopy softness. He closes his eyes and dreams of sitting on the front porch with his brother and playing mumbleypeg when it's raining too hard to traipse the cow-dotted fields. He already has memories; even this young, he looks back over his life. He takes a deep breath. They are moving on. He will be moving on.

30

Every Spare Moment

By early 1999, I had finished galleys on *Crossing Wildcat Ridge*. It would come out, as usual for me, in the spring, and when it did, reviews were solid, especially a lovely one in *The Sewanee Review* by the splendid writer Sam Pickering and another solid one in *The Bloomsbury Review*. Compared to *Silent Stars*, my UGA Press book sold modestly, but it was a strong volume and the second of two non-fiction books I had out in the space of six months. My body of work was growing.

I had also gone deep and deeper into the life of Hugh Kenner. We had arranged a number of video interviews with people who knew Hugh, including William F. Buckley, Jr., at his office in Manhattan. (I didn't get to go on that trip, but I met Buckley later.) By that time, the originals of Hugh's papers were at the famed Harry Ransom Center at the University of Texas in Austin, but he'd made copies for researchers. Some days when I was in the basement of Hugh's house studying letters from famous literary figures from the Twentieth Century, others would be there too, reading away with awe.

It turned out that one of the people I was desperate to get for the documentary was coming to Athens in late March: Mary de Rachewiltz, the daughter of Ezra Pound himself. Humphrey Carpenter's great biography of Pound, *A Serious Character,* had come out in 1988, and I read the covers off the hardback copy I bought. I was never an acolyte of Pound's, of course. The man was filled to the brim with crazy ideas about money and especially about Jews. I had always felt (and feel) a deep connection to the Jewish people, and found Pound's actions and writings about Jews beyond abhorrent. (If me saying I feel a deep connection to Jews seems like pressing the point, it is nevertheless absolutely true. I found out about the Holocaust when I was small, and my admiration and despair grew from there.) But it would be folly for me to deny that on a literary level, I was deeply attached to Pound and had been since my undergraduate days, as I noted earlier. I was also obsessed with *The Cantos*, since they combined art and history, just as I would many times during my literary life. Meeting Mary and getting to interview her about Hugh Kenner on videotape was an honor I wasn't about to pass up. She came into Athens on March 25, and what a lovely woman she is. She had written her own life story in a book called *Discretions*, which she signed for me. She also signed my pristine hardback copy of *The Cantos*. A delight to interview, she added immensely to our film, and I enjoyed dining out with Mary and the Kenners in April, during her long visit. By 2012, Ezra Pound was being held up as a hero in Italian neofascist politics, and poor Mary, by then eighty-seven years old, was fighting them tooth and nail over the use of her father's name. But in many ways, Ol' Ez brought it on himself.

By July I had looked through dozens of hours of our videotape and written the script for my documentary on Hugh's life. I knew even then that it would be yet another thinnish project because we had almost no budget. But no one else was doing anything, so I would. It turned out to be the only documentary project done on Hugh in his lifetime. I know he would have wanted a better job than what we managed, but he was gracious, and I was just glad to give something back to the man who had given so much to me. (Years later, I got to know the great novelist Richard Powers when I helped arrange a visit to campus by him, and he had been just as influenced by Hugh's book *The Pound Era* as I was. Rick and I have remained friends.)

Starting in April I was back on the road, at the South Carolina Literary Festival, to Raleigh, Boone (N.C.), Savannah, and yet again to the Nashville area. (This was for a literary festival, but it was also the time I accidentally wound up at the event for Tom T. Hall. One good thing that happened was that I sat at table with John Siegenthaler, a famous newspaperman who had served as Robert F. Kennedy's administrative assistant and who was beaten senseless by racist thugs in Montgomery when the heroic Freedom Riders came to town. For a long time, he had been the figure on the ground working with Dr. King to keep Civil Rights figures safe. I was too in awe of Mr. Siegenthaler to say much more than hello, and I've always regretted that I didn't just thank him.)

I had also been doing intensive research for some time on something that fit in with thoughts of Dr. King and the Civil Rights Movement. I had always been interested in Southerners who were against the South's position in the Civil War. I have spent my entire life in a part of the country that has some very fine people but an often vile history and in which so many with opposite views have been poor, wayfaring strangers. Even the good people (with a few notable exceptions) did little to fight against racism until the 1970s. The South is still no bastion of tolerance, but it's light years better than it was when I was a boy in the 1950s. Still, I had begun to find out more about the white people who knew, even as the country was heading toward war in the late 1850s, that the South's position on human slavery (and it *was* the central issue of the war) was immoral, unethical, and insupportable. The South's position that led it into the Civil War was *evil*. There is simply no way around this. I had tried over and over to write a Civil Rights novel, but the more I tried the less capable I felt of pulling it off. I did write, very early in my career, a novel about a friendship between a white boy and an African American boy, but I could never bring myself to publish it. I realized I could deal with the same issues by writing about white Southerners who knew how wrong the South was in the Civil War.

I first heard of Shelby Foote's *The Civil War: A Narrative* from Pete McCommons back around 1979. Although I've always loved military history (something I've passed down to my son Brandon and his son Caleb), most of my study had been on World War II and the Indian Wars. The veneration by white southerners for the Old South during my boyhood slowly began to sicken me as I grew up. But when I understood that I could write about Civil Rights in a second-hand way, I threw myself headlong into research and contemplation about the American Civil War. I came up with characters. I wrote spec chapters and threw them away. I read dozens of books, including Shelby Foote's magnificent trilogy. It is truly the South's *Iliad*. I designed characters and wrote dozens of pages about them and their relationships to each other.

I had one important advantage. My hometown of Madison, as I noted before, had a reputation as a progressive place, even as far back as 1840. During the Civil War, a local citizen who wanted nothing to do with the rebellion, flew the Stars and Stripes—the Union flag—over his home during the entire four years of the war without reprisal. Many people also don't know that both sides had a free press during the Civil War, so reporting became a part of the war itself and an invaluable resource for writers a century and a half later. So I could set my story in Madison and use actual research for background on my story. (I had set many of my books in a fictional Madison, which I called Branton, after our son Brandon.)

By late 1999, I had been working on this book for years, but as yet I had not written a word that would ever see print. I had begun to see the outlines of it clearly. I had also been talking with my friend Tom Dyer, a historian at UGA, who was in the middle of writing his own book (a history) about the same subject, *Secret Yankees*, which would come out from Johns Hopkins University Press in 2001. His book sped my research dramatically, and Tom and I shared research findings, though I doubt mine helped him much. His helped me enormously. (He was also one of the funniest humans who ever lived.) By 2000, I spent almost every waking moment thinking about the Civil War. I had also narrowed my focus to Sherman's Atlanta campaign from March through November 1864. And if I was going to write about it, I had to know it. So I developed an hour-by-hour canvas of what both armies were doing every day in that period. Want to know if it was raining in the Confederate lines at 2 p.m. on June 6? I could tell you. By far the hardest job I had was not disliking the South as I wrote. I tried as hard as I knew how to put myself in the shoes of southerners who supported *or* opposed the war. But in the end, justifications for evil are transparent, or, as Dr. King memorably and famously said, paraphrasing language used by 19th century abolitionists, "The arc of the moral universe is long, but in the end, it bends toward justice." I have to believe that. So I studied and I wrote and I planned. And it was pleasurable beyond anything I'd done as a writer before, but it would be several years before I managed to begin my novel.

The Kenner documentary premiered on Georgia Public Television on March 30 and aired numerous times. After so much work, it felt weak to me, but doing nothing would have been far worse. From a selfish point of view, the best part was that I got to spend a year hanging out with Hugh and Mary Anne. I was also still working half-heartedly with Agent X on several projects, none of which would go anywhere. In August, WUGA-FM, the NPR affiliate on the UGA campus, had a live-on-the-air stage show not unlike "A Prairie Home Companion," and I was invited to read a funny story. I went, looking forward to a fine time. One of my fellow performers was singer-songwriter Vic Chesnutt. I knew him slightly, and he was intense and edgy that evening, but we had a good chat backstage as we waited to go before a huge "studio" audience. (The event was in an auditorum at the Georgia Center for Continuing Education, where the radio station was also located.) Called "Once in a Blue Moon," the show had become an annual event on local radio, and I was honored to be invited. I was standing by myself about half an hour before I went on live when I had the the most savage anxiety attack of my entire life, bad enough to frighten me. I had had them before and had a doctor for the problem, but this was unlike anything I'd ever felt. For a few minutes, I thought I was going to die, then I was worried that I wouldn't. I finally just threw myself on to the stage and got through my story to strong applause. After it was over, I felt fine, but it was the last such live-audience radio event I ever did.

Mark and I took a canoe trip down the Oconee River near our houses that summer. The water ran laughably low. When I told my friend Hot Thomas, a barbecuist out on Highway 15, that we were going, he laughed and said we'd be less likely to drown if we changed our minds and just walked it. For most of it we could have. But as we were getting in, I somehow lost my balance and fell into a seven- or eight-foot-deep undercut-hole on the bank of the river, and a hydraulic took me straight to the bottom and held me there. I saw the wavering sky through the surface of the water, but I could not move. Finally I pushed myself upward, caught a root, and laddered my way higher and into the flow. Immediately blown downstream by the current and my exhaustion, I managed to grab on to low branches and pull myself, soaked, to shore. But I didn't quit, and when we pushed off for the second time, the trip became deeply personal and memorable. I wrote about it in my book of essays *In the Morning: Reflections from First Light*, which came out in 2006.

In October I was invited to be the keynote speaker for the annual meeting of two-year-college teachers of English in Virginia. The meeting was in Virginia Beach, and the town was absolutely *On the Beach* (last scene) empty when I pulled in to the Ramada Resort Oceanfront Hotel, having endured the hideous experience of driving all the way across North Carolina on I-85. *Hideous*. Earlier that year, Henry Hart's biography *James Dickey: The World As a Lie* had come out, and I enjoyed it and sent an e-mail to Henry telling him so. Some of Dickey's friends, family, and supporters absolutely loathed the book because it was severe on Dickey's alcoholism and philandering, and I absolutely understood that, but to me the book also told the story of one of the most interesting southern writers of my time. And of course the title of my first book came from one of Dickey's poems. I should note that Dickey's daughter Bronwen, a terrific writer herself, wrote a blistering assessment of the book, apparently for a publication at Clemson University. (It's online separately in a PDF file.) She also wrote a great essay on her father for *Newsweek* when he died. She is a writer worth watching. Anyway, a great many people I knew personally wandered through the book's pages. So Henry offered to drive down to visit me in Virginia Beach from the College of William and Mary in Williamsburg, where he was a professor. We had a delightful visit and chatted about Dickey—his failings as a person, which we all share, and his genius as a poet and talent as a novelist, which most of us decidedly do *not* share. A nice man, Henry, and I enjoyed his company very much.

In the middle of all this I was taking piano lessons and practicing every day, though I was worse than I was when I was seventeen. At my best I was maybe one-tenth as good as my sister Laura Jane was at her *worst*. In December I did autographings at the local Borders and Barnes & Noble, but it was pro forma, and few people came.

During all these years, paperback editions of my novels had come out, and most of them were well done. I was especially pleased with UGA Press's paperback edition of *Jenny Dorset*, which was published in 2001. I was as always deeply conflicted on what to write next, even though I continued to do research and scribble spec pages on the Civil War novel.

I stayed in touch with Kevin Meyer. In 1999, I gave him permission to write a screenplay based on *The Song of Daniel*. That proposed project, alas, went nowhere, either. "Nowhere" was becoming the final location of most film projects that had my name somewhere on them. In late '99, Jack Lemmon contacted David Valdes about *All the Western Stars*, but that project was long gone. My contact with Kevin dwindled as the years passed.

But by 2000, as I turned fifty, it was clear that I was approaching another now-or-never point. I had tentatively begun to turn back to composition and had composed a large-scale oratorio for orchestra, chorus, and soloists called *Sorrow and Light*. In the end, it was too "popular" to attract serious artists and too "serious" and large to be of much use as "community" art. I showed it to a faculty member in the UGA School of Music whom I knew slightly, and he was dismissive and hostile, and I fled. But a change in computer technology altered my plans. By this time, many musicians were using a scoring program called Fanfare, though many serious composers wouldn't go near it, or said they didn't. It was simply a way to create scores of any size or combination of instruments or voices on a computer and then print them. Even better, sampled sounds had come along so that one could play back an orchestral score in which the oboe part was "played" by an actual sampled oboe, not a computer-generated or synthesized sound. So, for the first time, I began to get a general idea of what my large-scale fully scored compositions would sound like with a full orchestra.

I had a small idea some ten years before when Linda and I hosted a birthday evening for my father, and I played for him a number of compositions I'd composed in his honor, including a "Birthday Symphony," a Mozartean piece with no more seriousness than a champagne bubble. Alas, the only computer sounds I had in those days made the pieces, when played back, sound like they were being made on a small portable organ.

My acquaintance Lewis Nielsen, a composition professor at UGA (he has moved on in the years since), suggested in 1999 that I might be interested in a notation program called Sibelius. It had been around since 1993 but only in 1998 did a version for Windows appear. (In the years since then, I've gone all Apple.) I bought it, installed it, and my life changed. For the first time since I had been a boy dreaming of being Shostakovitch or Wagner, I could compose large-scale pieces and listen to them on separate "sound sets" I could buy and install. I promised myself that the 2000s would be my decade of composition. Once again I began to study scores and to listen to the most contemporary music I could find. I went to concerts. And I studied theory and composition on my own as I always had.

So, beginning in 2000, I launched myself into the "career" I might have had back in 1968 if I had stayed in music. My ear was deeply imprinted with the work of mid-century symphonists such as Peter Mennin, William Schuman, Roy Harris, Howard Hanson, and David Diamond. But I also loved the more aurally adventurous music of George Crumb, Augusta Read Thomas, and many others. (I was an internet penpal with the hugely talented Thomas for awhile.) Since I worked at UGA, I went often to the music library and checked out scores to study, and I bought dozens of CDs, this in an age before streaming audio was common.

Two of my chamber pieces were performed in concerts on campus in the '90s, small lyric works for cello and piano, and they were well received. Once, I stupidly asked a campus string quartet to privately "read" a quartet I'd written, but the open dismissiveness of several of the players terrified me. I even videotaped it but never could bring myself to watch it because the event had been so wrenching. For anyone with some success in one field of the arts, there is a gallery ready to boo if you even try another. After that, I only got near the music school about my own compositītions two other times over the years, and it ended with a similar rudeness.

I decided that I would do it anyway: write symphonies and concerti, live the life, dream the dream. This was all I had wanted as a teenager when I read the same three or four histories of music dozens of times. But as time passed I read hundreds and hundreds of books on all aspects of music, and I really did know art music from chant to Carter. I knew that I would never compose something entirely divorced from traditional tonality. But I wasn't remotely as conservative as Howard Hanson (whom I loved) or Aaron Copland (whom I didn't). I suppose Mennin was my hero, but for many years the only work of his available in recording was his Symphony Number Five, which I still believe is one of the great masterpieces of Twentieth Century American symphonic literature. In the 2000s, much more of it has become available.

In an insanely short time, I became a virtuoso on Sibelius. I could "play" it like a Strad, and also worked like a demon to find and install the right sound sets. My violin section sounded very much like a violin section. My solo horn sounded like a solo horn. It was exhilarating, addictive. While I still tinkered with the Civil War novel, my composition was like falling, drunk and happy, down an elevator shaft with no bottom. I was the composer I had dreamed of being. Absolute heaven.

In 2000 I composed my first numbered symphony, and if it was a tad square-shouldered, it also had some strong writing. I followed it up with Symphony Number Two, "Easter." This symphony went back to my roots as a Christian and told the story, with orchestra and a soloist, of Jesus's death and resurrection. It is dramatic, tense, and, in the end more ethereal than triumphant. I am extremely proud of it. I called my third symphony "The Bridge" and based it on Hart Crane's long poem of the same name. Crane's elliptical and dense poetry had interested me since boyhood, and I was reading him as I wrote this. It's filled with such postmodern tropes as the butting of traditional and more pop approaches, something I'd known since Leonard Bernstein explicated Charles Ives's work on television when I was a teenager.

By 2001, I spent every spare moment composing. Ideas for the use of every instrument group flashed through my head all day every day, even wedged their way into my dreams. I composed symphonies four through nine that year, making up for decades of unquenched desire. I had been rescued starving from a desert island and given a feast. Symphony Number Six is subtitled "Andersonville," and was a working out of feelings I had about the Confederate-run concentration camp in my own state where 13,000 Union prisoners died, largely from starvation. Symphony Number Seven is "9-11-01," and its genesis is obvious. Symphony Number Nine is subtitled "Inferno" and goes back to the heart of my lifelong obsession with Dante.

In 2002, I composed symphonies ten through fifteen. I have a special fondness for my thirteenth symphony, subtitled "Gravity's Rainbow," an homage to Thomas Pynchon's great novel, and its three movements are titled "A Screaming Comes Across the Sky," "They've Cut Slothrop Loose Again," and "In the Zone." I was just as manic in 2003, composing symphonies fifteen through eighteen. But most of my compositional time that year was taken up by a dream project: a fully scored opera. It's called *Emma Devlin*, and it is a story of multiple family betrayals that lead to a tragic ending. I wrote the story behind it and then turned it into a dense and complex libretto. It is, I believe, exquisitely imagined, and I'm as proud of it as anything I ever did in my creative life. It will never be performed. But it exists, and I wrote and composed it.

In 2004, I was on the road with a novel, and so I composed very little, but I was back at it in 2005, with my Symphony Number Eighteen, "For the Civil Rights Martyrs" and a full *Requiem*, a work of which I am also intensely proud. In 2006-2007, I wrote concerti for flute, clarinet, trumpet, and piano (separately, not as a group!), as well as an unnumbered symphony called *King Lear*. I also composed my *Holocaust Symphony* as an homage to the Jewish dead in the Nazi inferno. Finally, as a thank you to Megan's wonderful piano teacher Jane Lester, I composed a large-scale piano-solo work based on *The Goldberg Variations* and *The Well-Tempered Clavier* and called it *The Bad-Tempered Clavier*. It's filled with jaunty good spirits and in-jokes by the dozens.

Exhausted, satisfied, I lay down my metaphorical pen after that, and I haven't yet gone back. I never expect to hear any of them, but I could not have lived my life without revisiting the dream about which I was so madly passionate as a boy. Copies of all my scores, along with CDs I made of their audio "realizations" are in the Hargrett Rare Book and Manuscript Library at UGA with my papers.

In late spring of 2001, an old friend came back into my life. I was attending some event at the UGA Chapel, and my heavyset friend from the *Athens Observer* days, Phil Sanderlin, was there covering it. Phil never married, and for a time he'd tried to get his health problems in hand. But by this time, he looked terrible. The *Observer* had been sold more than once and was as distant from the edgy, left-wing paper it had once been as you can imagine. He looked seventy or older. After the event, I waved him over, and we chatted a bit. He told me that he was being forced to leave what was left of the *Observer* and would probably be moving to Atlanta to live, at least for a time, with his brother. He asked if there were any writing jobs I knew about on campus, but there were none. I shook his hand as we parted.

On June 22, my friend Tom Jackson called me to ask if I'd heard about Phil. I sighed and leaned back in my chair. I said I hadn't, but I knew what was coming before Tom said it. Phil had been waiting at a bus stop in Athens that morning and had a heart attack, collapsed, and died. He was only fifty-two. If, in some ways, the *Observer* still came to me in dreams, that day ended the last tie I felt to it. The memorial service for Phil was painful, upstairs over a bar in downtown Athens. And needless to say, he came to the party, or his ashes did.

In August, I got a royalty check from Peachtree for $29.91, and Linda and I both reacted with glee about how far I had fallen. I pretended to be comically upset, but the truth was that I felt a freedom easing upon me. I was composing seriously and working on my Civil War novel, and time was no longer an issue. I worked hard at my art because it was my nature. But it was no longer such an unnatural need.

That summer, my journal shows, I had been seriously deranged about my writing. Though my composing went beautifully, I was like a fistful of sputtering Roman candles when it came to prose fiction. I would have a set of plans one day and toss it in a trash can the next. The odds of ever seeing in print the best things I'd written—*Almost Light, The Inner Kingdom,* and two other manuscripts I loved called *Dreams and Dust* and *Sunrise Boulevard*—began to seem remote. And they were such good ideas that I worried someone else would come up with similar plots and thereby make my novels garbage. (It had happened in Hollywood with *All the Western Stars* and could surely happen in Lit World.) So, to protect the copyrights, I printed them all with a self-publishing firm called iUniverse in a uniform black cover with red letters. Since copies would go to the Library of Congress, I was covered. I printed them under the name P.L. Williams instead of my own formal writer's name, so they wouldn't show up in online searches. Paranoia? Maybe. But the content-rats had attacked me before. (A decade later, pirates in other countries, mostly Asia and Africa, began to steal my books, scan them, and put them online. I hope with all my heart that readers aren't taken in by such thievery.) Maybe all content *does* want to be free. But I'm pretty sure it doesn't want to be kidnapped.

One signal event did take place that summer. I found a history called *Decision in the West* by Albert E. Castel, which is an intense and brilliant study of the Atlanta campaign in the Civil War. In the midst of my unhappy grumbling, I finally began to see my way clear to finishing the novel I would call *A Distant Flame.*

Meanwhile, back at the commercial trough, I had come up with an ingenuous idea for a murder mystery, with the hero being a newspaperman in a small town on the South Carolina coast. That year's version of Agent X loved *The Angel of Blades,* absolutely loved it. And that terrified me, because he/she said it would only go out with my name on it. Alas, it is a very creepy manuscript about a killer who idolizes famed Japanese writer and celebrity suicide Yukio Mishima, and it went out right after 9/11 when no one was in any mood to buy such a thing. We left the submission of my novel to editors play out, and it went away, to my relief. Years later I rewrote it and moved the setting to Cape Cod, but as of this writing, it's just another unpublished manuscript.

September 11 was shattering to us as it was to billions around the globe. Since Linda and I had been in the World Trade Center Buildings, it felt slightly more personal to us than others who had not, but that meant nothing. Our local library had asked me several weeks earlier to do a reading the night of Sept. 11, and after the attacks, I presumed it would be canceled. I talked to the nice lady in charge, and her point of view was that if we cancel things "we have let them win," meaning the terrorists. I was dubious, to say the least. I wanted to be home with my family. But it was too late to cancel the event easily, so I went through with it. I didn't read a word of my own work. I just couldn't. I read from the poetry I had loved as a boy, things my parents knew by heart: Wordsworth. Keats. Shelley. Shakespeare. And W.H. Auden, especially his famous "Funeral Blues," which had been memorably used in the film *Four Weddings and a Funeral*:

He was my North, my South, my East and West,
My working week and my Sunday rest,
My noon, my midnight, my talk, my song;
I thought that love would last forever: I was wrong.

Then we all went home to grieve.

It had been a superb year for my music, but for everything else it was at best a scratchy and annoying time. One good thing did occur late in 2002. My friend, the writer and UGA creative writing professor, Judith Ortiz Cofer, asked me if I'd be interested in teaching as an adjunct professor in the Creative Writing Program at UGA. Her predecessor, Julie Checkoway, had first broached the subject to me several years before, but I was under no delusions. I would have to do it *in addition* to my job in the College of Arts and Sciences, in *addition* to my writing, in *addition* to my composing, in *addition* to my family life. Only an insane person would have done it.

So, naturally, I said yes. It might be another year before it happened. But yes, I said yes, I said YES.

It is the summer of 1958, and he and Mark wander around the old Return community school where the Williams family reunion is underway. They both love the Coke chest filled with watery ice and bottled drinks. You can have as many as you can drink! A miracle! The old folks are ambrotype-slow. His father's brother, Vincent Astor, called Sambo, will die in less than three months, but that seems impossible here, now. He hangs out with his cousins Bob and Alice and Jackie, but they are older, and that distance makes him feel separate but not alone. He is fat and it embarrasses him. A few hundred yards away, the Return Baptist Church cemetery sleeps in the summer light.

31

Waiting for the Train to Crash

I've just been reading over my journal from this period in my life, and I don't know who that petty, sullen, depressed ninny is. I remember almost none of the things about which I wrote. They have fled from my brain like a peregrine falcon, which in a dive can hit 242 miles an hour. I'm not kidding. Go look it up. I was paranoid, overweight, and generally unhappy, seeing myself as a failure in all things. Ask Linda. She will tell you. But here, now, I don't remember the narrative of my life that way. Maybe everyone else I know does. Perhaps as we age we exchange our true life stories for more agreeable false ones, trade them out until what really happened no longer exists or matters. Maybe we each live two lives, the one we imagine and the one our friends and loved ones see. It's my nature to be hard on myself, but in the back of my mind, I feel as if I've done my best with whatever talent I had. But what if that's all a lie? What if my life's work is no more than a hissy fit pitched against the background of Western Art?

In fact, the life I lived, my true autobiography, was only tangentially about what I did. Of course, you know this. My life was about family and my eight-to-five job. More than anything, it was, first, about Mother and Daddy, Mark and Laura Jane. Then it was about Linda and Brandon and Megan. More than anything, the best, happiest, and most important parts of my life surround my relationship with my children. They saw me get up and go to work every day, just as everyone else's parents did. I wrote and composed almost exclusively before the rest of my family got up in the morning. My life at *The Observer* and UGA were more intertwined with my creative work than my life at home. People in the public world asked me all the time what the status of this project or that was. My family mostly ignored the whole thing, for which I will always be profoundly grateful. Mother was very proud of *The Heart of A Distant Forest* but quite unhappy with some of my later books. I knew this was going to happen, but I couldn't write *Heart* over and over and feel as if I'd grown in my creative life. When my little Christmas memoir *The Silent Stars Go By Came* out in 1998, she only said, "I wasn't that nice." And to her that was true. To me, it was ridiculous. She *was* that nice, and she always will be as long as that book is around. Before *Final Heat* came out, I warned her that she shouldn't read it. She did anyway, and her only comment was that it was "really rough." She was right, but I meant for it to be. Linda was always my first reader and editor. She pencil-edited almost every word I wrote. (Unlike many literary relationships, she was never my typist. In fact, I was *her* typist, right through graduate school. I had learned to type well by the time I was nineteen.) This was my life, the real one. And more, to wit:

*My favorite food is Jif Creamy Peanut Butter. Nothing else has ever been close.

*We always had pets, or rather, they always had us. We have lived with black cats since 1972 and have two now (Boston and Bambi). At the moment they live on the main floor of our house. Upstairs, our tiny tuxedo cat Cocoa, who hates all other animals, lives happily alone in Megan's former bedroom. Becky, a blue-cream tortie, regally resides in my study and writes with me. Alas, she had this bizarre curly-tail gene, and that huge tail is always going up my nose as I type. She belonged to Linda's father, and when he passed away, Becky adopted me.

*Laura Jane is the mother of two wonderful grown children, John and Anna. John wed Beth in 2013. Laura Jane is married to a terrific guy named Duane Kuncaitis, and he brought his lovely and brilliant daughter Alyssa to the family. Mark is married to the extremely intelligent and accomplished Anne Shenk, and they also have two grown children, Zach and Leah. Thus, Mark, Laura Jane, and I all had two children, and they came boy-girl.

*Linda's brother Brian and sisters Gail, Melody, and Donna all grew up with me. I've known them since Brian was six. They are all now adults, married with children, too.

From my journal:

> December 9, 2002
> 9:25 a.m.
> Sitting here in complete shock: Jim Kilgo died yesterday. I know he held on until a Sunday. I feel completely, utterly lost and breathless. I loved the man. I'm so sorry he didn't live to see his Africa book come out. Nothing seems important to me at the moment. I feel a deep happiness for him as a believer, but a deep shock, too. I think I knew Friday afternoon that he was going to die—a huge hawk landed in a tree next to the [UGA North Campus] parking deck and was majestically facing south in the sunlight as I left, and I thought—he's getting ready to fly. I guess he was. I loved you, Jim, and so did God. A full year since I saw him at the Georgia Writers' Hall of Fame event and he was so sick and frail, using a cane and coughing terribly. He lived another full year! He died at 10:30 last night. I found out about his death at about 8:50 this morning. Kilgo *and* Stan Lindberg. What sorrow.

James Kilgo was my friend from the UGA English department, a fine writer, and a wonderful human being. I published his first creative writing in *The Athens Obsever*, the pieces that, collected, would become *Deep Enough for Ivory Bills*. Linda took classes with him when we were undergraduates, and he was one of the best professors she ever had. Stanley Lindberg was the brilliant editor of *The Georgia Review* and a dear friend, too.

*I love golf and baseball. I'm now reduced to playing Wii golf and watching the Braves and Red Sox on TV. Linda loves sports as much as I do and can explain a Nickel Package, if you happen to like football.

*I still haven't read Proust's *In Search of Lost Time* and am ashamed. I've started *Swann's Way* a thousand times, but all that stuff about angling, over a hundred pages, to be invited to Madame So-and-So's Salon seems perfectly idiotic to me. Of course Proust is one of the greatest novelists in history. But his interests are so far from mine I can't follow him. I'd follow James Joyce and Vladimir Nabokov to the ends of the Earth.

*Incense: Patchouli and Nag Champa. Old hippies never die, man.

*I'm a neat freak. If I am not otherwise engaged, I will straighten things around the house into the position God meant for them to be: at right angles to each other.

*Although I'm ahead of my own story, Brandon and his wife Laura have three wonderful children, Caleb, Mollie, and Elliott. We absolutely adore our grandchildren. They all think I'm insane. Welcome to the club. Beautiful Megan is a student at UGA at this writing.

*Anything one writes about ongoing "real life" is dated before the writer hits "save." When you are reading this, I may be long long dead. Sort of. Changing my real life to the life I remember means I can come back from the Land of Shades if I want to.

*People are always saying, "I bet you can't choose between your books because that would be like choosing between your children." For the record, it is absolutely *nothing* like choosing between one's children. I would never choose between my children and would gladly step in front of a speeding train to save either of them. Any parent would.

*I've never liked Brussels sprouts, spinach, or turnip greens. My mother loved turnip and collard greens, and just smelling them cook almost makes me ralph.

*We eat very little red meat, but we aren't vegetarians. When I was teaching at UGA, my students were sometimes nutrition fascists: I'm a vegetarian. Yeah? Well, *I'm* a *vegan*. Oh yeah? *I'm* a *frutarian*! The only really pure position for them to take, it seemed to me, was never to eat anything. So I often brought donuts to class just to be perverse. The students glared at them as a Fourteenth Century priest might stare at a peasant possessed by the devil. Then slowly, one by one, my students would mangle the whole box until there was nothing left but crumbs. I'm sure they're still lean and fit as all Americans are.

From my journal:

> December 18, 2002
> 9:45 a.m.
>
> Absolutely nightmarish phone call from [Unnamed Potential Agent] regarding the Civil War novel. Hideous beyond words—nearly 90 minutes of lashing, and I almost hung up two or three times. He's supposedly sending me some suggestions, but I won't read them for a while. As far as I'm concerned, that's it for me. Absolutely, utterly, and completely sick of the whole thing. Rewriting? Of course. But not being bashed for more than an hour

> with a blunt tool—the single worst hour of my writing career—by a long shot. My hatred for the writing business is corrosive and bitter.

This is the kind of thing most writers say two…oh, three times a week for thirty years. I had sent him a working draft of *A Distant Flame,* and he was right. It was undercooked and not yet finished. But I told him that. A foul, nasty man. I never spoke with him again.

*I like to play rapid word games filled with bad puns and extremely arcane references to Mesopotamian history, Medici church politics, and TV Shows of the 1960s. It requires an intellectual nimbleness, an ability to improvise, and a willingness to waste the precious time we are given to live our lives. Laura Jane is as good at this as I am, and when we are really wound up, it's a chilling sight.

*I've undersold the number of personal appearances I made over the years. Dozens and dozens. And dozens.

*For most of my life, I've been like super glue, binding to ideas and creating poetry, fiction, and music with dramatic efficiency. In 2001-2002, I was more like kindergarten paste, thick, slow, and binding badly to almost everything.

*I still consider myself a feminist and am ready to give the country (and the world) to women at all levels. But I have always had a small voice whispering in my editorial ear that Virginia Woolf is a bit overrated. I apologize.

*I didn't mention the cover of the Random House edition of *Final Heat.* It's a studio photograph of a half-naked hunk of a young man in half-removed overalls being hung on to by a young woman who Wants It Now. It's also half-baked. I've always wanted to find the models and apologize. The jacket quote was much quoted, though. Again, it was from my friend Anne Rivers Siddons: "Philip Lee Williams reinvents the classic Southern novel, and William Faulkner would cheer. *Final Heat* is a study of love, rage, and redemption that makes us realize what we've been missing in fiction lately—passion and largeness of heart." One clever twist: The cover photo is reproduced on the back as a negative image.

*My brother Mark and I have been good friends all our lives, though we're too often going different directions. He got married to Diane Pallas in 1969, earned his bachelor's degree in anthropology from UGA in 1970 and then, because of a low draft number, joined the U.S. Air Force during the

Viet Nam era. After basic training in San Antonio and electronics courses at Keesler Air Force Base in Biloxi, Miss., he taught basic and advanced electronics in the USAF until the war began to wind down. He left the Air Force in March 1974. After that, he got his master's in anthropology from Florida State and then continued his work as the guru of the archaeology of the Oconee River Valley in north central Georgia. He taught at Georgia Southern University for a year and divorced in 1980. In 1981 he began running the Georgia Archaeological Site File (which he still does at this writing) and also started the non-profit LAMAR Institute. He earned his doctoral degree from UGA in 1983. He ran many archaeological projects through the Institute along with teaching classes at Mercer University and UGA. He married Anne Shenk in 1988, and their son Zach joined us in 1991 (the same year as Megan came to me and Linda) and then Leah in 1993. He began working full time with UGA in 1992 and was teaching a full load by 1995. He also directed summer archaeological field schools for UGA for more than a quarter century, and around 2002 was named director of the Laboratory of Archaeology. Along the way, he's published numerous books as editor, written dozens of scholarly papers and site reports, and in addition to all that, he's the most intellectually interested and accomplished person I ever knew. I've always been proud to be his little brother.

*My brilliant sister Laura Jane graduated with a journalism degree from UGA in 1981 and moved to Roswell, Georgia, to work for awhile but was back in school that fall, taking core courses from UGA to get in nursing school. In May 1984, she'd finished her second college degree, this one as a registered nurse from the Medical College of Georgia's School of Nursing Program in Athens. Told you she was smarter than I am. She married Scott Tankard in 1984 and moved to Macon, Georgia, working first at Coliseum Park Hospital and then for some years at ABC Home Health. John was born in 1987 and Anna in 1990, and both would grow up to be exceptionally bright students, too. In 1994, she started working as an adjunct clinical instructor for what was then Macon Technical Institute. She and Scott separated, and that marriage ended in 2000. By then, she was working full time for Macon Tech at its campus in Milledgeville, Ga. Shortly after that, she met the warm and kind Duane Kuncaitis, and they got married at the lighthouse on St. Simon's Island on Sept. 1, 2001. Since 2000, she's been a full-time teacher at Central Georgia Technical College in medical-surgical nursing. She's by far the best-traveled of us, having made, so far, five trips to England and Europe. I've called her *Lol* for decades, short for Lolly, her childhood nickname. In teaching new nurses, she brings more honor to our family every year than I have in my whole life as a writer. She's sharp, funny, and a joy to know. And I'm more proud of her than I can say.

*I love films. Passionately. Insanely. Almost carnally. And my taste is wildly eclectic, like my books. Everyone who knows me knows that my favorite film is, oddly enough, I admit, *Jeremiah Johnson*, an early Robert Redford / Sydney Pollock collaboration. Although I wish I could be Hubbell Gardiner in another Redford / Pollock movie, *The Way We Were*, I am really the volunteer isolate that Redford plays in *Jeremiah*. The list of Films I Love would take up about two hundred printed pages. If I had to save one film as Planet Earth was being destroyed by something monstrously and hideously large from space, I would probably take *Casablanca*. Sometimes I think that *Some Like It Hot* would have been a good picture if it hadn't starred Jack Lemmon. (In another Six Degrees from Kevin Bacon story: Mick Garris shared his screenplay of *All the Western Stars* with Billy Wilder, who directed *Some Like It Hot*. Wilder's only comment, according to Mick, was "I kept waiting for the train to crash.")

*From my journal:

> March 31, 2003
> 3:12 p.m.
>
> Completely finished first act of my opera, which I'm calling *Emma Devlin*. I think it's special. [I'm] in a period of Wagner madness. Going to re-do the small bedroom downstairs as an elegant music room, I think. New stereo system, etc. Opera very fine, but I'm more convinced than ever that I won't show anything to anybody again...Had an odd idea today—to write my autobiography, but an autobiography of a life I didn't live—as a great composer. Pretty funny thought....I want to create madly for the rest of my life; no interest at all in doing it for the public. Secret. Feel kind of languid and weird and funny today. Want to do my *Ring* more than ever—something huge that ties things together and would take several years to accomplish. Not sure what yet, but I will do it. Some day, some year, long after I'm gone, somebody is going to look at the bulk of what I accomplished—the novels, the poetry, and above all the music, and they aren't quite going to believe what I made. Some day, decades from now, I could be famous in death as I never wished to

be in life. That would be all right. But, like Mahler, my day will come.

And Linda chastises me for being self-involved! Hah!

*I never did write my *Ring*, meaning my version of Richard Wagner's Ring Cycle of music dramas. I do like *The Ring* and *The Ring Two*, but that is mostly because I have a thing for Naomi Watts.

*As I mentioned many pages ago, I have always painted. I have never had a show or exhibited in any way, mostly because, as I said, one isn't allowed to have more than one serious artistic career in the U.S., and I'm unwilling to be criticized for the wrong reasons. My hero Tony Bennett is also a fine visual artist and promotes that part of his life all the time, but I have the sense that it's a losing battle for him. I still, from time to time, will paint something in a realist manner for pleasure, but most of my canvases are non-objective and come out of the fact that I see migraine auras. In a sense, my canvases combine the world I see through auras with images from Hubble telescopy. The sense of science *and* art comes to me strongly when I am painting. I spend a great deal of time in the world of visual arts, from owning and reading dozens and dozens of books on it to my own sketching and painting. The Naifeh and Smith biography of Jackson Pollock was a work of genius to me. Their biography of Van Gogh was a tremendous disappointment. My love of art history is lifelong and avid. If there is one artistic movement my eye loves, it's abstract expressionism. I do admire the control of hyperrealism, but in the age of high-definition digital cameras, I'm not sure of its esthetic meaning. I see visual art the way I see fiction: chaos struggling toward a satisfying completion.

*Since I get up at three or four and have all my life, and since I love cold weather and loathe hot weather, I think it's self-evident that I was born at the wrong latitude and longitude. I should have been from Iceland, maybe.

*I hate all the blogs where people list the one hundred things they love.

*I subscribed for many years to the classical music magazine *Fanfare*. In 1992, they had a national contest for the best mock review done in the format of the magazine, somewhat along the lines of the Bad Hemingway contest. I was co-winner and almost flew up to Tenafly, N.J., where it is located, to get my prize. But since it was just a year's free subscription, I stayed home. My review was for an "unknown" Donizetti opera called *Don Corleone*.

*Linda and I, in the early Nineties, tried to start a congregation of the United Church of Christ in Athens. (This was the liberal denomination in which she was raised and in which we were married.) We worked hard at it for more than two years, and for a time we had worship services and plans for the future. But one by one, some of those originally involved dropped out, and in the end, we had to quietly go into that good night. I regret our failure, but it was an honest, possibly even noble effort. I am still a pilgrim, remembering that day the Starling from Heaven came down to celebrate my baptism.

*A few years back I fell and ripped the rotator cuff off my right shoulder. I also hit my right big toe on a door frame and tore it to smithereens. But surgery wasn't an option for either because of my artificial heart valve. Since I'm right handed, I can't throw the baseball anymore after my shoulder injury, so I'm learning to throw left handed. Linda bought me a gorgeous left-hander's glove by Rawlings for my birthday this year (2013). I'm breaking it in. I wrote my name on it (I told her) so none of the other boys would try to walk off with it.

*From my journal:

> April 28, 2003
> 9:26 a.m.
> Today's Monday. Got this Friday from Bill Contardi:
> Dear Phil,
> I am sorry for the delay in getting back to you. I have been so swamped with reading. And I have not yet finished A DISTANT FLAME. But what I have read—100 pages—is excellent. I will make finishing this a priority and get back to you with my thoughts within the week. Hope that is ok?
> My best,
> Bill

*Bill Contardi. The wonderful, warm Bill Contardi. The man who was to become my agent after my years with Agent X. And I should clarify for the several agents I have boiled into Agent X, I have nothing but affection and gratitude toward them all. One apparently doesn't feel the same toward me, so I am masking him/her in this way. Really successful writers often stay with the same agent their whole career, but ones who keep trying to create art while selling books often don't. That sounds precious and arrogant and silly, I realize. It's the truth.

*Even in a book this long, all one can do is skim high points of one's life and beg the gods not to forget a life-changing event or someone you loved.

*My journal again:

> May 12, 2003
> 2:53 p.m.
> Today was the first day of Maymester, my first day as a college classroom professor. And I passed with flying colors! Today was no doubt the hardest day—should be easy. Doing a [public] reading tomorrow afternoon. A year ago, I was scared to death at the idea, but it's gotten so much easier that there's hardly a worry. Plus, of course, I prepared fanatically. Sneezing, eyes watering, allergic, though. Yuck.
>
> Have 333 pages [edited] on the CW [Civil War] novel and suddenly wonder if there's a sale in my future or not. Can't worry.

*Without Linda, without my kids and grandchildren, without Mark and Laura Jane and Mother and Daddy, I would have been nothing. With them, I could fly.

ꙮ

An old man sits on the front pew in church. It is Sunday morning, and the boy watches the old man cup his ear with a trembling hand. He feels sad for the old man. He can tell by the man's expression that he hears little of Preacher Sheffield's sermon. The boy wonders if he will ever grow old. That is beyond imagining. He thinks in passing of cold milk and peanut butter sandwiches and Boys' Life. *Nothing else in this world sounds like a funeral home fan being waved against the heat on a summer Sunday morning. He opens his Bible to the back and looks over the maps of the Holy Land and imagines that gold is buried in some corner, in Samaria or Galilee. He would be the one to open a hidden crypt. He has already read parts of a book called* Gods, Graves, and Scholars, *and he could be that intelligent, the discoverer of passed civilizations. He wonders if the grave in Galilee belonged to a wealthy old man, one who cupped his ear to hear the last words of those he loved.*

32

Tramping on Holy Ground

In the summer of 2003, the grand funk that had railroaded me for the past two years lifted. And Linda and I planned a vacation to remember. We took Megan (who was eleven at the time) and drove slowly up the Blue Ridge Parkway all the way to the Gettysburg National Battlefield. The speed limit on the Parkway is forty-five miles an hour, and I love life at that pace. Megan wasn't fond of spending her vacation at such a speed, but she was a trouper. Even though *A Distant Flame*, which I had finished and Bill Contardi was then reading, was not set in the Shenandoah Valley or any of the Eastern-Theater battlefields, I needed to have that land in my head during rewrites and revision. (And it would be central for my next novel, *The Campfire Boys*.) The Parkway is a gray ribbon that wraps a green gift. I drove thinking of my *Distant Flame* protagonist, Charlie Merrill, just a boy, doubting the South's positions but finding himself in the heart of war. It had been my own journey, seeing this gorgeous land and aching at how my South had (and still did) fit into it. Even though I'd finished the manuscript and awaited Bill's verdict, I could not pinpoint exactly why I'd wandered into the American Civil War.

I know well enough that the South's obsession with the War baffles other Americans. And here in 2013, the public justifications and breast-beatings of other southerners during my boyhood are long gone. But any land's present is also its past. I have always been interested in mob-think, how the silently complicit allow evil to flourish. White pastors, from their Southern pulpits, before and during that War, claimed that the Bible actually *approved* of slavery, not unlike the way some current gun nuts appear to think that the Second Amendment actually *intends* for them to overthrow the government. The power of presumed moral authority was still being used a century later to condemn integration, Civil Rights workers, homosexuality, and many,

many other things. The past hadn't stayed in the South's mannerly box where some had tried to hide it. I remember, when Linda and I lived in Beacon Heights, reading a book about the Klan and Goodman, Cheney, and Schwerner, the Civil Rights workers killed in Mississippi—I remember reading it and growing so angry and upset that I sat sobbing in my study for nearly an hour. I had done the same thing when I really understood the Holocaust when I was about nine. And yet there were people in the South in the 1960s, and the 1860s, who knew it all was deeply wrong and morally offensive. Maybe, just maybe, I could be one to speak for those in the 1860s who suffered for standing against evil. This was not about the past.

The battlefield at Gettysburg is holy ground. Even though I had studied all three days of the battle and knew it from the first tentative engagement until the last of the slaughter, I was unprepared for the way I felt. On Little Round Top I had to clear tears to see the death-land below me. The low stone wall where Joshua Lawrence Chamberlain helped save the Union is still there, and I walked alone to its far end and tried to imagine those terribly misguided Southern boys as they fought their way up, killing, dying, firing, falling. We were there in summer, and it was hot, and there were so many Americans there, so many. I walked out into the field where Pickett's Charge had taken place and into the sudden silence of blood. My God. The next day we went to Antietam. The battlefield had just opened for the day, and virtually no one was there yet. We started at the Dunker Church and worked our way down to the famous bridge where a handful of courageous (yes, they were) Georgia soldiers had delayed the Union advance for hours, changing the course of that bloodiest single day of battle in American history. More than 3,600 Americans died there, and a staggering 17,000 were wounded. What a price we paid for the South's defense of the indefensible. At both Gettysburg and Antietam, I picked up stones to take home. I wrote the name of each site on the rocks with a Sharpie and put them on my desk.

Late that summer Bill Contardi called me. He loved *A Distant Flame,* and he felt sure we could sell it. He had some suggestions for rewriting, all of them well-considered, and I set to work with an energy I hadn't felt in a very long time. Two years before, when I thought I was nearing a final draft, I realized the book had gotten baggy with ambition, and over one weekend I cut out an entire subplot, well more than one hundred pages of text. Rewriting it just to cover that cut took me another six months. When I finally completed the book, Bill sent it to a strong list of possible publishers. By this time, my age and relatively poor sales overall had begun to weigh against me. I was fifty-three, and publishers understandably buy *writers,* not just writing, and I was not young, not pretty, not someone who could sell books just on my smile at a bookstore reading. Soon enough, we had strong interest from an editor named Peter Wolverton at St. Martin's. He saw exactly what I was trying to do. The advance they offered was modest, but Peter loved the book, and it would mean going back with a New York publisher. With a great deal of pleasure, I told Bill to close the deal.

This wasn't exactly a redemption story for me. And I knew well enough that it could be my last gasp in the Big Apple, so I decided to enjoy to the hilt the coming publication of what might be my best book to date. I had almost given up hope of publishing my most artful books, but that hadn't kept me from writing more. Maybe, somehow, the final act of the literary career Harvey said I didn't have would be the books by which I really wanted to be remembered. By this time I had added to my long list of obsessions Eugene O'Neill, and I knew he had written the greatest American play, *Long Day's Journey into Night,* while knowing he would not allow it to be published or performed in his lifetime. Perhaps in the arc of my own career I might just get back to the books I dreamed of writing when I was still a boy.

Sorrow finally found us late in 2003 when Linda's mother, Marie Rowley, died unexpectedly at home on a Sunday afternoon in November from respiratory failure. She had been ill for some time, but no one was expecting her death, and it hit us all very hard. We loved her—I loved her—and it was a difficult, dark time.

The promising year of 2004 began with a party for an anthology called *After O'Connor,* a volume designed to trace where the short story had gone in the South after the death of Flannery. Edited by Hugh Ruppersburg, the University of Georgia Press published this book, and I was glad to have a story in it, especially since my short form was poetry, which I continued to write when I could. (At least I *knew* one very great short story writer, Mary Hood.) One of my literary dreams—an epic poem—was still unfulfilled because I had not been able to find a subject that attracted me enough to spend months or years writing it.

On February 17, our grandson Caleb was born to Brandon and Laura. It was a difficult birth, but everyone was fine. Caleb would be a gentle joy in the coming years. Linda and I loved being grandparents far more than we had even imagined.

One interesting sidelight that year was a brief project with a would-be film producer and director in Athens. He seemed nice, we chatted several times, and I agreed to write a screenplay on spec. After my history with the movies, this might have seemed a little, well, nuts. But I liked the young man, loved his ambition, and I was between projects after spending years on *A Distant Flame*. So I wrote what I think is a fine, indy-type, character-driven screenplay called *Turtle*. I loved it, but as they say, complications ensued soon thereafter, and the project went nowhere. I have always had a lot of affection for *Turtle*, though. Someday, maybe.

My gentle, brilliant friend Hugh Kenner died in November 2003, and I was quietly pleased that I had originated, written, and co-produced the only documentary ever done on him: *Hugh Kenner: A Modern Master*. The memorial service on the UGA campus didn't take place until April 16, 2004, and the marvelous Mary Anne Kenner invited me to a luncheon at a downtown Athens restaurant beforehand for the large group of honored guests of the family and those participating in the event (I wasn't). The then-head of the English department, Nelson Hilton, and I sat across the table from William F. Buckley, Jr., who was a lifelong friend of Hugh's and best man at his marriage to Mary Anne. I couldn't stop thinking about how weird it was, since I was a political liberal, and Buckley was, well, not. But he was charming and didn't mind when I asked him about interviewing Allen Ginsberg on his television program "Firing Line" decades before. Buckley wrote a lovely piece about Hugh when he died in the fall of 2003 in his magazine, *The National Review*. I didn't even know about it until I was researching this book, since I tend to read things like *Mother Jones*. In his piece, Buckley said Kenner told him about the University of Georgia's quest in the '90s for a new academic excellence. Doing that in engineering or chemistry would have cost the university twenty-five million dollars, Buckley said Kenner told him. "If they want it in the humanities, they can just hire me." He also told Buckley that at UGA he taught the most talented students he ever encountered—and the dumbest. I laughed. One gets a little of everything at a large state university. While being goaded to tell tales at lunch, Buckley's hand slipped on his glass, and he sloshed red wine all over Dr. Hilton's tie.

Horrified, Buckley insisted that Nelson take off his tie *immediately* so he, Bill Buckley, could wash it off before the memorial event by dipping a cloth napkin in his water glass. At first, Nelson demurred.

"Let him," I said, leaning over. "People will be buying you drinks off this story for the next twenty years."

Nelson, though highly accomplished, is modest and quiet, and rather than causing more of a kerfuffle, he agreed, took off his tie, and Buckley went to work cleaning it. By the time we got to Hugh's memorial service, I had laughed more than once, something I think Hugh would have enjoyed greatly.

The only thing I told St. Martin's (the book was actually published under its Thomas Dunne Books imprint) was that I would *never* have a Confederate flag on the cover. I have always loathed that flag since it was hijacked by racists during the Civil Rights days. It still stands for something deeply unsavory in the South. So of course the first proposed cover they sent me had the rebel flag all over it. I managed not to explode, and they apologized and removed it forthwith. Pub date for *A Distant Flame* was August 26, 2004, and I knew I'd be on the road that summer and fall, so I bought a new car with a great sound system and, with the publicity people at St. Martin's, began to map an extensive book tour. Reviews didn't exactly pour in, but the ones we got were good, and I did a great many interviews and speeches before setting out toward Memphis. This time, it was to the Southern Festival of Books again, and though it had always been in Nashville, for a time it alternated between there and Memphis. This opened a chance to visit Oxford, Mississippi, and William Faulkner's house and grave. My friend and former publisher Judy Long from Hill Street Press needed a ride to a southern food writers conference in Oxford, and it was good to have her along. (Somewhere between Tupelo and Oxford, an insane person tried to run us off the road, but after having been passed and viciously flipped off, we journeyed safely.)

Judy knew the Oxford milieu well, and so she took me to Rowan Oak, Faulkner's house, on the day we got there. It was a gorgeous, warm October day, and I walked through the house not believing I was in the footsteps of this greatest of all southern writers. I was deeply, profoundly moved, and I cried. At St. Peter's Cemetery, I knelt and put my palms on Faulkner's cool granite tombstone, then left him a penny. Judy went on to her conference, and I drove around Oxford, visited Square Books (and bought something), took a long walk in the cool of the evening, and spent the night on the campus of Ole Miss. Lord, Oxford is a wonderful town. The next morning I drove up to Memphis for the SFB, and there, I was on a panel and did an autographing. Seeing the Mississippi River again, I thought of famed explorer, botanist, artist, and writer William Bartram and his eventful trip across the South that got as far as the Father of Waters.

The scrupulous research I had done for years on the Atlanta campaign paid off. Historian Thomas Dyer, whose book *Secret Yankees* I mentioned earlier, gave me a honey of a blurb: "*A Distant Flame* is the best story yet written about the Atlanta campaign and life on the home front in Civil War Georgia. It is also much more. It blends scrupulously researched history with powerful narrative to produce a compelling, multidimensional story of one man's life as shaped by the Civil War over a span of fifty years. It is a story of war, love, and community in a small north Georgia town, brilliantly told, full of insights into the complex impact of the Civil War on everyday Southerners." Coming from a respected historian, that means more to me than all the reviews combined. Some people have asked me if my book is the anti-*Gone with the Wind*, and it's not. I never read that book, though I did flip through it not long ago just curious to see how much of the war is actually in it. The answer: virtually none. Like everyone, I know the movie well and, except for its regrettable racial attitudes, love it.

Back from Memphis I had a major speech at the Carter Center in Atlanta, and Linda's father, Fred Rowley, came, which cheered me to no end. He was a fine father-in-law to me, and no man ever loved his grandchildren more. He gave each of them a nickname by which he always called them, and, for them, the nickname he gave himself was Pete. So he generally came to be known in his extended family by that name. It was an honor to be invited to speak in President Carter's center, even though he wasn't able to be present.

All that fall I was on the road for autographings and speeches, including a swing on November 10-11 back into the Carolinas and Quail Ridge Books & Music, where I'd met Charles Frazier while on tour for *Jenny Dorset* in 1997. The year ended for me with another party at my friend Peggy Galis's house with her book club, a cheerful, almost rowdy group who knew how to enjoy life.

In 2005, my work life at UGA took an interesting turn when I was named assistant dean for communications for the Franklin College of Arts and

Sciences. I still taught in the Creative Writing program and had even been approved by the English department to be a member of the graduate faculty.

One day that spring, in my office in New College on UGA's North Campus, the phone rang. At the moment I was teaching an independent study course to a single student, but I knew immediately the call was worth taking. Leah Jewett from United States Civil War Center at LSU was on the phone, calling to tell me that *A Distant Flame* was the 2004 winner of the Michael Shaara Award as the best Civil War novel published in the United States that year. It came with a cash award and a plaque, and would I be able to be in Boston in June to receive the award in person? You bet I would.

Winning a national literary award had been a dream of mine since I was a boy reading about the writing life. The Shaara had been started in 1997 by writer Jeff Shaara in honor of his father, Michael Shaara, author of *The Killer Angels*, a Pulitzer Prize-winning novel about the Battle of Gettysburg and widely considered one of the two or three finest novels ever written about the Civil War. I had loved the book for many years, and winning an award with Shaara's name on it was a joy to me. I immediately called Linda and then did something I almost never did: I told my work colleagues and the student in my office. (The award's name would later be changed to the Michael Shaara *Prize* and moved to the Civil War Institute at Gettysburg College from LSU.) I was delighted also because my writer friend and penpal Marly Youmans had won it for her fine novel *The Wolf Pit* from Farrar, Straus, and Giroux in 2002. Marly and I have remained friends for more than a decade now, and she is one of the best people I've ever known—go buy her books!

Linda, Megan, and I flew to Boston on June 15, and the event would be on the next day—Bloomsday—in this most Irish of American cities. Delicious. From hot Georgia we landed in cold, wet Boston, one of our favorite places. The event was held at the Massachusetts Historical Society on Boylston Street, and they had gone out of their way to make it a superb occasion, with special displays of materials from collections dealing with the Civil War. Jeff Shaara was kind and generous, and the people there from LSU could not have been kinder. Peter Drummey from the Massachusetts Historical Society was helpful and pleasant, too. We stayed in a suite at The Eliot Hotel on Commonwealth Avenue because I wanted to do things properly—it was something like four hundred bucks a night, and I was delighted to pay it. Linda and Megan had a great time shopping and visiting all the historical sites in the city. In yet another strange coincidence, all this was about half a mile from where Fred and Marie Rowley were living when Linda was born. Even more audaciously weird, *A Distant Flame* ends in that same area of Boston. I felt very calm and happy. And after the cheerful furor of the award's presentation, we drove down to the Cape for a week, visiting with Linda's relatives and having a fine time. The Shaara Award gave me more energy as a writer than I'd had in years. Finally, decades of hard work seemed to be paying off, not in terms of money but in respect, which was all I ever really wanted. The fact that I'd made a great deal of money was nice, but it was never why I wrote. The year I won the Shaara I had turned fifty-five. It was time to write for art alone, whether one word of it was published or not.

That fall, Hall County, Georgia, in the northeastern part of the state, made *A Distant Flame* the selection for Hall Reads Together, one of those events where a county reads and discusses one book. The whole event was staggering—and I had appearances at colleges, public schools, and community groups off and on for more than two weeks. Since *ADF* isn't appropriate for younger readers, I wrote and privately published a novella called *Casey's Sky* that dealt with many themes I knew to be current in Hall County, especially those dealing with the large Latino population there. The local daily paper also printed the whole story in several installments. The event was a joy from beginning to end. One thing I haven't forgotten is that during the Q&A at a middle school when the entire school was gathered in an auditorium, one student asked the name of my favorite *band*. I knew what I was going to say and was prepared for deafening silence. But when I said the Eagles, the place absolutely *erupted* in screaming, clapping joy. These were thirteen-year-olds in 2005! Oh to be Don Henley or Glen Frey or Joe Walsh or Timothy B. Schmit. Oh to be young and sexy and standing on a corner in Winslow, Arizona.

A number of new projects began, cheerfully, to poke at me during 2005. The most urgent was a book of essays that I would publish in 2006 under the name *In the Morning: Reflections from First Light*. It was to be, obviously, about morning, the time of day I had always loved most, from many perspectives: scientific, sociological, religious, and personal. In many ways, it extended the very personal tales told in *Crossing Wildcat Ridge* in 1999.

Both of these were, in a sense, proto-memoirs, rehearsals for the full autobiography I was certain at that time I would never write. My agent Bill Contardi liked the manuscript, but he rightly said it simply didn't look like a New York book. He was always truthful with me, always kind, and even though we disagreed on manuscripts over the years, the man seems incapable of being disagreeable. I wish for every writer an agent who is as fine a person as Bill.

I had been keeping my eye on a small university press only about eighty miles from where I lived. Mercer University Press would be an unusual choice for me as a publisher, since Mercer was then a Baptist school, and I had moved far away from my Southern Baptist heritage when I was still in college. The Georgia Baptist Convention voted in 2005, though, to break formal ties with the school, and the growing press at Mercer (by any standard a superb university with medical and law schools), already had one important thing going for it: Marc Jolley.

As Marc and I became friends over the coming years, I found a new literary brother. To my astonishment, he was beginning to add fiction and poetry to Mercer's list and wanted to start, naturally, from within the state of Georgia. Even more arresting, he loves postmodern fiction and its earlier avatars, especially the work of James Joyce. The man celebrates Bloomsday every year and loves Thomas Pynchon! (Bloomsday is the day on which all the action in Joyce's great novel *Ulysses* takes place, June 16, 1904. Every June 16, Joyce-lovers the world over celebrate.) But even deeper, he adores Thoreau and Emerson as I do and is an adjunct member of the department of philosophy at Mercer as well as director of the Press. A writer and editor who loves both Pynchon *and* periwinkles? This could get very interesting.

If you read my journals from this period, you'd think I was an edgy, crazy, well, *bastard*. I have a sense, though, that journals and diaries are supposed to be bitchery deposits. Meant-to-be published journals and diaries are different animals entirely. If elegant, well-reasoned journals are gazelles, mine in those years was a naked mole rat. Note to future researchers, if any: Don't take my journals (in my collected papers) very seriously.

So I began to think of Mercer, even though I'd never met or exchanged an e-mail with Marc Jolley. Although Bill worked with me in the usual round of evaluating and sending out manuscripts in New York, I began to think far more about writing and far less about publishing. I finished a draft of *In the Morning* that I thought was strong. (And it had a few of the stories I've told in this book, though in truncated and slightly different versions.) In its parts about the natural world, it drew heavily on my years as a science writer at UGA. But I had done so much research on the Civil War for *A Distant Flame*, that by sheer torque, I also wrote, not long after finishing the morning book, what may be my most underrated novel: *The Campfire Boys*.

As I said much earlier, I embody the odd combination of a strong belief in progressive politics and an enduring interest in military history. And as part of my studies over the years, I had become quite interested in entertainers during the time of war. One of Glenn Miller's last performances before he was lost over the English Channel was at my father's air base near Oxford. (My dad didn't bother going since he didn't like any music after, say, 1890, and he preferred stuff before 1830.) So I got quite interested in leisure time activities of troops during the Civil War. To the surprise of many people, the armies on both sides had long stretches when they did very little other than drill and try to stay busy. Nineteenth century roads were appallingly bad in the U.S., nothing more than muckworks in the rain. So very few battles or even army movements took place from December until March each year. And though there was no system of entertainment organized at the highest level of command for the armies, the troops did find ways to create their own entertainment. Often, battalions commandeered an auditorium in a nearby town and performed Shakespeare or follies of some kind. The records are full of it. After the intense, dark drama of *A Distant Flame*, I wanted to use the rest of the energy and interest I'd spent in the past ten years on something much lighter.

The Campfire Boys is a seriously funny and strange book, and it was designed, like *Jenny Dorset* to fall in the category of Postmodern Historical. I used as many different narrative strategies as I could work into it. And writing the book was a pure joy. Even though it ends in sorrow, for several hundred pages it's the crazed experiences during war of the entertaining Blackshear brothers from Branton, Georgia. I love this book, and many readers did, too.

On November 17, 2005, my parents celebrated their sixtieth wedding anniversary, the same day that I finished the first draft of *The Campfire Boys*. Laura Jane, Mark, and I gave our parents a private, emotional tribute with gifts and much love. Laura Jane found a World War II jacket from the WAVES for sale online and gave it to Mother. I arranged for the current minister of the First Baptist Church of San Francisco, where they had been married in 1945, to write them a letter congratulating them on their long marriage. And Mark had just built a dulcimer and played for them one of their favorite pieces, "Jesu, Joy of Man's Desiring" by Bach. They were deep in their autumn years, and we were entering ours. It was an achingly beautiful hour.

So by then I had in hand two new manuscripts I wanted to see in print. Though Bill Contardi continued to faithfully work with me, telling me gently when I sent him something he couldn't sell, I had begun to get more and more interested in Mercer University Press. I had an idea that they might just save my literary life. I knew that any books I published there would sell as books usually do for university presses. I also knew that if I could make Marc Jolley see what I was trying to do, the kind of books I'd wanted to publish since 1972 might, at last, have a home. So I decided to give it my best shot. As it turned out, my best shot was more than enough. The finest books I would ever write would soon start to come out from a press only sixty miles from Madison, where I grew up. I was circling back toward the place from which I started.

Atlanta is burning. She watches it with him in darkness, and he feels her shoulder touching his. His heart explodes with happiness, but he is confused, his palms damp. Ten-year-olds, and he can smell her hair, glance at her lovely oval face, touch the despair of the woman in the buggy on screen. He feels the music slice him from capillary to vein. She is reaching over, reaching now, and she takes his hand and slides her slender fingers through his, and what he feels is beyond imagining. He wants to hold her tight, to press his cheek to hers. He glances down. Her hands are so small. Her fingers are tiny. He has to focus to keep his hand still. Atlanta is falling down in flames. His homeland burns with war and arrogance. But he sees only her. Please don't let this ever end, he thinks. God, just let this go on forever.

33

The True Meaning of *Distant*

In 2006, my little book *In the Morning: Reflections from First Light* came out from Mercer University Press. A small book physically, it has value, I believe. I didn't expect to hear from so many people who absolutely and utterly *hate* morning. And those people reacted to my book like a werewolf to garlic. They didn't even want to *hear* about it, much less see it in the bookstore. Trendy young urbanites might have loved it—they are probably going to bed around the time I get up.

Every writer I've ever met goes through periods when she or he says that their writing days are over. It can be such a thankless endeavor with so much rejection and so little money, done alone, and with only sporadic encouragement, it's hard to understand why there are thousands of would-be writers out there still. I have talked to hundreds of wonderful people almost desperate to be published, intelligent folks from eighteen to eighty. I tell them to keep writing and to work as hard at the business of writing as they do at the writing itself. But I try not to encourage them to be delusional. The saddest ones are those with far more drive than talent. They have heard stories, though. Margaret Mitchell plucked from obscurity by an editor for Macmillan traveling the country looking for novels. First novels sold for a million dollars then made into epochally fine movies. *To Kill a Mockingbird.* If Harper Lee could do it, why couldn't I? Why not indeed. My advice is keep trying. But know that at more than one point, you *will* quit.

I quit writing in 2006. Even with *In the Morning* coming out, I was exhausted. Things had not been going well in my work at UGA for many reasons. I had hoped, stupidly, that after winning a national writing award and having published a raft of well-received books, my alma mater might want me to teach creative writing more and write science stories less. It turned out that UGA didn't mind if I wanted to work two full-time jobs for the price of one, but it didn't let me forget that I was essentially a science writer and that in the Creative Writing Program I wasn't at the bottom of the pole; I wasn't even in the room. I understood it then, and I understand it now. Institutions have very little flexibility in how they set out job definitions for faculty and staff. And I *was* staff, not faculty. In Creative Writing, I was an adjunct professor and no more. The real faculty had earned the right to be there, and I hadn't. So, for the time being, I decided to jump without a place to land. I quit teaching cold turkey. I was an excellent teacher. No kidding. I am still in touch with several of my students who went on to become published writers. (My student Ashlee Crews some years later won a Pushcart Prize for one of her stories and in 2013 took home the prestigious Rona Jaffe Award in ceremonies in Manhattan. So she has caught the eye of many editors and agents already. Lucas Klauss published a young adult novel with Simon & Schuster called *Everything You Need to Survive the Apocalypse*.) But I could not continue at the pace I'd set. So I went back to being a science writer only. I'm immodest enough to say I was very good at that, too. At the same time, I quit contacting Bill Contardi for a long time and wrote nothing. My journal is filled with whiny, pathetic things like this:

> December 7, 2006
>
> I am going to give up the writing life. No more speeches or appearances without a lot of money. Maybe something else to UGA Press, but that's it...But most likely the end of it all. I'm relieved.

I may have thought I was giving up the writing life, but the writing life had no intention of giving up on me. It was sitting in a chair across the table, smoking a cigar, drinking a whiskey neat, and calling me a pussy. I glared back, sighed, and started writing another book. This time it was a novel about Abraham Lincoln, narrated by Lincoln himself and dealing with the death of his beloved son Willie. I think it was and is a strong piece of work, but I only showed it to one press (not Mercer), and the reaction from their outside reader was so vile and personal that I never showed it to another living soul. Called *A. Lincoln & Son*, I'm proud of it and glad I wrote it, but it's yet another book of mine that will probably never see print. I spent almost two years of pleasant joy writing this book, feeling all along that it was for me alone. It was. And I am fine with that.

By 2007, the itch had become too powerful to ignore, and I began to talk with Marc Jolley again about my publishing future. His situation had changed somewhat, and he had more freedom in what he chose to publish. And we found out that we genuinely liked each other. Marc is an easy man to like. But any new books from Mercer would be a year or two down the road. I had begun, finally, to see the beauty of publishing less often, though it wouldn't last. While I was proud of the books I'd made so far, I still had not published *The Divine Comics* or written my epic poem. I had work to do.

Early that year I went to check the mail at our post office box in Watkinsville and saw a letter from the Georgia Governor's Office. I had been to the Governor's Mansion several times over the years and had my picture taken with a governor back in the Nineties for one of my Georgia Author of the Year awards. But this looked more formal, crisp and clean. I opened it in the car, and to my shock it informed me that I'd won a Georgia Governor's Award in the Humanities. These highly coveted awards are given to those whose life's work have made a significant contribution to the state's humanities areas, from writing to historic preservation. I was thrilled. That May, at ceremonies in Alanta, I received a framed certificate and a gorgeous silver and beribboned medallion with my name engraved on the back. There were a few other winners, too, and we all celebrated. And despite my unhappiness with the teaching situation, the dean of the College of Arts and Sciences and several others from UGA came to the event, which was a lovely gesture.

The award lifted me from my second extended funk of the 2000s. Unfortunately I had reached the age when I began to lose my past as well. That January, my old friend from the *Athens Daily News*, Plott Brice, died from lung cancer, only months after being diagnosed. He was just sixty and didn't have many months in retirement before he had to leave us. I remember him from 1972 when he was so full of energy (and himself) that his feet barely touched the ground. He was a first-rate journalist and one of the funniest guys I ever met. I remembered the day we only spoke to each other by singing lyrics from songs. He had charisma. In the coming years I also got back in touch with Johnny Futch from the *Daily News*, and he was in great health and still in the newspaper business in California. He and Plott all but created me as a writer. Bob Chambers, the publisher who hired me, died young, and our associate editor Larry Young is gone now. A good friend from *The Observer*, Joe Causey, died too young, also of cancer, in 2013. Those days when we were young and happy—so long ago.

While original books were slowly coming along, paperback reprints of other books kept me busy, too. St. Martin's/Griffin brought out a softcover version of *A Distant Flame* in 2005 with a pre-printed "sticker" on the front saying it was "Winner of the Michael Shaara Award." You cannot imagine the joy. My first novel, *The Heart of a Distant Forest*, had stayed in print since 1984, first from Norton, then in mass market paperback from Ballantine, and a trade paperback edition by Peachtree. When Peachtree's edition went out of print, I took it to my friends at the University of Georgia Press, and they were delighted to take up the torch with a new, gorgeous paperback edition. Publication of the book was made possible by a gift from legendary UGA dean of women and then state representative Louise McBee, a strong supporter of the Press. Louise was more than a friend; she kept my treasured first book in the stores. Bless her.

I need to say a word regarding two books with the word "distant" in the title. That was no accident, of course. The latter was an interior homage to how far I'd come as a writer in the twenty years I'd been a published author. If people thought I was getting senile or simply careless, I didn't mind. I knew that soon enough all the stories of my life would be distant, even to the people who shared them with me.

Early in 2008, my literary megalomania, which had been dormant for a time, began to metastasize again. Ugly. While I continued to hammer out *The Campfire Boys*, I decided to get back into composing with my own *St. Matthew Passion*. Bach's sublime take on the passion story from the Book of Matthew had been one of the background hymns of my teenage years. My father adored that deeply spiritual, most personal of all Bach's choral works. Bach's libretto, fashioned by a writer named Christian Friedrich Henrici, combined words from the Bible with his own narrative of Christ's final days. Re-setting the Henrici material seemed pointless, possibly blasphemous, and simply ignorant. So I wrote an entirely new libretto for my own *St. Matthew Passion*, taking a couple of months. In the end, I never composed all of the music and haven't yet. I also fashioned a libretto for a *St. John Passion*, but I haven't composed it, either. It was not a waste of my time, but after the explosion of the early 2000s, I was feeling as if I'd shifted, in my music, rather to automatic pilot, and I didn't care for it.

On April 23, the birthday of Shakespeare and Cervantes, our granddaughter Mollie was born. She was beautiful, and Caleb loved his little sister, treating her with almost heartbreaking tenderness. I found his love for her deeply moving. Later, they'd have the kind of rambunctious relationship all siblings can have, but early on, Caleb was protective and gentle. Linda and I had been coordinating with Brandon and Laura about Mollie's impending birth. That morning, Linda called me and said that our new grandchild was about to be born, and I leaped in my car and dashed from campus toward Athens Regional Hospital only to have my cell phone ring halfway there.

"Don't go to the hospital," Linda said. I froze.

"What?"

"The baby is already born! And she and Laura are fine. She had her at home!"

Mollie had, in fact, been born in an inflatable child's pool in Brandon and Laura's living room with a seasoned midwife in attendance. Laura has more guts in one little toe that I have in my whole body. And in 2010 our duet of grandchildren from Brandon and Laura became a trio with the birth of Elliott, the sweetest of children imaginable. (After one home-birth adventure, Laura gave birth to Elliott in the hospital.)

As my relationship with Marc became closer, I began to sense he might be open for a volume of poetry if I sweetened the deal with a novel. I had been working for some time on a book of poems I was calling *Elegies for the Water* after the title poem. Not exactly nature poems, since that category often implies feeling over craft, the individual poems were the kind an aging man can write—reflective, intensely personal, and filled with inner music. As I said earlier, the problem was that I refused to play the publish-twice game that is almost required for a volume of verse. Spend years placing poems in journals and little magazines, spend months getting permissions, and then publish the book and *still* sell only two hundred and eight copies. I have always believed it is a nutty model. So I polished my poetry manuscript until I could do no more, and submitted it along with *The Campfire Boys* to Marc. Five of the poems *had* been published, including "Cinnamon Toast," which had been in *Poetry* in 1995. But by and large it was new work.

Marc didn't take long. He accepted both books, and *The Campfire Boys* would come out in the spring of 2009, the poetry that fall. Because I loved both of these manuscripts, I was delighted. And because this was a small academic press, the pressure of publication, which I had found difficult for years, would be less stressful. Armed with success in placing these with Mercer, I began to dream of books I had always wanted to publish and write. At the top of my list was *The Divine Comics*, so the mice of ambition began to nibble and swarm with greater intensity as the weeks of 2008 passed.

But that was, in manuscript, a 1,500-page mammoth re-imagining of Dante's great work, and the idea that it might sell well never occurred to me. Above all I simply wanted the book in print. It was to say: I made this over a period of thirty years, and it was the best I had in me. And in truth it *had* taken that long, because I never stopped writing it. There are some dramatic differences, for example, between the self-published-to-preserve-copyright version called *The Inner Kingdom* and the final book. That book was largely finished though. I hadn't even started my epic poem, or one that I would publish. I had tried it numerous times over the years, first with the twin projects on the arts from the early 1970s, *Princeps Musicorum* and *Images*. Those were apprentice books, though, and in places undercooked. I had tried to write a long poem about science, but it was far more fun for me than it would be for any reader. And actually, the word "epic" is misleading anyway, since I wasn't interested in trying to recreate the traditional epic, with war at the narrative center. I did want to recreate the mythical hero's journey in Joseph Campbell's formulation, but I wasn't really interested in creating a story to write a long poem about. I wanted something based in history. How could I find the right protagonist/narrator, though? I knew I needed someone who was, in some way an artist who takes a journey of discovery and returns home to tell the story of his travels. I needed someone who was young and discovering the world as we would with him. And I wanted to write about the land that I knew best, the American South. One day I was looking at the spines of books in my study when I saw a volume whose green cover almost looked like a growing plant among duller volumes.

"Oh my God," I said out loud. Then, more softly, "Oh my God." I pulled the book out and sat on the sofa and held it before me, and I knew: *The Travels of William Bartram*. Of course. The much-loved Eighteenth Century botanist and artist who had spent four years on horseback riding around the South in pre-Revolutionary days, visiting Indian tribes and wealthy landowners, giving us a picture of the famous "Crystal Basin" in Florida, whose depiction in Bartram's book gave Coleridge the imagery of "Kubla Khan" until the person from Porlock intervened. This was *it*. But I could not simply turn Bartram's book into poetry. I *could* use it as a stepping-off point for a long meditation on nature and history and human loss, grief, and transcendent joy. I knew I was going to write it, whether anyone published it or not. The odds of any major commercial press in New York doing such a book were close to zero. It was too big a project for a small commercial press. And most academic presses have the much-dreaded contest-judging for their own tiny poetry lists. But Mercer just might be interested. That summer, though, all I had was an idea. That is my second-most favorite time in the writing process: the moment when I know I will write something from the sheer passion for it. (My favorite is when I finish a first draft and then begin the lovely process of intensive rewriting.)

Writing the long poem would have to wait, though. That summer I would be working simultaneously on *Elegies for the Water* and *The Campfire Boys*. The latter is a sprawling narrative, and despite my attention to plot, character, and setting, too many typos crept in, and a few people were unkind about that when the book came out a year later. But I had the solace of knowing the misprints in my book paled in comparison to those in the first edition of *Ulysses*. I read *Elegies for the Water* until my eyes almost bled.

Late that spring of 2008, though, Mother suddenly grew gravely ill, and I knew that soon I would have to say goodbye.

Against Fear While Standing in My Woods in March

Death, tell our stories in your dancing step,
Young and tender, old as late-night's clock;
Wind and sun will hide the trail to where we wept.

You search the keep where every light is kept,
Round and round each city street and block;
Death, tell our stories in your dancing step.

Upon the ice of madness you have slipped,
To rob all time of every gentle tick and tock;
Wind and sun will hide the trail to where we wept.

I do not fear the forest paths where you have crept
To steal the barred owl in his single sleeping flock;
Death, tell our stories in your dancing step.

All will fear and then forget your claim to be adept,
The trail of poults, the huddling hen, the cock;
Wind and sun will hide the trail to where we wept.

And all our lives we went to bed then soundly slept
Despite the key you bear to every living lock.
Death, tell our stories in your dancing step.
Wind and sun will hide the trail to where we wept.

34

Falling Rose Petals

My mother was beautiful. She had auburn hair and green eyes and an unguarded laugh that would sweep you along like a river current. She was far more social than I was, with a wide circle of friends from church and community who loved her as much as we all did. Growing up in the Depression in a tiny South Carolina mill village had left her with the joy of close-knit families and small towns. When Mark and I were boys, she played baseball with us, since she was naturally athletic. The kindergarten she founded and ran with her friend Barbara Engle was so successful that decades later, grown men and women would come up to her, call her "Miss Ruth," and say they'd been part of Magic Land.

She and Laura Jane were extremely close all their lives, and in my sister's laughter and intelligence I see Mother's life living on. My mother loved to watch the Atlanta Braves on television and had a restless love of knowledge and learning. She adored opera, and her favorite, until the end of her life, was *La Bohème* by Puccini. Every Saturday, we would all listen to the broadcasts of the Metropolitan Opera on a tinny little AM radio with an unsteady signal, that small box with heaven inside. Of all of us, she knew the most about opera. Her single favorite piece of music was "O mio babbino caro [O my beloved father]," from the opera *Gianni Schicchi,* also by Puccini. I listened to it a hundred times with her, and she was always smiling, rapturous. Mother also loved pop songs from the Forties and Fifties, and she especially adored Frank Sinatra in general and more specifically his late hit, "Strangers in the Night."

After Magic Land's twelve-year run, she was ready for something else and became a caseworker at the local Department of Family and Children Services. She had a deep compassion for the people she served.

My mother was a lifelong devoted Christian. Her faith was not the kind that demands constant public professions of faith. Rather, she lived her beliefs, and I always thought that God's light shone in her face. She constantly did things for other people, especially those in need. She taught Sunday School, sang in the choir, worked at Vacation Bible School. She had a beautiful voice when she was young, and she sang to all of us children and often just to herself. I have often thought that my own faith came straight out of hers. I have nothing but happy memories of church as a young boy and then a teenager, but I think it's because of the joy for it that I saw in her eyes.

Mother loved children in general. She attracted kids like a sock attracts lint. She especially adored her grandchildren and great-grandchildren, and I know they loved her. She enjoyed bright things: flowers, a lovely day, smiles.

She kept a journal for awhile in the early 1980s at my father's insistence. At that time her own mother was elderly but still living by herself in Seneca, S.C. (My mother's brother, Uncle Charles, and his family, lived only a few blocks away.) In the summer of 1982, Mother wrote this in her journal:

> Saturday morning, I took Mama to the grocery store. Got her favorite white fudge at Harper's, took her to the vegetable stand, the library, and got her more books than she wanted. I always pick out some for her and she fusses & says that I get too many, but sometimes it's a long time between her trips to the library. At her age she still reads a lot. I guess I take after her. When I was a child, one of our school teachers visited us & was impressed with our bookshelf. I guess we must have had 20 or 30. Most of the people in Newry had none except the Bible. Now we have hundreds of books. We all love books.

About the same time she wrote that, many of the older people in her family and my father's had begun to pass on, and she described a trip to the funeral of my father's Aunt Flora:

> When we went to Pickens Friday night to the funeral home, we crossed the Keowee Dam that overlooks Newry. I could see the empty mill, church steeple, & tops of a few homes. You can see more in the wintertime when the trees are not green. I felt so sad. I lived there the first 15 years of my life. I go often & drive by the last house

we lived in. It doesn't look the same & everything seems so close together. There was no River Road anymore where we used to take walks on Sunday afternoon & gather hickory nuts in the fall. We made hickory nut fudge—it takes forever to get the meat out of a hickory nut besides being hard to crack.

That autumn she wrote about the change of seasons with the kind of passion that she lived her life:

I love this time of year. There was a time when I didn't like Fall—it made me sad. But now I see the beauty in it all. The skies are blue & clear, cloudless. The mornings & evenings are cool—days are warm. Dogwood leaves are turning and the sweetgum tree in our yard is red and I like to stand still in our yard & look around me and up. It's a glorious feeling. I've always identified places & times with smells. I still smell burning leaves even tho we no longer burn them. As a child I remember the smell of burning leaves & the smell of apples. I remember in the cool evenings gathering sticks & kindling & making a fire in the fireplace. I'm amazed now that Mama let me do this when I was young. I still enjoy building fires—it's a sort of challenge & a pleasure, something satisfying about the whole process. *See,* I've made something wonderful from a few pieces of wood, paper & a match. Sit back & warm your hands. Stand up and warm your back in front of my grand discovery—no one has ever done it before!

In 1983, I gave her a manuscript to read before it was published, and she called me almost in tears. She mentioned it in her journal:

Phil had his novel, *The Heart of a Distant Forest,* accepted for publication by W. W. Norton Publishing Company in New York City. It will come out in May or June '84. It's one of the most exciting things that's ever happened to our family.... I hope it will be a smashing success.

Then, a few months later:

Yesterday, Phil brought us a copy of his book.... It's not in the bookstores yet. His inscription to Woodie & me is beautiful. The book is beautiful. I hope it sells a million copies. I'm so proud of Phil. He's worked so hard on his writing....

By 1985, my grandmother had had to move away from her home, and my mother and father drove to Seneca that August to attend to some details:

> Yesterday Woodie and I went to Seneca and Newry. We took pictures of our last home in Newry and of the store and mill, also the church. The place looks bad...Mama's neighborhood [in Seneca] is deteriorating badly. It is so sad. The place echoes for me. I couldn't stay in the house long by myself. Because the house has been closed up there was mildew everywhere.... In every room I can see Mama & Daddy. There are so many things that Mama made because she didn't have extra money. She baby-sat for a few years and made some spending money. She bought the dining room suit and several other things. She ordered the dining room chairs and finished them herself. She was always doing something. She sewed, even made sheets. Just a few years ago, she was still making pillows for grandchildren. She was so proud of her tomato plants in the back yard. Even when she could no longer dig holes for them, one of us would dig the holes and she would plant her Big Boys. She always had good luck with them.

My mother's health had been steadily declining for some years as she neared her mid-eighties, but my father took exquisitely fine care of her, making sure she got each pill at the right times, cooking for her, and cleaning. She wanted to do more for herself but simply was no longer able to. Yet she never complained and never felt sorry for herself. She lived with the grace and dignity of old age as if it were a queen's cloak, when we all knew she was in pain. She was diagnosed with Parkinson's Disease and then congestive heart failure. Doctors implanted a pacemaker-defibrillator after an episode when I am sure she came close to death. She lived with it, and on good days, she was as bright as she had been when Mark and I were boys, when Laura Jane was her darling little girl.

There is a point in our lives that we know is coming but dread: the ringing of the phone. Linda's mother had been ill, but her death was so unexpected, so unfair, that none of us had time to prepare for it. It was a storm that swept all our emotions out to sea. When my cell phone rang, I was standing in a stairwell of the Miller Plant Sciences Building on the UGA campus. It was June 2, 2008.

"Your mother's had a stroke," my father said. I slumped against the wall. I was fifty-eight, Mother eighty-four, but age dissolves when a loved one begins to slip away. Daddy had made her a sandwich for lunch, and she was eating when she began to choke. He dashed from the kitchen into the den, and it was clear from her face that something terrible had happened. He called an ambulance, and they took her to the emergency room of the local hospital. By the time I got there, Mark had already arrived, and they were giving her the so-called "clot-buster" drug that certain stroke victims can take. But the prognosis was not good.

She could not speak. But she made signs, and soon enough she would show us that she could write—her mind was clear, and I think she knew what had happened. But we could not tell her how serious it was because none of us knew. She remained calm through it all. She had long since made her peace with aging. She often said that sixty hit her hard, but after that, she rarely mentioned age. Fortunately, Laura Jane could tell us what we did not know—as a registered nurse, she was far ahead of us all the way.

The hospital in Madison isn't set up for critical care, so Mother was transferred to a nearby town. There, a twelve-year-old doctor said to us, while we were all standing around Mother, that we should just let her go. Even if he was right, his almost nonexistent bedside manner was shameful. Before I could think of how much trouble I'd be in for slugging a doctor, we all went into the hall. There, my father made it clear that we weren't giving up on her. The doctor backed down, and the staff took her to surgery to implant a feeding tube.

We got her transferred back to a recuperation center and nursing home in Madison, and the staff there worked hard to restore her health. Dramatically, her speaking voice came back. I asked her questions and made her answer me just to keep her mind agile. Daddy *lived* out there. A friend came by and sang "O mio babbino caro," *a capella* to Mother. By August, it was starting to be clear that things weren't going her way. She repeatedly asked my father to take her home, but he couldn't. One day when he had brought her in a wheelchair to a sunny quiet spot in the nursing home, she became violently ill and had to be transferred to the hospital, which is across the street.

By the end of her first day in the hospital, it was clear that she would not be with us much longer. Strangely, a dear friend of hers from church was dying in the adjacent hospital room. On August 15, we all gathered for a vigil, and, as often happens with the dying, a deep, transcendent peace came over her. She was not in pain, and she looked at us with such love and pity that it was almost beyond human strength to endure. Laura Jane was a rock. As a nurse, she knew what was coming, and she was able to tell us what to expect. The last thing I said to Mother was "I love you" as I kissed her on the forehead. She said "I love you" to me, too.

We spent the entire day with her, and around ten that night, Mark and I left to drive home—we live about half an hour from Madison. Laura Jane would spend the night with Daddy. I had just dozed off in bed when the phone rang, and it was my sister. The hospital had called, and Mother was slipping away. If we wanted to see her alive, we need to get out there. Dazed, upset, I got up and started dressing, but before I could leave the phone rang again. It was Laura Jane. Mother was gone. Fortunately, she and our father got back to the hospital in time and were with her as she passed on. By the time Mark and I got back, Mother was still in the bed, no longer sick, no longer in pain, no longer having to fear the inevitable. Daddy and Laura Jane were calm and in control of things. I kissed Mother and told her goodbye. She received military honors at her funeral, including the playing of taps.

She is buried in the Return Baptist Church Cemetery in the country outside Seneca, S.C. Our father will lie beside her when his time comes. I have taken my father up to visit once a month over the years since she died. When we go, we spread yellow or red rose petals on her grave. And we remember.

Roasting hot dogs on a summer evening. Running from one end of the yard to the other, Flipsy barking him along. He sees the first ones near the hen house, the flamy flickering, the Morse code of childhood. He stops and watches. Sometimes he thinks he can change their patterns with his mind alone. The world is filled with secret messages. He knows this from comic books, messages for which one needs a decoder ring, a new language. Ten flash their intentions, then a hundred. Now thousands float on invisible waves, ecstatic for slow summers, the slap of baseballs in oiled mitts. Everywhere he turns, lightning strikes softly, and he wonders if this is their language, their Christmas lights, their resurrection. He touches his dog on her head as she stands for petting. She speaks to him in a hidden language, too. Then, true beauty: his mother's voice, calling his name.

35

A Much Better Idea

I want to say that when 2009 came, the sorrow of Mother's death began to lift, but my occasional moments of private tears continued with regularity until 2010. That's the power of family. She was eighty-four when she died, and I was fifty-eight, but I might have been a little boy reaching for her hand as we crossed the street. All the same, I knew that I was lucky to have known her at all. Still, I finished galleys on *Elegies for the Water* and tinkered with last-minute changes on the manuscript of *The Campfire Boys*.

My first volume of poems was a long time coming. I won't deny that I am proud of this book. David Bottoms, a much-honored poet and novelist (and Georgia Poet Laureate for a number of years), wrote this about my book: "*Elegies for the Water* is a beautiful and mature book of poems steeped in the joys and mysteries of the natural world. At the end of a dirt road near Wildcat Creek, the world has been speaking to Philip Lee Williams, and the poems he has brought us from this place are lessons in the art of being human. They operate on the spirit like healing herbs. If I had to describe these poems in one word, I'd call them *wise*. They achieve a difficult and genuine wisdom that can only be won after ultimate resignation has turned into a wild and sustaining gratitude. Very few writers ever attain this. There is something here about the ultimate, maybe even the eternal. When we find this sort of gratitude for the world and our place in it, there is really nothing greater to accomplish."

Writers are supposed to be cynical types, but it took me days to get over that. From a writer as talented as David Bottoms, that came as one of the great affirmations of my writing life. Readers also loved the book. It sold strongly and made national poetry bestseller lists. I still get e-mails from people who have felt moved and even changed by it. One man had read it five times and wrote me to say how much he loved it. As usual, I did a number of readings, including a capacity one at the local Barnes & Noble, and readers were lovely and generous. Mercer University Press actually made money on the book. No, the old publish-in-a-journal-first model isn't necessary. What is good isn't made better by being in a magazine, and what is bad won't be made book-worthy by being there. I want to add to this lingering diatribe that I absolutely *love* literary journals, have been in many, subscribe to several (especially the brilliant *Georgia Review*), and can't imagine my life without them. It was where I began, and I continue to love them all.

The military history in *The Campfire Boys* is correct. And it encompasses most of the major battles of the Eastern Theater of the Civil War. No detail was too small to check centuple times. Half of that was a desire for accuracy. The other half was sheer paranoia. Much of what I knew about the war in general came from the years I prepared to write *A Distant Flame*. I managed to pull off a coup for *The Campfire Boys*, though, by getting the help of Robert K. Krick, for more than thirty years Chief Historian for the National Park Service for the battlefields around Fredericksburg, Virginia, and a brilliant writer. I told Bob I wanted him to be hard on me when he read my manuscript for historical accuracy, and he was. I had done a good job in my research, but since he knew about 45,000 times more about the Civil War than I did, I listened like a chastened pupil and made every correction Bob suggested. (He was especially annoyed by the often-repeated story that the blood of the wounded after the Battle of Fredericksburg froze in the night. Weather records exist, and the low that night was something like thirty-eight. No one's blood froze that night in *The Campfire Boys*.) I got many of the jokes the Blackshear brothers used in their shows the same way comedians get material today: I stole them. This, from my Author's Note at the end of the book:

> Finally, many of the jokes in this novel came from actual Nineteenth Century shows and skits, and Mike's [one of the characters] joke about the electric chair is from Henny Youngman. Some of the jokes in the latter part of the book are from Bob Hope himself, gathered at the online site containing material about his life in the Library of Congress. Considering how many stories Bob told over the years about stealing material, I'm sure he (and Henny) are laughing over my shameless thievery.

I should clarify that I know the electric chair hadn't been invented in the Civil War era. There is a frame story involving one of the Blackshears who lives to great old age and into World War II, when there *was* an electric chair. (It's worth a note here that I have opposed the death penalty my entire adult life, and I believe that it will, one day, be nothing more than a terrible memory of morality gone wrong in America. And no, I am not soft on crime. I just don't believe the state should be in the business of killing people.)

I also devised (I think) a new way of setting off dialogue: with a tilde. This sounds odd until you see it on the page. It looks whimsical and carnivalesque, exactly what I sought in a large-scale comic novel. But if anyone noticed, no one mentioned it.

I rounded up blurbs from the brilliant Ron Rash, whom I had known for years and who had become a national figure as a novelist, Pulitzer-winner Robert Olen Butler, and Civil War novelist Alden R. Carter. Mercer used Mary-Frances and Jim Burt (their business is called Burt & Burt) to design the book, and they did their usual brilliant job. I had not had a novel out in five years, and I worked hard to promote the book with a number of autographings and speeches. But nothing happened. The book was largely unreviewed, sold poorly, and disappeared without a squeak. Obviously I felt bad for Mercer and for Marc Jolley, but in terms of my career, I had begun to realize that I truly believed the old dictum that whatever is good lasts and what isn't will not. So many writers, famous in their lifetimes, are now completely unknown, with the name having died before the man. (Is there any reader or writer who really hates Housman?) My "career" had entered a sea change. I was starting to get old, and I had done the best I could. I didn't need sales or reviews to tell me that. I am proud of *The Campfire Boys* and writing it was a delight.

Marc Jolley had some time in 2008 asked me if I might be interested in editing an anthology of Georgia nature writing. I told him I would, but only if I could also include fiction and poetry that dealt with the natural world as well as nonfiction. He agreed, and I began working on the project, but I soon found that I wasn't terribly interested in it. Instead, I had begun to map my epic poem about the life of William Bartram. Why did I remain so interested in such an arcane form in the early Twenty-First Century? I addressed that in my postscript to the published poem:

All of my life, I have been obsessed with the epic poem. I first read the Robert Graves translation of *The Odyssey* in high school and was more deeply affected than I can explain. When I was a freshman in college I encountered the John Ciardi translation of Dante's *Divina Commedia* and that kicked off a lifelong obsession with that great epic poem, though I now prefer other translations. Many others followed, especially Ezra Pound's *Cantos,* a poem with which I have been wrestling for well more than forty years now. In fact I met Pound's daughter, Mary de Rachewiltz, a fine poet and author in her own right, and she graciously signed my pristine copy of the 1970 edition of *The Cantos* that I bought as a young journalist in 1974. [*Note: The date I gave for this printing, not edition, of* The Cantos *was wrong. It was actually the Fourth Printing of Cantos 1-117 in one volume and came out in 1973.*]

I have spent much of my life planning for my own epic poem, but I found it terribly difficult to nail down a narrative project that interested me. Pound, at the end of his life, came to regard his own epic as a "botch," which it is in many ways because of its method of collating fragments and using them to imply meaning that must remain elusive. It is also marred by Pound's admiration for fascism and for the anti-Semitism for which he apologized (too) late in life. To me it shows a lack of artistic discipline—he came around to that opinion, too. And yet it is a wild and magnificent beast.

Other epics have just as many problems. Charles Olson's *Maximus Poems* follows Pound's working method into the same power and the same impenetrable obscurity. James Merrill's *The Changing Light at Sandover* is more to my taste in many ways, but it also lacks a cohesive narrative and much of it was "written" by a Ouija Board, and that oddness hangs over it like a fog.

I began a lifelong study of other epics: Virgil's *Aeneid,* Ovid's *Metamorphosis,* Homer's other masterpiece, the *Iliad, Beowulf, The Seafarer,* and especially Milton's magnificent *Paradise Lost* which I read in its entirety on Milton's 400th birthday in 2008. (I've probably read it twenty or more times.) There were also *The Odyssey: A Modern Sequel* by Nikos Kazantzakis and *Omeros* by Derek Walcott. Of those two, I've never been able to get through the Kazantzakis book because there is no variation in presentation through 33,333 lines. I

> love *Omeros* and got to meet Walcott during the Cultural Olympiad at the Georgia Governor's Mansion, where I was a guest, as a Georgia writer, when all living Nobel laureates for literature gathered at the time of the 1996 Atlanta Olympic Games. And finally, I couldn't leave out *The Canterbury Tales*, which I adore and first began to learn in high school under the tutelage of my brilliant English teacher Florence Wagnon, who had an enormous influence on my life. I learned it first in Modern English and later in graduate school in Middle English, that gloriously musical variant I'm sorry that we lost along the way.
>
> Still, the narrative epic poem as it was once practiced, has, with a few brilliant exceptions, seemed dead and buried for a century or more. It seemed to me that I needed to find a way to acknowledge the great 20th century poetic epics while using my background as a novelist to establish a plot and give it a shape.

What I didn't say was that spending a year writing a 444-page poem would, to many Americans, seem like all the evidence one would need for involuntary incarceration. Even more, I carefully designed the poem to be chock-a-block filled with references to hundreds of unspoken things. Here is how I explained it in the postscript:

> I knew from the beginning that I also intended to create a work that operated on several levels because I wanted *The Flower Seeker* to take in many worlds, not just the one Bartram saw on his *Travels*. To this end, I studied the great poetic epics from *Gilgamesh* on, and deconstructed writing methods and approaches. I was struck by such things as the now-well-known use of so-called "Homeric epithets," the repetition of such phrases as "much-enduring," "great-hearted," and "wine-dark" in *The Odyssey*. Scholar Milman Parry understood early that these were not simply repeated phrases that are used when the hero of the poem appears. (Bernard Knox's introduction to the Robert Fagles translation of *The Odyssey* explains this beautifully.)
>
> But there was much more I wanted to accomplish. Even though I have only one other language, French (and I have it poorly, at that), I wanted to find ways to link Bartram to the great world of

scholarship of the past in all areas—science, art, literature, religion, and more.

To accomplish this, I did something akin to what owners of some ruby mines in North Carolina's Cowee Valley do to lure paying customers. (Bartram ended his journey into the Cherokee country at about that spot, so the comparison is apt, I think.) These mines do what's called enriching—putting pretty stones, some of value, most not, in the buckets that customers screen in water flumes. It's not a bad idea at all, and it certainly isn't deceptive—giving customers a chance to find *something* for their work, even it's not a native stone such as the ruby or sapphire. A gem hunter there simply chooses, to screen in a flume, buckets with only native stones or ones that have been enriched.

So I enriched my long poem with words, lines, selections, and excerpts from numerous other sources, none of which I choose to make public as notes with *The Flower Seeker* (though my editor knows the source of them all). It isn't necessary to understand them to comprehend the poem, but they do add another level of meaning so that those who wish to do so can read the poem as a scholarly text. James Joyce famously said of *Ulysses* that "I've put in so many enigmas and puzzles that it will keep the professors busy for centuries arguing over what I meant, and that's the only way of insuring one's immortality." I don't make any such fanciful claim, but I did want to write a poem that could not be completely "gotten" with one, two, or even three readings.

When I drove to Macon to visit Marc and report on where things stood, I told him I was having a terrible time with the assigned nature anthology, but I had a different idea he might like. And I showed him a title page I'd designed for *The Flower Seeker*, along with the first canto of the poem.

"Your idea is *much* better than mine," he said, words I would never forget. "I want you to try and do this."

With that, ideas for the book began to explode in my mind. I would design each of the book's twenty-four cantos differently. One would be made up of individual poems, using poetic forms from sestina to sonnet. Another would mimic famous poems from the past. And I would use artwork and music. (Bartram was a gifted painter.) Yes, there would be compromises. It would be impossible to use the incomprehensibility-by-design of some modern poetry. (And I need to admit here that I love dense, difficult poetry.) While I still wrestled with Pound, he had taken the poured-out-grab-bag of history as far as it could be taken. I wanted to use my skills as a novelist to give the poem a narrative shape, though I knew it must be informed by long poems since *The Waste Land*. I also knew that the poem would also have to be personal for me, and so my own experience with Bartram could stand for that of the many hundreds of thousands who had loved his *Travels*. I had been given a chance to do something truly special. And I would do my best not to blow it.

I hope that the two books I published with Mercer in 2009 helped bring it some notice if not a ton a money. Fortunately, the Press had other titles that sold well. By the end of the year, Marc had made a decision that widened the scope of what we would do with *The Flower Seeker*. In addition to publishing my book-length poem in the fall of 2010, he would bring out a similarly formatted new edition of Bartram's *Travels* along with essays on Bartram by many of America's finest nature writers. The only problem was finding an editor for this companion book.

"Have you contacted Dorinda Dallmeyer?" I asked Marc one day. He hadn't, but I did on his behalf, and what had originated as a small personal project for me suddenly turned into a major focus on one of the true heroes of American ecology. And it helped make 2010 one of the highlight years of my writer's life.

The oil heater cracks its knuckles. He sits and watches a comedy on the black-and-white television, holding a blanket and feeling utter contentment. The winter before, he had stumbled and fallen against the heater and burned his arm badly, and an oval scar still lives between his elbow and wrist. He is more proud of that scar, of others, than he can say. His mother reads her book. She is always reading something. His father comes through the room, holding a sheaf of papers, working on a new idea. He is always working. Mark lies on his stomach in front of the televison, coloring. A sudden burst of laughter comes from the TV set. An invisible audience is watching the family on the set, finds them wildly amusing. His own family loves its motionlessness. He looks at his mother and sees that she is still beautiful, still near. He is loved.

36

The Flower Seeker

It takes a lot of cheek or a load of delusion to write an epic poem in the twenty-first century. After all, it is an art form originally created as part of the oral tradition, when there wasn't much else to do around the fire after the beast was charred and the mead supped. Now, with our corporate attention span encompassing 140 characters, and a heartfelt message being "Tk cre luv U," the idea of writing a 450-page poem on a single topic seems prima facie evidence of self-regard bordering on Wagner's.

I love formal poetic devices, and like everyone who started with a pen and a notebook in his bedroom, I loved finding out that I could write a Shakespearian sonnet, even if it was screamingly inept. We somehow convince ourselves that it's easier to write fine free verse than richly imagined rhymes. But a long poem without *some* form won't hold many readers. Even *The Cantos* uses the progression of history through Pound's fractured lens as a homing device. We feel him always circling, occasionally screaming, and finally asking forgiveness for his terrible decisions. I know of no more wrenching sequence in modern literature than the *Pisan Cantos,* 74-84 in the whole sequence, written when Pound was interned in an Allied prisoner-of-war camp near Pisa after his arrest on charges of treason at the end of World War II. But if I used one overriding structural device, what would it be?

I wanted an idea that would fill the poem with music—the kind that lifts and floats on a gentle wind, not a blaring march or, in far younger writers, riff and a shout in the street. I wasn't about to pretend I was who I was not. So I began to tinker with variations of what I call back-rhyme. This is not an easily visible device, and the ear doesn't hear it as one does, say, the rhymes in Housman (below, since I just mentioned him):

Loveliest of trees, the cherry now
Is hung with bloom along the bough,
And stands about the woodland ride
Wearing white for Eastertide.

Now, of my threescore years and ten,
Twenty will not come again,
And take from seventy springs a score,
It only leaves me fifty more.

And since to look at things in bloom
Fifty springs are little room,
About the woodlands I will go
To see the cherry hung with snow.

I believed that in a very long poem, the formal metrical foot and obvious end-rhymes would too soon become a straightjacket. I wanted lines measured by breath units, not feet. And if I did use rhyme, it would have to be something hidden, the way some patterns remain delightful secrets in the natural world. I had in mind something like a continent's coast, rocky here, smooth there, but from space of a singular pattern that might be reduced to the recurrent rhythm of fractals. So I devised a format with paired eighteen-line stanzas that rhyme *backwards* from the *middle.* Here is the very beginning of my poem's "Preface":

Here in the last summer of my last year,
Here in the moontide garden of my lives,
I stand to walk before I lie. The dovecote
Fills with marbled wings. Our horses stamp
Near the coach house and the stone barn
With an aim toward adventure, a higher
Memory and one I now so desperately share.
This shade simmers with delicate shadows,
The architecture of swallowtails, a dancing
Buttress in the waning days of my life.
Ice-pit, cold-cellar, greenhouse, shed:
I see the walls of one man's existence
Crumble to imaginary dust: the dust is me,
Though, old man in a sparkling season

Who trod the swamps for one azure bloom.
The names still fill me as the rain will swell
A droughty well: *tube-rose, painted bunting,*
Quercus prinos, Keowee, and *dyeing indigo*.

Here is the last river and my final flow,
A life of tramping moods and flower hunting,
The mounds where alligators roar and dwell
Rising from the page of this diurnal gloom.
The Schuylkill River has it route and reason,
From Valley Forge to Philadelphia then the sea.
So I try to see the passage of the almost-dead
Backward to the Carolina days. I leave no wife,
No children, or their heirs to run along the prancing
Lawn; yet I am still the witness, meadow-
Green too bright for one old man to bear.
All my life when flowers rise, I, sigher
Of beauty, form, and structure, solid urn
For ideas in their flittering flight, will camp
To suit their summons, petal by petal, boat
Moored to my solitary need. Bees in their hives
Hum. I see the sudden eyes of bird and deer.

Let your eye light on the last word in the first line of the second stanza, "flow." It rhymes with the last word in the last line of the *first* stanza, "indigo." And if you go down in the second stanza, the last word in the second stanza is "hunting," and it rhymes with the last word in the second-to-last line of the first stanza, "bunting." So that would be my formal structure—back-rhyme. The ear does not hear it as it does the A-A-B-B scheme of the Housman poem. Indeed, I doubt the ear hears my rhymes at all. But I do believe the hidden music of the poem speaks to the eye and ear, the same way the natural world whispered (and shouted) to Bartram in his four years of traveling around the American South. That eighteen-line back-rhyme scheme is the recalibration position for the poem, a formal surveying point to which the poem's narrator constantly returns during his journey. From there, it opens and closes into a dozens of forms that in some ways replicate the history of poetry from its earliest days. It was the most difficult book I had ever attempted, and it was informed by every poem I had ever loved, every novel that had spoken to me from between the pages. I wanted to use drawings of plants within stanzas themselves to fill meaning until it overflowed. Could we obtain the rights to use some of Bartram's own drawings for each canto's title page? We could. I wanted to have actual musical scoring in the poem, as I had done in *Jenny Dorset*. That was possible, too, and I did it.

Bartram's *Travels*, that great mess of a narrative that straddles the Age of Reason and the Age of Romanticism, would be my guide, of course. But I needed something more deeply imagined that did not stop at taxonomy but went all way down deep into the DNA of the man and his age. When I realized that it was going to work, that whether it was published or not, I would write the long poem I'd dreamed of writing since I was a boy, I thought of little else for many months. As I explained in the afterword:

> I wrote much of it in a state of wild and grateful rapture. Many days I finished my work in tears. Sometimes I would cringe when I was creating incidents whole cloth from my imagination, but I knew it was necessary if I was to fill in motivation for his actions and to ferret out a deeper reason why he didn't leave home for the last half century of his life. (The standard reason is that he was injured in a fall in 1786 when he was 47 years old while pruning a cypress tree and that he suffered from the eye troubles he contracted on the western leg of the *Travels*—I didn't invent that part of *The Flower Seeker*.)

I had help from a great many texts and people while I was writing the book, all listed at the end. But in any context, this book exists because of Marc Jolley. Without him, it would be moldering in a box beneath a bed. My ambition didn't stop there. I also talked to Marc about publishing the book simultaneously in three editions: hardback, softcover, and in a limited edition with a color frontispiece. And in the hardback and limited editions I would like to have an audio CD that had music to accompany the book that I had specifically composed for it, a "Bartram Suite." I would also record the poem's last canto for the CD, and finally, I wanted to include on it one of the most haunting sounds I know.

In the spring of 1967, on a trip to South Carolina and about the time my brother Mark, our father, and I began working as volunteers to help excavate Fort Prince George, which Bartram had visited in its post-military days as a trading post, our father had an idea. He waded to the edge of the

Keowee River, which lay between the former locations of Fort and the Cherokee village of Keowee. And he pressed "record." Again, from the afterword:

> My father took a battery-operated reel-to-reel recorder there on April 13, 1967, to record the sound of that glorious river's flowing water. Now part of a hydroelectric impoundment, the river is gone, though, one hopes, not forever. This astonishing recording is a treasure.

So the flowing water is from a river that no longer exists and which Bartram would have heard on his visit there. When I presented this entire plan to Marc, I was sure he would laugh at me. Instead, he said yes. Now all I had to do was finish the poem. Marc's idea to widen the project by reprinting Bartram's *Travels* in a new edition along with many essays by fine writers was the swallowtail on the clover. And I knew only one person who could edit that part and pull all those writers together: Dorinda Dallmeyer. I had known Dorinda for quite a long time at that point. Her astonishing biography from The Southern Nature Center project is worth printing in part:

> Dorinda G. Dallmeyer is director of the Environmental Ethics Certifi-cate Program at the University of Georgia. A native of Macon, Geor-gia, she holds three degrees from UGA: B.S. and M.S. degrees in geo-logy and a J.D. Dallmeyer is a member of the Council on Foreign Re-lations and past vice-president of the American Society of International Law. At UGA, she teaches courses in environmental dispute resolution and marine environmental ethics. Since 2001 she has collaborated with a group of southern nature writers in creating the Southern Nature Project, founded on the conviction that writing can help us lead more human, profound, and courageous lives, thereby conserving the southern environment for generations yet to come.

That description doesn't even do her intellectual breadth and human warmth justice. So I e-mailed her one day, explained my poem and Marc Jolley's idea about Bartram. Would she be interested in editing such a book? We talked on the phone, and she was intrigued and said she would get back to me in a few days. But by that night she was in.

One thing was missing, though. Bartram was an artist, but the world had changed in two centuries since he had roamed the South. What we needed was a new hand and a new eye. One day the phone rang in my office at UGA, and it was Dorinda. She was so excited she seemed barely able to hold the phone.

"Have you seen the artwork of Philip Juras?" she asked.

"I don't think I know that name."

"Then get up right this minute and walk over to Caldwell Hall and go to the Circle Gallery in the basement. He's got a show up there now. You aren't going to believe it. This is the missing part of the project."

Caldwell Hall was a two-minute walk from my office, which by then was in the renovated Old College on UGA's North Campus. I went in the front door of Caldwell and walked down the stairwell to the small gallery tucked at ground level. What I saw inside knocked my proverbial lights out. Juras's paintings were gorgeous and insanely accomplished landscapes of areas that, in many cases, Bartram had walked. I was stunned. No one else was in the gallery, and I lingered for more than an hour, walking from painting to painting, shaking my head in wonder. I got brushstroke-close to the canvases. This guy was *great*. Back in my office, I called Dorinda.

"Good grief," I said. "Do something. This *is* the missing link for the whole project."

"I'm on it," she said. I knew Dorinda well enough to know two things: first, she was a fine writer and editor, and she personally knew every nature writer in the South and half in America; and second, she knew how to crack a whip on any writer who might even be remotely thinking of missing a deadline. Marc Jolley was understandably thrilled. Dorinda brought academic cachet and a deep knowledge of Bartram since she'd grown up in Macon, where Bartram had spent time on his travels (and which was, of course, the site of Mercer University). She also began to contact nature writers, and she also got in touch with scholar and noted anthropologist Kathryn E. Holland Braun, a Bartram expert, and all of them agreed, for the love of it and no compensation whatever, to write essays. And these essays would focus on the different places of Bartram's *Travels* across the South. The writers who did this for the joy of walking once again with Bartram, deserve to have their names mentioned: Janisse Ray, Whit Gibbons, John Lane, Roger Pinckney, J. Drew Lanham, Doug Davis, Gerald Thurmond, Braund, Christopher Camuto, Philip Juras (also a fine writer), Matthew C. Smith, Dixon Bynum, Thomas Hallock, Jan De Blieu, and Thomas Rain

Crowe. Never, in the service of the personal essay on the natural world, have so many done so much for so little.

Dorinda's book would be called *Bartram's Living Legacy: The* Travels *and the Nature of the South*. And I want to point out that in the whole project no one worked harder than Marc Jolley. I can't even begin to calculate the hours he put in on everything from permissions to use artwork from the Natural History Museum in London to editing Bartram's *Travels*, which hadn't been out, at that point, in a new edition in decades. Both our books were designed by Burt & Burt to look alike and thus be companion pieces. They are oversized, drop-dead gorgeous volumes, each with an original Philip Juras painting on the cover.

The first time I saw the painting for the cover of *The Flower Seeker*, I got quite emotional. With input from me, my father, and from Bartram's descriptions, Philip painted a landscape of what the Keowee Valley must have looked like when Bartram came through (minus the buildings that still stood at the remains of Fort Prince George and the Cherokee village of Keowee across the river). Philip's painting even has the ford over which Bartram no doubt crossed many times and on which my father recorded the sounds of the now destroyed river. Though we could use only an excerpt from the painting on my cover, I was not about to be without that canvas. So Linda and I bought it from Philip, though it was on tour for two years after it was on the cover of *The Flower Seeker*.

Proofing our books would have been a nightmare for Dorinda and me if we hadn't loved them so much. Linda has always been supportive of my career and read galleys with me on most of my books, but on this one, her attitude was noticeably different. As she read along, she became deeply engrossed in Bartram's story. And she loved it. My father told me he thought it was a masterpiece. My only regret (and it is a deep one) is that Mother did not live to read it. My sorrow on that count was joined by Dorinda's, since that summer of 2010 she lost her mother *and* father.

While we all had worked very hard on the project, we knew from the outset that a small academic press had no budget for lodging or travel expenses after pub date for both books on September 1. So we decided to put our joy into a few selected events that fall, especially a publication party at the Ogeechee River Mill, a scenic gristmill that has been in operation since 1826. It was a fine site to remember Bartram and to honor our books. Many of the essayists in *Bartram's Living Legacy* came and signed books with me and Dorinda. She, in her grief, arranged the whole thing, and we had a good crowd on that sunny autumn afternoon near Warrenton, Georgia. In all, I read from my book at ten or fifteen events, ending with an affair at Barnes & Noble on November 18.

I am as proud of *The Flower Seeker* as any book I've written. When I watch films or read books about the cynical young, about their disconnected, unhappy, lives, I know I was part of that, too, back in the late Sixties when I was in college and protesting the Viet Nam War. But in my heart I was a country boy, and that has been my True South for a lifetime. And that was what I really understood about Bartram: the glory of the woods and the beauty of solitude.

In October of 2010, a more poignant literary event came before me. Even though I had a heavy schedule that fall with *The Flower Seeker*, I was already thinking of ending (for awhile at least) my time on the road. While driving and flying all over the country to meet, greet, and autograph had helped make me known, I was never sure if all those trips sold many books. But there was one event I would not have missed if it meant crawling to the venue: the premiere of *Somebody Else, Somewhere Else*, a film on the life of my dear friend Raymond Andrews. It had been written, produced, and directed by Jesse Freeman, who is from my own hometown, Madison, Georgia. *The Georgia Review*, under the editorship of Stephen Corey, also produced an entire issue in honor of Ray, something that would have deeply touched my good friend. After a party and showing of the film at Ciné, an independent film house in downtown Athens, there would be a panel discussion about Ray, and I was asked to be one of the panelists.

Linda and I had known Ray and Benny since 1975. After Ray's suicide in 1991 and Benny's death from cancer only a few weeks after diagnosis in 2006, we thought of them often. But I wasn't prepared for Jesse's marvelous film. Many members of the Andrews family came, too, and it was a pleasure to see them again. The event and the issue of *The Georgia Review* were simply wonderful, and I felt honored to be part of both.

I formally retired from the University of Georgia in early 2010 but immediately went back to work part-time, since Megan had decided to attend Agnes Scott College in Atlanta after graduating from high school that year. She got a huge academic scholarship, but even after that, it was expensive. So my plan was to retire and then go back and work two days a week in the same job but just as a writer, not as assistant dean. The dean of the college graciously allowed me to do that. From my splendid office in Old College, I moved to an impossible-to-find warren in one of the buildings occupied by the chemistry department on South Campus. I did the best job I could, but as each day passed, I felt more and more alienated from my old life. I had been doing this since 1985 to pay the bills so I wouldn't have to write fiction for money. It was worth every moment I spent, too. I made so many good friends in the office and across the UGA campus, especially Ruhanna Neal, Sarah Baines, Cathy Owens, Hollis Yates, Linda Bachman, Suzi Wong, Alan Flurry, Hugh Ruppersburg, Kellie Borders, and so many more.

Linda retired from teaching eighth grade English in 2009 after thirty-five years as a much honored and much loved member of the Oconee County Middle School in Watkinsville, Ga., where we live. Soon enough she was back working part-time as the archivist for Morgan County, working with my father, who originated the position as volunteer in 1986. The two of them have worked together three days a week for several productive years now. She has grown to be extremely good as an archivist, something that hasn't surprised me at all.

One day late that fall, the phone rang in my office, and it was Marc Jolley. Someone had just called him and said that a national magazine called *Books and Culture* had named *The Flower Seeker* as Book of the Year. Shocked, I made Marc wait while I looked it up online, and it was true—what a lovely surprise! Marc was thrilled. The list of top books of the year along with the announcement that mine was Book of the Year was brief, but the website also had a long podcast between editor-in-chief John Wilson and an editor at large named Stan Guthrie. With John's permission, I'm reproducing some of what he said in the podcast:

> "Every year…I pick a list of my favorite books and my favorite [of the year]. And this year it is *The Flower Seeker* by Philip Lee Williams. It's an epic poem and an absolutely fascinating book, and its subject is William Bartram, the naturalist, who was born fairly early in the 18th century and lived into the early 19th century. He was 84 years old when he died.
>
> "He had a relatively unsuccessful career—didn't do well at all. But then in later years he took a trip down to the South—North and South Carolina, Georgia, Florida, and other areas in the South. And

he wrote a book about that jaunt, which has a very long title but which people simply refer to as his *Travels*. Bartram's *Travels* is a classic of nature writing, but at first glance you might not think of this work as inspiring an epic. It [*The Flower Seeker*] doesn't necessarily fit with what we think of as epic poetry in works like *The Odyssey* and *The Iliad*, Vergil's *Aeneid*, Milton's *Paradise Lost*, and so on.

"But this book is just an extraordinary book in several ways. I can't do justice to all those ways here, but let me try to give you a sense of what kind of a book it is. There's a certain kind of book that a writer attempts in which you might say he or she is trying to sum up what they want to say about life, about the world, bringing to bear all that they've learned in the course of their career....

"There's a wonderful passage in an essay by the poet Czesław Miłosz where he says he's dreamed of writing a single sentence in which he could somehow express everything that he's sensed and everything that he has experienced. And of course it's a totally impossible dream for a writer. It's the kind of dream that a lot of young writers have, and both for good and for ill it tends to get driven out of them. Because if you come to an editor and say, 'I want to write a book that pours everything into it,' most of the time the editor is going to get you out of the office as quickly as possible. And frankly, most of the people who try to do that can't bring it off, and it's better to try to take something small. But, I said, both for good *and* for ill. So in some ways, that ambition can be a vain ambition.

"On the other hand, it's also a magnificent ambition, and it's something that has driven a lot of great writers. Certainly, Milton would be an example, but there are also a number of examples that are important to Philip Lee Williams in the 20th century, above all, I think, Ezra Pound and his *Cantos*—it's that kind of work that builds over time, and you try to put everything in it—everything you know. Everything you care about, your sense of why we're here and beauty and suffering and all into this huge work. And in the case of Williams, you can get a good sense of what he's doing by starting at the back of the book instead of just plunging right into the poem. (You can do that as well.) He has a postscript in which he explains his lifelong fascination with the epic form and his desire to tackle it someday. And he chose as his point of departure Bartram's *Travels*, and he often works into the book quotations from Bartram. So there are passages here that have been taken pretty much straight from Bartram's journals with a little bit of tweaking of language and rearranging. And people who have read Pound's *Cantos* or Charles Olsen's *Maximus* poems or Ronald Johnson and other American poets who work in that vein, modern American poets, will recognize what Williams is doing.

"So on one hand he's working in a tradition that's very strong in modern and even in contemporary American poetry. On the other hand, he's very conscious of the whole reach of epic poetry going all the way back to the Greeks and coming up through Dante and Milton and all those great predecessors. So you can see already from these names I'm invoking (that he invokes himself in his postscript)—you can see already that it's a work of remarkable ambition. That doesn't mean, of course, that brings it off. I think he does, remarkably well.

"On top of that, it is a physically rich book. There are many variations in typography. It is a book that is a visually enticing, seductive poem that uses the resources of typography in a brilliant way. And then on top of *that*, not in the paperback edition, which is the one that I'm holding here and is very handsome, but in the hardback edition there is a CD in which Williams reads the poem, and so you have that audio. So you can see again his impulse to create the total work, to throw himself totally into this.

"The scope of it is magnificent because you have Bartram traveling in this land where he is very often the only person not an Indian nearby. And the Seminoles give him the name the "Flower Hunter," because they were amused at the fact that they weren't collectors of flowers themselves and they saw how much he gave to flowers and other fauna, so they gave him this affectionate nickname. And Williams explains in the postscript that he deliberately changed it from the Flower Hunter, which associates what Bartram was doing to hunting for game, with the Flower *Seeker* because Bartram's quest was not just for physical things. He absolutely loved—he was very much like John Muir in this—he loved the physical world intensely, and he was observant to minute detail."

I apologize for going on so long with that, but in many ways it serves as apotheosis to my entire career—what I set out to accomplish so long ago.

Stan Guthrie ends the podcast by asking Wilson what he imagined Bartram might have thought of *The Flower Seeker*.

> "I think he would have been greatly honored by it," said Wilson. "It doesn't treat him as a perfect being, which he certainly wasn't—none of us is. But I think he would be greatly honored by it. Who knows? Maybe some day, Philip Lee Williams and Bartram will have a chance to meet in a splendor that's just hinted at in some of these lines."

Another highlight of the fall was an invitation to speak at the national American Academy of Religion meeting, which was held in Atlanta. Apparently, a great many people were seeing a spiritual side of *The Flower Seeker*, something I had not deliberately put in it. Still, it was a nice meeting, and I was delighted to take part in another event on a national stage. The praise I received there for my book was frankly overwhelming.

The Flower Seeker would go on to win my fourth Georgia Author of the Year award the next year, but the greatest thing it did was open a door I had been trying to push in, kick in, break in since 1983: In the fall of 2011, Mercer University Press would publish *The Divine Comics*.

Who are you, old man, who sits to know his passing
Days? How can sweet spring find my garden when all time
Has grown autumnal around me? The pale grandeur
Of age is overrated; I have no gift of prophecy, seer-
Like qualities for the pilgrim. All I own is memory
And this green and flowered acre, this old serenity
In the time of my hermitage. The businessman, the trade,
The ledger books all fade. Now my currency is sunfall,
My music made of mill-race and the quiet adoration
Of hurtless things. I strain to bring back my boyhood
Days, the river-crossings, botanical adventures, faces
I could not in my own fancy imagine. I recall the loud
Insect uproar of the night, the shady vespers, the supreme,
Sabbath-loud shouts of swamps in the deepest darkness.
I want to travel past this much-earned melancholy to roads
Of seasonal delight. I want to be almost innocent in the way
My eyes seek to curve around the dusty paths before me.
Who are you to ask more than his simple passing days?

I was the Flower Seeker, the pioneer of sands and clays,
Of crystalline pools more splendid than the deepest sea.
I rode in the reflected genius of Nature, felt the spray
Of waterfalls on my face, inhaled the liberty that startles
Even free man. Shakespeare could not have dreamed
It all: islands roiled with brambles, seashells, rose clouds,
The hazel canopy of live oak. In my young man's races
I never found such animal riot. Rivers, sulfurous blood
Flowing from swamps, and on those trails the impatient
Youth mad for species, genus, the pleasure of one tall
Pine rigid with rapture in the breeze. What have I made
In this life? What knowledge gained, what old enmity
Forsaken? I want to bring back the strong and sensory
Equations of those days when I found no real fear
In each day's awakening, an old man's right to be sure
Of one sure thing, the sweetness of the rose and the lime
That lift me up to trails I have no hope for surpassing.

—From *The Flower Seeker*

37

Becoming the Poem

A writer's autobiography is bound to be out of order because novelists and poets don't think in a linear way. As you may have noticed, I started this book in 1991 and immediately went back to my boyhood. So I hope you'll forgive me for having leaped over one of the most important events of my career that happened in March 2010, just as Dorinda and I were getting our twin books ready for birth. *The Divine Comics* can wait for a chapter.

There are enough literary awards that one might suppose every writer will win at least one, given time and persistence. But no matter how small the award or how large, even the most faux-superior scribbler is happy to get it. No, winning Best Poem in your local writer's group for December isn't the same as winning the Pulitzer. But it can keep you going. It's cold in Writerland, and, like Everest, the higher you go, the colder it gets. I had started my career winning the Townsend Prize for Fiction, which no one outside Georgia knows, since it's awarded for the best novel published by a Georgian during the past two years before award-time. But it *is* a prestigious award, made so by the quality of the winners. (As I noted, Alice Walker won it just before I did.) I have felt honored to win four Georgia Author of the Year awards in three categories, but, again, most states probably have such awards. (The awards are given by a private group, not the State of Georgia.) I reached a new plane with the Michael Shaara Award for *A Distant Flame*. This is a national prize, named for a great novelist. The fact that I received it in ceremonies in Boston also made it a national event and very personal to Linda and me. But it was for a single book, not one's body of work. And I had reached the age where my life's writing was either worth honoring or not.

In 2000, the Hargrett Rare Book and Manuscript Library at the University of Georgia instituted the Georgia Writers Hall of Fame. This was at a different level from many literary prizes because it would be curated by a state organization—and a fine one at that. Here's how Hargrett is described on its own website: "The Hargrett Library, a leading repository on Georgia history and culture, holds 200,000 volumes in its rare book and Georgiana collections, 6 million pages of historical manuscripts and photographs, along with maps, broadsides, and UGA archives and records. Other areas of emphasis include performing arts and natural history. Holdings date from the 15th century to the present." The magnificent new Russell Special Collections Library Building on the UGA campus, of which Hargrett is a part, opened in 2011. The Hall of Fame is selected by a panel of judges named by the library. And so far, those selected are a magnificent lot, including Flannery O'Connor, Alice Walker, Dr. Martin Luther King, Jr., Conrad Aiken, and James Dickey. The members also include a number I have known or met during my writing career: Raymond Andrews, Coleman Barks, David Bottoms, Erskine Caldwell, Judith Ortiz Cofer, Pat Conroy, Harry Crews, Melissa Fay Greene, Terry Kay, Jim Kilgo, Judson Mitcham, John Stone, and many more.

In 2009, when the installation of the latest crop of winners took place, the board of judges met after the main ceremony to vote on new members. Immediately afterword, word began to leak out that I had been selected as a new member of the Georgia Writers Hall of Fame. I was deeply flattered, but in those days, the Board waited many months to announce the winners to be installed the following year. (The Hall started by installing two writers a year, then shifted to four for a brief time, and finally back to two.) So I had to wait quite a long time before hearing formally that I had indeed been elected to the Hall of Fame and would be installed in March 2010. Being honored for one's lifetime body of work is a wonderful feeling, I'm here to tell you. Georgia is physically the largest state east of the Mississippi River and has a population of around 10 million (eighth most-populous in the entire United States and about the same as Greece), so the honor is significant. I also got a small delight that the Hargrett Library is only a couple of hundred yards from the apartment on South Hull Street in Athens where my parents first lived when they came to UGA after World War II to earn their college degrees on the GI Bill.

I was selected for 2009 (installed in 2010) with Judith Ortiz Cofer, poet Georgia Douglas Camp Johnson, and pioneering Civil Rights journalist Walter Francis White. Johnson and White were long dead, and in general that has been the pattern for HOF recipients each year—two living and two gone. (Now it's back to one of each.) The event in Boston had been important to me, but none of my family was there except Linda and Megan At the Hall of Fame event on March 23, 2010, in Athens, many of my family members and friends came. The only ones missing were my mother, who had died in August 2008, and Linda's mother, who passed away five years before that. The pain of their absence was acute. Linda's father, Fred, was there.

Each writer new to the Hall is introduced and then is given a few minutes for remarks. Installing me was my dear friend Terry Kay, a fine writer, an even better man, and by then already a member of the HOF. No writer in my life was a better friend to me. I love him.

"Philip is among the finest writers the State of Georgia has ever produced," Terry said in his introduction. "For over fifty years, I have learned enough about writing to know when to stand in awe. Today I stand in awe." His entire introduction overwhelmed me with his respect and affection, and as I sat in the huge crowd in the rotunda of the Miller Learning Center at UGA (the new library was not yet built in 2009), I thought back to my earliest attempts at writing in the early to mid-1960s. It had been a long, crazy road. "I always believed that if Phil had never published again, this book [my first, *The Heart of a Distant Forest*] would secure his place as a major figure in Georgia's literary history," Terry added.

My remarks that day summed up my career.

> I stand before you today with humility that is as profound as it is deep. I keep asking myself, "What am I, Phil Williams from Madison, Georgia, doing in a hall of fame with Flannery O'Connor, Conrad Aiken, and Dr. Martin Luther King, Jr.?"
>
> I keep having in my mind, this picture of them sitting in a room and welcoming me warmly, while trying hard not to laugh. Flannery, no longer needing her crutches, walks over to me, shakes my hand, and says, "I know Madison's just up the road from Milledgeville, A Bird Sanctuary, but I didn't have no idea that anyone there was capable of wasting as much time as I did."
>
> And yet I can't quite imagine having lived a life that would have given me a tenth the joy for a hundred times the work. So if I don't quite feel I belong in the company of so many great writers, of the

Cofers and the Kays, the Margaret Mitchells and the Alice Walkers, that doesn't mean I'm not thrilled to be invited to the party.

In point of fact, this is one of the happiest days of my life. To be here, surrounded by a family I love and friends who are so dear, is the kind of thing about which we all dream but that seldom happens in real life.

Although I am in no sense allergic to money, the older I get the more I know that it is the least valuable thing we can leave to our children and grandchildren. Love, of course, is the first and best gift, but a close second is a life of the mind.

I was among the most fortunate of kids to grow up in a family that didn't care especially about wealth but cared passionately about Bach and Shakespeare, about Wordsworth and Beethoven, about poetry and science, music and visual art. On long car trips, my sister, brother, and I would give our father and sometimes our mother a category—*any* category—and then we would get a question to which we were expected to know the answer. Of *course*, we cheated. I asked for questions in classical music, and Mark would ask for something in physics or chemistry. Laura Jane, who would be the high school valedictorian, could ask for questions in *anything*.

And from that traveling quiz show, we all learned the answers to a thousand different things. My father might ask me a question about Romantic Poets, and as a coda, my mother would recite Leigh Hunt's "Abou Ben Adhem," memorized forty years before, without missing a word.

I knew, from the time I was fourteen, that I would live a life in the arts. I loved science and nature and sports, but I *lived* for the arts. For a long time I wanted only to be a great composer, but by the time I was in my late teens, I began to realize that the art I would most often try to inhabit was literature.

It wasn't hard to know why. When I read poetry, in many ways I *became* the poem. It wasn't just blood and sinew to me. It was marrow. It was the stone on which I was meant to stand if indeed I stood at all. I suppose my family was unusual in that my parents stressed a knowledge of and love of arts and sciences equally. From childhood I loved science, but as it turned out, my gifts lay more in explaining science than in doing it.

Albert Einstein once said, "The intuitive mind is a sacred gift, and the rational mind is a faithful servant. We have created a society that honors the servant and has forgotten the gift." Although I still doubt my own gifts in the presence of these great women and men, I do not for a minute doubt that I have lived largely with the intuitive mind and its grace and grandeur.

As some of you may know, my family has been connected to the University of Georgia for more than six decades. I have marinated among some of the best and brightest men and women alive during all my years here. I also awoke one morning in Reed Hall when I was a freshman and saw a chicken walking down the hall. Maybe it is that eternal confrontation between the epic lunacy of the real world and the slopes of Parnassus that makes a life of the mind such an unending joy.

I can imagine very little that would give me more pleasure than knowing I will be in this magnificent Hall of Fame. For that and so much more, I want to say thank you to the University of Georgia and the UGA Libraries.

Trying to explain what one does as a creative writer can often sound a little strange, I admit. Once, when my daughter Megan was very young, she came up to me and said, "Let me get this straight. You make up one person (*makes sock-puppet hand*) and then you make up another person (*makes another sock-puppet hand*) and then you make them *talk* to each other? (*The hands "speak" to each other.*) I admitted that was about right. She looked at me sadly and turned and walked off. Now that girl who didn't believe in such foolishness is already an accomplished artist who has exhibited her photographs at the High Museum of Art in Atlanta and will be a freshman at Agnes Scott College this fall.

I'm equally proud of our son, Brandon, who would have held his own in the traveling quiz program, especially in Asian history—the focus of his degree from UGA.

"There is no use trying," said Alice, after she'd gone down the rabbit hole. "One can't believe impossible things." "I daresay you haven't had much practice," said the Queen. "When I was your age, I always did it for half an hour a day. Why, sometimes I've believed as many as six impossible things before breakfast."

To this day, I believe in things some people find impossible even to consider. I believe that poetry matters. I believe that a life without art is intolerable. I believe that those who would destroy education, especially education in the arts and music, are guilty of *crimes* and that people in the future will remember their names and hold them accountable.

But mostly I believe in the power and necessity of writing. And needless to say, when I began as a writer, I only knew where the road lay, but I had no idea how to travel it. When I was in my early twenties I wrote a novella that had to be one of the worst things committed to paper since the invention of movable type. My second work, a six-hundred-page novel, was so bad that I pictured Johann Gutenberg slapping himself on the forehead with the most profound regret imaginable.

At that point, I was publishing poetry with some regularity and could have given up on fiction. But I decided to make a list of everything I loved in the world and to try and write about that. The manuscript was a quiet novel called *The Heart of a Distant Forest*. And I was off in a life I could barely believe as it unraveled.

Along the way I have most often written about people at the margins of society, those out of the mainstream because of age or social position or race or beliefs. My last two novels, for example have been about southerners who were against the South's position in the Civil War. It hasn't been the easiest course.

The Pulitzer-Prize-winning writer Dave Barry put it most succinctly when he wrote, "The problem with writing about religion is that you run the risk of offending sincerely religious people, and then they come after you with machetes."

No one has come after me with machetes, not yet. On the contrary, people have been more than wonderful to me and have treated me with respect and kindness that continually humbles me.

And so I stand before you today deeply moved to be here. Mark Twain once said, "Grief can take care of itself, but to get the full value of joy you must have somebody to divide it with."

So today I want to share with all of you here the joy I feel, to divide it among us as readers and lovers of books. And if we listen closely enough to the sound of that inner grace and joy, it may well sound like Flannery O'Connor laughing, healed by what we are allowed to become, even when time has taken us away.

Bless you all for being such wonderful partners in the joyous pilgrimage of this writer's life.

In the end, awards are not why we write. But in a profession largely done alone and filled with rejection and pain, as well as intermittent delight, an honor such as the Georgia Writers Hall of Fame is the kind of quiet joy that endures.

At the same time I was honored with induction in the Hall of Fame, the Georgia House of Representatives passed a resolution honoring me. Among its kind statements:

> "Whereas Mr. Williams is among the finest writers the State of Georgia has ever produced and his induction into the Georgia Writers Hall of Fame is an honor befitting his talent as a writer and supporter of the arts....
>
> "Now therefore, be it resolved by the House of Representatives that the members of this body commend Mr. Philip Lee Williams on his incredible literary works and congratulate him upon his recent induction into the Georgia Writers Hall of Fame."

Nice.

That March, I was awaiting the publication of *The Flower Seeker* and had every reason to believe it was the apex of my writing life. But in the wings, blasting at its own pages like barrage of fireworks, was the book I'd been trying to get into print for three decades. And it's time was now.

He and Mark take croker sacks and fill them with dirt for bases. In the windswept field beside their house, they make a baseball diamond. He imagines Mickey Mantle smiling out toward them, taking practice swings. Mickey will be kind and strong, and when you throw him a pitch, he will hit it all the way to the woods, until the red laces are no larger than the smallest dot visible. He really wants Yogi to come though, hero of heroes, that odd little man who lifts everyone around him. The Yankees are different when Yogi comes to bat. He imagines himself as Yogi, hears the crowd shouting hopefulness as he comes to the plate. No. He will never be Yogi Berra except in imagination. But in imagination he can be anyone, President Eisenhower, Howard Carter, even Hercules. No. He is just Phil Williams, a boy in blue jeans straightening croker sacks in a field where cattle come to call.

38

Paving the Road to Hell

I'd heard of Dante's *Divine Comedy* before I got to high school, but I didn't read it in translation until 1969 when I was in my last quarter as a freshman at UGA. I still have the New American Library's Mentor Classic paperback edition of *The Inferno,* the first part of Dante's epochal masterpiece. In the front I wrote "Philip L. Williams, 1969-70." I don't really recall the circumstances under which I read it, but the double date I wrote in the front makes it seem I bought it (cover price: 95 cents) for a class. It was also at the same time I got my greedy palms on *An Anthology of New York Poets,* and so I was actively feeling my way through the past and present of literature, vocational preparation for a life's work.

There are times in our lives when we aren't ready for the book we hold in our hands, when experience and desire and knowledge block it from us. There are also times when a text explodes in the mind and imagination, when a book is so overwhelming that it is literally life changing. When I read *The Inferno,* I was nineteen and kindled so highly that any spark would set me ablaze. By then, I had begun to know an inner world that was inaccessible even to friends and family. In literature, I felt I could see through *walls.* I had felt that way with classical music for years, but since I knew by that time that music would always be an avocation, my interest in books was pinwheel-bright, addictive. O *God,* what a time of joy it is to be young and suddenly, wildly in love with serious literature! Everything was as new to me as spring's first rose. I'm sure I bought the paperback of *The Inferno* expecting nothing. But when I finished the book's last words, I was a different young man, and I knew it. In short order I saved my money and bought (also in the Ciardi translations) the *Purgatorio* and the *Paradiso,* the middle and ending sections of Dante's imaginary journey from hell to paradise. On first readings, they did not enthrall me as the *Inferno* had, but that's probably true for everyone who's read the books over the past eight hundred years as well. In contemporary times, the *Divinia Commedia* (its proper title in Italian) has been a source of inspiration for, among others, Beckett, Pound, Eliot, Joyce, and dozens of others. My hero (and serious nut case) William Blake did illustrations for it. As a teenager I'd obtained a badly water-damaged copy of the Henry Cary translation with engravings by French artist Gustave Doré. I was far more in love then with the artwork, which was hideously wonderful and made the ghastly perils of Dante's hell come alive with a giddy delight. I don't even remember having read it, but the Cary translation is snooty and pedestrian. Not until I read Ciardi's lively translation with his version of Dante's *terza rima* verse form did I begin to understand the poem. And from there, I began to explore other translations and to pick my way through it in Italian.

By the time I was in my mid-twenties, I wanted in the worst way (alas, the only way I was capable of dealing with anything in my writing in those days) to use Dante as a jumping-off place for some work of art. I had, for years, a similar obsession with the Italian Rennaisance in general and Michelangelo in particular, so all of Italy's artistic heritage is buried deep in my DNA. The first thing I tried was an orchestral-vocal piece, and to that end I boiled down the Ciardi *Inferno* to a usable length and wrote my own transitions between sections. I don't think it ever occurred to me that I was using copyrighted material, but of course copyright is only theoretical when one is writing (or composing) for one's cats and aquarium fish. In those days, I could only hear my music in my head or a piano reduction, so after maybe thirty pages of full score I lost interest.

After that, I wrote occasional poems dealing with Dante. And my *Inferno* madness led me to a deep (so to speak) love of caves. I went into every commercial cave in the Southeastern United States and some noncommercial places, and I found out that among my many mental and emotional quirks, claustrophobia wasn't one of them. Indeed, I loved being in small, confined spaces deep in the Earth and felt no fear whatsoever. (While I love a safe view from high places, I am terrified of insecure heights. Once, while Linda was driving us through Rocky Mountain National Park near Estes Park, Colo., and pointing out scenery, I was in the shotgun seat looking straight down about forty miles on the side of the road with no rails, screaming, and banging my hands on the dash in front of me. She couldn't understand what my ruckus was about.) This love of caves, which began with the *Inferno*, was translated years later into *Blue Crystal*. When *BC* came out, a review in the bulletin of the New England Speleological Society said I was either a caver or had really done my homework. Thrill time.

What I needed was the right form to cast out the demons of Dante. The right moment. I had been edging that way in reading Joyce and Kenneth Patchen, in collecting dogeared experimental fiction of all stripes from used bookstores. *Don Quixote* and *Tom Jones* were paths to follow. I discovered Sterne's *Tristram Shandy* as an undergraduate, and my love for that book would ripen years later with *Jenny Dorset*. I knew and liked John Barth from near the beginning of his career, though my favorite book of his, *The Tidewater Tales*, didn't appear until 1987. Nabokov can't really be considered a postmodernist, and I was late coming to him anyway, not even reading my first VN novel until about 1978. Since then, I've become the most wild-eyed Nabokovian imaginable. I believe with all my heart and soul that he is one of the greatest writers who ever lived. Of course, I was far in advance of fiction with my love of *An Anthology of New York Poets*. But as a twenty-year-old I was so ripe for that volume that I was falling off the tree. While Frank O'Hara was a wonder and worth gold to me, the poet from that volume whose voice has stayed with me the strongest and longest is John Ashbery's. I love poetry and fiction that seem to be part of some obscure code. I love a narrative that comes to a reader from a hundred directions at once and only on the last page can be seen as a fully assembled jigsaw puzzle.

While I have read enough to admire and study realist fiction, and the well-made story with a perfect beginning, middle, and end, I have never liked that neatness of approach as a writer myself. My mind does not work the way realist fiction does. And yet I also knew that I had to follow my own lights as a writer if I wrote prose fiction. I was not a bitter person who wanted to meditate on the hopelessness of life and "humanunkind," to use e.e. cummings' word. Even though I'd been an "actor" in the first act of *Waiting for Godot*, Beckett's reductive bleakness didn't interest me. I wanted passion—big, sprawling, messy passion on a canvas filled with culs-de-sac, tunnels that lead nowhere (or somewhere), and verbal delight in every sentence.

So I was at least headed in the right direction when in 1976, I bought Thomas Pynchon's novel *Gravity's Rainbow* on one of our trips to New York City. I had never heard of the book or Pynchon. When I opened it in the store and read "A screaming comes across the sky," I was hooked. It was set during World War II in London and Europe and dealt with...well, *everything*. When I got home, I read it with increasing excitement. As I finished, I was sure of a few things. First, Thomas Pynchon was (and is) a genius. Second, his mixing of history and postmodern techniques attracted me like a Siamese to catnip. And finally, this was a narrative direction worthy of a writer's (or reader's) time and life.

Over the years, I've been rather amazed at how angry Pynchon and other postmodern novelists can make selected readers. He simply infuriates some, as if he knows a riddle whose solution is shared by a group of snickering acolytes but kept from the larger public as a personal insult. I remember being in an apartment in New York City and a woman asking me what I was reading. I said Pynchon. She turned on me in a rage, and I was seriously happy she wasn't armed.

"You *like* that intellectual bullshit?" she almost shouted at me.

"Uh, yeah, I do," I said meekly. I haven't been a serious physical coward since I escaped the shark, but I found out that day I had to be careful to whom I divulged this particular passion.

Naysayers aside, I love *Gravity's Rainbow* and in short order read the rest of Pynchon's *oeuvre*. I also began to spread out from there, reading as much fiction in the same vein as I could find. This was a language I could speak, and in which I thought I might one day be fluent. So, by 1982, I had begun to start writing sentences and then pages that saw the world through a similar smashed and then casually reassembled prism. And then one day it hit me: *Dante*. My new technique would be a perfect platform from which to tackle a new, bizarre, and comic version of the *Divina Commedia*. So I began writing what I then called *The Inner Kingdom*, and which was my version of the *Inferno* only.

I'm proud that I was writing fiction as a postmodernist well before many of its later, famous practitioners did. I was also writing more traditional fiction, though not the Realist novel as such. *The Heart of a Distant Forest* used the fragments of a journal to tell a story. But long before I'd started showing *Heart* to anyone, I was working on *The Inner Kingdom* in a voice that I knew could be mine for a literary life. The manuscript was read and rejected by a number of presses, but by the mid-1980s I had learned that literary rejection had many meanings. Sometimes it's a matter of what else is on a publisher's list. Often it's the very real worry that the submitted work won't sell. And a lot of the time, the editor simply hates the book. An editor in Manhattan once rejected a novel of mine because he said my dialogue made his *teeth* hurt. I didn't know fiction even *had* a medical pathway to dental health, but if so, I feel sorry for editors in the 1840s when bad teeth were a part of daily life.

I finished the first part of my novel in the early 1980s, the second in the mid-1990s, and the final part in the mid-2000s. But I never stopped rewriting and polishing the whole thing. After the literary success of *The Flower Seeker* and its winning national Book of the Year by *Books and Culture*, I had what might have been my last chance to publish a volume I'd spent three decades writing and most of my life imagining. I had talked to Marc Jolley at Mercer about it off and on for a long time, but since other projects intervened, I'd never made a formal submission.

Marc said to send to him in late 2010. I did.

On December 20, he sent me this e-mail:

> "*The Divine Comics* is too ambitious, too large, and too expensive. Can't wait to see it next fall! Merry Christmas."

I exploded with joy and answered him:

> "I have been waiting my whole creative life to see this e-mail. Since before my first book was published. You have no idea what this means to me. Or maybe you do. *Ecstatic* doesn't even come close. If you promise not to hate me, I'm going to send you one of my long emails tomorrow. Until then for me it's PARTY!!!!!!!!!!!!!!!!!!!!!!!!!!!!!"

When I say "party" I meant it in the quiet, metaphorical sense, because I haven't had a serious drink since 1994. But, oh, did I party that night.

The idea for the cover was mine—a winking harlequin juggling three balls—one with a fire image of hell, another with mountains for purgatory, and finally a blown-wind image for paradise. It was brilliantly executed by Mary-Frances Burt and won graphics awards (as did her cover for *The Campfire Boys*).

In the narrative terms of autobiography, this is the place where my lifelong obsession triumphs, I win the Pulitzer and the Nobel, and I get my picture on the cover of *Rolling Stone*. Alas, when it came out in November 2011, nothing happened. At all. The book was completely and utterly ignored. Part of that was simple economics. A thousand-page novel isn't cheap, and most people simply aren't going to pony up a lot of money for a book. But it went beyond that. It was unsold, unreviewed (with one exception), and unread. An online critic and writer named Malcolm Campbell gave it a rapturous review which meant a lot to me, but as far as I can tell, no one else reviewed it.

In theory, I suppose, a good way to complete the story of *The Divine Comics* would be for me to jump off a cliff holding a copy and screaming about the world being unfair. But the truth is that I fully expected the book to be ignored. I was writing now for a world that wouldn't include me. I would be long gone before the book was read or discovered, but I'm sure it will be some year. Copies of it are in selected libraries around the world, including the Zentralbibliothek Zürich, only a couple of miles from where James Joyce is buried.

He stands beside his mother at the clothesline. She is bringing in the sun-dried shirts and pants, and she wears a skirt and blouse, and over her skirt is a pocket-apron, and as she taken off each clothespin, she drops it with a clack on to others there. He thinks it sounds like one twig being dropped on another. He is small, maybe five, and he has to shade his eyes as he looks up at her. Nothing has ever smelled more lovely than these warm cotton clothes that she drops in the plastic basket. She sings to herself, something from the radio that he can't quite place. The sound of falling clothespins moves him in a way he does not understand. He comes close and looks into her apron pocket, and he is still looking when she drops another. That sound means he is safe. He feels the sun warm his own head. She touches his back, pulls him to her once, and then turns to gather more clothes. Nothing can harm him now. They will all live forever.

39

Who I Really Was

I have focused in this book on my life as a writer and composer, but that is just one small sliver of the life I lived. Obviously, I would not be who I was without my mother and father, my brother Mark, my sister Laura Jane. Together, we were a fine quintet and made lovely music. But even closer in my life have been Linda, Brandon, and Megan.

Telling my story without including them on every page seems incomplete or even wrong. Linda never dove into a roaring river to rescue me, but she saved my life more times than I can count. Without her, my life would surely have been a wandering thing, and I might still be writing only an occasional bad poem. She pushed me to be better than I thought I could ever be in this life.

A teacher of the year at her school, director of an award-winning school newspaper, remembered well by thousands of former students over a thirty-five year career as a teacher? Priceless. I have often told her that she touched far more lives and did more good in any one year of her career than I did in my entire life. She helped generations of children learn to love words and writing and to know why the strong and proper use of language is a ticket to a fuller, richer life.

With every book I wrote, she was at my side, reading drafts, listening to me ask about plot changes and narrative devices. She told me when something wasn't good and why. When she was really moved by something I wrote, she rarely said so in a conversation. Instead, she left a note on the desk in my study, and I saved them all and to this day take them out and read them when my work is going poorly. Howard Carter in his greatest days as an archaeologist in Egypt never found anything half so fine as those early morning notes.

She loves the color yellow and Westerns—films, TV series, and books. For years we have watched re-runs of fifty-year-old episodes of "Gunsmoke" while eating dinner each night. She knows sports inside and out and probably loves college football the most. She enjoys *my* great sports passions, baseball and above all, golf, and lets me watch the Braves every night in season and almost every golf tournament—men's and women's—on TV. She doesn't like movies as I do, but she will gamely enjoy them with me from time to time. When we were first married in 1972, she could barely boil water. Within a year, she was an exceptionally fine cook.

She was born with a green thumb and loves to garden. Every spring, the miracle of her annuals and perennials begins again—gorgeous bulb plants, creeping greenery. And she finds sunny spots in our shady land in the woods to grow tomatoes and cucumbers and other vegetables.

Linda gives money to every charity on Planet Earth. I'm forever getting thank-you notes from Save the Vampire Squids and similar groups. We have steadily given to environmental and progressive causes for decades, but no cause is too unworthy (or obscure) for Linda. We've gotten free tote bags from everyone but the Rodeo Clowns of Armenia. (When we lived in Madison from 1970-74, I was one of only two or three white members of the local NAACP, and we have kept contributing to it and similar groups for decades.)

She will go on a major shopping excursion with Megan or her sisters and come home with $9.12 worth of miscellaneous stuff from seven different stores and be just as happy as if she'd bought the Hope Diamond.

Linda is exceptionally intelligent, well-read, and altruistic. She loves Classic Rock, but her favorite musical genres are Folk and Folk Rock. She turned me on to great many artists that I should have known before I met her, including Cream, Joan Baez, Joni Mitchell, and a hundred more. I know the lyrics to dozens of old songs and sing along with them on the car radio, and Linda doesn't ask me to stop the car and let her out. She is not a singer, though she has a perfectly fine voice.

She is obsessed with the geology and archaeology of our seven acres. I have called her the Crystal Queen in print before—she is a genius at finding quartz and amethyst crystals lying in what should be clear sight—but she is the only one who finds them. She can take one look at a huge patch of clover and go straight down and find one with four leaves. She first performed this trick for me when we had just started dating and were sitting on the UGA campus in front of Park Hall. I was sure she had cheated, but she has since then done it for me at dozens of places around the country over many decades. I can only assume it is a gift. We pick up Indian pottery sherds but only out of our creek bed, where they have no real provenance. We are scrupulous about not disturbing artifacts where they might have a context for some future archaeologist or historian. Linda always finds the biggest and most beautifully decorated sherds in the creek bed, no matter what I happen to find.

Linda fears and hates snakes, even the tiny and lovely ring-necked snakes we have on Wildcat Ridge. I rather like them and forbid any harm coming to them. I have in my life regrettably killed three copperheads near our houses, but I never kill non-venomous snakes. She makes up for it by loving every other animal, and she has an almost hyper-human connection with birds, something she got from her Grandma Rowley.

She loves to travel, and I enjoy staying home, since most of the time I am living deep inside my imagination. Most of our married life, we had too little money or time to go very far, but my literary career somewhat changed that.

We throw the baseball together and have since we first met. She takes no prisoners and has a ferocious fastball that will leave my glove hand stinging for days. As I said earlier, when my right shoulder no longer worked, and I could no longer throw, she bought me an expensive Rawlings glove for the right hand so I could learn to be a lefty. I wrote my name on it with a pen "so the other boys won't steal it." I was sixty-three at the time. This is all worth repeating.

Linda is a political progressive as I am, and together we have supported losing candidates (especially in the South) since the early Seventies. We have together been ardent feminists and supporters of women's rights. I am glad that we have lived long enough to see some of the bleaker days of racial hatred end. We are also cheered that little by little hatred and discrimination toward people for their sexual orientation is ending in the U.S., though we have far to go.

She had never had a pet cat until she met me. When we were living together in Athens just before our undergraduate graduation, we found three kittens sleeping in a barbecue grill, and she took the small black one we eventually named Africa. She called me from Decatur one night and said

"Little Black," as she was calling him then, was deathly ill. I was taking the bus to Decatur to visit her the next day, and I said I'd check it out.

"It mostly happens when you rub him," she said the next day when I got there. "Listen." She rubbed Africa's belly, and the mystery sound—*purring*—came off him like audible love. After that, she grew to be a cat lover in full, and now cats everywhere flock to her because they recognize her as one of the feline tribe.

In so many ways, this is her book, too. Without her, my life could not have been filled with such joy. I feel fortunate just to have known her. To have been her partner in life feels like grace.

Brandon and Megan should also be on every page of my life starting with our son's birth in 1978.

Brandon is a wonderful—really wonderful—father. The three children he and Laura brought into the world, Caleb, Mollie, and Elliott, are lucky beyond imagining. Laura is an equally fine mother. Brandon has some of the same odd quirks that I have, including the fact that he's a political progressive who loves military and family history. He got a degree in history from UGA, and his main interest in those years was Asia. But from his early boyhood he was fascinated with computers. He ran the computer labs in UGA's classics department for his last two years in school, and from that he got his job as a computer specialist in UGA's Lamar Dodd School of Art. He's now director of IT for the art school.

He is funny, loves the small beauties of the world, and has always been an outdoors person. He took wilderness survival training in the scouts, and it almost killed him, but he refused to back down or quit. I taught him animal tracking and woodcraft as a young boy, and he learned it and more, and he has since taught it to his own children.

He played cello for years in the Suzuki program in Athens and performed in numerous recitals. He became quite a good guitarist and played in high school with an interesting rock band that once opened a major show at the local high school. Music was one of the things that drew him to Laura, who as I said earlier is a spectacularly gifted and accomplished violinist. He is well-read and deeply attuned to current events, but his life is in his young family.

Megan is the most altruistic person I've ever known, and at this moment she's a twenty-two-year-old college student. She cares deeply about others. I have never once heard her use a swear word, not even a mild one. *I* have to watch *my* language around *her*. She has a sweet disposition but doing things right is never far from her mind. She might be mature for her age, but she will still admit she loves Disney World and the best of the Disney animated films. She and I must have watched the masterpiece *Beauty and the Beast* a hundred times together when she was growing up. She is a world-class expert on the TV series "Little House on the Prairie," and she, Linda, and I have watched episodes of it hundreds of times together. She also knows the "Little House" books inside and out, and she's turned me on to *The Hunger Games*.

She is also ambitious. When she was in band, from the eighth grade through high school, she worked harder than I could imagine to be a fine player and leader. She was a tremendously gifted tympani player and section leader in the Athens Youth Symphony for several years. She also performed as pianist for AYS during its concerts on stage at UGA, too. She has done everything from teaching Sunday school to volunteering as a poll worker during elections here. She has had numerous jobs over the years and distinguished herself in them as well. At this writing, she is a senior at UGA, majoring in history while at the same time working at the Hargrett Library and teaching swimming lessons. But her real life's ambition is to be a children's librarian. She would be wonderful at it.

But most of all, Megan was the shining gift of our late life, the girl who kept us young even as the years have begun to feel a little heavier.

I worked hard as a literary man. What I have reported in this book leaves out about ninety percent of what I did as a writer and as an author and as a human being. But my true life, the one that mattered and matters most to me, is the one I lived first with my parents, brother and sister, and then later with my beautiful wife and wonderful children. Look for me there.

From The Babyhood Record of Philip Lee Williams*: I was born on January 30, 1950, in Athens, Georgia, at St. Mary's Hospital. I weighed 8 lbs., 2½ oz. I was 19½ inches long. Complexion: fair. Color of hair: brown. I remained at the hospital for six days. Name of physician: Dr. Tom Dover. Crawls anywhere at 5½ mos. on stomach, hands, and feet. Almost sits up at 5½ mos. First tooth at five mos. 3 weeks. Philip had chicken pox at 3 mos.*—In the handwriting of Ruth Sisk Williams

40

Every Moment, Every Object

On February 1, 2012, I retired, finally and completely, from the University of Georgia. As you may recall, I had formally retired in 2010 and then gone back to work two days a week. I owe a great deal to UGA for my job all those years. It helped give us a good standard of living, solid health insurance, and a comfortable retirement. But what I did there was not my profession. It was my *job*. And I took that job so I would not have to use my creative writing talents to make money. It did mean I had to get up at 4 a.m. or earlier most of my life, but it was worth it. Professors have a profession. I had a job. When I was a teacher, I, too, briefly had a profession, but I was beneath the bottom on the academic totem poll as an adjunct professor, and it was clear that I couldn't do that *and* my job forever. I thought being an adjunct would at least bring me a little prestige. But I was wrong about that, too. Still, I have nothing but fondness and praise for the faculty in the English department and the Creative Writing Program. I came along a generation early for the MFA track, though, and making my way into fiction through journalism is an honorable tradition of which I'm proud.

In 2011, Marc Jolley and I decided to publish my next novel, *Emerson's Brother*, in the spring of 2012. I have always had a deep interest and sympathy for the siblings of famous writers and composers. And it's astonishing to me how many "great" writers of the past have troubled brothers and sisters. (And I use "troubled" to encompass everything from physical illness to catastrophic mental problems. And I need to point out the obvious, that most brothers and sisters of famous writers are perfectly normal and always have been.) Often, when I read biographies, I begin to poke around and learn what I can about the siblings of the subject—how was that brother the same or different? Did he see the world through a window so similar one could complete the other's sentences in conversation? That's how I came to be interested in Bulkeley Emerson.

One of the finest gifts my father ever gave me was the directive to read two of Ralph Waldo Emerson's most famous essays, "Nature," and "Self-Reliance." I must have been about fourteen, and they overwhelmed me. We had a copy of Emerson's most famous works in our house, and the man's voice, his gentleness, and his self-assurance mesmerized me. I read *Walden* for the first time about then, too, and I gave myself, wholly, to the Transcendentalists, a love that, like most first loves, has endured for my lifetime. I knew from my earliest sentient moments that I was designed for a solitary life and that I somehow intuitively understood nature from sepal and petal to her most intimate molecules. I think we readers tend to love Thoreau more strongly than we love Emerson, because he's more approachable, and, honestly, less stuffy. To a Twenty-First century ear, Emerson's long, slow sentences take patience (which of course is well rewarded). He seems like the paterfamilias of our clan. Henry seems like our slightly nutty brother, the one that today would be given Ritalin and sent to therapy. In other words, he's more like we are. But I loved them both equally and have bounced between them like a ping-pong ball on the green table of a lovely meadow.

Waldo suffered terribly in this life. His father died of stomach cancer when Waldo was only seven years old. (My own father's father, as I have said, died when Daddy was twelve.) Three of his siblings, John Clarke, Mary Caroline, and Phebe died as children, something that was sadly common at the time. William, Edward, and Charles lived into adulthood with Waldo, but their lives were anything but easy. Waldo lived to be seventy-eight and was at his death the grand old man of American philosophy and literature. He died in 1882 on April 27—the date sixty-eight years later on which Linda would be born. Bulkeley had a life that was as unfortunate as his unpronounceable name. In some way, Bulkeley was mentally ill, and I began to wonder if perhaps in his own fractured manner he saw and dealt with the same things that Waldo did. How would this strange, damaged brother of Ralph Waldo Emerson see, for instance, self-reliance or the natural world?

In order to know as much as I could about Bulkeley I spent several years combing Waldo's letters and journals, his books, and other papers. I was fortunate that the University of Georgia Libraries have an enormous collection of Emerson materials. Bulkeley had received almost no attention from scholars, though, so I had to make a meticulous search for mentions of him. This is from the postscript to my novel:

> So what was Robert Bulkeley Emerson's illness? I am not a doctor or a scientist and more than a century and a half have passed since Bulkeley died. My research has been intentionally limited, too, because this is a speculative novel that needed the framework of history but not all its details.
>
> Still, I have read through Emerson's collected journals and essays and examined every passage about Bulkeley in the standard biographies, and the picture I gain from the biographies is at odds with what I glean from the letters. In his final, posthumously published book, *Emerson Among the Eccentrics*, Carlos Baker hedged his own bets, calling Bulkeley "mentally retarded" in one place and "mentally challenged" in another.
>
> In their wonderful book, *The Emerson Brothers: A Fraternal Biography in Letters*, scholars Ronald A. Bosco and Joel Myerson (Oxford, 2006) say that "a growing number of Emersonians have speculated privately that Bulkeley may have been a victim of what is now know as `Tourette's Syndrome,' a disease that manifests itself in tics [and other symptoms]..." They go on to say, "Unfortunately, other members of the Emerson family, including Bulkeley's brothers, were never specific in their characterization of his symptoms...." He was, they admit, a "shadowy figure."
>
> In fact, Bulkeley wasn't the only Emerson with mental problems. Edward, blue-eyed and fair-haired, was once confined to McLean's at the same time as Bulkeley after suffering a nervous breakdown. And Edward did not go gently into that good Asylum—he was described as violently deranged and had to be physically restrained. In his journal, Waldo sadly referred to Edward's mental illness as "the constitutional calamity of my family," though tuberculosis was just as bad. (Waldo's first wife, Ellen, died from an all-too-common disease of the time, consumption.) Edward's demise was considered far more tragic than Bulkeley's, since Edward was a Harvard graduate and the family's fair-haired boy in more ways than one....
>
> Whatever the cause and course of Bulkeley's illness, it seems improbable that he could have written the letters that I have given him in the novel. Still, I am intrigued by the possibility that Bulkeley

likely dealt with the same issues that make up the bulk of his brother's writings (such as nature and self-reliance). I have carefully interwoven many of Waldo's ideas through the prism of his brother's sorrow throughout the book.

I believe that Bulkeley's time with the Hoars [the family that Waldo 'placed' him with near the end of Bulkeley's life] was a happy way to end his life. I hope that in those days he was able to live in the way Waldo describes at the end of "Nature":

Every moment instructs, and every object: for wisdom is infused into every form. It has been poured into us as blood; it convulsed us as pain; it slid into us as pleasure; it enveloped us in dull melancholy days, or in days of cheerful labor; we did not guess its essence, until after a long time.

My novel is a book of letters surrounding the last year of Bulkeley's life, and I believe it is deeply moving. I was fortunate to have the help of Joel Myerson, unquestionably the top living Emerson and Thoreau scholar. He generously offered to chat with me online about my research and my book, and in the end, gave me this sweetheart of a blurb:

"This fascinating novel about the least known Emerson brother brings to life the Transcendental currents of the time and shows how hard it was, for all the Emersons, to live up to the expectations of their forefathers. Fans of Henry Thoreau and Waldo Emerson, as well as anyone with a brother, will find this novel an emotional recreation of an important period and place in our history."

Emerson's Brother came out from Mercer University Press in May 2012 and was universally ignored. It sold only a few copies and was unreviewed. I do not even think my close friends knew it came out. By this time I had run out of a desire to be constantly pressing my own name into the public limelight and had stopped blogging, though I did try to keep my website up to date. For a time, I felt myself slowly begin to fade into past-tense, at least as a public figure.

But I had hardly quit writing. Since *EB,* I have written a massive postmodern comic novel titled *Thoreau's Last Theorem* and a cycle of five plays about the decline and fall of a Southern family from 1890 until the present. Called *In a Southern Garden,* I'm probably more proud (and certainly more vain) of these plays than anything I've done in years. Without question, *Thoreau's Last Theorem* is my masterpiece. I hope to publish it a year after this volume. My fingers are crossed. For one six-month stretch after I retired, I wrote nothing but love poems, and we plan to publish *The Color of All Things: 99 Love Poems* in the spring of 2015. And to my surprise, I decided to write my autobiography, something I always swore I'd never do.

The need to publish, once a roaring inferno, is now no more than candlelight in a window on a winter's night. The need to write, though, still flames in my soul, and each morning as I come to this computer, the world is bright, sparkling with dew, and I am here, by the light of my own history, meant for this path, these words.

41

What I Didn't Lose

It is impossible for a writer to judge his life's work. I have books that I love because I was happy when I wrote them. *Speak Again, Bright Angel* was one of those novels, and I was disappointed when no one appeared to like it but me. I'm sure it does still need work. Almost every novel does, shy of *Madame Bovary* (and Nabokov even found problems with it!). But "disappointed" is about the strongest word I can use. I moved on to another project, another world.

In my mother's journal, she mentions how hard I had worked on my writing. And this was just before *The Heart of a Distant Forest* came out. Most people seem to think writers have an apprentice period, and then they are professional artists or commercial writers. That's not how it works, at least not for me. I have been learning how to write my whole life. And let's face it, even after winning seventy-eight tournaments, Tiger Woods still had a swing coach. One area that I disliked at first and then grew to love insensibly is rewriting. In typewriter days, rewriting and retyping a manuscript was the work of many agonizing months. Now the concept of a "draft" is almost arcane. A writer does go through complete drafts, of course. But just as often, we start over from page one and tinker our way through a manuscript. I have "passes" I do for all my manuscripts. For instance, one pass will look at nothing but verb tenses. Another will examine only nouns. In a third, I will study sentence rhythms.

I do have books of my own that still evoke a passionate response in me. My latest two manuscripts at this writing, the very long novel *Thoreau's Last Theorem* and the play sequence *In a Southern Garden* jazz me more than I really want to say. Other books of mine do little for me years later. But you must understand that this is not a judgment based on careful study and re-reading of the books and unpublished manuscripts. Once a book is published, I never go back and read it. And unless one of my manuscripts is a project with which I can't stop tinkering over vast geological time periods, I rarely look at it, either. No, my reaction is based on memory of writing and having written. Even though it largely got respectful reviews, I've always felt that *Blue Crystal*, for instance, is a weaker effort. When *Final Heat* came out, I was physically sick for weeks, and after the local lifestyle magazine in Athens savaged it, I wanted to hide. I think it's an obvious book, and I try hard not to be an obvious writer. So I learned from it. All along, starting with my first poetry, I have gone from project to project trying to improve. I read constantly and write every day. I can say for certain that the list of my works at the end of this volume isn't everything I have done, not by a long shot. There are dozens of other partial manuscripts and even more pages of character descriptions for novels I never wrote. I wrote hundreds, if not thousands, of letters and e-mails dealing with my writing. One trait that has deeply marked my time is the fact that I never even thought about developing one character or one genre to carry throughout my career. For many years, the words "John Grisham thriller" meant an idealistic young lawyer trapped in a nexus of crime and inescapable tragedy. And readers responded. But I didn't want people to be able to locate me quite so easily. There's something a little unartful about fulfilling expectations. In that sense, Nabokov, always flitting in directions for which a reader is wildly unprepared, is a hero of mine. The only genre I ever read with pleasure was the Raymond Chandler mystery, and so I did my own homage with *Slow Dance in Autumn*. But I was no mystery writer. So there wouldn't be a detective series.

One thing that distinguishes my work is that I have for much of my life been a country man. Most of my sensibilities are attuned far more to someone like Wendell Berry than John Ashbery. And yet my creative impulse is deeply informed by a love of forms more associated with cities than the country. From my first days as a reader, I loved the avant garde, even while recognizing much of it is too affected to read. What I grew to love is a voice that roams the history of Western thought and literature and that does not write *down* to a reader. I believe my readers are intelligent and well-read. I think they bring a wide knowledge to the page. I also love many of the methods of postmodern writing, especially the unstable and evolving narrative and narrator. I will say it once more: I like to think of a story as a perfect stained-glass image that is shattered into a thousand pieces and then reassembled at random with pieces from other windows shoved in to make the image whole. I enjoy using an enormous toolbox of narrative devices. Check out *The Divine Comics* to see what I mean.

From the beginning, there are two poles to my art: the poignant and the comic. Both are devilishly hard to handle properly. The poignant can devolve into sentimentality faster than you can say *Love Actually*. The comic can become brittle and unimportant as a Borscht Belt one-liner. As one of my books comes together as comic or poignant (or both), there is a third rail that is always close in my narrative approach. That is the size of the life that's contained within. When I was in my early teens I discovered Mahler and Bruckner and Bach, and with them I discovered ambition, though I did not then know its price. I just knew that I was constitutionally attracted to long and complicated works of art and not just to a three-minute pop song. (Yes, I know it's only rock and roll, but I like it, too.) The idea of endless compression never interested me. While I see the art and craft in Raymond Carver's work, it seems to me little more than a sputtering that never even quite begins. To me, minimalism hit its high point with Hemingway's short stories almost a century ago. It was not new in the 1980s. I was also weary of fashionable pessimism even as an undergraduate. I tried it out and found it was great fun, but it is also a neighborhood with nothing but dead ends. And you can see a whole neighborhood quite well in a short time. No, give me a huge canvas. Give me the ceiling of the Sistine Chapel, not a four-by-six-inch canvas. I want to *smell* the life, not sense it by inference.

So what did I write *about*? I have said before that I largely write about people at the edges of society, about the elderly and those marginalized by race or income, for instance. I can't even remotely imagine writing about the people John Cheever knew—wealthy suburbanites drowning in their own well-supported agonies. Cheever's most famous story, "The Swimmer" is about a man who swims back to his house in the pools of neighbors, one after another. It's a staggering, brilliant work, a jaw-dropping masterpiece. And yet I could never write about a neighborhood where everyone has a swimming pool. I don't even know how those people speak, much less think. (Read Blake Bailey's *biography* of Cheever, however, to find out about those people if you're not one—it is one of the greatest literary biographies ever written.) These days, I marginalize myself to be a rural writer. Everyone assumes that the only people who live in the country are extreme right-wing gun nuts or off-their-rockers conservatives. And that is demonstrably untrue. I love the country. I also love Penderecki and de Kooning, Franklin Roosevelt and the Rev. Martin Luther King, Jr. I also know small town America quite well, and that's another point where writers are marginalized. The thinking goes: If you're so smart, why would you live in (Fill in the Blank), Illinois? New Yorkers can be brutal about rural folk just because of such assumptions. They can also be kind and generous and supportive. Neither Molly nor Harvey nor Bill Contardi ever made me feel less because of where I lived. But living in a rural area *is* a hurdle for a serious writer, not a help. There was a period in the early- to mid-1970s when living in the country was hip, and we're seeing glimmers of that again, with the interest in local foods and home-grown free-range chickens. Maybe someday I'll be seen as a pioneer, not a man apart. I can hope and pretend, anyway.

In A Southern Garden goes far beyond much of my earlier work and deals head-on with race, homophobia, family, and poverty. It's about the decline and fall of a Southern family and the one house in which its generations live from 1890 until 2010. Its five plays slowly unwind the desperation that comes over a family when it becomes the voice of racism and hatred. The first play, *Deeper, Wider, and Washed Away* is set in 1890, and the second, *The Righteous in Their Rage,* in 1925. The third, *Summer Darkness, Winter Light,* moves the story forward to 1959 and the Civil Rights Era, and the fourth, *If I Could Save You,* is set in 1985. The cycle ends with *Toward the Green Palace,* which takes places in 2010. It is my backwards love letter to my homeland. I designed it to be performed on five consecutive nights, so it is obviously the Ring Cycle that I finally *wrote* but never *composed*. It is something that took me a lifetime to know and write, though I have been making quixotic stabs at it all along, most notably in *A Distant Flame*. Yes, the South has artistic riches, fine people, and generations of hard-working, loving men and women. And though I don't care for most of its weather and climate, it is a demonstrably beautiful place.

If *In a Southern Garden* is dark, then *Thoreau's Last Theorem* is as light and giddily unstable as a swallowtail in flight, though postmodern and very long. I designed it using thousands of portmanteau words—giddy mutants of standard English that are readable and understandable, and filled with more meaning that I could get with normal locutions. Its characters have their comedies and tragedies, but in the end, as they take a journey across America, they come to love both the internal and external lamps lifted beside our somewhat golden shores. Though we now know these shores are tarnished (and no one knows this better than a Southerner), I hope this book shows why there is still plenty of glitter in them thar hills.

All the Western Stars (1988) was such a great idea that as soon as it came riding into Hollywood, people began to steal the plot, lock, stock, and smoking barrel. I had a sense this would happen, and when it did, all I could do was shrug. If you have a short fuse about such things, don't go to Hollywood. Because any *thought* you have *will* be stolen. In a sense, even *All the Western Stars* has familiar elements, though I didn't really know it at the time. The story of two old men going out for one last adventure certainly didn't originate with me. Sam Peckinpah's glorious film *Ride the High Country*, starring, oh my God, Randolph Scott and Joel McCrea (honestly, Western fans, does it get any better than that?) came out in 1962. But even that great film (which I didn't really know well until the '90s) didn't have the slant I did—two old men escaping from a nursing home for one last adventure as fuller human beings. You might say they were living out their *Bucket List* (2007). I will just nod and say it's all right, but remember me.

My novel *A. Lincoln & Son* was impossible from the start, and I knew it. I mean impossible in the sense that people feel proprietary about Lincoln—okay, I'll just go ahead and say it: We love the man desperately and always will. It got one reading, as I said, at an academic press by someone who didn't have a clue what I was trying to do. That was all it took to make me withdraw it forever. But I got to spend a year with one of the finest men anyone every met. I lost absolutely nothing.

The Shape of Rain, also unpublished at this writing, is one of my favorite manuscripts, and I have worked on it for many years. It is about the relationship between fathers and daughters and is in the form of twin journals, each one reflecting the other. It *is* a dramatic book, but for the most part, nothing happens in Twenty-First century terms—no hot sex, no explosions, no back-stabbing and greed. Just a dying man trying to win the love of his estranged daughter, and his daughter, though she doesn't quite know it, trying to win his love, too. It is *present* and powerful and unpublished. Some day.

Of all my published books, only *Final Heat* and *Blue Crystal* are out of print at this writing, and I have made no effort to resurrect them. Neither is badly written, and each has its value, but for now I'm just as happy with them sleeping in the out-of-print bin. Obviously, though, nothing is *really* out of print any longer—both can be readily and easily bought online from used book dealers. But they *are* out of print in the sense that I won't make a penny when they sell as used books. This brings up another point I want to make: To be a published writer and to *stay* a published writer requires a skin harder than medieval armor. I have known so many people, some of them talented, who give up at the first rejection. You have to be prepared to keep going after the *hundredth* rejection if you want to make it. And then after you publish one book, you may have to start all over again. And again. And again. My trick, if one wants to call it that, was that I decided early that *no one* would out-work me, and that I would never, *ever* give up. I might have to shift strategies—like changing agents or publishers—but I *would* find someone who would take my work. But while I was working angles, I was often my own worst enemy because I was too restless to stay long in the same literary neighborhood. I wrote a "road" novel with *All the Western Stars*. I created a poignant novel of aging with *The Heart of a Distant Forest. Slow Dance in Autumn* is a mystery starring an alcoholic detective. *A Distant Flame* focuses on the moral dilemma of having views wildly out of step with those of most people where a person lives. *In the Morning: Reflections from First Light* is about how we are all affected by things we take for granted, like the time of day in which we feel most alive. *In a Southern Garden* is my final working out of sorrow at what the American South willfully let itself become and how it has surely but too slowly moved toward the right end of the moral universe's arc. *Elegies for the Water* is an old man's book of healing verse, yet, I hope, one informed by a deep and close knowledge of contemporary voices and methods. *The Flower Seeker* is about the flora and fauna, geography and geology of my South. And it is also about the Native American nations who lived here before we killed them or drove them away. African American slavery, the forced removal of Indian tribes, and the Civil War—that troika of moral failings gives the South something to work against for the next hundred years. And in such efforts, we can begin to peel back the light on the best of what we are. We have moved in that direction already. *The Color of All Things: 99 Love Poems*, which we plan to be my next published book, focuses intently on love between an older man and woman. I worked for more than a year on it, checking, double-checking, and testing each word to make sure it is the best I could write.

In addition, I have published dozens of others pieces over the decades, poems, fiction, and journalism in magazines and newspapers. A *catalog raisonné* of my entire works would be astonishing in its length. I always worked hard.

The gauge I use on bad days to judge how I have done as a writer is the holiest of places for all readers: the public library. As I mentioned before, a great many of my books are in the Central Library in Zurich, not far from the grave of James Joyce, meaning nothing to anyone but me. One can find *The Heart of a Distant Forest* in the Frankston Public Library in Frankston Victoria, Australia, as well as the American Library in Paris and the British Library. All of my books are in libraries from one end of Australia to another. G'day, mates! *A Distant Flame* is even in the Cooloola Shire Library Service in Gympie, Queensland. A patron can find *All the Western Stars* in the National Library of New Zealand, the U.S. Army Library at Schofield Barracks in Hawaii, and the Union Catalog of Polish Research Libraries. *Perfect Timing* can be checked out at the National Library Board of Singapore. You might find *Slow Dance in Autumn* at the Ealing Central Library in London. English libraries in particularly seem to love *The Silent Stars Go By*, but it's also available in libraries in New Zealand, among many other places. *Blue Crystal*? Pick it up at the library in Hoofddorp in the Netherlands if you're up that way. *Crossing Wildcat Ridge* can be checked out at the American University of Sharjak in the United Arab Emirates, and while studying at the University of Cambridge, look up my poetry collection, *Elegies for the Water*. And if you're in Morocco, pick up *The Song of Daniel* at the Al Akhawayn University Library in Ifrane. The French translation of *Final Heat*, titled *Coup de Chaud*, is at the main library in Alexandria, Egypt, a place known for another library from another time. The German translation of *All the Western Stars*? Libraries in Slovenia have it to check out, too.

My books are in hundreds of libraries all over the United States and can be found at Harvard, Yale, Stanford, and the libraries of most major universities. Of course, the writer judged by a panel of his peers as the Worst Writer in Human History may well also have books next to mine in libraries all over the world. That is the democratic promise of the library—it is the winnowing ground for the wheat from the chaff. But I have enough confidence (and arrogance) to think that in some corner of Planet Earth a reader is deep into one of my books, wondering who I am (or was) and what caused me to write the book she holds close. (Visitors asking questions about me on the Internet often wonder what year I died. Well, as of 2014, not quite yet.) I discovered the world that way, book by book, in the Regional Library in Madison, Georgia.

This is just one life I lived, from one perspective. Each of us, if given time and energy, could tell of our own lives from a hundred places. The truly famous never run out of names to drop and, by comparison, make having lunch with Jessica Tandy look downright ridiculous. But for my place and my time, I lived a life that many others coveted. I was a serious writer; I saw my work published and translated into other languages; and I sold my books to the movies. I gained notice for the best of what I have been.

I really did, once upon a time, live my dream in the Big Apple as I rode across town in a taxicab to a party thrown by Random House. All told, it was a marvelous life to live.

I'm going for a walk now. Come on and go with me. I'll tell you a story.

Addendum

The following is a list, as complete as I can make it right now, of my finished literary works. Copies are in my papers in the University of Georgia's Hargrett Rare Book and Manuscript Library.

Fizz. Novella. 1972. Unpublished.

Princeps Musicorum. Poetry manuscript. 1974. Unpublished.

Images. Poetry manuscript. 1974. Unpublished.

A Farm in Central Georgia. Poetry manuscript. 1975. Unpublished.

Lips of the Night Wind. Play for one performer and tape. 1976-77. Unpublished, unproduced.

Mercenaries. Full play. 1977. Unpublished, unproduced.

The Boys of Deathshead. Full book, poem sequence. 1977. Unpublished.

Let Us Have Madness. Full novel. 1977-79. Unpublished.

Asphodel. Full novel. 1979 or so. Unpublished.

The Heart of a Distant Forest. 1980-81. Full novel. Published first by W.W. Norton & Co., 1984.

Edge of the Current. Full novel. 1982-84. Unpublished.

Southern Light. Full novel. 1980s. Unpublished.

Darkness. Full novel. 1983-84. Unpublished.

Children of the Country. Mid-1980s. Partial novel and outline. Unpublished.

All the Western Stars. 1987. Full novel. Published first by Peachtree Publishers, 1988.

Slow Dance in Autumn. 1987-88. Full novel. Published first by Peachtree Publishers, 1988.

The Song of Daniel. 1988. Full novel. Published first by Peachtree Publishers, 1989.

Speak Again, Bright Angel. Full novel. 1988-90. Unpublished.

Declared Dead. Full novel. Second Hank Prince mystery. 1987-88. Rewritten 2010. Unpublished.

Perfect Timing. 1989-90. Full novel. Published first by Peachtree Publishers, 1990.

Final Heat. 1990. Full novel. Published by Turtle Bay Books (Random House), 1991.

Almost Light. Full novel. 1990-91. Privately printed in 2003 but unpublished.

Blue Crystal. Full novel. 1991-92. Published by Grove Press, 1993.

Dreams and Dust. Full novel. Privately printed in 2004 but unpublished.

Tomorrow Shall Be My Dancing Day. Full novel. Early 1990s. Unpublished.

All the Western Stars. Screenplay for The Zanuck Company / MGM based on my novel. Late 1990s. Unpublished and unproduced.

Beyond the River. Full novel. Privately printed under the pen name Samuel Leigh, 2002. Unpublished.

The Growing Season. Full screenplay. Mid-1990s. Unsold, unproduced.

Dreamer in the Sun. Full screenplay. Mid-1990s. Unsold, unproduced.

A Gift from Boonie. Seymour, and Dog. Story. Early 1980s. Published as a chapbook by Maypop Press in 1994.

The True and Authentic History of Jenny Dorset. Full novel. 1995-96. Published in 1997 by Longstreet Press.

The Silent Stars Go By. Christmas memoir. 1998. Published in 1998 by Hill Street Press.

Crossing Wildcat Ridge. Memoir. Nature essays/memoir. 1997-98. Published by The University of Georgia Press in 1999.

The Travels and Adventures of Anthony Clark, Viscount. Sequel to *Jenny Dorset*. Full novel. 1998-1999. Privately printed in 2003. Unpublished.

The Angel of Blades. Full novel. 2000-2001. Unpublished.

Summer Light. Full novel. Optioned by Meg Ryan for Polygram Television by her Prufrock Pictures. 1990s. Unpublished, unproduced.

The Seventh Secret. Full novel. Early 2000s. Unpublished.

The Shape of Rain. Full novel. Mid-2000s. Unpublished.

Flight. Full novel. Early 2000s. Optioned for film by producer Mike Fischler. Unpublished and unproduced.

Night Wings. 1975-1995. Full poetry collection. Privately printed 2003. Unpublished.

Psalms for the Earth. Sequence of poems. Late 2000s. Not yet published.

Sunrise Boulevard. Full novel. Late 1990s. Privately printed 2003. Unpublished.

The Growing Season. Full screenplay. Mid 1990s. Unpublished and unproduced.

Turtle. Mid-2000s. Full screenplay. Unpublished and not yet produced.

A. Lincoln & Son. Full novel. Mid-2000s. Unpublished.

Casey's Sky. Young adult novel. 2005. For Hall Reads Together event. Privately published, 2005.

In the Morning: Reflections from First Light. Nature essays. 2004-2006. Published by Mercer University Press in 2006.

Emma Devlin. Libretto to full opera of the same name. 2005. Unpublished and unproduced.

The Campfire Boys. Full novel. 2006-2008. Published in 2009 by Mercer University Press.

Elegies for the Water. Poetry collection. 1994-2008. Published in 2009 by Mercer University Press.

An Early Snow and Other Stories. 1995-2008. Short story collection. Unpublished.

The Flower Seeker: An Epic Poem of William Bartram. 2008-2009. Published by Mercer University Press in 2010.

The Divine Comics. Full novel. 1982-2010. Published in 2011 by Mercer University Press. Privately printed in 2003.

Emerson's Brother. Full novel. 2009-2011. Published in 2012 by Mercer University Press.

The Color of All Things: 99 Love Poems. Planned to be published in 2015 by Mercer University Press.

It is Written: An Autobiography. The volume in your hands. Published in 2014 by Mercer University Press. Written 2010-2014.

Thoreau's Last Theorem. Full novel. 2010-12. Not yet published.

In a Southern Garden. A cycle of five plays: *Deeper, Wider, and Washed Away; The Righteous in Their Rage; Summer Darkness, Winter Light; If I Could Save You*; and *Toward the Green Palace*. 2010-2013. Not yet published or performed.

History of Holy Cross Lutheran Church. Church in Athens, Georgia. Mid-2000s. Published in church documents.

There are also dozens of partially completed manuscripts of novels, some more than two hundred pages long. And there are thousands of unpublished poems, as well as hundreds of stories and personal columns as a journalist in a career stretching more than fifty years. My work has also been published in numerous anthologies.